Enigma Books

Also published by Enigma Books

General Mark W. Clark

Calculated Risk

Enigma Books

ISBN-13: 978-1-929631-59-9
ISBN-10: 1-929631-59-6
Printed in the United States of America

Front cover: February 23, 1943. General Mark W. Clark after receiving the Grand Cross of the Order of
Ouissam Alaouite Cherifien (First Class) from His Majesty The Sultan of Morocco.
All photos courtesy of The Citadel Archives & Museum.

Library of Congress Cataloging-in-Publication Data

Clark, Mark W. (Mark Wayne), 1896-1984.
  Calculated risk / Mark W. Clark.

  p. : ill., maps ; cm.

  Includes bibliographical references and index.
  Originally published: New York : Harper, 1950.
  ISBN-13: 978-1-929631-59-9
  ISBN-10: 1-929631-59-6

1. World War, 1939-1945--Campaigns--Africa. 2. World War, 1939-1945--
Campaigns--Italy. 3. World War, 1939-1945--Personal narratives, American. 4.
Generals--United States--Biography. 5. Clark, Mark W. (Mark Wayne), 1896-1984. I.
Title.

D766.82 .C5 2007
940.542

This book is dedicated to the men and women of many nationalities who fought and who died serving with the Fifth Army and the 15th Army Group in Italy. Never did a commander have more to be proud of than I in being associated with these selfless individuals.

M. W. C.

In the preparation of this book I was greatly aided by having the expert advice and assistance of Joe Alex Morris, to whom I wish here to express my deepest thanks.

It is with great pride that I thank my daughter, Ann Clark, for her assistance in preparing all maps and illustrations.

M. W. C.

Contents

Foreword

by

Martin Blumenson

General Mark W. Clark was a major figure in World War II. He was prominent as one of the top American commanders. Together with Dwight D. Eisenhower, Omar N. Bradley, and George S. Patton, Jr., Clark was widely regarded as being responsible for victory on the European side of the conflict. That view is true today, and it will stand for all time.

He was noted as having been outstanding in two areas during the war: training troops for combat, and leading the American Fifth Army in the Italian campaign. At the conclusion of the struggle, he was a full or four-star general officer.

For his rise in rank, he owed much to the U.S. Army Chief of Staff, General George C. Marshall. Admiring Clark's personal integrity, good sense, and energetic application to duty, Marshall brought Clark to Washington, D. C. as war threatened and marked him for promotion and high responsibility.

Clark owed much also to Eisenhower, the Supreme Allied Commander, because they saw solutions to problems in much the same way. Their close association resulted in a deep friendship and, for Clark, great opportunities to advance.

In the final analysis, however, Clark owed his success to his own habits of work, his clear-headedness, and his exemplary judgment.

His book, entitled *Calculated Risk* and first published in 1950, is among the best accounts of the military events in which he participated and which he largely shaped. His narrative is exciting and accurate, reveals an insider's knowledge, and is authoritative. It deals also with conditions continuing beyond his lifetime. Examples are the activities of guerrilla warriors and the command of multinational forces.

Yet he tells his readers little of himself before the war. He starts his presentation in the middle of 1942 and uses a flashback to indicate what he did at his previous duty station. Who was he? And how did he prepare himself for greatness and fame?

His father, Charles Carr Clark, graduated from West Point in 1890, and was a Regular Army officer on active duty, and served during the Spanish-American War in Puerto Rico, Cuba, and the Philippines. He remained in the United States during World War I, retired in 1920 as a colonel, and died ten years later. His mother, Rebecca Ezekiels Clark, born in San Francisco, was the daughter of an eastern European who had immigrated to America. Attractive and energetic, she lived many years in Washington, D.C. after her husband's death.

Their union produced a daughter, Janet, and Mark. He was born in 1896 at Madison Barracks (later known as Pine Camp, then Camp Drum) near Watertown, New York, on the eastern edge of Lake Ontario.

When Mark was an early teenager and at Fort Sheridan, close to Chicago, he saw from afar the slim and handsome Lieutenant George S. Patton, Jr., who was serving at his first post. Mark gazed upon him with wonder and hero worship.

He entered the Military Academy in 1913. Joseph Lawton Collins and Matthew Bunker Ridgway were his classmates. Eisenhower, two years ahead of him, was cadet sergeant of Clark's company and became a valued acquaintance.

Assigned to the 11th infantry upon graduation, he served as a platoon leader and company commander. As part of the 5th Division, the regiment arrived in France in mid-1918. After a month of further training, the men marched to the front to relieve a French division. Clark's battalion commander fell ill. He turned his organization over to Clark, his best company commander. As Clark supervised the entry of his units into the trenches, a German shell exploded nearby and seriously wounded him.

Hospitalized for six weeks, then declared unfit for service in the infantry, Mark Clark joined the First Army Supply Section. He performed his duties proficiently and with a pleasant personality. Although recommended for promotion twice, he remained a captain.

Clark commanded infantry companies at Fort Snelling, Minnesota, and at Fort Crook, Nebraska. He then became head of an eight-soldier entertainment detachment that performed on the Chatauqua circuit. For two years, he traveled constantly from Florida to Ohio, putting on shows devoted to Americanization. His experience taught him to speak extemporaneously and to understand the nature of public relations.

Next, Clark worked in Washington, D.C. for the Assistant Secretary of War, specifically for the Director of Sales, who was disposing of surplus War Department property, including buildings, houses, lands, factories, and installations no longer needed. Clark traveled extensively again for two and a half years, conducting publicity campaigns and finding purchasers for abandoned plants. His superiors rated him "an exceptionally capable officer." He was, they said, "an able, conscientious, and efficient executive" who employed "sound judgment and care in the expenditure of public funds."

He married Maurine Doran, who was from Muncie, Indiana. The marriage was exceptionally happy. They had two children, a son William and a daughter Ann.

Clark attended the Infantry School's Advanced Course at Fort Benning, Georgia, then joined the 30th Infantry at the Presidio in San Francisco. There Colonel Frank. C. Bolles, the regimental and post commander, recognized Clark's efficiency and affability and relied upon him for everything. Promoted to brigadier general and assigned to Fort D. A. Russell near Cheyenne, Wyoming, as 4th Brigade and post commander, Bolles took Clark with him because Clark, he said, was "efficient, dependable, and energetic" as well as "a very presentable officer." As brigade Executive Officer, Clark again looked after everything.

The War Department sent Clark to Indianapolis, Indiana, where he instructed the 38th Infantry Division, a National Guard unit. Promoted to major in 1933, Clark attended the Command and General Staff College at Fort Leavenworth, Kansas.

Bolles, now a major general commanding the 7th Corps Area headquartered at Omaha, Nebraska, insisted on Clark's transfer to his command. Clark again worked closely with him as Assistant Chief of Staff G-2 for Intelligence, as Assistant Chief of Staff G-3 for Plans and Training, and as Deputy Chief of Staff for the Civilian Conservation Corps. In the latter capacity, as Bolles clearly proclaimed in a published order, Clark had the authority "to make all the decisions and to take all necessary action" normally the province of the commanding general. Throughout Clark's tour, Bolles wrote to prominent officers advertising Clark as "one of the ablest young officers" in the Army.

Probably as the result of Bolles's campaign, Clark attended the Army War College in 1936–37, the ultimate educational step after Forts Benning and Leavenworth for eligibility to high rank and responsibility. Clark's student committee looked into the structure and functions of the infantry division, a massive and unwieldy organization suited for trench warfare in World War I. Since then, the emergence of automobiles and trucks indicated an increasing need for mobility. Clark and his group recommended a smaller division by eliminating the brigade level of command and reducing the number of soldiers. The proposal was forwarded to the War Department, which appointed a board of three general officers to consider the idea. This foreshadowed the reorganization of the division by General McNair in 1940.

In July 1937, after graduation, Clark reported to the 3rd Infantry Division at Fort Lewis, Washington. As international relations deteriorated, American military budgets began to increase and the U.S. Army started to prepare seriously for war. In this endeavor, Clark played a prominent role. He earned an Army-wide reputation.

As the Assistant Chiefs of Staff G-2 and G-3, Clark was in charge of intelligence and training, a normal combination at that time. The intelligence function was minimal, but associated with it was public relations, that is, promoting understanding between the civilian and military communities. Clark spoke often to fraternal, patriotic, and civic clubs in the area.

His main responsibility was as G-3, to prepare individuals and units, including nearby National Guard and Reserve groups, for war. He prepared training programs and field exercises. Able to try out his favorite tactical theories and concepts, Clark had to be certain that his ideas were practical. He needed a mature and experienced counselor. He found his mentor in Marshall, then a brigadier general, who commanded a brigade at Vancouver Barracks, Washington, several miles from Portland, Oregon.

Marshall had been a superb officer in World War I. As the First Army's Chief of Operations in France, he had planned the St. Mihiel and Meuse-Argonne offensives. He was happy to look over Clark's projects and to offer advice. He came to appreciate Clark's clear mind, refreshing outlook, and energetic application to duty.

Called to Washington, D.C., Marshall became the War Department Assistant Chief of Staff. A few months later, he was elevated to be Deputy Chief of Staff. On September 1, 1939, the day that World War II opened in Europe, he was appointed U.S. Army Chief of Staff. He had continued to receive Clark's plans and to comment on them

Clark, meanwhile, had received many tributes. One superior judged him to be "a hard working, conscientious, highly efficient officer with a pleasing personality." Another called him "one of the most brilliant all-around officers I have known in forty years of commissioned service."

In the summer of 1938, Lieutenant Colonel Eisenhower, Douglas MacArthur's assistant in the Philippines, visited the United States. He stopped in Tacoma, Washington, to see his brother. He called on the 3rd Division commander, an old friend, at Fort Lewis. He ran into Clark, whose experimental training projects impressed him.

From Manila, Eisenhower sent Clark a Christmas card. They began to correspond. Eisenhower managed to separate himself from MacArthur and to obtain assignment to the 3rd Division at Fort Lewis. When Eisenhower arrived, he found that Clark had arranged for him to command a battalion of the 15th Infantry, a choice position.

Clark drew up two large training operations involving amphibious and air components that were forward-looking and modern. Generals Marshall, McNair, and other high-ranking officers came from Washington, D.C. to observe the exercises. All were impressed with Clark's energy and clear-headedness. His West Point classmate, Collins, also present, was enthusiastic over Clark's work.

In 1940, promoted to lieutenant colonel, Clark was transferred to Washington, D.C. As war clouds gathered over the United States, General Marshall pulled together around him a group of young and talented officers. He assigned Clark to be with General McNair.

This is where Mark Clark's book begins.

A note is required to clarify the environment in which Clark functioned in Italy. When his Fifth Army landed in Salerno to start the Italian campaign, the Mediterranean theater of operations was an American-run area under Eisenhower, the Supreme Allied Commander. Appointed in December 1943 to head the Allied cross-Channel invasion of Normandy, Eisenhower departed the theater and traveled to England. Replacing him was General Sir Maitland Wilson, who took charge of what became a British-run theater. Prime Minister Winston S. Churchill now had the primary responsibility for the activities there. For that reason, Churchill could and did exert pressure to put on the Anzio operation, which military planners and technicians had earlier vetoed as being too risky.

Churchill's appointment of Mark Clark, an American officer, to command all of the Allied troops engaged in Italy toward the end of 1944 was an immense compliment to Clark. As an army group commander, he directed both the U.S. Fifth and the British Eighth armies.

Had he departed Italy early in 1944 to command the forces preparing to invade southern France, as the authorities in Washington and Eisenhower wished, Clark would certainly have been an army group commander serving with Sir Bernard L. Montgomery and Bradley under Eisenhower in the main arena. But Clark was trying desperately to reach and take Rome and believed it would be a mistake to abandon Italy for France.

Yet Italy had always been a subsidiary theater. The strategic objective was to keep the Germans occupied in order to prevent them from shifting additional forces to the Soviet Union. From the conquest of Sicily in August 1943 to the landings in Normandy in June 1944, the Allies fought in Italy to maintain an active front in Europe.

The lack of a real strategic purpose in Italy, that is, a guide to victory, is why so much controversy developed over Salerno, Anzio, Monte Cassino, Rome, and elsewhere. The Allies were seen to tie down the Germans, but who actually tied down whom remains controversial.

After serving in Austria, Clark was the Sixth Army commander at the Presidio. When the Korean War broke out, he became the Chief of the Army Field Forces, and, like McNair, trained the soldiers headed for combat overseas. He then succeeded Ridgway as Commander in Chief of the United Nations Command in Tokyo. Much against his will, for like MacArthur he believed there was no substitute for victory, he signed the Korean Armistice Agreement in 1953.

Retiring from the Army shortly thereafter, he became President of The Citadel, the Military College of South Carolina, at Charleston. He served for eleven years, raising funds for upgrading old and building new facilities on campus and inspiring the cadets. He supported and campaigned for conservative candidates for political office. He visited Eisenhower in the White House and called him Ike until he realized that his old friend preferred to be addressed as "Mr. President."

Mark Clark died in 1984 in Charleston. His career was distinguished. His achievements were exceptional. His influence on his times was enormous. His book, as he hoped it would be, is a mighty good read.

Calculated Risk

1.

The Road Back to Rome:

May 1949

By Way of Introduction

A soldier's life in combat is an endless series of decisions that mean success or failure, and perhaps life or death for himself or his comrades. The rifleman crawling through the rubble of a bombed-out street must decide on the best moment to escape enemy fire as he dodges from one doorway to the next. He must take a chance. The general seeking to break an enemy defense line and destroy his forces must decide just when and how to strike and precisely to what extent he dare weaken one sector of his front in order to mass overpowering strength at the main point of attack. He, too, must take a chance, although, in the stilted phraseology of military communiqués, he calls it a "calculated risk."*

The Allied campaign in the Mediterranean during World War II was, from the beginning, a gigantic calculated risk. We had to open an initial front against Germany and Italy in 1942 and, after weighing the odds for months, we took a chance on what Prime Minister Winston Churchill called "the soft underbelly of the Axis." We risked stripping the British Isles of fighting power. We took a chance—and a grave one—that the French in North Africa would join us instead of fighting us. We risked a German counter-

---

* A calculated risk is an action taken or contemplated, the outcome of which is uncertain, but which is undertaken after weighing all the factors for and against, because the reward that may be gained is sufficiently important to outweigh or overbalance the objections, hazards or losses that may be involved.

attack through Spain that would have severed our supply lines. We risked untried American forces against veteran enemy armies at a time when defeat would have been an almost fatal disaster.

But most of all, I suppose, we took a chance on Churchill's persuasive eloquence, his conviction that we could "slit this soft underbelly of the Mediterranean." It turned out to be not so soft.

The theory was widely held at the beginning of the Mediterranean campaign that the German armies could not fight effectively in Italy. It was believed that our superior air power could quickly destroy the enemy's supply lines through the Alpine passes and down the long, mountainous spinal column of Italy, and that, being unable to maintain himself logistically, he soon would find it unprofitable if not impossible to give battle.

This was wishful thinking. Throughout the Italian campaign, the Allied armies had to fight for almost every foot of ground against a determined, homogeneous, experienced and powerful foe. The enemy was able to capitalize on the great advantages given him by ideal defensive terrain and long periods of rainy weather. He had a cohesive, mobile fighting force and if he suffered from lack of reinforcements or supplies, it never was evident from our side of the battle line until the closing days of the war.

On the other hand, the Allied offensive wallowed in the mud and ground its way against mountainsides where only a pack mule and sometimes only a man could carry ammunition and food. Against the tightly knit German armies, we were an unavoidably awkward collection of Allies from a dozen different nations, speaking different languages, believing in different Gods, using different equipment, and, on occasion, seeking different goals in accord with our different nationalistic backgrounds and ambitions. Ours was a hodgepodge army in Italy and one of the miracles of the war, it seems to me, was the fact that instead of splitting into fragments under the stress of battle, it became the first army in history to advance from the toe to the top of the Italian boot, taking Rome in its stride.[*]

I believe I should mention here that some responsible persons have doubted the wisdom of the Italian campaign, or have expressed belief that the long, costly drive up the Italian boot should have been halted after we had established our control over the Mediterranean life line by capturing the

---

[*] The Fifth Army was the second ever to take Rome from the south and the first to overcome organized resistance along the Liri Valley approaches to the Eternal City. In A.D. 536, Belisarius marched from the Messina Straits to Naples, which was captured after a siege of twenty days, and then continued to Rome through the Liri Valley. By the time he reached Rome, the king had fled and the city fell without opposition.

great port of Naples and securing the air bases that we needed, principally Foggia. The argument in support of this theory has been that the expenditure of lives, equipment and effort could have been better directed toward the defeat of the Germans on their home grounds.

To me, this argument ignores the basic purpose of our Italian campaign, which was to engage and attack—always attack—as large a part of the German Army as possible in order to prevent the enemy from bringing his full strength to bear against the Allied fronts in France and Russia. It is true that, particularly after the Allied invasion of France, we were a "forgotten front," which until the spring of 1945 never had enough men or enough equipment to mount a quick, decisive and fatal blow at the enemy; but throughout the campaign we were able to tie down approximately one million of the enemy (800,000 Germans and 200,000 Italians) in a manner that made other Allied offensives more crushingly swift.

We were more or less in the role of football guards and tackles who had the task of blocking and "taking out" the enemy forces, which might have made a tremendous difference in the Red Army's advance from the east or General Eisenhower's drive across France and into Germany. This assignment was a vital but hardly a glamorous one, particularly when we were short of men, short of ammunition and equipment, short of everything that was needed at some stages of the campaign, and when we seldom started a battle with better than a fifty-fifty chance of success. Yet, I believe, our mission was fulfilled and, save for a high-level blunder that turned us away from the Balkan states and permitted them to fall under Red Army control, the Mediterranean campaign might have been the most decisive of all in postwar history.

My decision to write this book was confirmed four years after the end of the war when I returned to the Mediterranean as a guest of the Italian Government on the fifth anniversary of the liberation of Rome and the third anniversary of the founding of the Italian Republic. With Mrs. Clark, I flew from Washington on the morning of May 27, 1949, in a B-17, across the Atlantic again, bound for Africa and Italy. I was delighted to be returning, particularly as representative of the Fifth Army, to the scenes that had remained so vividly in my mind and to friends who had lived with me a series of experiences not easily forgotten.

But I must confess that another thought also was in my mind. I had never been a good writer of letters to my family; at least, I felt I had never been able to write letters during the war, which permitted them to share many experiences that I valued. Perhaps no one could. Now I felt that as we retraced the paths of the campaign, it would be easy to explain to my wife what had happened, to give her a better idea of how I felt about people and events that were so intimately connected with the scenes that we would visit and over which we would fly. I could, I thought, now tell her the whole story. Henceforth, we would talk about the same things, have the same interests.

When the coast of Morocco was a bright and glistening strip of surf and sand ahead of our plane, I reminded Mrs. Clark that we were going to be the guests of General Alphonse Juin, the Governor General of Morocco.

"Now I want to tell you about Juin," I began. "He goes way back toward the beginning. There was that day in Algiers when I first saw him . . ."

I looked down as the seashore flashed beneath us. I looked forward toward the big, flat, sun-baked airfield beyond Rabat where the flags were colorful dots above the runways. We were almost there. How would I have time to explain about Juin, the vivid little man of whom I had not been too sure on that day when I first roared and pounded my fist on the table in a furious frustration over the Darlan affair? How could I explain how he had become one of my best friends; how he had miraculously cracked open the German defenses in the mountains before Rome; how he had reacted on the day I told him he was about to be deprived of the thing he wanted most—to lead his men back into France?

"Yes, Wayne," my wife prompted. "About General Juin."

"Well, he's one of the best," I said. "I'll tell you later. We're ready to land."

There was another time when I pointed over to the northeast and said, "Gibraltar must be about in that direction. I've been meaning to tell you about the night General Giraud and Captain Jerry Wright of our Navy came into Ike's office under the Rock. They hadn't shaved for days, or at least Jerry hadn't, but he was grinning like mad because . . ."

I tried to collect my thoughts about that night when we had feared our carefully laid plans to smuggle Giraud out of France in time for the African invasion had gone haywire. And how, like a black-bearded pirate, Jerry Wright came striding down the long tunnel to Eisenhower's headquarters deep under the Rock of Gibraltar, bringing with him the tall, dignified Frenchman, who had escaped at the last moment by submarine from Vichy France.

I wondered how I could explain our anxiety, or our elation at the sight of Giraud, and our amazement as we sat there in a little office and heard him expound an idea that threatened to wreck our whole plan of attack on North Africa. And I was still wondering—and Mrs. Clark was waiting patiently for the story—when we flew over a familiar coastline and I barely had time to point and say:

"See! There's Cherchel. The little port . . . those houses . . ."

What was the use of trying to explain while an airplane whisked us in minutes over the paths that had taken hours and days and weeks and even years to cover in wartime? It would take thousands of words to tell about Cherchel, where we landed from a submarine at night on hostile shores; where I lost my pants in the surf; where the Vichy police searched the room above a wine cellar in which we took refuge. At the moment all I could think of was the startled expression on the face of a British Commando captain when I grabbed a wad of chewing gum from my mouth and thrust it into his to stop a coughing spell that almost gave away our hiding place.

"Cherchel?" Mrs. Clark said. "Oh, that's where you met General Mast."

"Yes. I'll have to show you later. We'll come back and see it afoot."

It was like a time machine running too fast, as we traveled the road back to Rome. From day to day, as we crisscrossed over the scenes of battle, or as we paid official calls at Italian cities, I would try again to tell the story. Once I shouted: "Why, there's Piccolo Peak!"

"But what a peculiar name," my wife said. "I never heard of it."

Few people ever heard of it, by that name or any other, but for me it was a kind of memorial to the day we almost lost the battle of Salerno beachhead—the day even the piccolo players dug in with guns in a last desperate effort to prevent the Germans from driving us into the sea.

But the days moved too rapidly to do more than remind me fleetingly of the story behind the landmarks like Piccolo Peak. We could get no more than a glimpse of the furrowed Apennine Mountains where the Fifth Army literally clawed its way through mud and snow to within sight of the lush Po Valley, yet could only cling there in terrible exhaustion, unable to muster that last ounce of strength to get over the final rocky ridge. Even when we walked down the streets of Anzio, the bright new houses around the sunny port made it difficult to realize that once we had crouched here in the rain-soaked rubble while enemy guns and planes battered every square yard of the town in an effort to carry out Hitler's order to wipe out this "abscess" on the coast of Italy. And at Naples, where we had a wonderful dinner at Giacomino's Restaurant, it seemed incredible that the short, loquacious, irrepressible Giacomino himself had once cooked spaghetti, goat meat and hot peppers for me over a campfire in the woods of Capodimonte, alternately singing "Santa Lucia" and hurling imprecations at the German bombers over his beloved city.

Thus, in one sense, my trip along the road back to Rome tended to impose new scenes that blurred my sharp memories of the war in Italy—until on Memorial Day we visited the American cemetery at Anzio and saw the curving rows of white crosses that spoke so eloquently of the price that America and her Allies had paid for the liberation of Italy. If ever proof were needed that we fought for a cause and not for conquest, it could be found in these cemeteries. Here was our only conquest: all we asked of Italy was enough of her soil in which to bury our gallant dead.

The story I would like to tell, I thought then, is the story of the men who lie here. Nothing can blur my memory of their courage and tenacity and devotion to duty, of their refusal to be awed by seemingly insurmountable odds, by the swirling dust of Salerno, by the treacherous mud of the Liri Valley, or by the stinging snows of the high Apennines. Some chapters of their story I could not hope to tell. No one could tell them who was not there day after day in the foxholes that filled with water before they were half dug, and on the rocky peaks where not even a pack mule could find a footing.

But I can tell part of the story. I can tell how and why the turn of the wheel of war took the men of the Fifth Army to Italy and what was behind the orders that sent them into battle at Salerno, on the Volturno, at Cassino, and on the flat and barren little strip of hell known as the Anzio beachhead; and I can give at least a glimpse of the bravery and sacrifices, not only of the Americans but of men of a dozen other nationalities who fought their way into the not-so-soft underbelly of the Axis. They are men who paid heavily for their page in history. Testimony to their courage is the fact that they won 56 of the 255 Congressional Medals of Honor awarded in our Army during the entire war. I am proud to have had an opportunity to share in their calculated risk in the Mediterranean.

2.

Getting Ready for War:

July 1940–June 1942

One day in the spring of 1942, when I was chief of staff to the commander of the Army Ground Forces, Lieutenant General Lesley J. McNair, in Washington, D. C., General George Marshall called me on the telephone. The British, he said, wanted to find out whether the United States Army was really getting ready to fight in Europe. Could I, he continued, arrange to show our Allies what we were doing? I said I could.

"Very well," the General said. "There will be Lord Louis Mountbatten and Sir John Dill." Then, after a brief discussion of details, he said he would go along too.

I made a few telephone calls and then put our distinguished guests and General Marshall into an airplane at Washington. We flew to Fort Benning in Georgia, where I took them up on a hilltop that provided a good view of an infantry assault. Artillery using live ammunition covered the advance. Tanks and fighter-bombers supported the realistic attack. In the afternoon we flew to Camp Gordon in Georgia, where the 4th Division at a review gave our visitors a close-up of the material of which the Army was made. I loaded them in the plane again and took them to Fort Bragg to see the 9th Division and to witness a parachute drop in which eight hundred men plunged from transports and spectacularly demonstrated how to seize and defend an air-port. By the end of the second day, Mountbatten and Dill were back in Washington, a bit breathless but, I believe, impressed by what they had seen. So was General Marshall.

Even on that brief two-day journey they were able to get an idea of the speed with which we were building new divisions only six months after Pearl Harbor. They also seemed to be impressed by the enthusiasm and high character of the officers in command of this newly created Army and by the kind of matériel with which it was equipped. The quality of leadership was always in Marshall's mind, and during the trip he had taken a hard look at the major commanders with whom we came in contact. Some of them, he felt, failed to measure up to requirements and his first act upon returning to Washington was to replace them. We were on the eve of events that General Marshall knew would test our armed forces to the limit and he intended to take chances only when they were unavoidable. A great and selfless soldier, he was also a tough taskmaster and a strict disciplinarian. He wanted to see rugged, physically fit commanders who knew their stuff and who got out and saw things on the ground, men who had the courage of their convictions and who would speak their minds.

The training system that we observed briefly on that trip was, of course, the key to our nation's ability to put into the field an Army that was ready to go up against the veteran German troops within less than a year after the United States got into the war. Since sound and intensive training of troops is normally the deciding factor in the final test of battle, it seems to me a brief glimpse of the methods we employed is essential to the reader's under-standing of events that later made wartime headlines during the Medi-terranean campaigns.

In the late 1930s our General Staff, conscious of the danger of war, was making as much progress as conditions permitted toward preparing the armed forces for an emergency. At that time I was Plans and Training officer (G-3) of the 3rd Division on duty at Fort Lewis, Washington. General Marshall had instructed Lieutenant General John L. DeWitt, commanding the Pacific Coast area, with whom I was closely and happily associated in World War I, to make the first large training test of landing forces, and the 3rd Divi-sion was selected to carry out the joint exercises by the Army and Navy. It thus became my job to do the detailed planning for embarkation of the divi-sion at Fort Lewis, its transportation in convoy by the Pacific Fleet to Monte-rey Bay, California, and its landing in small craft against simulated enemy opposition.

We had almost none of the special equipment that was later developed for such wartime operations, but the three-day exercise went off well, and General Marshall, who witnessed the landing, later ordered me transferred to the Army War College in Washington, D. C., as an instructor. I was promoted from major to lieutenant colonel, and at the beginning of July 1940, I went around the post saying goodbye to my friends and associates.

It was not exactly a cheerful departure. I hated to be leaving the 3rd Division, which had a brilliant record in World War I, and my associates at Fort Lewis were an unusual group of men. In a period of a few years, there had been Brigadier General George C. Marshall, who commanded one of the brigades. There was Major General Walter C. Sweeney, the able and understanding commander of the 3rd Division. There was Colonel Robert Eichelberger, who commanded the 30th Infantry and was to set an enviable record in the war in the Pacific as commander of the Eighth Army. And there were many others who were to come into prominence within the next few years in various theaters of action.

It also was true that our family—my wife, our son Bill, and our daughter Ann—were unhappy about leaving Fort Lewis, for we had enjoyed our tour of duty there. We regretted the journey that would take us so far from Camano Island in Puget Sound, where we owned a few acres and had spent many happy vacation days. But the thing that really kept us from being cheerful was the tenseness that was building up everywhere as the war danger increased.

I dropped in on one of our friends, Lieutenant Colonel Ike Eisenhower, on my farewell rounds, and we talked briefly about the drift toward trouble as a result of the European war. Ike was a friend of long standing. He was two years my senior at West Point, but we had been in the same company and had lived in the same division of barracks. We saw a lot of each other. He later had been chief of staff for General Douglas MacArthur in the Philippines before returning to Fort Lewis to take command of a battalion of the 15th Infantry. I had long admired his sterling qualities, but of course never foresaw that we would serve so intimately together as we were to do in World War II. No more did I foresee that he would be primarily responsible for the opportunities that were later to come to me.

There had been a rumor that the Army War College and other educational institutions of the Army might fold up in order to release large numbers of military personnel for duty with the troops, and for once it sounded like a sensible rumor. I didn't much like the idea of setting off on a transport from San Francisco via the Panama Canal to Washington when there was such an intense feeling of uncertainty. Who could tell what might happen while I was circling slowly around the coast?

We left Fort Lewis by automobile, planning to pay a short visit to Camano Island before heading for San Francisco, and had gotten as far as the downtown district of Seattle about an hour and a half later when I turned on the radio to get a news broadcast. The first announcement was a dispatch from Washington saying that the Army War College had been closed. The Clark foursome suddenly felt as if it had been cut adrift in rough seas. I pulled over to the curb without saying a word, got out and went into the Olympic Hotel, and telephoned General Sweeney, the commander at Fort Lewis.

"Look, General," I said when I heard his voice on the telephone, "they've closed the War College. I want my house back."

"Well," he answered promptly, "you only left it two hours ago, so I think you could come back and move in."

I did not do it, however. I took the family to Camano Island and then returned to Fort Lewis to report for duty, but when I wired General Marshall explaining the situation and requesting further instructions, I received in reply a crisp message telling me "comply with your orders." When I finally arrived in Washington, I found that a General Headquarters of the Army (GHQ) was being set up directly under General Marshall. Major General Lesley J. McNair was the chief of staff for this GHQ and about fifteen officers from the various branches were assigned as his staff. The new GHQ was described as the field headquarters to organize, equip and train our Army for combat, and I was told that I was to be one of McNair's assistants. That sounded good to me, but when I tried to report for duty I couldn't find McNair. As a matter of fact, for the next couple of years it was pretty hard for anybody to find McNair because he always was on the go; in one year I traveled 80,000 miles by air with him.

I never had met my new boss, but I had corresponded with him not long before when he was in charge of the Command and General Staff School, and he had taken a great interest in the 3rd Division's amphibious operation at Monterey Bay. I also had heard a great deal about him. He was highly regarded throughout the Army and, for a general officer, he was on the younger side. He had distinguished himself in combat as an artilleryman in World War I, had passed rapidly from the grade of captain to brigadier general, and had dropped back to major immediately after the war as one of the "busted aristocrats." Now he was up toward the top again and I, naturally, was eager to see him.

When I inquired where I could join him, I was given a message saying to forget it, because he was on an inspection trip and he knew I wouldn't have the equipment with me for sleeping in the field for the next couple of weeks.

I appreciated his thoughtfulness, but I didn't have any intention of sitting around in Washington for two weeks. I began borrowing equipment, which was comparatively easy, except for the fact that I am six feet two inches tall. Everything was too short for me. My arms stuck out of borrowed jacket sleeves and my feet were too long for the sleeping bag, and I wasn't always sure that everything met in the middle.

I got aboard a plane and caught up with McNair at Pine Camp, New York, where the First Army under Lieutenant General Hugh Drum was conducting maneuvers that involved the National Guard and Reserve components, along with Regular Army units. I arrived before McNair and was waiting for him on the airfield. He gave me a quick, surprised look when he found out who I was, and then took me in his automobile to the scene of maneuvers. For the next three days, I hardly left his side.

When we got back to Washington, McNair began working on the organization of his new GHQ. He made me the G-8, which had responsibility for the training of troops. I found McNair one of the most brilliant, selfless and devoted soldiers I ever knew. He was a man who always wanted to see at first hand how things were working out, and there was never a time when he even considered the possibility of sitting back and getting information at second hand. Later, in Tunisia, he insisted during a visit to the battle area that he wanted to get up front and determine why the advance was slowed up, and he finally made his way to the most forward elements, where he was exposed to enemy fire and severely wounded. And still later, in Normandy, it was because he insisted upon seeing how the front line action was going that he was caught in the tragic bombardment by our own airplanes that, owing to a slight miscalculation, caused casualties among our own men and fatally wounded the General.

At GHQ, the small staff immediately became busy preparing programs that would enable all units to conduct their training along similar lines intended to achieve certain standards and specified objectives. Our goal, of course, was to integrate and speed up training in order to develop an Army for combat in the shortest possible time. My own feeling then was that we were eventually going to need a hundred divisions, but it was not easy to convince the War Department that our planning should be on such a scale. In fact, there was a continual and stubborn struggle with the General Staff, which took the position that we were trying to move too fast and that we should slow down the rate at which we were trying to expand.

The greatest problem that confronted the staff, I suppose, was to formulate a system for building new divisions at a high rate of speed when the time came. At that time there were only nine divisions activated in the

Army, and these only partly trained, but when an emergency arose we would be called upon to produce fifty or a hundred divisions as quickly as possible. In laying the groundwork for our job, we devised tests to determine the proficiency of each Army unit, and we planned the advance schooling of officers and noncommissioned officers. The system we evolved, briefly, provided for the careful selection ahead of time of key officers, which included the division commander, his two brigadier assistants, and regimental and separate unit commanders and their staffs. Likewise, a noncommissioned cadre of several hundred selected corporals and sergeants was earmarked for the new division. All were sent to appropriate schools, and several weeks before the date the new division was to be activated these key people were assembled at the new camp. They were given a brief period in which to work as a team, then the draftees poured in, and a new division was born of good parenthood. It was born with a pretty solid backbone, too, since one out of every ten was an experienced soldier.

The division immediately plunged into a fifty-two-week training program, the details of which had been fully worked out at GHQ long in advance for infantry, cavalry, and armored divisions. In practice, this method made it possible to create as many as four new divisions each month.

The GHQ eventually was abandoned in favor of a similar organization called Army Ground Forces. General Marshall announced this move as McNair and I returned from a long inspection trip. As usual when we landed at Bolling Field after one of these exhausting journeys, McNair asked me to ride with him to the Army War College, which now is called Fort McNair. And as usual, Master Sergeant George R. Williams, who was McNair's driver and now is my driver, brought the General's official mail out to the plane. There was a sort of set procedure about this. McNair would read a letter and invariably hand it on to me without comment as we drove in from the airfield. On this occasion, everything went along as scheduled until he came to the last letter, which he read, folded up and put in his pocket without saying a word.

I was not only surprised; I was a bit miffed. All the way home I kept wondering what could be so secret about the letter that he should keep it to himself. When we pulled up in front of his quarters Mrs. McNair was waiting on the steps, and as soon as we were out of the car she yelled, "Congratulations!" McNair flushed and began fishing around in his pocket for the letter, which he handed to me. It advised him that I had been promoted to brigadier general, but he had intended to give it to Mrs. Clark so that she would be the first to tell me. That was a kindly idea, but as long as it didn't work out I was glad to get the news in any fashion.

Shortly after my appointment as brigadier general, I was made the first chief of staff of the new Army Ground Forces. Our headquarters became the center of planning for a number of operations that never got beyond the planning stage. Just for instance, Major General Joe Stilwell and later Major General Lloyd Fredendall were designated to command operations for the seizure of Dakar and the Azores. Their groups worked in our offices, which was about as close as they ever got to those particular objectives.

It soon became increasingly important to give commanders a chance to handle large units of troops in the field, and McNair wanted to test the soundness of our logistical doctrines in large-scale maneuvers, where the men could sleep and live and work as near as possible to combat conditions. He asked me to plan maneuvers in Louisiana and, a bit later, in North Carolina in the autumn of 1941 when for the first time air and ground forces with infantry, artillery and armored units would test medical and signal facilities and all the other complicated apparatus essential to the maintenance of large bodies of troops in the field.

The Louisiana maneuvers were typical of such tests. There we pitted Lieutenant General Ben Lear's Second Army against the Third Army commanded by Lieutenant General Walter Krueger. "Keep the directive," McNair said, "as simple as possible."

With this in mind, I got an automobile map of Louisiana and drew a big goose egg in the Shreveport area, where Lear would assemble his army. I drew another for Krueger's forces, and in front of each I put a broad line that no troops would be permitted to cross before a given signal. I gave each army a mission that would bring them into contact; McNair said that was fine and to go to it, limiting the maneuvers to the state of Louisiana. Except for one disappointment, these maneuvers proved to be invaluable in giving us experience in moving troops rapidly and efficiently, giving new commanders and staffs a chance to handle large units in the field, with the complicated logistics involved, and providing an opportunity for the various arms—the infantry, artillery, cavalry and armor—as well as the services of the army and air, to work closely together and to develop team play. The experiences learned greatly simplified our work when after Pearl Harbor it was necessary to move large numbers of troops quickly to the West Coast. The disappointment referred to above was suffered by Krueger's chief of staff, who turned out to be Colonel Ike Eisenhower. He had a fine plan for making a huge envelopment around and through Texas in order to get at the rear of Lear's Second Army, and it doubtless would have been the most spectacular maneuver of the pre-Pearl Harbor era if we had not limited the operations to Louisiana.

As McNair's deputy at this time, I conducted the critiques that followed these activities in the field, and just as I was concluding one of them an officer handed me a telegram from Washington listing the names of a number of officers who had been nominated by the President for promotion to the grade of brigadier general. I took a quick look at it and noticed Eisenhower's name well up on the list. I took a quick look out in front and saw Ike sitting in the first row. It was too good a chance to miss. I announced to the officers in attendance that I had just received the list of promotions and would read the names. There was a silence as thick as a Turkish rug in the big recreation hall where we were meeting. I read the names, but when I came to Ike's name I deliberately skipped it and read all the way through the list before I paused, studied the paper briefly and added: ". . . and Colonel Dwight D. Eisenhower." He was watching me closely with bright, alert eyes as if he might have been expecting something of the sort, and, as I read his name, he dropped one eyelid in a broad, pleased wink. I noticed as the meeting broke up that it was Eisenhower who got the most congratulations.

It was not long afterward that General Marshall came down to observe our field training operations. One evening when we were sitting alone, he told me about certain changes he was making in the staff in Washington. "I wish you would give me a list of ten names of officers you know pretty well and whom you would recommend to be chief of Operations Division of the War Department General Staff," he said.

"I'll be glad to do that," I said, "but there would be only one name on the list. If you have to have ten names, I'll just put nine ditto marks below it."

"Who is this officer of whom you think so highly?" he asked.

"Ike Eisenhower," I said.

"I've never met him," Marshall said, but he quickly added that he knew of Ike's brilliant record. Not long thereafter Eisenhower was ordered to Washington as chief of War Plans Division, and was soon made a major general.

By the time Pearl Harbor came along—I got the news, like almost everybody else, over the radio—I was in on a great deal of top planning in Washington, partly because McNair happened to be hard of hearing. He made up for this by reading the other fellow's lips, and usually his mind, if there was anything up there worth reading; but he was reluctant at times to become involved in large conferences because of his handicap, and it fell on me to represent him at many sessions in General Marshall's office.

After we were in the war, and I had been made a major general, a number of these conferences were devoted to our plans to send an army corps to the United Kingdom at an early date for the purpose of commanding, receiving our forces, selecting training sites, and handling the training of troops that would be flowing into that island base off the European coast. McNair was of the opinion that any one of three men could do the job admirably. They were Major Generals George Patton, Stilwell, and Fredendall. I presented his views on the candidates and on the plans generally when these matters were discussed in conference.

Nothing had been decided, however, when Eisenhower gave me a ring one day in May of 1942 and said he was flying to England the next day on Marshall's instructions to study the situation at first hand.

"Will you go along?" he asked. "We'll be gone about three weeks."

I quickly accepted the invitation and secured McNair's consent. General "Hap" Arnold, then chief of staff of the Army Air Forces, and his assistant, Colonel Hoyt Vandenberg, now Chief of Staff of the U.S. Air Force, were to go along. I went home for lunch, told Mrs. Clark the good news, and quickly packed my suitcase. I had considerable business to clean up, so I returned to my office and sat at my desk for several hours, dictating most of the time. McNair sent for me about then and I got out of my chair—and discovered I couldn't stand up. The whole six feet two inches of me was doubled over, and no matter what I did, I couldn't straighten up. I was, among other things, horrified. This seemed to me a hell of a way to start off for the war.

It eventually developed that I had dislocated my sacroiliac. I managed to get home and into a hot bath. That did no good. I tried everything any of us could think of, with no results. In desperation I got myself into a chiropractor's office and after he had wrapped my legs around my neck a few times, I was able to navigate again. I still was barely able to walk and, incidentally, only with considerable pain, when I got out to Bolling Field the next day and climbed aboard the plane for Gander Air Field in Newfoundland.

My back gradually improved despite a bad flight. We were almost halfway across the ocean from Gander when weather forced us to turn back. The next day we tried again and landed at Prestwick, in Scotland, but flight conditions were so bad we had to take the night train down to London. We were quartered at Claridge's Hotel and quickly got down to work, the main result of which was a recommendation by Eisenhower, Arnold, and myself that an experienced officer, who was familiar with Washington's new plans for action in Europe, should replace the U.S. general then in command in the United Kingdom.

The next most important thing about the trip—or at least the thing that sticks in my mind most firmly—was our meeting with General Bernard L. Montgomery, who was then the general officer in command of the British army in the southeast of England. This was known early in the war as the "invasion coast" because it was there that the German invasion had been expected for so many months. Montgomery was then engaged in maneuvers that had the code name of TIGER, a nickname that often was applied to the dapper and harddriving little general himself in those days. An invitation was extended to Ike and me to observe the maneuvers, and we drove down to Montgomery's headquarters, where we were shown into a small office lined with war maps to await the arrival of the distinguished soldier.

He came in briskly, was introduced, and promptly began to orient us with a crisp lecture on the development of the maneuvers. There were several other officers in the room and everybody gave his full attention to Montgomery's remarks. After a while, Ike decided he would like to smoke a cigarette. He quietly fished around in his pocket, pulled out a pack, and offered one to me. I declined with a shake of my head, but Ike lighted up. He had taken about two puffs when the lecture broke off in the middle of a sentence. Montgomery sniffed the air without looking around and in a loud voice asked: "Who's smoking?"

"I am," Ike said meekly.

"I don't," Montgomery said sternly, "permit smoking in my office."

Ike put out his cigarette, and the lecture proceeded. At the conclusion of that first meeting between Montgomery and Eisenhower we got a good laugh out of the incident, but not until we were well out of Montgomery's hearing.

It was after we had returned to the United States that General Marshall asked me to arrange the two-day airplane journey that gave Lord Mountbatten and Sir John Dill a chance to observe the training methods we had initiated. On the last evening of that trip, Marshall gave a little dinner for the party at Pinehurst, North Carolina. I sat next to him and we discussed in detail the new divisions that had been created and the necessity for getting a corps overseas at an early date.

"It seems to me it would be a good idea to include one of these new National Army divisions among the first sent to England," I said at one point. "I think it should be done even if the division selected is only part way through its training and not actually ready for combat. It would stimulate the interest of other divisions that are still in training, and there is a good chance that training under semi-war conditions existing in the United Kingdom would speed up the process." This was never done, however, because available shipping had to be used for divisions immediately available for combat.

In the course of several conversations on this subject during the month of June, 1942, the question had come up of who would command the corps which would be sent abroad. I always had assumed that it would be either Patton or Fredendall, but near the end of our talk at the Pinehurst dinner,

General Marshall said, "I am going to send the II Corps to the United Kingdom very soon and I may send you as its commander." I almost fell out of my chair.

The next day, back in Washington, Mountbatten telephoned me and offered congratulations. I still wasn't sure, but he said that he had just been at a meeting with Marshall and that I would lead II Corps to England. Marshall confirmed this a short time later. He recalled that earlier when we had discussed the need for a new commander in the United Kingdom I had said that my choice would be Eisenhower.

"I had already decided to send Eisenhower," he said. "A few days ago I had him in here and told him he was going and asked him whom he would recommend to be his principal subordinate in command of II Corps. He said, 'Clark.'" Marshall gazed at me speculatively. "It looks as if you boys got together. How soon can you go?"

Instinctively I looked at my wristwatch. He said, "Never mind; that's soon enough."

Before we departed, however, I had to go down to Jacksonville, Florida, to visit II Corps headquarters, then under command of Fredendall. I wanted to see the staff and to augment it with some men of my own choice, men with whom I had been associated for some time. And there was one thing about which I was particularly determined: I did not intend to take old officers on this arduous duty. I was forty-six years old at the time and I had prepared a list of all the staff with their ages. One by one, I called in the key chiefs of sections, interviewed them, and told each of them immediately whether I was taking him abroad. There were only a few men in their top fifties who were thus eliminated, but these interviews obviously were not a pleasant task. I did, however, stick firmly to my predetermined plan. Well, I almost stuck to it.

At the end of my list was the name of the corps chaplain, Colonel Marius S. Chatignon. He was fifty-eight years old. By the time he came in—a fine-looking, vigorous man—everybody around headquarters knew what was going on and that there was bad news if you were born too soon. Chatignon saluted and I asked him to sit down.

"I suppose you know what's going on?" I said.

"I do."

"You understand why I am taking this course of action?" I continued.

"No, I do not."

"Well," I said, "you are just too old, Chaplain. I'm sorry, but I feel that I must take younger men."

He bristled and looked me steadily in the eye. "May I speak freely,

General?" he asked.

"Certainly."

"Well, General, I think you're too young for this job. And as far as physical qualifications are concerned, I believe I could put you on your back right here in this office if you would like to give me permission to try. If you don't take me, I'll go with someone else. I'm going to get into this show."

"You win, Padre," I said. "We'll go together."

We did go together. Padre Chatignon was with my Fifth Army throughout the war. He was a magnificent man among a large number of men to whom magnificence was routine in those days: a courageous character, selfless in his devotion to duty and to care of his men. I don't know where he is today, but I know that I am proud to have been associated with him and that he kept me from making a grave mistake by inviting me to wrestle.

By the time I had returned to Washington to complete preparations for my departure to England, I had made a good many changes in II Corps. Mainly, I had increased the size of the staff until it was now a reinforced complete headquarters staff.

"It seems to me," remarked McNair when we talked things over, "that you and I have been spending the last year insisting to everybody every day that all staffs must be kept to a minimum. But here you are, in command of the first staff to be sent to Europe, and you've got yourself the biggest staff of all."

His chiding was gentle, but I could only agree with him. There was, however, what we both considered a good reason. My headquarters would be the first and only large staff group in the United Kingdom under Eisenhower for some time to come. Eisenhower would have to build up his Allied staff, and I wanted to have an excess of good officers with me to fill his needs in the coming months.

A couple of days prior to my departure for England, I conceived what seemed to me a brilliant plan for easing the pressure of work that I knew would be great during the first few weeks abroad. I called in Sergeant Kenneth G. Merrill, an efficient clerk and stenographer, who had been with me at Fort Lewis and later joined me in Washington, locked the door of my office, and sat down to dictate. My idea was that, having just returned from a three-week visit to England, I was familiar with the various places of interest and could get a head start on the job of writing home. I simply would dictate a few letters to Mrs. Clark, describing the sights around London and in the countryside, file them in the proper order, and then, after I reached England, mail one of them every third or fourth day, or whenever I didn't have time to compose an on-the-spot letter home.

I explained my plan to Merrill, impressed him with the necessity for secrecy, and proceeded to dictate five separate letters to be dated after I arrived in London. I was so pleased with my plan that when I finished dictating, I gave him a friendly little lecture on how efficient I was being and how much time it would save me later on. Merrill was going to England by boat, but since he had to join II Corps headquarters at Indiantown Gap, Pennsylvania, he left Washington before I did. He had known our family for several years and, naturally, went around to the house to say goodbye. As he was leaving, Mrs. Clark told him, "Don't forget that you have one very important job to do over there. Be sure that the General writes to me at least once a week."

Merrill had just finished typing the five letters and listening to my remarks about efficiency, and the combination was too much for him. He burst into hysterical laughter. It didn't take Mrs. Clark long to force a confession out of him, and of course I had to destroy the five letters I had prepared.

There were a couple of other things that stand out in my memory about those last days before my departure. I knew a number of officers scattered around the country who wanted to get overseas and in whom I had a lot of confidence. I could not tell them what was happening, but I knew their way of thinking well enough to call them on the telephone and by indirection find out whether they would like to go with me. One of them, for instance, was Colonel LeCount Slocum, who was in the field artillery and stationed on the West Coast. I got him on the phone.

"Do you," I asked, "want to go places and ring doorbells?"

He didn't even hesitate. "Yes, sir," was the reply. "What's the timing?"

"You'll have to be here tomorrow," I said. Slocum got there and so did some of the others, such as Colonel Lowell Rooks, Infantry, an old friend of mine and an outstanding officer with a fine record of accomplishment in our peacetime Army. I made him chief of staff. I took Lieutenant Colonel Edwin B. Howard, Infantry, and Major C. Coburn Smith, Field Artillery, both promising officers who had demonstrated ability with the 3rd Division at Fort Lewis. I summoned Lieutenant Jack Beardwood, a reserve officer whom I had known at Fort Lewis when he was with the Associated Press in Tacoma. He later did a fine job as my aide and helped keep the diary that provides the source material for this book.

My hurried packing also attracted the attention of Sergeant William C. Chaney, a Negro, who had been assigned as orderly at our house after I came to Washington. He knew I was going overseas and although he had no idea where I would be, he went to Mrs. Clark and said he would like to go with me. She told him to speak for himself.

"How does a fellow get to go along with you?" he asked me.

I told him that it was impossible to know what kind of assignment this would turn out to be and I asked him if he was sure he wanted to go. He was sure, so I had him assigned to II Corps Headquarters. Chaney was with me from then on. He hardly left my side. When I lived in a trailer in Italy for many months, he pitched his tent beside the trailer and did everything from press my pants to cook my dinner. He served Winston Churchill, King George, and other famous personages as nonchalantly as he turned out a plate of beans for a hungry lieutenant, and was decorated for bravery at Anzio. I suppose the war would have been won without him, but it would have been far more unpleasant for me.

On June 23, Mrs. Clark, Ann, and Bill, who was then prepping for West Point, came down to Bolling Field to say goodbye. Ike and I took to the air at 9:10 a.m. for our second trip to Europe. It would be five years before I returned for duty in the United States.

3.

We Decide on TORCH:

June 1942–August 1942

The approach to Britain by air on a pleasant day is always an exhilarating sight, and on that 24th day of June 1942, the first glimpse of the beleaguered islands was both inviting and forbidding. We had awakened far out over the Atlantic Ocean, and about an hour off the coast of Scotland we flew over a convoy of ships that steamed a zigzag course with a naval escort hovering nearby. Then ahead of us was Scotland and almost at once we could observe hutment and troop camps in both Ayr and Prestwick. Beyond Scotland, we knew, lay the great military camps of England and Wales waiting grimly and hopefully for the reinforcements that were coming from America.

We landed at Prestwick at 11:30 a.m. and after lunch continued with a Polish pilot-guide and several additional passengers to Northolt Airport near London, where we were greeted by Lord Louis Mountbatten, chief of British Combined Operations; Major General John C. H. Lee, head of the U.S. Services of Supply in England; and other staff officers. We were taken immediately to quarters at Claridge's Hotel.

The next few days were taken up with conferences, which quickly included Admiral Stark, commander in chief of U.S. naval forces in the European Theater of Operations, and Major General Carl Spaatz, commander of the Eighth Air Force. Most of the discussion was devoted to preparations for the reception and training of the forces that would soon arrive from the United States. Making these arrangements was a tremendous job because the British military establishments already were crowded and now large areas would have to be given up for the quartering of our troops, further jamming the facilities of the island and often making us feel that another shipload would burst the seams. The ships kept on coming, however, and in one way or another we managed to keep the seams together then and under far more crowded conditions later.

The morning after our arrival we walked over to the big converted apartment house at 20 Grosvenor Square where Ike's Allied headquarters was to be located, except when he moved them to the various fields of campaign. Photographers were waiting for us, since Eisenhower's arrival had been announced, and there was a furious popping of flashlight bulbs as we went in. The next morning the photographs appeared in the newspapers with my picture carefully cut out by the censors, as it was not, of course, to be disclosed that my II Corps headquarters was being established in England.

I wanted to get my headquarters set up before the troops started to come from the United States, so on June 27, with my staff, I made a reconnaissance of the Salisbury Plain area, about eighty miles southwest of London. We visited the headquarters of the British V Corps and made arrangements to locate II Corps headquarters at Longford Castle, some three miles southeast of Salisbury. Later, after inspecting training areas near Plymouth and agreeing on tentative arrangements, Ike and I, accompanied by Colonel Lowell Rooks, my chief of staff, flew over to Northern Ireland on the first of July to inspect troops and installations of our V Army Corps, which then was engaged in a joint exercise with British troops. Thinking that the Americans seemed fat and pudgy in contrast to the lean, hard look of the British soldiers, I came to the conclusion that the II Corps was going to have a period of grueling training after it arrived in the United Kingdom to prepare for battle.

When I returned to Salisbury, Ike asked me to look into a minor problem that had come up. Near Salisbury was the American Red Cross Harvard Field Hospital, which had been established in the summer of 1942. It now was proposed that the American nurses attached to the unit should enter the American Army's Nurse Corps, but there seemed to be considerable reluctance on the part of some of them to do so.

I went to their quarters one evening to see whether anything could be done and was greeted by a lively and good-looking bunch of girls who invited me into the drawing room, gave me a place of honor on the divan, and gathered around as if they wanted to hear what I had to say. I suppose I would have been flattered in any circumstances, but since I had not been expecting a warm welcome I was quite set up by all the attention.

The conversation had hardly started when the directress, a very sedate and straight-backed woman, came into the room and gave me a long look.

"Well," she said, "I see the General has already captured all the girls."

I didn't know whether I was being bawled out or congratulated, and I never did find out for sure. One of the girls deflated me before I had a chance.

"Oh, it ain't him," she said scornfully. "It's them pips on his shoulders."

I should add that, despite my deflation, most of the nurses did later join the Army.

There was so much to be done that both Ike and I were on the go all the time in this period, but on July 5 we took a break and accepted an invitation for an overnight visit with Prime Minister Winston Churchill at Chequers. Churchill bounced out to meet us, wearing a baggy smock and carpet slippers, and beaming happily. He led us down a winding path through the woods until we came to a secluded bench where we sat down and talked about coming events.

At that time a controversy was just starting that was to last for several months and involve periods of rather bitter recrimination. It had to do with the question of whether the Allies should try to open a second front by crossing the English Channel to invade western Europe, and centered on whether such an invasion should be attempted immediately in order to relieve the German pressure on Soviet Russia's endangered armies.

It was typical of the Prime Minister that he lost no time in stating his views. He stressed to us that he was in favor of postponing the cross-Channel operation and undertaking an invasion of northwest Africa at the earliest possible date. A European operation, even of a limited nature, would be too hazardous, he said, until a later time. Both Ike and I felt that direct action was the best idea and that it was necessary to carry the war to the European continent as directly and as quickly as possible. We were, therefore, noncommittal about Churchill's suggestions because we felt that his African plan would detract from whatever hope there was of striking directly at Europe with a limited invasion program in 1942, or of mounting a large-scale invasion operation in 1943.

Later the Prime Minister showed us over the beautiful old house, but he never bothered to change from his smock and carpet slippers either for cocktails or for dinner, at which the only ladies were Mrs. Churchill and Lady Portal, wife of the head of the British Air Command. Churchill admonished us not to worry about talking about war plans during dinner because "my wife and Lady Portal know everything."

The conversation, however, didn't turn immediately to war secrets because the Prime had another idea.

"Where," he challenged me as we sat down to dinner, "is your short snorter?"

At that time, the short-snorter racket was in full swing and its participants were not numerous. It was a nebulous organization of individuals who had flown one of the oceans. A new member could join if after flying an ocean he paid a dollar to or bought a drink for one or more persons who already were in the club. Then they would give him a certificate of membership consisting of a dollar bill (or a pound note) on which was written the date of his ocean flight and to which they signed their names. Members were required always to carry their certificates, to which they had other members add their names from time to time, and any member unable to produce his certificate upon demand had to pay a dollar fine or buy drinks for all short snorters present.

In this instance, I produced my dollar bill, duly certified, and then demanded that Churchill produce his. He fumbled in his pockets. No bill.

"All right," I said, "pay up."

"No," he replied. "I won't pay up. I have it here somewhere." There was more searching and we again demanded payment, without success.

"The rules," I insisted, "are that if you don't have it on your person you are fined. Pay up."

"I make my own rules in my own house," he snapped. "Here everybody has an hour in which to produce his bill."

With that he got up from the table and went shuffling away into another part of the house. In ten minutes he was back, flushed and triumphant, with the bill clutched in his hand. I later saw this performance repeated on several occasions when the Prime always was caught short, but went scurrying around until he found his bill. We never collected from him.

The war news at that time could not be described as good, and Churchill mentioned several times during the evening that he soon must have something favorable to "report to my people." Once, after dinner, it appeared that he might have something. A report came in that a Russian submarine had scored a torpedo hit on the German battleship *Tirpitz* during action to protect a thirty-three-ship convoy that was then en route on a hazardous and highly important voyage from Britain to Archangel with supplies for the Russians. Churchill was elated for a while, but eventually it developed that the report was false. In fact the situation was far worse than we realized that evening.

The convoy represented the first real attempt to move supplies through to Russia, the Prime Minister pointed out. Murmansk had been bombed almost out of existence by the Germans and the Nazi fleet was concentrated on the northern coast of Norway, supported by land-based bombers, in an effort to prevent any supplies from getting through by that route. The entire British Home Fleet had accompanied the convoy almost halfway to Archangel but then was forced to turn back to avoid attack by the Nazi bombers, and the convoy had to go on accompanied only by destroyers, submarines and armed trawlers. It was some time later that we received news that only four of the thirty-three ships got through to Archangel.

News was not good from the African front either. The Nazi Afrika Korps under Field Marshal Erwin Rommel was pounding a path into Egypt, and the dispatches that reached the Prime Minister and his generals during that evening were not encouraging. Churchill, in spite of this, was full of bounce and he made the evening a lively one. He told about walking alone in the woods that afternoon and meeting a man and his wife and their three children. He stopped to chat and asked whether there were any other children.

"No, just three of them," the man replied.

"Well," said the Prime Minister, assuming a stern attitude, "I think you should have four. Get busy on that right away!"

After a session of motion pictures in the mansion, the Prime Minister introduced Ike and me to his staff, made up mostly of officers of the Cold-stream Guards, and while we were chatting to them he trotted out of the room. In a minute he came back carrying the rifle he had used during the Boer War.

"Gentlemen!" he exclaimed, adjusting his baggy smock and shuffling forward in his carpet slippers. "I'll show you how we used to do things." And, grinning happily, he went through a snappy manual of arms with the cumbersome old rifle.

Things went on that way until about three o'clock in the morning, with bursts of gaiety, serious talk about war plans, and frequent interruptions by the Prime Minister to ask Eisenhower: "Have you seen my paper on that point?" We had never seen his papers, so he would send out each time for documents embodying his own particular ideas on a certain operation. I was deeply impressed with his detailed knowledge of every subject of discussion. When we finally turned in, I found on the bedside table a book telling about the famous old house, which is almost a thousand years old, and I discovered a lot of important people had once slept in the bed I was occupying. I had a bit of trouble getting to sleep.

After breakfast the next morning, Ike and I went to inspect the Chequers guard. As we were going down the line, Churchill, still in his nightclothes, stuck his head out of a bedroom window and hollered: "Ain't they a fine body of men!" We agreed.

As a result of my repeated visits to Chequers and conferences at No. 10 Downing Street and elsewhere, I had many opportunities to study Winston Churchill at first hand. I consider him to be the greatest man I have ever met—dynamic in the extreme, full of charm, persuasive, with plenty of ability and drive, and a profound understanding of global affairs. He had a surprising knowledge of tactical and strategical problems, but the military factors always were subordinate in his mind to political considerations. Once he had decided that a certain course of action was proper and would produce the best results for the Allied cause—and particularly for Great Britain—he relentlessly pursued that course, ruthlessly eliminating obstacles in his path.

We drove back to London, with only about a week left in which to complete arrangements for the arrival of the first American troops. I went up to Greenock, Scotland, to meet the convoy on July 12. The light cruiser *Philadelphia* and then the battleship *Texas* led the ships into the Firth of Clyde. There were in all seven big, gray troopships and twenty escort destroyers in addition to the *Philadelphia* and the *Texas*. Every foot of deck space seemed to be covered with khaki-clad men as the ships moved into the channel, which already was crowded with merchantmen, warships, small boats, and a couple of British submarines coming in from sea duty.

I went out in a launch to the *Monterey,* which was the lead troopship, and also boarded the *Argentina,* talking to as many as possible of the II Corps men. Late in the afternoon, the *Maid of Orleans,* a channel steamer that had made five trips to Dunkerque during the famous British evacuation of that port, took most of II Corps headquarters staff ashore and they entrained for London, thence to temporary quarters at Tidworth near Salisbury.

The following day I addressed all officers of my headquarters for the first time, outlining in a general way the task facing them and our men. There were about 180 officers and I had to stand up on a wooden bench to see all of them.

"You are the advance echelon of the American Ground Forces in England," I told them. "There is opportunity for all of you because you are in on the ground floor."

I devoted a good deal of my talk to the need for making a good impression on the British, for neat and soldierly appearance, meticulous conduct, and courtesy, in order to establish an attitude of confidence in our forces. I also told them that they would hear many ill-founded rumors, most of them emanating from enemy sources, about the British and that they must remember that cooperation with the British was imperative.

I made a similar speech of welcome to the enlisted men on July 15 as they began getting settled in their quarters. By that time, the 2nd Battalion of the 16th Infantry, 1st Division, which was the advance group of combat troops, was on the ground and seemed to be in good spirits. Within the next few days American troops began marching the roads of England for the first time, making long hikes with packs and rifles as the first step in the rigorous training schedule that I was determined to carry out.

The headquarters of II Corps was rapidly established at Longford Castle. I doubt that anybody has had a more remarkable headquarters building since the days of Cromwell, who, incidentally, almost lost his life capturing the castle in 1645. The castle, seat of Lord Radnor, who leased it to the United States Army, was started in 1588 and built on the site of the original manor, which dated back to 1166. It stood at the bottom of a dish-shaped valley, hard by a branch of the River Avon where there were excellent trout and where, by his lordship's edict, only he and I were permitted to fish. I appreciated the permission, but never got a chance to take advantage of it.

Nissen huts and tents quartered troops in the wood to the north, and carpenters were always noisily at work refurbishing or expanding surrounding buildings to make room for an increasing number of headquarters personnel. One such converted building, called Cowesfield, was promptly renamed Moo Manor by its American occupants.

The castle, which had walls three feet thick, had been built as a city within itself, and it included a chapel, a great dining hall, billiard and game rooms, a gigantic kitchen, many salons and countless chambers that were all converted now to offices, assembly and lecture rooms and communications centers. My own office on the third floor was reached through a maze of twisting walls and opened off a corridor that ran between two of the five great turrets on the castle. Other officers occupied four of the towers, and the fifth was reserved as the quarters of "The Lord," as we called him. He stuck around through most of the period of our "occupation" of the historic landmark, and we all got along pretty well despite the tremendous confusion and the occasional unearthly racket of antiaircraft guns that we had mounted atop the towers because they provided a good field of fire for defense against low-flying German planes. The Germans never got a bomb very close to the castle, but apparently the sixteenth-century architects didn't have antiaircraft weapons in mind when they built the towers; for several years after the war we received a claim from The Lord for damage to one tower, allegedly caused by vibration of our defensive guns.

We hardly were established at Longford Castle when word came from Eisenhower's headquarters that General Marshall, Admiral King, Chief of U.S. Naval Operations, Harry Hopkins, special assistant to President Roosevelt, and Presidential Secretary Stephen Early were arriving by air from

Washington. Their visit could mean only one thing: Mr. Roosevelt wanted a decision on when and where American forces were going to get into action. It was known that he insisted on some kind of operation before the end of 1942, because he was opposed to having our troops wait idly in crowded and food-rationed Britain. He wanted the weight of American arms to be felt by the Germans.

Ike told me to come up to London and to bring along my top-ranking officers. I arrived with eight colonels of the II Corps on July 17, and the next week was spent in threshing out a decision with the British, who were most conscious of the fact that comparatively few American troops could be transported to the United Kingdom for an assault on France in 1942 and that, therefore, they would be required to furnish the bulk of the necessary man power.

Since these conferences have been described in considerable detail by other participants, I shall merely say that the point of view of the Americans in favor of opening a second front in the fall of 1942 was based primarily on the idea that the Russians might collapse at any moment under the furiously renewed German offensive, and, in that event, we would have lost forever a favorable moment for an invasion. Also, being new at the job and impatient to get into action, by and large, we were ready to tackle anything. The British, however, with bitter experiences behind them, knew better.

In the course of this discussion, I was asked by Marshall, King and Hopkins to explain what I thought the American Ground Forces could do to alter the situation if the war in Russia developed to a point where the collapse of the Red Army appeared imminent. I pointed out that all we could count on using would be the 34th Division, then in Northern Ireland, if an assault across the channel were attempted on a date such as the often-mentioned D-day of September 15. The 34th, however, had had little amphibious training, it lacked antiaircraft support, and it had no tanks. The 1st Armored Division, also in Ireland, was not yet fully equipped, nor would any other units scheduled to arrive before September 15 be prepared for battle. I said that there would be a difficult problem in getting the men and their equipment together and that there seemed to be no possibility that invasion boats would be ready by mid-September—to say nothing of bad weather conditions prevailing at that time of year.

"I am in favor of doing something if the Russian situation is as black as President Roosevelt and others believe it to be. But opening of a second front at an early date means that the brunt of the invasion must be borne by the British. The American forces will be able to contribute comparatively little until the spring of 1943."

After a week of the London sessions, it seemed to be pretty well decided that no operations against the French coast could be undertaken in 1942, but that all our attention would be concentrated on preparing for a major invasion of Europe—a project that was known under the code name of ROUNDUP—in 1943. I returned to Longford Castle on July 25 and explained the situation to my staff, emphasizing that we must go in for a period of vastly intensified preparations and training.

Just to get the idea across, I told them that the enemy doubtless would employ all kinds of heinous devices against our invasion troops, and I described some of the anti-invasion equipment that the British had set up when they were expecting a Nazi invasion. Along the Dover coast they had installed huge reservoirs of gasoline on the sand dunes and had run dozens of pipes down to the most likely landing beaches, extending the pipes as much as a couple of hundred feet out into the water. The pipes ended in an upward curve so that the nozzle, which had attached to it a small explosive charge, was barely above water at high tide. In the event of an attempted enemy landing the gasoline would be permitted to run for a few minutes to cover the nearby surface of the water, and then the explosives would be set off in order to ignite the gasoline. A continuous stream of gasoline would then pour down from the reservoir to keep the waters afire. Some of these devices when tested by the British had set up a roaring wall of flames all along the waterfront, and may even have had an effect on the thinking of German observers who were not too far away on the French coast to get some idea of what was going on.

"Our training must be such," I said, "that we will be prepared for anything."

In line with this program, we canceled all half holidays and leaves and staggered the weekly day off of members of the staff so that work would not be interrupted. I also arranged with General Spaatz for Brigadier General Robert C. Candee to set up headquarters near Longford Castle and unify the work of the VIII Air Support Command with II Army Corps, and I selected Colonel Mike O'Daniel to head our amphibious training program. The Colonel had been with me in World War I when I commanded Company K of the 11th Infantry Regiment in the Argonne. After I was wounded by shrapnel there, Mike took over command and by his gallant conduct on the field of battle won the Distinguished Service Cross. He recently had headed up amphibious and commando training at Ground Force Headquarters in Washington.

I returned for the conclusion of the London conferences the next day, when it quickly developed that plans were being drastically changed.

Churchill's insistence on an invasion of Africa—a project that was known under the code name of TORCH—had borne fruit, and it was finally agreed that, while plans for ROUNDUP would be continued, the main immediate effort would be directed toward the Mediterranean Theater. We therefore were instructed to be prepared as fully as possible for an emergency attack against the French coast late in 1942 if the Russian situation became so critical that such action was essential, and we were told to proceed with broader plans for a 1943 invasion of Europe. But it was soon obvious that our real effort at this time was going to be against North Africa, with American forces coming directly from the United States to take over the major invasion role.

It seemed to me then that it would be a great calamity if the African operation acted as a sponge to draw off ships, matériel and men from the United Kingdom and weaken our preparations for the 1943 European invasion. I could not, of course, foresee that the European attack eventually would be delayed until 1944 and that, meanwhile, I would be operating in the Mediterranean Theater.

Just before General Marshall and Admiral King returned to the United States, General Charles de Gaulle requested a conference with Marshall. He knew something was in the wind and evidently hoped to get some information about the Allied war plans. General Marshall agreed to see de Gaulle, but he knew that the British had been reluctant to give the Free French any highly secret information, in the belief that there might be some leaks to the enemy. Marshall had no intentions of going counter to the British policy of secrecy. He therefore invited Admiral King, General Eisenhower, Brigadier General W. Bedell Smith, and me to Admiral King's room for the conference.

De Gaulle arrived, accompanied by a stiff-necked aide and interpreter, expecting to see only Marshall. When he found four other officers present, he was obviously displeased. After a curt handshake with each of us, he shrugged and lowered his tall, gaunt frame into a chair. Throughout the conference, his attention was directed almost exclusively to Marshall.

Admiral King had ordered a bottle of champagne in honor of the occasion, but General de Gaulle refrained from drinking. He told Marshall that he was placing at Marshall's disposal the French troops then in England, French North Africa, New Caledonia, Syria, and other distant French possessions. He stated through his interpreter that the Free French fighters would welcome with great joy the opening of the second front. He then asked what Marshall could tell him.

The American general made a polite and complimentary but noncommittal speech. So did Admiral King. Neither of them told him as much as he could have learned by reading the morning newspaper. De Gaulle was becoming impatient.

"*Dites-moi,*" he exclaimed with emotion in his deep bass voice. "*Qu' est ce que vous pensez faire pour le deuxième front!*"

"Tell me," parroted the interpreter, "the second-front plans!"

General Marshall and Admiral King nodded pleasantly, but again both made noncommittal replies. Perceiving that he was not to obtain the information he sought, General de Gaulle arose stiffly and announced that he would not take up "any more of your time." Then, after a cool handshake, he marched out with his aide close behind.

Undoubtedly de Gaulle had a keen military mind, but none of us had been impressed with his diplomacy or personal charm during this interview. Nevertheless, we were agreed that the cooperation of the French people was essential to the success of our invasion plans and that de Gaulle's collaboration was necessary.

We discussed for some time the difficulties of the French situation, recalling the British raid on St. Nazaire, which had been timed to coincide with an uprising by French patriots on shore. The French dutifully rioted and shot German soldiers and police; but when the British Commandos had withdrawn from the port, the Germans killed hundreds of rioters and took other repressive measures to crush the rebellious spirit. I remember saying that it seemed to me there was only one good revolt left in the French people and that there must be careful timing to bring it to a peak at the moment of our invasion operations. We already were planning at that time methods by which weapons and ammunition could be dropped from the air to the French patriots, and there had been developed a tin .45 pistol that looked like a dimestore toy but was extremely effective at close range and made an ideal weapon for such operations.

The presence of our Army Ground Force Headquarters in England was officially disclosed, and we had thirty-nine newspapermen swarming into Longford Castle on August 7. On the following day the bulk of the 1st Division arrived aboard the *Queen Mary* at Gourock, Scotland. The big liner, carrying more troops than had ever been loaded on one vessel before, made the trip from New York in six days, and without an escort except during the first and final stages of the voyage. There were 15,045 persons aboard—the entire 1st Division, except for the 16th Infantry, which was already in the Salisbury-Tidworth area, and the 601st Tank Destroyer Battalion.

Major General Terry Allen, the division commander, reported that morale was good; and as I witnessed the debarkation proceed smoothly and swiftly, I felt that here was an outfit that was certain to play an important role in the forthcoming fight. The censorship had timed the release of stories about

U.S. Army Ground Force Headquarters to coincide with the arrival of the troops on the *Queen Mary,* and on August 10 the newspapers were full of news about the interviews with the Americans. I had put emphasis on the idea that we were "not going to sit here on our backsides" during my talk with the reporters, and as a result all the articles had an aggressive tone that suggested the American forces were going to take the initiative as quickly as possible.

I had returned to Longford Castle on August 9 and was deep in conferences with my section chiefs about the reception of the 1st Division at Tidworth and plans for getting started at once on amphibious training when a call came for me to go to London to see Eisenhower. The next day knocked all my plans into a cocked hat.

4.

Deputy to Eisenhower:

August 1942–October 1942

I went up to London on August 10 and had lunch with General Eisenhower, Major General George Patton, and Lieutenant General Sir Kenneth Anderson of the British Middle East Forces; and by the time we had gotten around to the coffee, the entire war picture was undergoing a drastic change from my viewpoint.

As a result of the recently concluded second-front conference in London and of discussions after General Marshall's return to Washington, it had been decided that TORCH, the North African invasion project, would become a major instead of a minor operation and that it would be substituted for the proposed 1943 invasion of France. My fear that TORCH would drain off the strength of our French invasion plan was only too well grounded. The entire available resources of both the United States and Great Britain were to be thrown into TORCH, leaving nothing for ROUNDUP.

As Ike outlined these changes to me, I saw my plans falling apart like a handful of confetti. There wasn't any question now that Prime Minister Churchill's views had prevailed and that only future events would determine when or whether ROUNDUP would be revived.

"I am being buried under the demands that are being made on me," Ike said, turning to me. "How would you like to be my deputy commander in chief on TORCH?"

I began to feel better, but of course it was not easy suddenly to give up command of II Army Corps after all the work and planning we had put into it.

"The question is," Ike continued, "whether you want to stay at Longford Castle and sit on a dead fish."

That wasn't really a difficult question to answer. I said I wanted to do whatever Eisenhower wanted me to do and that I didn't want to run a risk of sitting out the war in a relatively inactive theater. In other words, I wasn't interested in sitting on a dead fish, and being second in command of the North African expedition sounded just right.

General Eisenhower immediately put up to a meeting of the British commanders the proposal to make me his deputy, and it was approved. The War Department was advised of the decision by cable, but it was decided that the action must be kept secret generally for a while in order to avoid arousing speculation. In fact I temporarily retained command of the II Corps because if I gave it up suddenly for some unannounced assignment, it was certain to arouse suspicions that some operation was in the making.

It was decided that Patton would command the American army corps that would make the attack on Casablanca by ship directly from the United States. I was pleased with that decision because I had known General Patton for a long time. My father had made the Army his career and was a major at Fort Sheridan, Illinois, when Georgie, as I called him, reported for his first duty in 1909 from West Point. He was then a fine-looking fellow, a good athlete and a dashing cavalryman. I being thirteen years old, he was my ideal of a young soldier. When I was chief of staff of the Ground Forces, I had many pleasant contacts with him, as he was our foremost American expert on tank warfare. We got along fine together.

Command of the British half of TORCH had changed three times in the four days previous to my appointment as deputy. In the beginning, General Sir Claude John Eyre Auchinleck had been in complete command of the British Middle East campaign, but the load was so great that Lieutenant General Sir Harold R. Alexander, who had been earmarked for TORCH, was designated instead to assist Auchinleck. So we lost Alex. Next it was decided that because of the growing importance of the African campaign, Lieutenant General W. H. E. Gott would be sent to take command of the British Eighth Army in Egypt. Gott's plane was shot down and he was killed while en route to Egypt.

Lieutenant General Sir Bernard L. Montgomery had been designated to succeed Alexander in active command of the British section of TORCH; but when Gott's plane was shot down, Montgomery was assigned to command the Eighth Army, leaving the TORCH assignment open again. On the day I was named deputy, the post had been given to Lieutenant General Sir Kenneth Anderson.

"I hope," I told Ike, "that the turnover of American generals in Africa is less rapid."

From my point of view, it turned out that the assignment of Anderson was unfortunate; although he conducted the operations of his British First Army in a competent manner during the North African landings and Tunisian campaign, he had an unhappy disposition that made planning very difficult.

I had to return to Longford Castle to clean up various problems and to explain developments to my top officers. The 1st Division was just getting settled at Tidworth and the Germans apparently were trying to find out something about our activities. On the afternoon of August 11, two Focke-Wulf fighter-bombers suddenly were sighted from the castle towers, although no air alert had been sounded as they covered the twenty miles between the coast and our headquarters.

The reason they had escaped detection, although it was a bright, clear day, was that they had flown at terrific speed barely above the trees, a maneuver that came to be known as hedge-hopping. Anti-aircraft batteries had no chance to open up on them and, because the weather was so fine, the Salisbury barrage balloons were not up. The planes dropped bombs near Salisbury and machine-gunned some trucks, but they failed to spot about half of our officers and enlisted men who were under the trees engaged in gas mask training. They did, however, make the British a bit jittery because of the failure to spot them in time for a warning, and the next day we canceled plans to mass the troops of the 1st Division for my welcoming speech. Instead I toured the area with Major General Terry Allen, the division commander. Here was a colorful officer. I had known Terry for many years. He had the reputation of being both a "hell raiser" and an unconventional "hot-shot operator." He was a typical cavalryman, full of dash, firepower, mobility and shock action. He shocked everybody—the enemy, his troops who loved him, and his superiors. He was ably supported by one Brigadier General Theodore Roosevelt, Jr., his assistant division commander. Their troops looked fine, and we were all pleased by their attitude and bearing.

That night I proceeded to London to take up my duties as Ike's deputy, establishing my own headquarters for joint planning of TORCH with the British at Norfolk House and temporarily moving to the Dorchester Hotel to share an apartment with Ike. Later, when the work became so pressing and the crush of night conferences became so great that we both needed more room, I moved to a small but comfortable apartment, which had been converted from an old stable on Hays Mews. Naturally, the place quickly became known to my friends as the Cat's Mews.

Word had come back from Washington approving my appointment as deputy commander in chief and I immediately began work with General

Anderson, Brigadier General Jimmy Doolittle, General Lee and others. There were many problems and considerable apprehension. Anderson seemed to me to be concerned about the wisdom of the whole TORCH project. The French were reported to have around 150,000 troops in the areas where the principal assaults would be made. Nobody seemed very certain about what the French attitude toward our forces would be. There were many reports that the Germans were planning to move in on the French North Africa area in the near future, a possibility that added to the pressure for speed on our own part.

Ike laid the problem of picking personnel and pushing preparations in my lap; he told me to make my own decisions and merely to report to him what was being done. One of the first decisions that had to be made concerned air support. I asked Doolittle to come around to my office and we went over the problem in a general way.

"Who do you think should handle the American air end of this operation?" I finally asked him.

"That," said the hero of the Tokyo raid, "is a pretty tough one to answer. There are a lot of good men."

"Do you think you're one of them?" I interrupted.

"Well . . . yes, sir. I think I'm the man for the job," he said.

"You're it," I told him. "Get going!"

Even the irrepressible Doolittle was a little surprised by the quick decision, but he got going. From then on we followed a racehorse schedule of conferences and inspection trips in which Patton, Doolittle, British Admiral Sir Bertram H. Ramsey (later killed in an air crash) and Air Vice-Marshal Sir William Lawrie Welsh, Anderson and Gruenther were the principal participants. This was my first close and intimate association with Al Gruenther, who later became my Fifth Army chief of staff and who remained with me throughout the war period. In him I found a close and loyal friend, a brilliant, tireless and efficient assistant from start to finish.

The problems that arose were both endless and formidable, and on a great many occasions we had serious differences of opinion. Anderson fretted a great deal about air support for his British operations. He felt that the United States forces scheduled to land at Oran were monopolizing the air support and that there would not be enough left over for his First Army operations around Algiers, which was farther east and probably would be more vulnerable to heavy Axis attack. Anderson also was concerned, as was everyone, with the probability that the French would react less favorably to a landing by British forces than by Americans and, although some American units were assigned to his command, he was eager to have a larger proportion of United States troops in order to foster the impression that it was an American operation.

There was a great deal of concern about the use of Gibraltar as head-quarters for the initial invasion, since it was so easily observed from Spain that any unusual activity there was certain to arouse suspicions and attract the attention of German spies.

"If Gibraltar is made use of on more than a very small scale before operations commence, it will be practically impossible to conceal that some form of operation is being mounted," the commanding general at the Rock advised the British Chiefs of Staff. "There is no doubt that any evidence in this direction will cause profound concern to the Spanish authorities. It is urgently desirable that TORCH should not only have initial success, but should not lose momentum; otherwise the temptation to the Spaniards, if we find ourselves held up or in difficulties, might be too great to resist. Both the naval base and air station would go out of commission completely and at once should Spain decide to attack."

In mid-August, General Marshall cabled from Washington that "there is a unanimity of opinion of Army officers here that the proposed operation appears hazardous to the extent of less than a fifty percent chance of success. To what extent are you prepared to meet possible German air assaults launched from Spain or Spanish Morocco? Give me your completely frank view and similarly frank expression from Patton."

Eisenhower replied that we believed the TORCH plan had more than fair chances of success "if Spain remains absolutely neutral and the French offer only token resistance or are so badly divided by internal dissension and by Allied political maneuvering that the effect of their resistance will be negligible."

"It is our opinion," the message continued, "that Spain will stay neutral at least during the early stages. We think there will be considerable resistance from certain sections of the French and that the Algiers operation at best will have less than fifty percent chances of success. If Spain enters in the results can be serious."

Our reports showed that the French had about five hundred airplanes in Africa and, while they were not modern, they were superior to the usual type of British and American carrier-based planes. We were planning to use about 160 of these, both British and American, for air support, and the rest of our air strength would have to be based at Gibraltar, which meant we would have to have good weather in order to use it. The French had about fourteen divisions in French Africa, but they were poorly equipped and there was considerable doubt as to their willingness to oppose us enthusiastically.

Rear Admiral Sir H. M. Burrough of the British Navy, who was to lead our naval convoy into Algiers, came in to talk to me on August 18. He was a grand fellow with a splendid battle record and had led a much-battered convoy through the Mediterranean to beleaguered Malta early in the month. A husky, stern-faced man, he said that Axis planes and submarines had been lying in wait for his fourteen merchant ships because they knew that Malta was about out of food and that a convoy would have to try to get through. Burrough had had no illusions about what he was getting into, and had figured that his job would be successful if he got half of his ships through. Actually only five of them reached the little island; but they carried enough to keep Malta going until January, and it was hoped that by then our invasion of North Africa would have changed the situation drastically.

Admiral Burrough's report was not designed to build up my optimism; in fact, the only really optimistic person around London in those days seemed to be Churchill, who was completely sold on the wisdom of TORCH and kept on being sold. Some of the rest of us occasionally had our doubts, even if we didn't admit it. I had dinner that evening, after my talk with Burrough, with General Sir Hastings Ismay, the Prime Minister's military adviser, and his questions about our progress suggested that even he was a bit apprehensive. Ismay, however, always had his chin up and lived up to his nickname of "Pug." He was enthusiastic, cooperative, helpful and always trying to ease our difficulties or smooth out the problems that grew out of the conflicting British and American methods of staff procedure.

At dinner, I talked to Pug about the tremendous pressure that was piling up on our planning staff as TORCH took shape. I told him that Dicky Mountbatten had invited me to go on a British Commando raid on the French coast that night, but that when I asked permission I was refused on the grounds that the operation was too hazardous. "Okay," I had replied, "but considering the fire I'm facing every day at the office, I think I'd welcome something as quiet as a Commando raid."

The pressure, of course, kept getting worse even after we were able, toward the last part of August, to see TORCH shaping up in vague outline. There was a continual crisis over shipping space and frequent changes in plans had to be made to overcome what was always a shortage of vessels. We could not get out of our minds the possibility that the Germans or the Spaniards would strike at our supply lines, cutting off and isolating whatever Allied forces landed on the North African coast. There was always the danger that the Germans would get wind of what we planned and rush their troops into Tunisia and Algeria before we could make a landing. And there was the fact, as I frequently remarked in those days, that the Allied forces in Africa would still be a long way from their real objective of invading the Continent and coming to grips with the bulk of the German Army on their home grounds. In that, I was at least partly correct. It was going to be a long time before we got to German soil.

Patton completed his conferences in London and returned to the United States the third week in August to start assembling the force that would sail directly from America for the invasion of North Africa. General Doolittle returned to Washington a few days later for conferences on the air-support problem. On August 22, the date of October 15 was tentatively set for the launching of TORCH, with assaults planned simultaneously at Casablanca, Oran and Algiers.

General Anderson was pushing for the inclusion of Philippeville, eastward toward Tunisia, as a fourth point in the attack because he felt that he would need an additional port; but on August 25 I was called out of bed at 3 a.m. to receive a cablegram from General Marshall to Ike saying that the American Chiefs of Staff in Washington felt that TORCH was on too big a scale and should be contracted to eliminate the Algiers-Bône area because of "the limited military forces available."

"The hazard is too great, especially considering the extreme seriousness of the effect on the peoples of occupied Europe, India and China if the United States should fail in its first major operation," the cable said. His message said that the operation should be limited to an American attack on the Casablanca-Oran areas, with the British forces following later.

This was the most depressing news of the summer. The entire American planning staff of TORCH immediately sat down to draft an answer for Major General Tom Handy, who was chief of War Department Operations Division, and visiting us in London, to carry back to Washington on the first available plane. In general we pointed out that with the proposed limited operation we would not be able to impress the French sufficiently to bring them in on our side. The big thing, however, was that we would be offering the Axis plenty of excuse and opportunity for moving into French North Africa and seizing Tunisia, but we would not be in a position to oppose such Axis moves. Even if we took the Oran and Casablanca sectors we would not have improved the strategical position of the Allies in the Mediterranean-North African Theater, which was the whole purpose of TORCH. We said we were "ready and anxious to proceed with any operation directed" but we added that there was "urgent need for an early decision." There was no question in our minds that landing as far east as Algiers or Bône was a calculated risk, but it was well worth taking if we wanted to use North Africa as a springboard to attack the continent of Europe.

We were in a gloomy mood that evening when Eisenhower and I went to No. 10 Downing Street to dine with Prime Minister Churchill, who had just returned from a 14,000-mile trip through the Middle East and to Moscow. Wearing his smock as usual, Churchill greeted us with high enthusiasm and almost at once began talking about TORCH. Since only Americans had been at our conference earlier that day regarding Marshall's message, we didn't tell him specifically what had happened.

"TORCH offers the greatest opportunity in the history of England," the Prime Minister exclaimed, unaware that Washington had just about counted the British out of the African invasion. "It is the one thing that is going to win the war. President Roosevelt feels the same way. We're both ready to help in any way we can; but the important thing, the first battle we must win is the battle to have no battle with the French."

I don't know whether the Prime Minister sensed any change or not, but he emphasized that "this thing must go over" and he said he was ready to fly to Washington at a moment's notice to talk it over with President Roosevelt if necessary. Then, abruptly, he asked us what was on our minds. I was feeling a bit fed up with developments, I suppose, for it seemed to me we were floundering around too long trying to find out exactly what we were going to do.

"The greatest need," I said bluntly, "is for someone with the necessary power to make some decisions. We're in the middle of day-to-day changes. We must have had ten sets of plans. There have been so many changes we are dizzy. We'd like to get one definite plan so we can go to work on it."

The Prime Minister was interested. He said he would get in touch with Mr. Roosevelt at once. As he talked, he walked around the room restlessly. Once he walked over to a corner and rubbed his broad back up and down on the jutting edge of the wall. "I guess I got them in Egypt," he observed with a grin. A little later he rang one of the many bells beside him and a valet came in.

"Change my socks," the Prime Minister commanded. He held up one foot and then the other while the valet took off his socks and put on socks of a lighter weight, but he never stopped talking to us.

"When I was in Moscow," he said, "Stalin and I talked very bluntly and sometimes I had to squirm a bit. Stalin says the war over there has shown that the German Army isn't as tough as it's cracked up to be. He said to me: 'Why don't you do something?' And I had to admit we can't get across the Channel yet.

"Then I tell him about the TORCH plan. I tell him we are going to do it. Stalin was disappointed that there would be no second front in Europe this year. But the more he thinks about the North African attack, the more he likes it.

"There was a formal state dinner in my honor in Moscow. I attended it in my smock. I thought I'd show them how proletarian I was!"

On the night before he took off from Moscow, Churchill was invited to Stalin's apartment in the Kremlin. "Stalin told me there would be just the two of us for dinner and we could do a bit of drinking. When I got there, Joe started uncorking bottles. After a while he says: 'Let's call in Molotov. He's a good drinker.' So we sit up until four o'clock and talk. At five o'clock I take off for home."

He paused and thought for a moment. Then he said that while he was at Stalin's apartment, the Soviet Premier's nineteen-year-old daughter came in. "And do you know," he said, apparently amazed that anyone could be affectionate toward Stalin, "she walked right up and kissed the bloke!"

Churchill's enthusiasm, which never lost its fascination for me, extended to his eating. Watching him at the table was an event. When the soup was put before him, he tackled it vigorously, his mouth about two inches from the liquid and his shoulders hunched over. He ate with a purring and slurping and the spoon went from mouth to plate so rapidly you could hardly see it until he was scraping the bottom of the bowl and bawling lustily, "More soup!" Turning to his guests, he'd say, "Fine soup, ain't it?"

After dinner we talked about transportation difficulties for TORCH, and although it was at night the Prime Minister sent for Mountbatten and Sir Dudley Pound, the First Sea Lord, to participate in the discussion. His habit of summoning high officials out of bed to answer his questions at such times always amazed me, even after I had seen it done many times. On this occasion, I had said I was puzzled by reports I had that it would take twelve days for combat loading of vessels and eighteen more days for the voyage from the United Kingdom to assault points. Churchill turned the heat on Sir Dudley.

"Why is it going to take you eighteen days to get to this point when it will take the Americans only fourteen days to get from New York to the African coast?" he demanded. The First Sea Lord said it was planned to have the convoy start out as if it were headed around Africa for the Middle East and then switch back to Gibraltar Straits. He said it would take only ten days if this cover plan were changed.

"Do it!" Churchill exclaimed. Then he turned triumphantly to me and said, "See, I've saved you eight precious days already." He turned back to Pound, "Now, Sir Dudley, you can turn in."

Churchill added, "I want troops pouring into the new area. I want them to come through the walls, the ceilings—everywhere! The French will go with us if we are going to win, but they can't afford to pick a loser.

"When Stalin asked me about crossing the Channel, I told him 'Why stick your head in the alligator's mouth at Brest when you can go to the Mediterranean and rip his soft underbelly.'"

The talk went on that way until two o'clock in the morning and reached a point where jokingly I told the Prime Minister that we should have paratroopers landing with parachutes made of American flags, and aerial skywriters inscribing against the heavens the words "*Vive la France!* Lafayette, we are here again—for the second time." But as the meeting broke up, we were serious enough.

"The planners of TORCH," I told Churchill, "are tired of piddling around. Every minute counts. What we need now is a green light."

The Prime Minister promised action.

The next day our planning sessions were resumed as if the TORCH operation were going ahead without change. The British, however, were feeling a bit slighted because they had been left out of our American meeting to draft a reply to Marshall's cable, and I had to try to smooth that over with an explanation that we had a communication that required only American consultation until it was presented to the British Joint Mission in Washington.

Eisenhower and I went down to Chequers to spend another night with Churchill on August 29, and while we were there a courier arrived from London with a cable from General Marshall. It said that President Roosevelt appeared to have decided definitely that the attack on North Africa would be made by American troops exclusively and would be directed at Oran and Casablanca. The President felt that 80,000 troops could do the job and that within a week they would be able to arrange so that there would be no complications regarding the landing of British forces to reinforce the Americans. Marshall said that Mr. Roosevelt planned to advise Churchill of the decision on the following Monday and that meanwhile the British must not hear a word of what had been decided.

Since we were at Chequers when the message and that meanwhile the British must not hear a word of what had been decided.

Since we were at Chequers when the message was received, this admonition to silence came at a difficult moment. General Ismay, General Sir Alan Brooke, Chief of Staff of the British Army, Foreign Secretary Anthony Eden, and Lord Mountbatten were all present that weekend and all conversation revolved around the plans for a British-American operation in Africa on a big scale. Churchill enthused. Eden expressed optimism. I fidgeted and boiled inside, and I imagine Ike did too.

We had no desire to air the latest word from Washington. In fact, it would have been embarrassing, but I must admit that I was getting awfully tired of the mind changing that kept going on back home. It seemed to me that it showed a timidity and uncertainty that might make our African venture more difficult because it would be on too small a scale to encourage quick French assistance.

Arrival of Marshall's cable aroused Churchill's curiosity, but we stalled him off and returned to London on Sunday afternoon. There we found that the British suspected something was in the air, but we went ahead with planning as usual and answered no more questions than necessary. On August 31, the message from President Roosevelt to Churchill was received, expressing the desire to make TORCH an all-American operation and omit the attack on the Algiers-Bône sector.

I remember that on the following day I assembled thirty-seven British and American officers engaged in the planning and said, "Some of you men are less confused than others about TORCH. Let's all get equally confused." That was about the way all of us felt at that point, because we couldn't be sure what the two governments would finally agree on and we were forced to base our work on several plans known as "Plan A," "Plan B," and, as somebody remarked in a burst of irritation, "maybe we better start calling one of them Plan Z." We also were being urged to be prepared to make the invasion during October, which, incidentally, would mean news of some kind of action by American forces prior to the November Congressional elections. The date that had been most mentioned about this time was October 30, although that was less than two months away and we still didn't know exactly what the governments in London and Washington would finally agree on as our immediate objectives in TORCH.

Later in the day we were told that Churchill had answered the Roosevelt cable, agreeing to the proposal generally but iterating his desire that British troops participate in the invasion by landing at Algiers. By this time it was more than obvious that military personnel and military plans were completely at the mercy of political decisions resting in the hands of the two heads of state in London and Washington. In fact the whole TORCH operation was primarily political because both the Prime Minister and the President had promised that a second front would be opened in 1942, and it was obvious that the North African area was the only place where this promise could be carried out.

I do not want to give any impression that I object to or deplore the political phase of military operations. It is often the deciding factor between success or failure. Every commander in battle must strive to conduct and win his battles in such a manner as to leave his forces best disposed to further the best interests of his country; but I emphasize politics at this point because it seems to me that most Americans look on an operation such as the invasion of Africa as a matter entirely in the hands of officers of the Armed Forces and consider that the entire responsibility for success rests on them. This, of course, is far from correct; it should be realized that political factors not only are always important but, in the African campaign, were often dominant. I find that I summed up my thoughts on the subject in my diary on the night of September 2 as follows:

> For many weeks we had been working on a plan reported to both govern-
> ments, and one that was approved, apparently, by both of them. The plan had
> almost reached the point where we were ready to go ahead loading for the North
> African assault when the delays started. During this period of indecision we have
> had at least a half-dozen plans, but before we could even start laying a
> foundation for one we got another.
>
> Those who delay us keep reminding us that TORCH must be carried out at the
> earliest possible moment. However, we're still waiting for the mission directive.
> And there is an urgent need for time to plan, time to train, time to assemble for
> the assault.
>
> The longer we wait the less chance we have of security and without security
> we can't get full success. And particularly we can't plan until we know definitely
> what we are planning for.

The security factor probably added to our nervousness in this period. About that time, for instance, we learned that General de Gaulle, who was then in Syria, had cabled his London headquarters that "the Americans have planned a landing in North Africa" and that the Vichy French "know all about it and have kept the Germans informed." We also were informed that Free French sources in Vichy, Gibraltar, Tangiers and elsewhere had told de Gaulle they had information concerning an imminent attack in North Africa and that active opposition would be encountered unless a prominent French-man was identified with the operations.

In view of all these factors, it was a relief when on September 3 the two governments finally reached an agreement. President Roosevelt cabled Churchill that the United States agreed to the triple-landing plans, including British forces, which would follow up an assault by 10,000 Americans on the Algiers beaches. The other two landings would be by 58,000 Americans at Casablanca and 45,000 at Oran. The President added that his information was that an American landing would meet little French resistance, but that an attack by British or Gaullist forces would "meet with determined resistance" because of the earlier joint British-Gaullist attacks on the French Navy in

African ports.

That afternoon the Prime Minister summoned Ike and me to a meeting of high officers for discussion of a reply to the President. After an hour of talk, Churchill, looking tired but dogged, said, "Well, let's get the cable off." He led General Sir Alan Brooke, Ike, and me into a secretary's office, and calling for a "shorthand writer" he began dictating directly to a stenographer at a typewriter, with frequent stops to consult us about details. In general his message agreed to the basic arrangements and at the end added: "Delays due to changes already have extended [D-day] three weeks. The Free French have got an inkling and they are leaky. Every day saved is precious."

When he had finished, he rested for a minute and said, "It's great not to argue when you get into a tight place. It makes you appreciate the accord between us. I know we all want to get the plan and get going."

I remarked that we were just about back to where we had been two months before, prior to the period of indecision and plan changing. "That's the tragedy of this thing," Churchill said. "We could have settled it two months ago, but it is one of the tangible difficulties of having our two staffs separated by all those miles of ocean."

He got up to go, taking a final look at his completed message and chuckling heartily as he read aloud, "The Free French . . . are leaky. . . ."

The next month was a period of hectic preparation, of endless conferences and consultations, of constant struggle to get supplies and matériel, and of worry about what the French in North Africa and the Spanish would do when TORCH got under way. There was, perhaps, more worry about the Spaniards than the French.

"The temptation [to the Spaniards] to cut our lines of communication will be very great," Sir Samuel Hoare, British Ambassador to Spain, said in one communication regarding the safety of our projected supply line through the Straits of Gibraltar. "We shall appear to have put our neck between two Spanish knives and Spanish knives are traditionally treacherous. The Germans will be on General Franco's back, dinning into his ears 'Now is your time.' Let no one underrate the power of this temptation or think that because nine Spaniards out of ten do not want war, General Franco might not risk it for the big stakes that it might offer him."

In these days of hard work at Norfolk House the supply problem often seemed likely to wreck all our preparations. There were unexplainable shortages, particularly in spare parts for weapons and motor vehicles. There were whole shiploads of equipment that seemed to get sidetracked in the United States, and, of course, there were the inevitable losses of ships to enemy submarines. One cargo of vitally needed combat equipment for the 1st Division started out three times from New York and each time was lost or otherwise diverted. There were never enough ships either to supply our needs in the United Kingdom on schedule or to assure that the great mass of supplies essential to the success of the invasion would be kept moving steadily to Africa after our landings.

So confused was the logistical situation that by mid-September it became obvious that it would be impossible to launch the invasion at the beginning of November; even the eager Prime Minister agreed that a delay of a week or more would be necessary. I remember that on September 12 the combat weapons for the 1st Division had not yet arrived, and apparently had not even been shipped from New York. At that time I discussed the snarled SOS (Services of Supply) situation with Colonel Everett Hughes (later Major General Hughes and our Army Chief of Ordnance) and told him that these weapons must arrive in the United Kingdom by September 26, which would "allow the bare minimum of time for the weapons to be distributed and combat loaded" by the deadline of October 8.

"You must make it vividly clear to Washington," I told Hughes, "that if the weapons are not here by September 26, the assault teams will have to attack with insufficient arms and ammunition. Something must be done and done fast or those men will be going in virtually with their bare hands."

I suppose that all planners encounter the same period of confusion and pessimism in such an enterprise, or at least that has been my experience, but it is difficult to exaggerate the depression we sometimes felt during that critical month of September. I know it would have been an almost intolerable situation for me if it had not been for my good fortune in having a close personal relationship with Eisenhower. This, of course, was the result of the fact that we had been friends for a long time and had previously worked together on many problems. There was a great advantage in this because we knew each other well, knew how to work together, and were able to discuss our problems intimately. I usually felt that I knew what Ike thought on most questions, and he always seemed to know what my attitude would be.

And he had a fine way of helping to smooth ruffled tempers.

"Now just keep your shirt on, Wayne," he said frequently when I would become particularly discouraged by delays, or on other occasions when I wanted to get some new project under way in a hurry, "Just keep your shirt on."

On various occasions that was good advice and, feeling that I knew how he felt about my ideas, I was able to concentrate on my work without worrying over what was going on in the office of the Commander in Chief. It was, I always felt, a good team combination and a solid thing to cling to in those hectic, unpredictable days.

Too, there were occasional diversions in the midst of the routine work of logistics, air support, naval support and all the other phases of a major assault. One of them was a strange request from Marine Colonel Eddy, the U.S. naval attaché at Tangiers, Morocco, who had come to London temporarily for espionage conferences. He submitted to me a memorandum that included the following proposal:

> I recommend that on D-day, when the landing operations actually begin, I be authorized to arrange for the assassination of the members of the German Armistice Commission at Casablanca [this was the commission dealing with the Vichy French] and for any members of the German or Italian Armistice Commissions who may then be in the city of Oran. About twenty of the German Army and Navy officers live in a hotel in Casablanca and the assignments have already been made for this job to men who have the demolition materials already in their hands. I might add that our principal agent in Casablanca is the father of a boy who was shot as a hostage in Paris recently and the father is impatiently awaiting permission to carry out this assignment.

I wrote on the margin "O.K. Looks good to me," but of course the proposal actually was out of bounds and was squashed at a higher level.

When our problem of getting ammunition and arms to the United Kingdom in time for combat loading was at its worst, Churchill again asked Ike and me to Chequers to talk over things with him and a dozen of his top officers. After dinner a report came in that ten Allied ships had been sunk by German submarines in the Atlantic, reminding us all of our shortage of ships for TORCH and reminding Churchill in particular that our African invasion was going to require so much shipping that it would be impossible to send any more convoys to Russia in 1942.

"I can't bring myself to tell Joe [Stalin] that there just ain't going to be more convoys this year," Churchill said, in reference to the perilous North Sea route to Archangel where very heavy losses had been suffered. "I don't like to tell you this. It hurt me more than a little, but when I was in Moscow last month, Joe turned to me during a discussion of convoy losses and said, 'You have no glory left in the British Navy. Your Navy only runs the British convoy halfway to Russia, then turns around and dashes back to England while the merchant ships get slaughtered.' Imagine me having to take that kind of lashing from Joe."

A few days later, Robert Murphy, the State Department career officer who was to play such an important role in our affairs and in the African invasion for the next few months, arrived incognito by air from Washington to confer on political aspects of TORCH. Ambassador John G. Winant, Averell Harriman, British Brigadier Eric Edward Mockler-Ferryman, Ike and I conferred with him and were astonished to learn that President Roosevelt had drafted a letter for almost immediate delivery to the Free French, telling them that "we're coming into North Africa at an early date." It was a cleverly hazy letter, revealing no details but proposing that General Henri Honoré Giraud, who had escaped from confinement in Germany and was then in France, should be made commander in chief of all Allied troops in North Africa, including the French.

The letter, which was never sent, seemed a highly dangerous idea to me and, I believe, to others at the conference. However, it developed that Murphy had been in contact with sympathetic French leaders in North Africa, where he had been stationed until several weeks previous, and he felt that upon his return to Algiers he could complete the organization of groups that would seize coast-defense batteries, radio, and telegraph stations, and other key points to aid our assault.

Murphy's visit was encouraging and at that time various other problems including logistics began shaping up better. Enthusiasm began mounting. Admiral Lyster of the British Navy, a salty officer picked to command aircraft carriers in the Mediterranean during the invasion, came in with some interesting suggestions. He said that we had to "exploit, exploit, exploit" after the landing and that we should drive eastward to Tunisia with the greatest possible speed to prevent the Germans from concentrating there. He suggested that some 5,000 troops on Malta, with fighter-plane support, could be moved in an attack on Tunis at the beginning of our invasion and proposed that we strip down some bombers and "stuff them with soldiers" to fly into Tunisia at once. His ideas seemed a bit reckless at the time, particularly in view of the trouble we had had overcoming timidity from Washington about landing at Algiers, but a long time later when I thought back on the conversation, I was pretty sure that Lyster was on the right track. Greater daring at the start would have saved us many weeks of hard fighting later.

The staff at Norfolk House was growing rapidly, and Brigadier General W. Bedell Smith arrived on September 17 to be Eisenhower's chief of staff, with Gruenther as his deputy. I had known Bedell Smith for a long time and knew he was able, aggressive, and capable of assuming an important place in the headquarters setup. I felt when Bedell moved in as chief of staff that perhaps before long Ike would not feel the need of a deputy and I could move to a command, perhaps my old II Corps. I didn't particularly like the idea of spending the war period as a staff officer. In a military career there is no substitute for battle command, and my only battle experience had been as a captain in World War I. Ike knew how I felt about it, and if the idea arose in our talks he would repeat his often-used admonition, "Now just keep your shirt on, Wayne." I agreed with his attitude, but I had been in the entanglement of planning so long that I had "ants in my pants" and wanted action. Neither Ike nor I knew it at the time, but plenty of action was coming up—action of a kind I wasn't expecting.

But first I had to make a flying trip back to Washington for final consultations on TORCH and to make sure that our operations from the British Isles would be coordinated with the expedition that would move directly from America to the African beaches. In the few days before my departure, I went over almost every phase of preparations and took up a host of small problems that were plaguing TORCH. Generally, the SOS phase that had given us so much trouble was looking better as the long-scattered pieces of the gigantic puzzle began slowly to fall into place with the arrival of many ships in British ports bearing arms for the African battle units. The air support and shipping problems for TORCH were straightening out and we were getting down to such little headaches as the fact that the fasting requirements of the Moslem religion complicated waging any warfare during the latter part of the year, meaning that unless we invaded Africa before November 10 there might be complications in getting the help of some French colonial troops. Finally we arrived at November 8 as a definite date for the invasion.

This decision and the progress of our preparations had a strange effect on Prime Minister Churchill. Instead of arousing his enthusiasm, he began to worry, mostly about shipping complications. One reason, of course, was that he was approaching the day when he had to decide how he was "going to tell Joe" that the next convoy to Russia wouldn't be coming through. He said that was going to be "frightfully embarrassing" for him and he expressed some alarm about the fact that American troops would be leaving Britain. Walking back and forth, warming his back in front of the fireplace, stopping from time to time to address directly an American or British officer, the Prime Minister reviewed the whole situation and remarked that he wanted to start planning at once for an attack on Norway to protect the convoy route to Russia.

"It is very disheartening," he said, as if carrying on a debate with himself. "I feel the next convoy to Russia should go through. I just can't tell Joe it's not coming when his people are bloody and dying and holding the enemy. The convoy is all loaded—I guess I just got to tell Joe."

Then he jumped back to the question of invading Europe and to various plans, which, it seemed to me, made it obvious that he was already thinking of ways to bring more and more American troops into action on the various fronts. "We should," he exclaimed, "be able to rip at Hitler's mouth [in France] at the same time we are ripping at the Axis belly [in the Mediterranean]."

That night we covered problems of strategy on every front, including India, and by the time we were ready to leave Churchill was in a better mood, delighted with the great Russian defense of Stalingrad (which he believed would fall, although he didn't think the Red Army would crack up) and cheered by news that the last convoy to Archangel had lost only eleven of fifty ships. "I'll bet Joe is drooling at the mouth over that package we delivered to him," he chuckled.

Later in the evening—I believe it was the same night—Churchill, following his usual routine, checked us on every detail of our planning, endeavoring primarily to find out if anything was going wrong and how he could help. On this occasion, I was explaining the lack of air support for the Oran landing. We badly needed another airplane carrier, and with our Navy preoccupied in the Pacific, it obviously would have to be British. I had discovered that the Royal Navy had one in the Indian Ocean that to my way of thinking was not contributing much to this all-out Allied effort in North Africa. Churchill called in Sir Dudley Pound, the First Sea Lord of the Admiralty, and asked what could be done. Sir Dudley indicated that about everything was already committed to the North African operation. I chimed in that I heard there was a carrier in the Indian Ocean. The Prime Minister questioned Sir Dudley closely on this point, found it to be correct, and told the First Lord of the Admiralty to order it to the Mediterranean at once to be thrown into the battle. It arrived in time and added materially to our successes.

With the date of November 8 set for the invasion, I departed for home on September 23 for final consultations. A couple of days later, in Washington, I had a long talk with General Marshall in which we discussed the entire TORCH project, and he seemed pleased. I found Secretary of War Henry L. Stimson worried, however, about the success of the African invasion. He also was apprehensive that it would have the effect of greatly delaying any invasion of Europe, which he believed must be executed. He suggested doubts of the soundness of Churchill's judgment regarding the "soft belly" of the Axis and pointed out that the success of TORCH depended on a multitude of suppositions—that Spain would remain neutral; that the French would not resist strongly; that the Germans would not seize the African airfields. He was a determined man, however, and now that we were committed to the invasion he was ready to go to any length to assure its success. He came around his desk to shake hands as I was leaving and said, "God bless you, my boy. We're all anxiously waiting."

President Roosevelt was away from Washington on a secret tour of defense industries, and after I had talked with Harry Hopkins and Admiral Leahy, the President's Chief of Staff to coordinate military and naval affairs, I spent the rest of my time in Washington conferring with the men who would lead the American section of TORCH. General Patton had a tremendous office set up in the Munitions Building, where all visitors were double-checked at both ends of a corridor. Inside things were humming and Patton was all over the place. It had been decided that the 3rd Division (Truscott), specially trained in amphibious operations, would spearhead the Western Task Force assault, carrying out the same role on the African west coast that our 1st Division from Britain would carry out at Oran. The 168th Infantry Combat Team already had been assigned to spearhead the Algiers attack.

Later I discussed fifth-column operations with Colonel William (Wild Bill) Donovan and with Robert Murphy, who was still in Washington, and Murphy was given a list of installations and establishments to be either destroyed or secured by our French friends prior to our invasion.

I flew up to West Point to see my son Bill, and because of unfavorable flying weather that delayed my return to Washington I had a chance to visit my family. Mrs. Clark and Ann had accompanied me to the Academy. On September 29 I started back to London, landing at Hendon Airport at 6:48 p.m. the following day. Ike was at the field to meet me and eager to get a firsthand report on developments in Washington.

While I was back home, news had come from Spain that made us jittery. Just before my departure for Washington, I had sent a Top Secret letter to the governor general of Gibraltar, giving him full information of our attack, the date of the establishment of our headquarters at Gibraltar, and other final information on the North African assault plans. This letter had been turned over to the British Intelligence chief for transmittal by officer courier via airplane to Gibraltar. The letter was to be carried in a special container with a self-destroying bomb in case the plane should strike the water. The word that we had received upon my return was that the plane had been shot down by German planes off the Spanish coast and that the body of the courier had been washed ashore in Spain. The Spanish authorities had delivered the dead officer to the British at Gibraltar. Upon searching his body, they found this Top Secret letter, still sealed, inside his tunic. This caused a great "flap" in London. Conferences were held to evaluate the possibility that the Spanish had found the letter, opened it, and carefully sealed it up. If this were the case, all our plans might be known to the enemy. I can tell you we went through many worrisome days just prior to the invasion. However, there was no leak through this unfortunate event.

One of the final stages of planning for TORCH concerned the use of paratroopers. The British, particularly Air Marshal Welsh, were doubtful about the use of paratroopers at Oran, pointing out that the men would have to fly over occupied France or Spain if they followed the shortest route from England, and that if any were shot down en route the security of the invasion might be menaced. It also was pointed out that the paratroopers would have to be transported approximately 2,000 miles in darkness and hit a pinpoint target at a scheduled minute, involving a rather remarkable feat of navigation and timing.

The proposed drop of some 800 men of the 509th Parachute Battalion involved the use of scores of transport planes and might easily result in a heavy loss of planes as well as men. This assumed important proportions in our overall planning because we were having a difficult time with all forms of transportation, especially in securing the shipping necessary to get enough munitions, trucks, gasoline, and other supplies to Africa for the use of combat troops. There is always in such an operation a tug of war between various units for use of the limited space available, and the British, who had had experience with paratroopers in combat, foresaw that the loss of transport planes could be a heavy blow. They felt that the planes could be better used, logistically, to fly in supplies to captured air bases and they discouraged us as much as possible.

I always felt that the paratrooper operation was worthwhile—all things considered—and Ike seemed to have the same viewpoint, but he was under heavy pressure from the British and for a while there was doubt that the 509th Battalion would get a chance to show what it could do. Our paratroop officers, particularly Lieutenant Colonel Edson D. Raff and Major William P. Yarborough, were confident that they could carry out the assignment, and they finally got their way. They were men who always took the attitude that they could do any essential job, and they proved their worth on D-day and later under the brilliant leadership of Raff in operations against Tunisia.

A month before the invasion date, our whole plan of operations was sufficiently advanced for Eisenhower to tell his triweekly conference of top officers that "things are getting buttoned up."

"All of our problems are being settled by the fundamental rule of common sense," he added. "Each day I see more evidence that we are getting together—getting better organized. And each day I get a little more hopeful."

Among other things that made him hopeful was a conference he had held with an unidentified "clandestine person" who advised him that the

Italian people were ready for peace at any price. High Italian government officials, Ike was told, were "at last convinced that they cannot win even if the side they are on wins," and were so eager to avoid antagonizing the United States that Italian submarines had been withdrawn entirely from the Atlantic seaboard.

Churchill also had encouraging reports on the difficulties, especially a shortage of ammunition and food, that were being encountered by the Nazi Afrika Korps in Egypt where General Sir Harold Alexander and General Montgomery were about ready to strike back at Marshal Rommel with a big-scale offensive coordinated with our landings and scheduled to open prior to the beginning of TORCH.

The Prime Minister discussed his news when we attended a dinner at No. 10 Downing Street in honor of General Jan Smuts, the seventy-two-year-old South African Prime Minister, who had just flown in from Cairo. I thought Smuts one of the most remarkable men I met during the war and it was invigorating to hear him report on the excellent effect of Alexander's leadership in the Middle East.

Smuts' personality was of the magnetic kind, but in addition he impressed me as a "can do" man; the sort of leader who always takes an aggressive and optimistic viewpoint in tackling a job or a problem. Just looking at him, you knew Smuts was not going to sit back in South Africa and merely do his part; he was going to get out and do things. There was a great comradeship between Smuts and Churchill, who incidentally had fought on opposite sides during the Boer War, and they worked well together.

During dinner, Churchill proudly showed us a dog that had just been given to him and which was happily exploring the Prime's official residence.

"I don't know what to name him," the Prime Minister said. "He's an important dog and he needs a good name."

Nobody could suggest anything that appealed to Churchill, but a few minutes later when I saw the not-yet-housebroken pup using the leg of a costly chair as a substitute for a tree, I had an idea.

"Why don't you call him Paderewski?" I asked.

Churchill and Smuts both looked at me.

"Why Paderewski?" asked the Prime Minister.

"Because," I said, recalling an old joke, "he's quite a pianist."

Both of them stared at me for a moment, and then Smuts broke into hearty laughter. Not Churchill. He gave Smuts a puzzled look and said, "I don't understand."

I tried to explain. He shook his head. Smuts tried to explain. Same result. Churchill just shook his head and muttered, "I don't understand."

Some days later, a question arose of who would take over command of TORCH if anything should happen to Eisenhower—a question that was quickly answered by the chief of the British General Staff, General Brooke, when he said that there had never been any question that "the command goes to General Clark." I mention the conversation, however, because the point was raised by General Anderson, who had brought up the matter of seniority, since he was a lieutenant general and I a major general at that time. It also developed that Anderson intended to send battle reports directly to Churchill, which caused us to worry over the possibility that separate communiqués might be issued in London. It had been arranged for Allied Force Headquarters to send complete reports to the Prime Minister for his information, but not for use in communiqués.

In a broad way, our work in that period, and later, keenly felt the differences between American and British methods, regardless of Ike's strenuous efforts to coordinate the two teams. The British favored large staff conferences and committee meetings. When a decision had to be reached, the British procedure was to have a conference where all interested agencies were represented. The subject was thoroughly discussed by each representative. These meetings were long and tiresome, and usually resulted in delayed decisions or none at all. The American system used a more direct approach. The commander used his staff officers to give him advice, usually individually and not in large open meetings, and after receiving their various recommendations and points of view, made his decision and published it for the information of and implementation by all concerned.

Ike succeeded in overcoming the differences between these two systems to a great extent; though as a result of his effort to be impartial naturally some of the concessions were from the American side. By mid-October, however, all our technical problems seemed to be shaping up well, and following the arrival of Admiral Sir Andrew Cunningham from the Mediterranean to head TORCH naval operations, Ike held a conference of all commanders, at which for the first time everybody seemed to be satisfied with the preparations.

"Surely," Ike insisted at the conference, "some of you have things that are bothering you." Nobody did, or at least nothing important enough to discuss there.

In the next few days we completed work on several plans to mislead the enemy regarding our convoys moving to the Mediterranean and regarding our intentions in general. Brigadier Mockler-Ferryman, in charge of public relations at Headquarters, arranged for news to "leak out" that Ike was returning to the United States, and a plan was devised to have a British destroyer in the Mediterranean send out a message that could be decoded by the enemy and which would indicate that the Algiers convoy was really en route to Malta or Egypt.

There still was a busy hubbub at Norfolk House, but now there also were frequent departures by officers who had specific duties that would not permit them to rejoin Headquarters until after the invasion; it became routine to say, "So long. See you in Algiers," or, "See you in Casa next month."

We all had been working at such a stiff pace that I told the staff it was about time we began catching up on our sleep in preparation for the job ahead. As a result, I ordered them all to stay away from the office on Sundays until 10 a.m. Other days, we would proceed as usual, which meant that they stopped for sleep only when they were ready to pass out from fatigue.

In line with this order, I strolled into the office at ten o'clock on the morning of Sunday the 17th of October and found only General Gruenther present.

"I've got a message for you," he said. "It's red hot."

It was a cable addressed to Eisenhower and signed by General Marshall in Washington. I had just started to read it when the red telephone on my desk rang. The red phone was a direct scrambled line to Eisenhower's desk at 20 Grosvenor Square. I grabbed it up.

"Come up," Ike said crisply. "Come right away."

He hung up without waiting for an answer, but I already had had a glimpse at Marshall's message and I made a beeline for the door.

5.

Secret Mission to Africa:

October 1942

On the two-mile ride to Grosvenor Square, I kept turning over in my mind what I had read of Marshall's message and thinking that this was it—this was a job I wanted to do.

"When do I go?" I said to Ike as I walked into his office.

"Probably right away," he answered, and I knew again that our minds were working together and that he had agreed with my desire to go.

The cable from Marshall was for the most part the text of a cable that Bob Murphy, then in Algiers as Counselor of Embassy on special mission to French North Africa, had sent to Washington. It disclosed an almost unbelievable plan that might give the whole TORCH operation a much better chance of quick success, if it could be pulled off. If it should fail—well, why think about that?

Ike and I began going over the message in detail while waiting for the response to a telephone call to Chequers, where Churchill was spending the weekend. We hadn't gotten far when Major General Sir Hastings Ismay answered the telephone.

"Pug," I said, "we've got a hot message here."

"How hot?" Ismay wanted to know.

"Well, it's too hot for the telephone."

After a pause, Churchill got on the phone. "What do you have?" he asked. "This phone is secret."

I handed the telephone to Ike, who said that the message was too important to talk about over the phone. When Churchill suggested that we come to Chequers, Ike said there wasn't time. The Prime Minister stiffened up a bit at this informal procedure and said formally: "Very well. Should I come back to London?"

"Yes, sir."

"All right," Churchill said, "I'll meet you at Number Ten late this afternoon."

We sent for charts of the North African coast, summoned a number of staff members and got back to a study of the message. Murphy said that he had been in close touch with General Charles Emmanuel Mast, then French commander in Algiers and our best contact in North Africa, and that Mast wanted an American delegation to come secretly to a rendezvous near Algiers to confer on plans for Allied operations in French North Africa.

This made it plain that there was a possibility of arranging for cooperation instead of resistance when we invaded North Africa and it implied that General Henri Honoré Giraud, then in Vichy France, might be able to reach Algiers and participate in the conference. Giraud, who had been captured by the Germans early in the war but escaped, was regarded as the most likely man to take over French leadership in the area in cooperation with our forces.

A specific rendezvous was given as a lone house on the shore at a definite latitude and longitude, about sixty miles west of Algiers, and we were able to find what we thought might be the house marked on our charts. The date set was the night of October 21—only four days away. Mast also had stipulated that the American delegation should travel by submarine and that it should include a "senior general officer," which was where I came in.

The War Department cable stipulated that the general officer in charge of the mission should be accompanied by one man thoroughly familiar with the details of TORCH operation, one supply man, one Navy man, and one political expert—the last to speak fluent French. Brigadier General Lyman L. Lemnitzer, head of the Allied Force Plans Section; Colonel A. L. Hamblen, our shipping and supply expert; Captain Jerauld Wright of the U.S. Navy, who had been our Navy liaison man since TORCH was started; and Colonel Julius C. Holmes, a former State Department officer, who headed up our Civil Affairs Branch of the TORCH plan, seemed to fill these specifications. I knew them all well, they had great ability, and could be relied upon in a pinch. Until late afternoon we were hashing over the details of our trip. We would fly to Gibraltar in two Flying Fortresses. The air people pointed out that there was danger in this. No B-17 had ever landed at the Gibraltar field, and we did not know if it could be done. The party would split into two planes, so that if mine were lost, General Lemnitzer could carry on for me. From Gibraltar we would be taken to the Algerian coast in a British submarine. The cable was very specific about how the final rendezvous would be made; a latitude and longitude some fifteen miles west of the tiny port of Cherchel was given. On the night of October 21 our submarine was to surface off the position given; a single, steady white light would be exhibited from a seaward dormer window of the house if the coast were clear and the landing should proceed. This light would not be visible from the land side. Unfortunately, nothing was said about what was to be done if we could not make it by airplane and submarine in the short time granted—four days—and we immediately asked Washington to send a secret message to Murphy and his associates, urging them to set up an alternate time of rendezvous if we could not make the October 21 date.

By the time General Eisenhower and I were ready to take off for No. 10, we were well briefed on the complex contents of the Murphy cable. It covered a lot more than just the details of the rendezvous. Murphy reported that when he had returned to Algiers from his visit to Washington, he had been asked for a secret interview by the head of the French Intelligence. The interview took place at an isolated spot outside of town to avoid German notice. The French said that both German and Japanese sources had reported that the Allies were planning early military operations against Dakar, Casablanca, or both. The Germans were urging the French to take every precaution against this, likewise giving indications that this could constitute a pretext for Axis occupation of French North Africa.

> "The Germans," Murphy cabled, "appear determined to settle the western Mediterranean issue during the coming weeks and will have the use of the Spanish mainland and of Spanish Morocco for this purpose. Gibraltar is under constant surveillance. In French opinion, definite action is not a question of weeks, but days. The French political situation is extremely delicate and collapse may be expected in as little as ten days. There is no question that the situation in French North Africa is moving fast. Information indicates the Axis has raised about 100,000 troops along the Tunisian frontier."

Murphy's message also brought up the question of the attitude of Admiral Jean François Darlan, who was then perhaps the strongest figure in Marshal Pétain's government at Vichy. Because of the shaky political situation in France, the message said, Darlan "is faced with a decision"; and it appeared that he might be willing to come to Africa and bring the French fleet with him if, as commander in chief of the French Armed Forces, he could be assured of American ability to supply large-scale material and economic aid. Murphy pointed out that if Darlan did cooperate, the French military and naval forces in French Africa would undoubtedly obey his command.

Because of the political furor that later arose over Darlan's role in the occupation of North Africa, I think I should make clear at this point certain statements in Murphy's message that were later generally overlooked or omitted in the millions of words written about the episode. The message said that Darlan, spurred by persistent reports of plans for an American invasion of Dakar or Casablanca, had instructed the French intelligence officers to make the contact with Murphy when he first returned from Washington to Algiers. They were told to advise Murphy that he might later receive a message from Darlan.

Murphy then specifically asked advice on how far he could go in replying to Darlan's representative, who desired to know, first, were we willing to cooperate with Darlan; and second, if we were, would we be able to do so quickly and on a large scale in Africa and Europe? Murphy recommended encouragement of Darlan in an effort to secure his cooperation with Giraud and noted that Darlan was expected to arrive in Algiers the following week. (The position of our government on the record was that we did not want to dictate to the French whom they should select as leader in North Africa. Actually, it had been hoped we would not be confronted with the necessity of supporting Darlan.)

At the same time, however, Murphy's message said that General Mast made it clear that Giraud "desires that he be dealt with instead of Darlan, who, he feels, cannot be trusted, but who is extremely desirous of climbing on the band wagon." Mast felt that the armed forces would go along with Giraud, but not necessarily with Darlan, according to the message.

Murphy concluded: "Mast asserts we can gain entry practically without firing a shot through Giraud's command. It is suggested that the United States supply an American submarine to pick up Giraud and his party at night on the French Mediterranean Coast."

When General Eisenhower and I arrived at No. 10 Downing Street, there was about as dazzling an array of Britain's diplomatic, military and naval brains as I had yet seen. The Prime Minister, without knowing exactly what was on our minds, was as enthusiastic as a boy with a new electric train. When we read the cable, he broke into a big grin behind a giant new cigar.

"This is great," he kept saying.

We discussed the implications of the trip at some length with Clement Attlee, Lord Louis Mountbatten, Admiral of the Fleet Sir Dudley Pound, and Sir Alan Brooke. Foreign Secretary Anthony Eden chimed in on the political phase. What Ike wanted was a specific British opinion on how much I could tell the French about TORCH. We knew Giraud would want an important spot in the command setup, and I offered, if it would help matters, to step down as deputy commander to Ike in favor of Giraud. That was rejected. At the end we told Mr. Churchill, happy as a detective-story fan, the more fantastic details of our plans for this secret rendezvous on which the fate of thousands of British, American, and French soldiers and sailors might hang. Almost as an afterthought, I asked the Prime Minister if we should wear civilian clothes or uniforms.

"Do you have civvies?" asked Mr. Churchill. "If you have, take them along."

I eventually left the civilian clothes in the submarine. It would have made things just that much harder had we been picked up without uniforms on shore. Escorting me to the door, Mr. Churchill emphasized Britain's entirely cooperative spirit. We would have the submarine, destroyer, amphibious airplanes, and facilities at Gibraltar, which we needed. He has an unaffected way of speaking in ringing phrases at important moments.

"The entire resources of the British Commonwealth are at your disposal," he said in parting. "I want to assure you once more how important it will be to get this information and to cut down French resistance. You have my genuine support. Keep in mind that we'll back you up in whatever you do." He shook hands gravely.

By this time, General Carl Spaatz already had provided the two B-17s with specially selected pilots. The weather people said we had better not try a takeoff until morning. We spent the night sleeping very little, but getting a lot of details and equipment together in a minimum of space and weight. Army Finance had scurried around to get money—a thousand dollars in Canadian $5 and $10 gold pieces for possible use in buying our way out of a jam. We had no bribing to do, but at the end of the trip I had left only three of the gold pieces I carried, and I purchased them for souvenirs for General Eisenhower and Admiral of the Fleet Sir Andrew Brown Cunningham. The third I still carry for a luck piece. We got money belts for the whole party and divided up the gold pieces. I had some United States dollars along too, but the whole amount was about $2,000—not the much larger sum later mentioned in news dispatches. I had been scheduled to leave with General Eisenhower on the morning of the eighteenth for an inspection trip of United States forces training in Scotland. In order not to attract undue attention to my mission, General Eisenhower left on his journey as planned.

It was not until dusk of the eighteenth that my four colleagues and I arrived at the Eighth Air Force bomber base at Polbrook, seventy-three miles northwest of London. I replaced my stars with lieutenant colonel's insignia on my shoulders when I left London. Even most of the people at headquarters thought I was on my way to join General Eisenhower in Scotland.

The weather was bad on the evening of the eighteenth and precious hours slipped away while we all waited in a tiny barracks, keeping out of sight of personnel on the field so as to attract a minimum of attention. I was plenty keyed up, and although I went to bed I didn't sleep much. What disturbed me most was the time element and the difficulty of communicating, not only with Murphy, but through him with the French, who might already be on their way to the rendezvous. I was afraid that if we did not arrive on time, the French would feel badly let down and might question our good faith. I must admit I also was pretty worried about the personal safety of all of us; the whole deal could be a trick. If we fell into Nazi hands, it would be far from pleasant and, of more importance, would jeopardize the whole operation. I had left a short note behind to be delivered to Mrs. Clark if I did not return. I had carefully gone over procedures with General Lemnitzer and Colonel Holmes so that either of them could carry on if one or more of us dropped out for any reason. A final cable had been received from Washington saying that "AGREE," a code name for myself, "is to proceed at once with the mission." But nothing was said to allay my gnawing fear that we could not make it in time.

I was sleeping at last when they called me about 6:30 a.m. We had some breakfast and climbed into the planes for a quick takeoff. General Lemnitzer was carrying all the secret documents in a heavily weighted tube. I instructed the pilots that under no circumstances was either plane to land in Spain or Portugal. The base commander had received some word about German fighters along the coast. We didn't have an escort—as possibly attracting too much attention—but the guns of our two B-17s were fully manned. My ship, the *Red Gremlin,* piloted by Major Tibbets,* broke above the clouds and flew out of sight of earth for three hours. By the time the overcast broke, there was nothing below but open sea. We sighted only one ship, a small sailing vessel somewhere off Portugal. Even before we had identified Gibraltar, Spitfires were shooting up to look us over. General Lemnitzer's plane, the *Boomerang,* went in first and we were all relieved to see the big bomber make it safely on Gibraltar's limited strip. One of the pilots had already climbed out of my plane when the British rushed up and motioned to everybody to stay inside. They explained that the Gibraltar field was always under full observation by German agents in Spain. (The runway is only about 300 yards from

---

* Later, as Colonel Tibbets, he was the pilot of the B-29 that dropped the atom bomb on Hiroshima.

Spanish territory.) The arrival of two B-17s—the first sent there—would give the Nazis enough to think about without their spotting high officers aboard. The British suggested that we leave off our coats and hats. A big car with drawn curtains pulled up as close as possible to the plane; we jumped swiftly into it to be whisked off to the governor's house. Here the governor, Lieutenant General Mason-McFarlane, and some British admirals, including Vice-Admiral Collins and the commander of British submarines in the Mediterranean, Captain Barney Fawkes, welcomed us. I asked my four colleagues to stay in their rooms—the less seen of any of us on the Rock, the better. I conferred alone with General Mason-MacFarlane and his naval associates. I have hardly ever been less certain of the success of an operational mission in my life. I needed support, but got little encouragement. The Navy people were taking a rather dim view of this whole crazy American adventure. They talked of thick shore patrols, plenty of spotting planes, and a French Navy and Air Force bolder than it had been before. What I needed was someone to say, "Okay, we'll get you in there and get you out, too."

They talked on until I said, "Gentlemen, there is no help for this. We are going. It has been decided by our two governments and I don't intend to call it off."

The most encouraging person I met at Gibraltar was Lieutenant Norman Ambury Auchinleck Jewell (we called him Bill later), commander of the submarine H.M.S. *Seraph*—one of the smaller and slower British undersea boats. He was described to me as a "fine youngster with plenty of experience in doing soundings along the North African coast." When I asked to see him, they brought in a handsome young man with plenty of self-confidence. I asked if he knew what this was all about.

"All they told me was that I was to take some Americans some place and land them at night on the African coast," he said.

I explained some of the details. Jewell was pleasantly reassuring: "I am sure we can get you in there and get you off again." He bucked up my confidence considerably. He told me he had three British Commandos and four folbots—little collapsible, wood-framed canvas canoes—on board. If we were to arrive at the rendezvous in daylight and submerged, we would have to get going immediately. At that, Lieutenant Jewell warned, considering the number of hours we would have to run submerged at very slow speed, he wasn't going to guarantee arrival on time. I had dispatched another message to Washington, through Colonel Eddy, our military representative in the international zone of Tangier, urgently requesting that the reception party wait for us from 9 p.m. the night of the twenty-first until dawn, and saying that if we did not show up that night we would attempt a landing the night of the twenty-second. None of us took to the idea of lying close to shore in shallow water where planes could spot even a submerged sub.

There was no time to lose. We wanted to leave Gibraltar in darkness, and we didn't want to lose any of the night and its valuable opportunity for running on the surface. They took us down to the submarine tender *Maidstone,* where we had a drink and a quick dinner in Captain Barney Fawkes' cabin. The *Seraph* (P-219) was tied up to the *Maidstone.* They were casting off her lines as we arrived aboard.

I had never been aboard a submarine before. I soon realized that they were not made for a lanky six-foot-two man. All the time I was in the P-219 I had to bend over and watch my head. The officers' quarters, which the submarine crew had hospitably given up to their passengers, was only a cubbyhole alongside the middle catwalk. When I went to the "head," I had literally to crawl on all fours. The submarine crew, almost all youngsters, welcomed us aboard. All they knew was that "we're going on a screwy mission with some Americans." While we were running on the surface that night, we passengers spent a lot of time on deck. A British destroyer led us the first fifty miles. Lieutenant Jewell and I, poring over the charts, agreed we couldn't possibly make the rendezvous if we had to run the entire trip under water. We decided to try as much as possible to stay on the surface where we could make ten to twelve knots compared to only two or three submerged. We would be ready for a crash dive at any time if spotted by an enemy ship or plane. During our first afternoon, slipping smoothly along and sighting nothing, we had a detailed conference with our Commando officers on embarkation and landing procedures. General plans concerning signals and possible action ashore were studied carefully. The submarine would go as close to the beach as possible and survey it by periscope in daylight.

Our radio was alert for word from Gibraltar, but apparently nothing had been received from Murphy regarding a secondary rendezvous.

In the late afternoon we played some bridge, and at 9:30 p.m., when it was fully dark again, Lieutenant Jewell stopped the submarine for a rehearsal of folbot embarkation. The sea was choppy. Colonel Holmes and Commando Captain R. P. Livingstone launched their boat first, after practicing stepping into the frail and very tipsy craft on the dry deck. They paddled noiselessly away, and from a distance of several hundred yards tried out the infrared signal light with which we had been supplied. This light cannot be seen by the naked eye, but with a proper sort of glass it becomes a useful signal light. The light worked perfectly. Holmes and Livingstone returned to the submarine, with General Lemnitzer and Lieutenant J. P. Foote trying the next trip. The general got pretty wet, but they made it all right, Colonel Hamblen and Captain Wright in their turn as well. Captain Godfrey B. (Jumbo) Courtney was my small-boat pilot, and we tried it last. He was the expert on these boats and was in charge of instructing all of us.

With small-boat exercises complete, the submarine was quickly under way again. I managed to get some sleep this night, in spite of the stuffy interior of the submarine, but at 6:20 a.m. the dive klaxons sounded. We were too close to the North African shore to venture running on the surface again in daylight.

There was still no word from Gibraltar.

I fell back on another bridge game to pass some pretty worrisome hours moving along at slow speed under the Mediterranean. Our submarine was a rather old type, and by afternoon the air within it was warm and lifeless, leaving us inexperienced landsmen feeling rather dopey.

It was not until the early morning hours of October 21 that we came in sight of our rendezvous point. We could spot a light that we thought indicated the correct location, but it was too near dawn to risk a landing and we were not sure enough where we were.

Submerged again, we prepared for another day of discomfort in the overcrowded undersea craft. When it was light enough, we ran up a periscope for a few seconds at a time and made sketches of the shore, visible from three to four miles. We were sure we had our house spotted. Soon after daylight two Algerian fishing boats came out and anchored right in front of "our" beach. They worried us, and we slowly moved out to sea.

Then a radio came in from Murphy. Since we had missed the first night's rendezvous, I was hoping word of our alternative plan had gotten to the French. The first "flap" about this message was when we got hold of a wrong codebook. The first word that came out was "police." I had a sinking feeling that the people on shore had been detected. We finally decoded the message correctly with great relief. Mr. Murphy understood our difficulty, but had changed my proposal and set the second rendezvous for the night of 23/24, thus skipping a night to make it two days later. However, to my relief, part two of the message said the "interested parties have been informed to expect you night of 21/22 and that if no contact then made to expect you night of 22/23 as well. You should assume, therefore, that you are expected tonight and tomorrow night."

That left us not knowing whether we were actually expected on the night then approaching, or twenty-four hours later. However, there was nothing to do but stick it out. My feeling of working against time was by no means allayed by the knowledge that on this day some units of the TORCH operation under General Patton were actually on their way from the United States.

We had another conference and outlined some special plans for trouble ashore. If we arrived safely, we would signal the fact to the submarine by turning off the guide light. If we wanted to reembark later the same night, we would start it flashing. The submarine would stay off the beach directly in front of the house the whole of the first two nights we were ashore. Then, if no radio communication was established and no word received from shore, the submarine would take a station five miles off an alternative rendezvous point a few miles away along the coast, staying there for another full twenty-four hours. If nothing was then heard the *Seraph* would return to Gibraltar without us.

As darkness approached, I speculated on what would happen that night. We surfaced as soon as it was fully dark; but there was no light showing from the shore. At 10 p.m. I was feeling plenty low with the prospect of another full day to "sweat it out." Just to keep things going, I bet each of my associates ten dollars the light would come on "tonight." In case something should be doing later, I decided to get all the sleep I could. At 10:30 I turned in.

At midnight they called me to say a light was showing from the shore. There was feverish activity on the submarine, getting the small-boats on deck, as the craft pulled shoreward within a bare two miles from the surf. The embarkation was calm and pretty well organized. We followed the drill Captain Courtney had worked out for us and counted "one, two, three, four" as one after the other of each boat's occupants arranged his gear and stepped carefully into exactly the right place.

If we had not been so keyed up at the time, it would have been pretty laughable that Jumbo Courtney was the one who capsized his boat and lost his gear. The stalwart Commando was absolutely devastated at this accident at such a crucial moment. I had to call Arch Hamblen back to swap boats with him while Jumbo repaired his boat to follow a little later.

We approached the beach in a V formation, Julius Holmes and Livingstone ahead. My boat and the others waited about 200 yards offshore until, through the darkness over the feathery surf, we saw the letter *k* flashed by a flashlight—the signal that the first boat had made it ashore and all was well. We followed, coming pretty dry through a quite moderate surf. For a moment there was no one at all in sight on an embarrassingly wide beach on which we nocturnal arrivals felt very exposed to unknown danger.

There was a steep bluff at the other side of the beach. It was covered with scrub vegetation and knotty olive trees, and on this dark night looked just plain black. We rushed for the cover of this darkness, carrying our boats and gear.

Just as we reached the edge of the bluff, Bob Murphy and his French associates came down. No one showed any light. Murphy said, "Welcome to North Africa."

I had had a speech all figured out for prompt and, I hoped, dramatic delivery in French. But somehow the whole idea escaped me. What I really did was to puff with relief from the exertion of clambering over the beach and say, "I'm damn glad we made it."

We climbed quickly up a steep and stony path over the bluff to the house. This was a rather typical French colonial villa of red-roofed white stone built around a courtyard, with the main highway to Algiers only thirty yards away. Its owner, M. Teissier, had sent his Arab servants away so that we would be undisturbed and unreported.

Teissier was a well-to-do owner of farmlands; a little, disheveled and rather frightened-looking Frenchman when I first met him. He was a true patriot and risked his life to let us meet at his house. Later I helped him enter the French Army and arranged for him to be assigned on liaison duty at my Fifth Army Headquarters, where he remained and served me well throughout the Italian campaign.

The house was pretty messy by our standards and it certainly was not an impressive setting for a conference of any sort.

General Mast and his staff were not yet there when we reached the house, and we were told by his representatives that they could not arrive until almost 5 a.m., coming by car from Algiers some sixty miles away.

I directed our Commandos to store their folbots in a downstairs room off the courtyard where they would be thoroughly out of sight, and to lock the door to that room. I asked the Commandos themselves, being British, to keep out of sight, as the French had made something of a point of this being strictly a French-American affair. They were not feeling too friendly toward the English after the naval attacks at Dakar and Mers el Kebir. Teissier took me to an upstairs bedroom where an unkempt and much-used bed was awaiting me. A lot of my doubts of previous days had slipped away and I was relieved enough to sleep a little until 5 a.m. when I was called and told that Mast had arrived.

General Mast spoke little English, but said, "Welcome to my country." One of the first things he told me was that he had once been a military attaché at Tokyo, where he had come to know an American, Colonel William C. Crane. He wanted to serve with him and I later arranged to send this colonel as liaison with Mast.

Mr. Murphy, General Mast, and I ate a typical French *petit déjeuner* of coffee, bread and jam, and sardines in the living room while we talked military strategy and North Africa. What I could not tell Mast, and had to be extremely careful not to reveal by any slip of the tongue, was that the TORCH operation, or anything like it, had actually gotten anywhere beyond the planning stage—and this with the leading elements of our armada actually at sea. I could not tell him why North Africa had been selected for the first American offensive in the war.

I was very impressed with Mast's sincerity. He certainly sold me on the idea that he was entirely at our disposal and would do everything possible to help us carry out an operation that to him was only a hope. Before we called together our respective staffs, I asked Mast, "With reference to a hypothetical landing, how would you do it?" I was very pleased that his conception was very close to ours, although it called for the south France bridgehead that I already knew to be impossible.

Later when things got hot, General Mast delivered all the goods he had promised me. He took great personal risk in ordering the French troops defending the Algerian coast to help the Allies. I consider him a great French patriot.

About 9 a.m. we brought our staffs around the dining room table for a frank discussion of the situation. Remembering my instructions not to reveal the facts of the impending operation, I was in a difficult position. Mast asked how big an American effort could be made. I tried to keep a poker face while saying that half a million Allied troops could come in, and I said that we could put 2,000 planes in the air as well as plenty of United States Navy. Mast was pretty impressed. (We actually put 112,000 Americans and British ashore in the first landings.)

Mast suggested that Giraud be picked up in an American submarine as quickly as possible. I was convinced that none of the French realized the imminence of an operation. Although they knew something was in the works, nothing definite had leaked to them. Much later Mast told me this was precisely the case.

Mast said that he was afraid of a German attack on French North Africa. "If they do attack," said Mast, "we will fight immediately, no matter how little we have to fight with." Mast said, with what seemed like utter sincerity, that the French Army would implicitly follow his and Giraud's orders, with resistance expected only from the French Navy.

While we conferred, some lieutenants from Mast's staff kept watch out of the windows and periodically walked around the gardens and patio, keeping an eye out for interference of any kind. No one had appeared by lunchtime when Teissier, with the help of one of the French, cooked chicken with a hot Arab sauce and served it with some red wine and oranges. General Mast was forced to leave at lunchtime to return to Algiers to tend to his duties as commander of the Algerian Division.

Before lunch I wanted to stretch and went out to the patio for a bit. I told one of the French guards I should like to see what it looked like around the house. He offered to change uniforms with me. I put on his French uniform and left my hat off while I walked around outside the wall and in view of the highway. Fortunately, no car came by during my tour of the garden.

During the early afternoon we split up into special groups for detailed discussions of various phases of our plans. The French were ready with voluminous written information, which later turned out to be accurate in every respect. They gave us locations and strengths of troops and naval units; told us where supplies, including gasoline and ammunition, were stored; supplied details about airports where resistance would be heaviest and information about where airborne troops could land safely.

I had said in the morning we would have to get out to the submarine the following evening, but as conversation piled up after Mast's late arrival it became increasingly difficult to see how we would make it. Furthermore, I had the surf on that wide flat beach always on my mind. Through the windows I could see the sea showing more and more whitecaps as the day wore on. There was a windmill near the house, and its increasingly rapid clacking told me audibly that a light breeze was building up into a fresh onshore wind.

It was midafternoon when the phone rang. Teissier answered and quickly turned from the instrument, yelling, "The police will be here in a few minutes." Instantly a full-scale French flap broke out. Officers ran in every direction. Some of the Frenchmen changed into civilian clothes with a speed I have seen exceeded only by professional quick-change artists. Before I had quite decided what was going on, one of General Mast's officers ran past me with a suitcase in one hand out to his car, which immediately took off in the direction of Algiers. Other Frenchmen went out the windows and disappeared into the brush along the beach. I can't say that I blamed any one of them, for their lives would certainly be in jeopardy if caught.

Finally only Teissier and one French officer, Murphy and his assistant, Ridgeway Knight, remained behind. I was feeling pretty deserted, as well as pretty agitated about just where we could go to escape the police. I knew it would not be safe inside the house and I had strong anxiety lest some telltale object be left around our meeting room by accident. Furthermore, our British Commandos were sleeping upstairs. I flew up the stairs and called them. To their question, "Where shall we go?" I said, "Take to the woods on the beach and get the boats out of here—fast."

But there was no time! Only one, carrying the walkie-talkie radio, made the beach to warn the submarine of what was happening. Teissier relocked the room containing the boats just as the police car pulled up.

"Where can we hide?" I asked.

He motioned all of us to rush down through a trap door in the patio into a wine cellar. There was no time for discussion. We had our musette bags with us, stuffed with the incriminating French documents, which, if found upon us, would make it pretty tough.

Teissier, his French associate, Murphy, and Knight remained visible to the police.

It was pitch black in the small cellar at the foot of the steep, open stairway. We could hear so plainly every word and every move above us that we knew it was imperative to keep absolutely still.

Teissier, Murphy, and the two others put on a good show for the police. They clanked bottles around, sang a little, and were very jovial indeed.

It turned out that the Arab servants had been suspicious about being sent away; then, when they had seen footprints on the beach, they had told the police about it.

Murphy identified himself as the American consul in Algiers. He boldly indicated that a little party was in progress and that there were women in the upstairs rooms, and urged the French police not to embarrass him. We could hear the police tramping around looking in corners and behind furniture. Every time their feet approached our trap door, seven hearts popped into seven throats.

I knelt at the foot of the stairs with a carbine in my hand. It was my intention, if they came down the stairs, to try to fight our way clear without shooting; but all of us were prepared to shoot if it were necessary. I whispered that no one was to fire unless I did. It might be hours before we would be able to get through the surf to our submarine, and anything we could do to avoid further police trouble was of the utmost importance.

Poor Courtney, who had had the trouble with the overturned boat the night before, was seized with a coughing fit. He choked and sputtered in the darkness and finally whispered to me, "General, I'm afraid I'll choke."

I answered, "I'm afraid you won't!"

I slipped him a wad of chewing gum on which I already had worked for a while. This quieted him, but he later expressed surprise that "your American chewing gum" had so little taste, and I had to tell him I'd chewed all the taste out of that piece. The police were moving around above us for a full half hour. They finally agreed to go back to town and check with their chief for further instructions. They frankly were suspicious and they told Teissier so.

Finally there was quiet up above, but we did not dare move until Murphy opened the door and said, "This is Bob. They've gone, but they'll be back."

"How long?" I asked.

"Just a little while," he said. "Better clear the house."

We got the boats down to the beach and hid them in the woods, keeping ourselves out of sight.

Captain Livingstone had made contact with the submarine with our walkie-talkie and told them we were in trouble. Later we learned they were pretty excited on board. It was just dusk and we could easily see that the waves were too high to take off in small boats.

Teissier and the remaining Frenchmen were pretty frantic too. We were a terrible liability to them and there was nothing they wanted more than to get rid of their remaining guests.

The waves looked impossible, but we had to make a try during the full darkness or risk ruining the whole mission. I decided to make the experiment with Courtney. I knew I was going to be soaked, so I stripped to shorts and my o.d. shirt. It was cold paddling around in the water. We tried one spot and immediately were overturned by a wave. I had put my money belt—containing several hundred dollars in gold—in my rolled-up trousers, not wishing to be weighted down by the gold in a turbulent surf and heavy undertow. My pants and the money—later described as a large sum in news dispatches—were lost at that time.

This attempt convinced us that a launching was impossible under those circumstances. We went back into the woods to wait, posting sentries in each direction. The French kept rushing back and forth to the house, but reported that nothing had happened there.

We sent one Frenchman to Cherchel with a pocketful of gold to try to buy or rent a fishing boat to take us out to the submarine. He had no success. The fishermen were afraid to take a chance on such a mysterious mission, even for any amount of money.

We talked about possible alternative ways of getting off. Somebody proposed false papers and an automobile ride to Spanish Morocco; but I vetoed that as too risky. I had told Lieutenant Jewell that we might have trouble and to stand by at the second rendezvous one mile east on the second night if we didn't make it the first. We had pretty good radio contact with the submarine by walkie-talkie, using coded phrases. The sub was then only a dangerous three-quarter mile off shore—almost at the edge of the breakers. This was risky, but Jewell was a "can do" boy. It was getting toward midnight. The police had not returned. I was cold, wet, and almost naked, to say nothing of being hungry. None of us had had anything to eat since Teissier's impromptu luncheon. I decided to climb up for a look at the house and to see what I could do about some food and possibly a sweater.

Teissier was very upset. He didn't want me in the house and urged me to get out as quickly as possible. I held out for some bread and wine, a pair of pants, and two of Teissier's sweaters, all uncomfortably tight. I had just started to put the bread and a couple of bottles of wine under the sweater when the police arrived again. Teissier was the most frightened man I had ever seen. He said I dare not use the path, but "please, for God's sake, get out of the house." I was barefoot and my feet already were cut up from the stones on the path, but I jumped over the cement wall on the sea side of the house and dropped painfully some ten feet to the path over the bluff, making my way down to the beach. I groped my way back to the waiting party about 1:30 a.m. Captain Wright, our Navy man, had been making a careful study of the beach to see if there was any place where the surf was a little lighter than elsewhere. The submarine was telling us over the walkie-talkie that they needed a guide light and that none was visible from the house. By this time, the French reported that the police had gone away again, and I sent one of the men to make Teissier turn on the light in the window. He had turned it off during the excitement after the police search.

We surrounded our little party, like the plainsmen in covered wagon days, with sentries, armed with carbines, lying down at all sides. At 3:30 a.m. I felt I could not remain inactive any longer.

"Maybe you and I," I said to Jerry Wright, "can make it. Let's have a try."

At 4 a.m., Knight, Teissier, and Murphy all stripped and carried our boat out into the cold water to try to steady it through the breakers. We passed the first one all right, and I heaved a sigh of relief. Just then the second loomed up ahead, gleaming just a little in the starlight and appearing about a hundred feet high. I knocked Wright's Navy hat off trying to call his attention to what was coming, and he grabbed it in mid-air. We made it and were in the clear after we had passed the second breaker. The other boats followed immediately, but without exception capsized. Our musette bags and brief cases loaded with the secret papers were soaked, as were the papers I had stored inside my borrowed sweater. We seemed to be paddling for hours without seeing anything before we spotted the loom of the *Seraph* in the blackness.

The others finally arrived; the last being Holmes' boat. A big wave knocked it against the side of the submarine and broke the framework of the folbot. Colonel Holmes just barely made it up the side as the boat filled and disappeared with his musette bag in it. This was a dangerous clue to leave behind. A folbot has an air pocket at each end, which might keep the wreck afloat. If it washed up on the beach, either with or without the bag of papers, it could cause us and our associates ashore plenty of trouble. Worst of all, the bag contained secret letters Murphy had given Holmes to deliver in England. They would reveal Murphy's presence at our rendezvous. My anxiety that this material might possibly be found overshadowed my elation at having completed the most delicate part of the mission.

I wanted to stay and look around a little, but the sky already was glowing with approaching day, and Lieutenant Jewell said we must submerge. We reluctantly went below and started back toward Gibraltar.

We were all soaked and exhausted. I asked Lieutenant Jewell, "Haven't I heard somewhere about the British Navy having a rum ration, even on submarines?"

"Yes, sir," answered the lieutenant, "but on submarines only in emergencies."

"Well," I said, "I think this is an emergency. What about a double rum ration?"

"O.K., sir," said Lieutenant Jewell. "If an officer of sufficient rank will sign the order."

"Will I do?" I asked.

It seemed that I was a satisfactory signer and I actually put my name to a formal written order for a double rum ration to crew and passengers of the P-219.

As the morning wore on, my worry increased. I felt I simply had to get a message back to General Eisenhower for relay to Murphy. Much against Lieutenant Jewell's better judgment, we surfaced long enough to send a coded radio to Gibraltar in which I reported the lost boat and urgently requested Murphy to have the beach searched. The boat and musette bag were never found, although my trousers and a light raincoat lost at the same time did turn up on the beach later.

Throughout the following night we traveled on the surface, and after drying ourselves off and sleeping a bit, my group devoted themselves to sorting out wet equipment and carefully drying the secret papers and maps in the submarine's engine room.

On October 24, we ran on surface again. I sent a radio to Gibraltar asking for one of the two flying boats the Prime Minister had assigned to us to pick us up as soon as practicable and fly us to Gibraltar.

The Catalina picked us up by mid-afternoon. We transferred in folbots, taking off for Gibraltar while Lieutenant Jewell and his gallant crew gave us a cheer from their deck.

I had the following cable ready for immediate coding and transmission:

Following cable from CLARK TO COMMANDING GENERAL, EUROPEAN THEATER OF OPERATIONS LONDON FOR EISENHOWER EYES ONLY.

Begins:

Brief summary of events to date are given below pending more complete details to be furnished on our arrival. It was necessary to stand off rendezvous point all day submerged under water waiting signal to land because had not heard from MCGOWEN [Murphy], as to exact time of meeting. Finally made definite contact with him and weather being favorable we went ashore in four canvas canoes about midnight 21/22. Held conference with General Mast who represented General Giraud, and five staff officers commencing at 0700 hours on twenty-second. Following general line anticipated by you our discussions are considered satisfactory. Mast is contacting Giraud today. Giraud expected to give definite decision by Tuesday, which is anticipated to be favorable. I base this conclusion on their favorable reaction to the size of the force the United States could make available for such an operation. All questions were settled satisfactorily except for the time the French would assume supreme command. My view on this question was submitted to Giraud through Mast for his consideration with the definite understanding that my proposal must yet be confirmed by you. Have obtained extremely valuable intelligence data which will be prepared as soon as I return for immediate radio transmission to commanders concerned. Our operations plans appear to be sound considering discussions and information received. Necessity for our being prepared promptly to occupy Tunisia with airborne units confirmed abundantly. Anticipate that the bulk of the French Army and Air Forces will offer little resistance whether Giraud assumes leadership in North Africa or not. I promised during conversation with Mast delivery of two thousand small arms with ammunition by submarine at earliest practicable date to vicinity of our landing. Also promised to furnish submarine to bring Giraud from France to North Africa. French insist this submarine must be American. Initial resistance by French Navy and coast defenses indicated by naval information which also indicates that this resistance will fall off rapidly as our forces land. Detailed conferences continued throughout day until afternoon when local police intervened having become suspicious of increased activity in rendezvous area. This event brought conference to abrupt conclusion. While Frenchmen flew in all directions our party hid in empty repeat empty wine cellar of the house while an argument ensued with the police. We made for woods near beach during lull in conversation with police. There we awaited favorable surf and conditions to permit us to reembark. One boat capsized and was damaged in our first effort to reembark and further attempt was futile in view of high waves. Remaining in hiding we made another attempt to embark at 0430 on the 23rd. After two had capsized at beach all boats reached submarine but one was broken while boarding submarine. Except for brief surfacing to send message to Gibraltar ran submerged during daylight hours of 23rd. With conditions ideal for the transfer to flying boat available morning 24th Gibraltar was asked to dispatch Catalina to rendezvous with us at sea to expedite return. Will inform you time and place of arrival in UK. ENDS.

Gibraltar offered us a number of pleasures, not the least of them hot baths and the opportunity to be a little smug with the admiral who had taken such a dim view of our mission.

Our B-17s took off for England late on the night of the twenty-fourth.

On arrival after a rough, cold trip, I went directly to Telegraph Cottage, General Ike's country place, where he and Bedell Smith were waiting for me. I gave them a complete account of the affair. Ike was delighted and phoned the Prime Minister to tell him that I was back. Churchill asked us both for supper that night. I was too tired to accept.

6.

The Darlan "Deal":

November 1942–December 1942

The next few days were busy ones, but I seemed to spend most of my time talking. I had to tell the story over and over—to the King, to Churchill, to countless officers who were vitally interested in what they should expect when they hit the beaches in North Africa. An example was the next day's conference in the office of the Commander in Chief. "The American Eagle," said Eisenhower, using the nickname by which Churchill often referred to me, "is going to tell us all about it."

On October 29, Ike and I went over to Buckingham Palace at the invitation of King George, who wanted to say goodbye to us before we left for our Gibraltar headquarters, and I repeated the highlights of the story there. The King was quite familiar with TORCH plans and when I was introduced, he said, "I know all about you. You're the one who took that fabulous trip. Didn't you, by the way, get stranded on the beach without your pants?"

By that time, my missing pants had become the subject of a lot of joking among those who knew about the trip. The King obviously had read the cable in which I reported on the journey and said he had "thoroughly enjoyed your statement that you were forced to hide in an 'empty repeat empty wine cellar.'" He talked about Giraud and Darlan, remarked that no one trusted Darlan and that he had shifty eyes. He was kind enough to compliment me on a trip "well done" and as we left there was real emotion in his voice as he said, "Goodbye and Godspeed."

Meanwhile, General Eisenhower had recommended me for the Distinguished Service Medal and there were some kind words in various messages from Washington. There also was an amusing message from Murphy saying our French friends regretted exceedingly that the end of the party's stay was so uncomfortable, and informing me that my pants had been washed up on the shore and that I would find them cleaned and pressed upon my return. And sure enough, I did, but the salt water had shrunk them so badly that they came just below my knees.

I had made arrangements to transport Giraud from southern France to Africa, and on the basis of word he had received by courier the general seemed to be in accord with our plans. Giraud insisted, however, that an American submarine come for him. We had none in the Mediterranean, so we did the best we could by putting an American naval officer in command, technically, of the British submarine P-219, which had taken me on my secret trip to Algiers. The American officer—who knew nothing about submarine operation—was the same Captain Wright who had made the Algeria trip with me. The *Seraph* was instructed to proceed to a rendezvous off the French coast to pick up Giraud. Everything seemed to be working out smoothly and we were in a period of comparative lull before departing for Gibraltar when a message on November 1—a week before D-day—threatened to upset our plans.

The message, from Murphy, said that it was impossible for Giraud, who was known by the code word KINGPIN, to leave France until November 20 and that Mast supported this delay. Murphy said he was cabling President Roosevelt a recommendation that the date of the invasion be postponed, because without help from the French it would be a catastrophe.

"The delay of two weeks, unpleasant as it may be and involving technical considerations of which I am ignorant, is insignificant compared with result involving serious opposition of French Army to our landing," he added. The message also said that Mast was surprised to discover how soon we planned to land and that such short notice amounted almost to "an ultimatum of hostile action."

Although we had been through the adventure of the submarine rendezvous in Algeria together, I didn't know Murphy well at that time. I presumed he was well qualified for his post, but his message indicated he was not well informed on military matters. Later I not only became very well acquainted with Murphy, but I developed a great admiration for his ability, and I greatly value his friendship. When I read his message, however, I certainly was upset, and I immediately began dictating a cable to Washington for Ike's approval. Pacing back and forth in my office as I dictated, here's what I proposed:

It is inconceivable that Murphy could possibly recommend such a delay with his intimate knowledge of the operation and the present location of troops and convoys afloat. It is likewise inconceivable to me that our mere failure to concede to such demands would result in having the French meet us with serious opposition. Such opposition for the reason stated would amount to a double cross by Mast. I cannot believe that he would degrade himself to this extent. Recommend Murphy be advised his suggested action is entirely out of the question and impracticable; that we will proceed to execute this operation more determined than ever to blast our way ashore. He should be directed to tell Mast that we are coming as planned; that all hell and the North African Army can't stop us; that if he uses the information already furnished him on the operation as to the time of its execution to our disadvantage either by regrouping his troops to more effectively stop us, by disseminating the confidential information Murphy has entrusted to him, or otherwise betraying our cause, we'll hang him higher than a kite when we get ashore.

I stopped and thought things over. The message indicated the tension we were under and my feelings at the time, but it seemed a good idea to try again. The cable that finally went off to Marshall was a far more diplomatic statement of the same idea and added that the submarine that had been sent to the Gulf of Lyons to take Giraud aboard would remain available until further notice.

The next day was scheduled to be my last in London before we left for Gibraltar, and we were somewhat reassured when Mast sent through Murphy instructions on how Bône should be attacked, pointing out that the town must be taken from the rear. It also developed that Mast had managed to get his lieutenants into key spots at airfields and elsewhere to facilitate our operations. Still better news came from Commodore Douglass-Pennant, who was chief of staff to Admiral Ramsey, with a report that our convoys were moving ahead of schedule and that there appeared to be no important submarine activity in the areas they were traversing.

After a luncheon with Churchill and a few farewell gatherings, I drove to Addison Road Station to board a special train for Bournemouth where six American Flying Fortresses were waiting at Hurn Airport to fly our party to Gibraltar. British bobbies and British and American military police guarded the little-used station where our train waited. Each officer and man was checked through the gates and then escorted to the eleven-car train. The only lights we could see were flickering coal-oil lamps, which were fuzzy in the drifting fog. The train was completely blacked out, but inside British and American officers were gathered informally at a long table running down the middle of one car. They were quietly excited and there was a spirit of comradeship that was pleasing evidence of the results of Ike's integration program.

Just as the train was pulling out, the best news was received. A cablegram informed us that Giraud would board the submarine waiting in the Gulf of Lyons and be taken to Gibraltar. We set off in an optimistic mood. Then the weather interfered, delaying our departure from Hurn until the morning of November 5. Even then we set out in a pouring rain, flying low to prevent radio detectors on the French coast from picking up the engines of our six craft. Ike was in the *Red Gremlin,* which was first to depart; I was in the *Boomerang,* which was second; and our key personnel was distributed in other planes to lessen the effect of any accident en route. British fighters met us over Gibraltar at 4:20 p.m. Below we could see the harbor filled with all kinds of ships and seaplanes, while the airport was crammed with planes parked wing to wing. It was a prime bombing target and we had a moment of concern when the "yellow alert" was flashed just before we landed, but no enemy planes appeared. Five of our craft landed, but the sixth, carrying General Doolittle and General Lemnitzer among others, had turned back to England because of motor trouble.

Our temporary invasion headquarters was inside the Rock. We entered past two guards and found ourselves in a five-hundred-yard tunnel bored through the solid rock, with our offices opening off the end. Ike and I shared an office about eight feet by eight feet. It had two desks and behind one of them was a cot. At ten o'clock that night, we advised London and Washington that Allied Force Headquarters on Gibraltar was opened.

By the morning of November 6 our rabbit warren of offices under the Rock was functioning smoothly and, so far as we could tell, all TORCH operations were progressing just as well. Admiral Sir Andrew Cunningham came in for a long conference and then looked the place over with enthusiasm. He was one of my favorite figures throughout the African campaign, a fine friend and a great naval commander. Nothing could have been more encouraging than to see him striding confidently through the Gibraltar tunnels, wearing a turtleneck sweater and rubber boots. He was a man who was always ready for anything and you had the feeling that he would be pretty sure to bring it off, too.

Ike called top officers, including Cunningham, into a talk about the handling of Giraud and what should be done if he balked at our plans. Cunningham laughed at our fears. "He's thrown his coat over the fence," he exclaimed heartily. "He will do what he is told." It was decided that we would fly Giraud into Algiers as quickly as possible after I had had an opportunity to go by plane either to Oran or Algiers to report on conditions. Ike would remain at Gibraltar headquarters for the time being to direct overall operations. After these problems had been talked over, someone brought up the question of whether Mast would carry through if Giraud were delayed or balked, and it was Cunningham again who gave the answer. "He must. He's gone too far to draw back."

Our sixth Flying Fortress, which had had to turn back to England, arrived on November 6 with Doolittle and Lemnitzer, after having a fight with three German Ju-88s which attacked it. The enemy planes, however, apparently were near the end of a long patrol and low on fuel, for they were unable to follow up and succeeded only in putting a few bullet holes through the craft, wounding the copilot.

While we were waiting for developments, we checked over the late news from the Middle East where General Alexander previously had opened his campaign to drive the Afrika Korps out of Egypt and Libya and to keep the Germans busy while we made our landings. It had gotten off to a splendid start and later dispatches told of the capture of 20,000 Axis prisoners and 350 tanks and advances that were faster than we had expected.

Then at midafternoon we received a message from Captain Jerauld Wright's submarine. "Task gone," it said. "Radio failing." That was all and we could only guess that there had been an error in transmission and that it should have read "Task done." Within an hour that guess was confirmed when a flying boat reported that it had taken Giraud from the submarine and was bringing him to Gibraltar. We arranged to receive the French General in our office.

The whole episode took a dramatic, weird and almost tragic turn as soon as Giraud arrived. He was a tall man in wrinkled civilian clothes—a man with hollow cheeks and a dark growth of beard straggling across his face, but with a beautiful handlebar mustache, which also seemed to be drooping. At first glance he hardly seemed a figure that would fit easily into the important niche in history that might be awaiting him; but he was also a man with patience and dignity and we soon recognized it as we exchanged formal but elated greetings. That he was stubborn, too, we were soon to learn.

Captain Wright, grinning and heavily bearded and pleased with the success of his submarine mission, accompanied Giraud. Wright had been invaluable to us on our submarine mission, and on my return to London I had sent a message to the Navy Department, attention of Admiral King, then Chief of Naval Operations, telling of Wright's great assistance and demonstrated ability and recommending him for consideration for promotion to rear admiral. Apparently Admiral King did not like this way of doing business, for he took the message to General Marshall with a remark, "who the hell is Clark?" General Marshall told me about it later and we both had a good laugh over it. Incidentally, Jerry Wright later was promoted to rear admiral and I am sure his participation in the submarine safari did his record no harm.

As soon as Wright left our office, Colonel Holmes joined us as interpreter and the red light above our office door was switched on to signify that no one was to enter. We got down to business. Ike did the talking at the start and he was both suave and persuasive, up to a point.

Sitting there in the little office far below the Rock, he explained our plans and said that we had prepared a message to the French people in North Africa, to be signed by Giraud, stating in rather vague terms that the United States, anticipating the plans of the Axis to seize North Africa, was intervening and calling upon all officers and soldiers of the Army of Africa to do their duty. Of Giraud's role, it merely said, "I resume my place of combat among you."

Giraud sat up stiffly. "Now," he said formally, "let's get it clear as to my part. As I understand it, when I land in North Africa I am to assume command of all Allied forces and become the Supreme Allied Commander in North Africa."

I gasped, and I thought Ike had probably never been so shocked and showed it so little. It was rather like a bomb explosion.

"There must be some misunderstanding," Ike said cautiously.

Giraud got a stubborn look on his face, but neither then nor later did he lose control of his words or temper, although at times he became coldly formal. There was no question in my mind that he was stating what he believed to be the agreement: that he would become the top Allied commander in North Africa. Furthermore, he was under the impression that there would be an almost immediate Allied effort to invade France proper to forestall German occupation of Vichy French territory.

Just how he had gotten this impression was something that I was never able to clear up. In my conversation with General Mast, I had been extremely careful not to divulge our exact plans to the French and I had particularly not promised that Giraud would have the top command. Murphy had been in the position of wanting to offer almost anything in order to persuade Giraud to join us, because it was of such vital importance to have a man of his caliber to prevent French resistance. Mast, who was so deep in the scheming that he had to pull every string to get favorable results, could not easily have misunderstood my position because at that time I had even gone so far as to suggest that I would be willing to step out and let Giraud become Ike's deputy if that were approved by Eisenhower.

All I could ever figure out was that there had been some exaggerated promises made to Giraud in order to make sure that he joined us. Mast, for instance, may have told him not to worry about the command; that it could be straightened out; and since such messages had to be taken to Giraud by courier, it is not difficult to see where he might have got the wrong impression. I am sure, at any rate, that Giraud, when he discovered the situation, was as shocked as Ike and I. As we talked it over, it became obvious that we were in for serious trouble.

We sat there for three hours, and at the end of that time Giraud still had not agreed to sign the message or to accept our arrangements. The meeting broke up for dinner. Giraud dined with General Mason-MacFarlane. Meanwhile, we grabbed something to eat, had our bedrolls moved into the office so we could spend the night there, and tried to catch up with the messages that were coming in at a terrific rate. Automatically, the "warning order" that TORCH was about to start had been sent out while we were talking to Giraud. It confirmed that the invasion would start the next morning, November 8, and ordered release of broadcasts and communiqués that had been prepared in advance.

There was nothing new in regard to the convoys, which obviously had had miraculous luck in escaping detection by the enemy. A cable from the Casablanca area brought the good news that the high surf that had been reported there was dropping and that conditions would be good for Patton's landing force.

After dinner we resumed our talk with Giraud, without making much progress. There was no question that he wanted top command of the gigantic operation that had been planned and was now being executed by the British and Americans, although he had arrived at the scene of action only a few hours earlier. I was amazed by his obstinacy and time was getting short.

Ike explained, through Holmes, that Giraud didn't have the means to assume command in such a situation. He argued for a while and then wearily nodded for me to take over. I decided there wasn't much to do except get tough.

"We would like for the honorable general to know that the time of his usefulness to the Americans and for the restoration of the glory that once was France is *now*," I said.

"But what would the French people think of me?" Giraud asked in resisting our pressure to take a subordinate role. "What about the prestige of Giraud; what about my family?"

"It shouldn't make much difference," I said, "whether he is governor of North Africa or general of the armies. After all, we made all the military preparations."

I emphasized that we were prepared to see him command French forces in North Africa as soon as practical, but that we could not give him a higher military command.

"Then," replied Giraud, "I shall return to France."

"How are you going back?" I asked.

"By the same route I came here."

"Oh, no, you won't," I said. "That was a one-way submarine. You're not going back to France on it."

It began to dawn on us that Giraud really was now playing a waiting game. He wanted to see how things would work out in our invasion. I felt that he was planning to stall along a couple of days and then, if all went well with our attacks, come around to our viewpoint. There were several moments when the conversation might have been amusing if we had not been under such a severe strain.

I know that I tried to put over the idea that Giraud should not let his personal ambitions and interests stand in the way of the best interests of France. When this brought no results I said to Holmes, "Tell him this—if you don't go along, General, you're going to be out in the snow on the seat of your pants."

At some point or other, Ike intervened and said that since we were all pretty well exhausted, we had better break it up and get some sleep in preparation for D-day. Giraud departed without changing his mind.

It was obvious we weren't going to get much sleep. The invasion was about to begin. Ike sent a long message to Washington explaining what had happened in regard to Giraud, pointing out that he had made every possible concession and that both British and American officers who had been consulted regarded Giraud's position as unreasonable and preposterous under the circumstances. He said that Giraud insisted there was no possibility that he could guarantee nonresistance to our attacks tonight and that he would not attempt to do so.

"He is obsessed" the message said in part, "with the idea of moving immediately into France and implied that if he were made commander he would promptly use the entire Air Force coming into North Africa in neutralizing Sardinia and in transporting troops into Southern France and would transfer the fighter and bomber units to airfields in Southern France.

"Eagle [Clark] and I are bitterly disappointed, principally because of the help Giraud could have rendered. Latest news that we have been able to gather indicates that we may expect considerable resistance, which, if true, shows that Mast, operating in the name of Giraud, has not been very effective. The Chief of

Staff of the Oran division has just reported that their plans have been discovered and that an intense alert is being conducted."

There was a message from Patton that cheered us up. Just prior to D-day, Ike and I had worried over unfavorable reports from Casablanca about the high surf there, which might make a landing by Patton's forces extremely difficult if not impossible. We radioed him that if events dictated, he should be ready to come on through the Straits of Gibraltar without attacking at Casablanca. The message we got back was typical of Patton. He said that if conditions prevented him from landing on the west coast of Africa, he would go on to land somewhere, and if necessary in Spain. We liked the sound of that message.

Brief messages also were coming in from the landing forces. The first, at 2:38 a.m., said that the Eastern Task Force assault had been successful and that landings had been made on the three beaches at Algiers. Then, half an hour later, it was reported that Sidi Ferruch had been captured. After that the messages came in rapidly and most of them looked good. Before dawn three enemy planes came over Gibraltar and aroused a tremendous clatter of anti-aircraft fire, but dropped no bombs. Our long tunnel quickly filled with people, for we were constantly expecting the Germans to strike back. However, the planes were probably merely trying to find out what was going on, and we were grateful that it took the enemy so long to do it.

Ike and I lay down for an hour in our office, and when we checked in again it was to find more favorable reports. Rear Admiral Henry K. Hewitt, commanding the Western Task Force naval operations, radioed just before 6 a.m. that the attack was proceeding on schedule and Fredendall reported from Oran that "landing continues unopposed." At 7:45 a.m., General "Doc" Ryder reported the Algiers force had captured Maison Blanche Airport.

These optimistic reports continued for another hour or so; then we began getting news of resistance. Fires broke out at the Oran airport, where thirty-nine planeloads of paratroopers from England were scheduled to land, and they had to come down some distance away in the desert. There also was strong opposition reported from the Oran harbor, where shore batteries opened up on our forces. Four French destroyers and mine sweepers sortied from Oran and engaged the British naval forces, which promptly sank two of the ships and drove the rest back to port.

The important thing, however, was that we were meeting less opposition than we were prepared for and, although we regretted the necessity of any fighting, the whole TORCH operation was off to a good start. It was decided that I should leave by air as quickly as possible for Algiers to establish advance Allied Force Headquarters. Ike believed I could go the following morning.

Meanwhile, we had another two-hour talk with Giraud. During the period in which our attack progressed, the French general had been under heavy pressure from the British to accept our proposals and let everybody get on with the liberation of French North Africa. These talks brought about a change in Giraud's attitude, and the change became more pronounced when he saw how our invasion operations were progressing. He decided to play ball, and in a comparatively short time we worked out the broad outline of our deal. Ike cabled Murphy in Algiers that a complete agreement had been reached and asked him to send a French plane to Gibraltar to carry the French general to Africa, where he would become commander in chief of all French forces in the region, working in close collaboration with the Allied troops. Giraud also agreed to do his utmost to stop resistance and to organize French assistance in our drive toward Tunisia.

So it was all set—or at least we hoped it was all set. I had previously given up my bed at Government House to Giraud, so I went to Ike's room and got a brief sleep in his bed since I was scheduled to take over the night trick at the office under the Rock. When I got back to work, my desk was piled high with reports from all sectors, including one that gave me real pleasure.

On November 7, the naval commander of the Eastern Task Force, Rear Admiral Sir Harold M. Burrough, had radioed that the U.S.S. *Thomas Stone,* heading for the Algiers beaches, had been torpedoed about 300 miles east of Gibraltar and around 130 miles from her goal. The vessel carried the 2nd Battalion of the 39th Regimental Combat Team. She was badly crippled, with her propeller and steering gear torn away. Tugs were sent to her assistance, but later that day the Task Force commander reported that in order to carry out his mission in TORCH he had been forced to leave the *Thomas Stone* after giving her antisubmarine protection and making sure she was in no danger of sinking.

We counted it out of the invasion, if not in danger of being destroyed by Nazi planes, but we counted too soon. A later message from the rescue tugs said that the battalion commander had decided there was no sense in being left out of the fight, so the battalion had gone aboard their motor-driven landing craft and headed for the shore 150 miles away. The message I received late on D-day showed they made it, accompanied by one destroyer. They landed some distance west of Algiers and a couple of boats capsized in the operation, but they got in on the fight.

Not long afterward word came from General Ryder that Algiers had surrendered and that, starting at 9 p.m., our forces had occupied the city. I gave the news to American and British reporters late that evening when they crowded into our little office. I also explained developments regarding Giraud and my plans to proceed the next day to Algiers. Major Joseph Phillips, our public relations officer, then asked me to tell them the story of my submarine journey to Algiers on the clear understanding that nothing would be written about it until an official release was obtained. I gave them as much detail as I could and they faithfully kept our agreement to withhold it. Major Phillips felt—and from the viewpoint of the Public Relations Office I suppose he was right—that I should tell it because I was leaving the next day, and if any accident should befall me the full account of the adventure would be lost.

Since I was leaving the next day for Algiers, I was busy until a late hour with my preparations. I asked General Mason-MacFarlane to sound out Giraud on a question that had been worrying me—the presence of Admiral Darlan in Algiers. The governor later reported back that Giraud had been asked about his attitude toward Darlan, who seemed likely to be the key man in any effort to get the French fleet to come over to our side, and that Giraud had grudgingly said a place might be found for Darlan if in exchange we could get such a prize as the fleet. He didn't, however, have much regard for or faith in Darlan.

The next morning the military situation continued to improve and Giraud departed for Algiers by airplane. I was ready to follow him immediately, but the weather closed in and my departure in the *Red Gremlin* was delayed until shortly after noon. The *Boomerang,* another B-17, carried the rest of my party, and we were accompanied by thirteen Spitfire fighters. The flight was made in close formation, at an altitude of only 500 to 700 feet above the sea. I opened the panel top over the radio room and, in goggles and helmet, stuck my head out and watched the approach to Africa.

We landed at Algiers at 5 p.m., just as a dozen German Junkers 88s came over the field at about 6,000 feet altitude. They flew through heavy antiaircraft fire and dived on the crowded harbor, where we could hear the dull *pung!* of their exploding bombs. Two of the enemy aircraft appeared to have been hit; and as I climbed into a Bren-gun carrier that had come out to our plane, I could see one of the Junkers wavering just south of the airfield with two Spitfires on its tail. Everywhere around us Americans and British ran out onto the field, yelling and cheering the Spits on. One of them flashed up under the Junker's belly and in a moment we saw the enemy engines begin to smoke. He crashed and the Spits darted away in search of other prey. Other Junkers were still over the harbor, and a solid wall of ack-ack fire was going up, the orange balls of fire looking like strings of Christmas tree lights across the sky. Guns around the airfield raised a tremendous clamor, and just as we drew up beside the airdrome buildings a stick of three bombs fell on the field within a hundred feet of the tail of the *Red Gremlin*. We'd had a peaceful flight over, but we got quite a welcome after our feet were on the ground.

The final touch in the greeting was a German plane that was caught in the flak directly over our heads while we were still in the Bren-gun carriers. It plunged like a rock toward the airport and seemed to be headed exactly for the spot where we had stopped. Our legs were over the sides and we were looking desperately for cover when the plane exploded into thousands of pieces at an altitude of about 1,000 feet. The rear half, grotesquely twisted, landed about a quarter of a mile from our position. We got our legs weakly back into the carrier and drove on into town and to the Hotel St. George.

The city was comparatively peaceful under an armistice, but there was a strong feeling of uncertainty and a political turmoil such as I had never before encountered. Everybody connected with the French administration and the leaders of the armed forces were clamoring for an immediate settlement of the status of the new regime and for as favorable a position as each could get. I found General Ryder haggard and grim.

"I'm glad you're here," he said. "I've stalled them off about as long as I can."

By the time he had sketched in the bare outline of the situation, I knew it wasn't going to be easy to bring the French together, particularly because Admiral Darlan was in Algiers. And also because some of the most powerful figures in French North Africa would have nothing to do with Giraud. They wouldn't even meet with him. I finally arranged to see Darlan, General Juin, Admiral Fenard, and other officers on the following morning.

Later Murphy came to the hotel in an excited state.

"Congratulations!" he shouted. "Glad you're here, but where are all your tanks?"

He couldn't understand why we were not making a great show of force to impress the French, who hadn't yet quite decided which way to leap. He had trouble understanding that our armored strength at Algiers was slight and that what we had was busy outside the town.

"Run your tanks through the main streets," he urged. "Show them some force. Give them a big parade."

"Okay," I finally said, "if you insist I'll have all three of our available tanks put on a show."

Things went on that way for quite a while and when I finally got back to my hotel room all I could say was, "What a mess! Why do soldiers have to get mixed up in things like this when there is a war to be fought? It's awful!"

I had talked briefly to Giraud and found he had quickly discovered that his relations with the French officers in North Africa were none too good. He decided to await developments and instead of trying to seize the leadership he practically went underground, moving in with a French family in an obscure neighborhood, after letting us know where to get in touch with him.

I had brought a small party of officers with me, including Colonel Darryl Zanuck, who was supposed to be taking pictures, but who, in the emergency, was one of my most helpful aides. He acted as an intelligence agent, an intermediary in many difficult situations, and as a courier when need be. All of these things he did with a great deal of skill. The ability of Zanuck, Colonel Slocum, and several other officers to take on almost any job and handle it successfully made it possible for me to devote most of my time to the major problem that we faced.

The next morning—the tenth of November—I met with the French in a small room off the foyer of the St. George Hotel. I had a platoon of infantrymen stationed outside the hotel, mostly for psychological effect. I wanted everybody to know that we meant business and I adopted a formal attitude. The conference room overlooked a peaceful garden filled with flowers and palm trees, but there definitely was a strained atmosphere when I took my place at the head of the table and looked over the assembled officers.

At my left was Darlan, a little man with watery blue eyes and petulant lips. He seemed nervous and uncertain, obviously ill at ease. Again and again he pulled a handkerchief from his pocket and mopped his balding head. He shifted in his chair and his hands fumbled with the papers on the table in front of him. On my right was General Juin, commander in chief of the French forces in North Africa, who was later to become one of my best friends, but who, at that time, was no help in my negotiations. Several years later Madame Juin told me that her husband had pessimistically returned home following our conference and reported that he had been dealing with a "big American who does nothing but shout and pound the table."

The others at the conference were, Navy: Vice Admiral d'Escadre Moreau, maritime commander of the Fourth Region; Vice Admiral Fenard, Secretary-General of the North African government; Rear Admiral Battet, Chief of Cabinet to Darlan; and Rear Admiral Reboul Hector Berlioz, Chief of Staff of the Fourth Region. Army: General Koeltz, commander of the 19th Military Region, and General de Brigade Sevez, Chief of Staff to Juin. Air: General Mendigal, Superior Commandant of Air in North Africa. The Americans present were Murphy, who acted as interpreter, Colonel Holmes,

Captain Wright, Commodore Dick and Lieutenant Jack Beardwood, my aide, who sat near me and kept a detailed diary of the conversation.

I believe I should stop here and explain some of the circumstances regarding Darlan, whom I have mentioned only occasionally so far, but who soon became the center of a great political controversy in both England and the United States. Darlan was an opportunist. He had, after the fall of France, collaborated with the Nazis as one of the strong figures in the Pétain government in Vichy. He was still an opportunist, as shown when he tried through Murphy to feel out the American attitude toward accepting his assistance prior to our African invasion. Nothing came of that, but it is quite possible that Darlan knew enough of our plans to be in Algiers at the right time on a visit to his son, who was stricken with infantile paralysis. That might well have been the way of an opportunist. Darlan had shown signs of being ready to jump our way if given any encouragement, or when assured of Allied success in North Africa. We therefore were not particularly shocked to find him there; in fact, General Ryder had advised Ike as early as November 8, while I was still at Gibraltar, that he was acting to take Darlan into protective custody.

The surprise in regard to Darlan, therefore, was chiefly the fact that the French officials with whom we had to deal looked to him as the man with the greatest authority in North Africa. I have said earlier that Murphy was not too familiar with military operations. I should now make it clear that I was in the same position in regard to politics, particularly the complex, involved, and intriguing sort of politics that the French practiced in North Africa. I took a great deal of blame later for dealing with a collaborator at Algiers. Ike backed me up, but I suppose he must have had many moments of doubt when the heat was really on from Washington and London. There is only one real answer that I can give—as Ike's deputy, I was charged with fighting a war, or, more specifically, with preventing a war against the French and getting on as rapidly as humanly possible with the war against the Axis in Tunisia. That meant I was trying to save American, British, and French lives—a great many of them. That meant that every day, every hour, was important not only in ending French resistance but in getting our forces into French Tunisia, some four hundred miles to the east. And to carry out this mission, I was ready to deal with anybody who could do the job.

Several things were obvious not only to me but to almost everyone I talked with in Algiers. Mast and other French officers had helped our invasion in various ways—some of them indirect. They had been able to issue orders—which were obeyed—to certain trusted units, instructing them not to oppose our landings. They had provided us with guides. They had pointed out gasoline dumps and cooperated in many other ways. We were grateful to them; but it immediately was apparent that Mast and the others who had negotiated with us were regarded as traitors by the other officers of the French armed forces. And, unfortunately, it was these other officers who were, for the most part, in command of the French defenses and who were in a position to order a cessation of firing, which had continued sporadically in a few sectors and might, of course, be resumed generally if our negotiations failed.

This situation was emphasized by the change in Giraud's position. Whereas he had previously felt he could influence the turn of events, he discovered as soon as he arrived in Algiers that he was looked upon by some French Army elements as almost a traitor and that he could exert very little influence on the immediate situation. He had, in fact, told me the night before that it seemed likely that only Darlan could issue a general cease-firing order that would be obeyed by all elements concerned.

I looked coldly at the stubby, ingratiating little man on my left and asked Murphy to explain to him the necessity of getting to the point of the conference at once.

"We have work to do to meet the common enemy," I said. "Is he ready to sign the terms of the armistice? It will cover all French North Africa. It is essential that we stop this waste of time and blood."

Darlan evaded. "I sent a résumé of the terms to Vichy," he replied. "Laval [Premier Pierre Laval] was away. There will be no reply until the Council of Ministers meets [in Vichy] this afternoon."

Looking back on this conversation, I imagine my table pounding, which was noted by Juin, began almost at once. There was, of course, no possibility of getting results by dealing with Vichy.

"Do you understand," I asked, "that diplomatic relations between France and the United States have been broken off in the last twenty-four hours?"

"I've had no confirmation officially," he replied, "but I want to see hostilities stopped as soon as possible. I have been given strict orders [by Vichy] to enter into no negotiations until orders come from Pétain or the Council of Ministers. My associates and I, however, feel hostilities are fruitless."

"I do not propose to wait for any word from Vichy," I snapped.

"I can only obey the orders of Pétain," Darlan said.

"Then I will end these negotiations and deal with someone who can act," I told him.

I will quote the remainder of our talk from the shorthand notes taken at the time.

Darlan: I have asked Vichy to give me an answer to your terms as soon as possible.

Clark: What you propose is not possible. I will end this conference in thirty minutes.

Darlan: I understand what this means, and I want to tell my government of what has happened.

Clark: This is impossible. It will be necessary to retain you in protective custody. I hope you understand.

Darlan: I am giving my opinion that it is stupid to continue hostilities here. I urged acceptance of the terms. I am confident that Pétain will agree.

Clark: That is fine, but do you understand that we cannot sit here while governments agree and ministers debate? If the Admiral will not issue instructions for the cessation of hostilities, I will go to General Giraud. He will sign the terms and issue the necessary orders.

Darlan: I am not certain the troops will obey. This will only mean the loss of more time and there will be more fighting.

Clark: Are you so sure of the decision from Vichy? Pétain has already informed President Roosevelt that he considers our landings aggression. If you think Pétain will agree with you that hostilities must cease, why can't you issue that order now?

Darlan: I can't assume the responsibility for such an order. It would result in the immediate occupation of Southern France by the Germans.

Clark: We all agree concerning the great danger of the occupation of Southern France, but it will not be because of this order. What you are doing now means the killing of more French, British, and Americans. I presume you know that Oran is already in our hands. This all boils down to one question. Are you going to play with the Vichy Government or go with us?

Darlan: I am simply bound by an oath of fidelity to the Marshal to obey his orders. I can't take the responsibility of giving an order to cease hostilities.

Clark: This is the time when we must lean on our inclinations and not on our orders. You are under domination. Here is an opportunity for all Frenchmen to rally and win the war. Here is your last chance!

Darlan: I am willing to send an urgent message to Marshal Pétain, recommending an armistice for Algiers and Morocco.

Clark: You already have done that.

Darlan: I have not done so in specific terms.

Clark: We haven't time. All Frenchmen and all Americans have the same interests at heart, and here we are fighting among ourselves, wasting time. I know that the Admiral wants, deep down in his heart, to stop this fighting between our troops. We all want to do the same thing, and we must get an order for cessation of hostilities this morning. We have the means. We have 150,000 American and British troops in French North Africa. We have the means of equipping the French Army and making this the base from which we can go into France. How anybody can fail to join us in an operation that can mean the liberation of France is beyond my understanding.

Darlan: I am completely in accord with your point of view, but I still can't act until I hear from Pétain.

Clark: Giraud will sign the terms of the armistice.

Darlan: The Army is still with me.

Clark: We will make it as easy as possible for you.

Darlan: I would like five minutes with my staff for discussion.

Clark: You understand that no one is to leave here or to communicate with anyone outside.

At this point, General Ryder sent me a message that at one of the French barracks an American captain had gone to the French colonel and told him that unless the armistice we were discussing was signed, the barracks would be bombed. I sent General Ryder with a French general to work this out with the French and American commanders. I was anxious not to have any such action on our part complicating what we were doing across the conference table.

As soon as we resumed the session with Darlan, he laid copies of an order before me and asked if I would accept it. It said in substance that the Americans would not accept his refusal to declare an immediate armistice, that further battle would be futile, and that he wanted to tell Marshal Pétain that, as a result of fighting, the French would probably lose North Africa. Admiral Darlan wanted to cease hostilities and merely take an attitude of complete neutrality.

I insisted again that what I must have immediately was a clear and specific order to all French troops as well as to the Navy and Air Force. Darlan finally agreed to this and to passing an order to Juin, Noguès, and Barre, the Air Force and the Navy. He began writing the message in his own hand, asking questions of me as he went along. I told him that each of our commanders would decide the terms of his armistice in his area, negotiating with the French commanders concerned. General Patton would meet with General Noguès in French Morocco and offer terms to him. Not until firing had ceased would terms for the whole territory of North Africa be discussed.

Then, for the first time, Darlan raised the question of Giraud's status. I answered, "What Giraud wants is to help France; in this big setup there is room for everyone. Right now I am trying to stop the fighting." Admiral Darlan handed me the draft of his order. It ordered all land, air, and sea forces in North Africa to cease firing immediately against American and British troops, to return to their bases and to observe neutrality pending further instructions. In it Darlan said that he took responsibility for North Africa in the name of Marshal Pétain, that present military commanders would retain their commands, and that political and administrative authority would remain unchanged for the present.

"This will stand," I said, "unless otherwise changed by the Allied Commander in Chief, General Eisenhower. It may be necessary later to make changes and for that reason I have asked you to insert the words 'for the present.' You understand there are some British forces involved, but all of them are under American command." Then Darlan, with some bitterness, asked, "What disposition will be made of the French generals who disobeyed orders? I mean Mast and the others. I think they should be given no French military command."

Clark: That is one of the things I want to discuss.

Darlan: I don't want to treat with those men. It is in your own interest to agree that I can't tolerate these men not obeying my orders. The other officers don't want them to have anything to do with French command.

Clark: I think I can handle this soon. As I understand it, you do not want these men under your command.

Darlan: Yes, that is right!

Mendigal: You had better put them in some safe place. They are bitterly resented.

Clark: I don't understand. They helped us so much. However, I do understand your resentment against their not obeying orders. We must see that these orders to cease hostilities are carried out. The order is not worth the paper it is written on unless carried out.

I O.K.'d the final draft of Admiral Darlan's order and everyone left the room except Darlan, Murphy, and myself. I was anxious to get some immediate reaction from the admiral concerning the powerful French fleet at Toulon. Darlan was vague and would make no hints or commitments, but he went so far as to tell me that he had personally issued orders to the French fleet to be prepared to move on short notice should the Germans enter unoccupied France. He said emphatically, "Under no circumstances will our fleet fall into German hands."

I also took this private opportunity to tell Darlan that it was of the utmost importance that he and Giraud reach a working agreement, and that I had arranged to bring the two together at the St. George that afternoon. I told the admiral that while he was not in our custody, I would like his word that he would not leave his residence for the present.

As soon as the meeting broke up, I sent a cable to General Eisenhower. One paragraph of this read:

I have now two Kingpins [this was the code name originally used for Giraud] but hope to wiggle out of it somehow. I deemed it of the utmost importance to do anything to secure an order which would be obeyed to cease hostilities. I have not announced Darlan's order over the radio, so as not to tip our hand to the Germans.

By afternoon of November 10—and before my Giraud-Darlan meeting at three p.m.—the news came from Vichy that Marshal Pétain had fired Admiral Darlan as head of the armed forces. He had appointed General Auguste Noguès, governor general of Morocco, as Darlan's successor. I immediately went to see Admiral Darlan. Pétain also had rejected the North African armistice. The admiral was very dejected indeed. He acted like a king who had suddenly had his empire shot out from under him. He stared at the floor as he said, "There is nothing I can do but revoke the order which I signed this morning."

"You will do nothing of the kind," I replied. "There will be no revocation of these orders; and to make certain, I shall hold you in custody."

With this, I directed that a platoon of Americans be thrown around Admiral Fenard's house to see that Darlan did not leave and that there was no communication.

I was immensely relieved later to learn from our field commanders that the Darlan order had already been widely obeyed and was continuing to be observed despite the contradictory news from Vichy. This convinced me all the more that Darlan would have to be our man for the present; in an out-and-out trial of strength with Pétain, Darlan had prevailed. Furthermore, time was running out. We knew that the Germans were moving reinforcements into Tunisia and we wanted French forces there to resist them as well as facilitate rapid movement of our forces to the scene.

I brought Generals Giraud, Juin, Koeltz, and Mendigal together to get their reaction on Darlan's rejection by Pétain. I knew of the French reverence for the chain of command and wanted to make no mistakes. Giraud, stroking his mustache pensively, told me that he had received information that the Germans were about to invade unoccupied France.

"We are at the end of our rope," he said. "It is an appalling situation. It is time for all Frenchmen to get together. It's our responsibility to get together to save North Africa."

Personally, I didn't have much hope of harmony at that time. The Darlan wing still looked upon Giraud as a traitor. Admiral Darlan had a disappointing reverence for Pétain. At our first meeting Darlan's people had refused even to shake hands with Commodore Dick of the Royal Navy. The delicate matter of French resentment of the British attacks on Oran and

Dakar was another fly in an increasingly complicated ointment. One comfort I did have was that up the line in Gibraltar General Eisenhower was absorbing the political heat from Washington and London, where a public uproar had broken out against our doing any business at all with Darlan or any other Vichyite. All sorts of rumors were floating around, including one that Pétain himself would come to North Africa to attempt to assume command.

While we were waiting to see how well the Darlan "cease-firing" orders would hold up to pressure from Vichy (which by now included direct messages to French field commanders contradicting Darlan's orders), I tried again to talk out with Giraud his exact position in our French setup. He had now modified his claims to command. What he wanted now was to be named "Commander in Chief of all French Forces in North Africa or any place in the French Empire." At least he was no longer asking for command of all Allied troops in North Africa, but it was still too big an order to be digested by other French leaders at the moment. My main encouragement at the end of that first day was that the occupation of southern France, which had already been started by the Germans, was tending to bring the divergent factions together in Algiers.

The next morning, November 11, I went out to the home of Admiral Fenard to talk again with Darlan. I was mainly interested in trying to get the French fleet, which was concentrated at Toulon, to join us before it fell into German hands. Darlan was evasive; I was unhappy at the way I was being forced to bluster and push people around, and I was irritated by the fog of French personal and political "honor" that seemed to be holding up our military plans. I simply had to find a sound instrument through which we could get the French to cooperate with us in Algiers and in Tunisia, into which the Germans were now pouring with little opposition. I didn't care much if that instrument were named Darlan, Giraud, or Pétain himself.

I was struck by how miserable Darlan looked that day, but I added to his woes by being as tough as possible.

"You've told us repeatedly that you want to free France," I said, "but you've given no visible indication or decision in support of us or the Allied cause. There are two ways you can demonstrate your good faith—by summoning the French fleet to a North African port and by ordering the governor of Tunisia [Admiral Esteva, who eventually was convicted by the French of treason] to resist the German invasion."

"I have no authority to summon the fleet," he replied, "and in view of my dismissal by Pétain I am not certain that any orders given by me will be obeyed. I am, however, sure that the fleet will follow orders to scuttle itself rather than be seized by the Germans."

"There is danger," I said, "that there will not be time to scuttle the fleet and, in any event, that will be an act against the Allies as much as against the Germans."

I then demanded that he issue orders to the fleet and to Esteva. He refused both demands. By this time, I was as angry as at any point in the negotiations and Darlan knew it. We must have made a strange picture—a furious six-footer, towering over the little baldish admiral, who usually seemed to cower even when things were peaceful—but I was not conscious of it at the time.

"This," I said, glaring down into his pale eyes, "merely verifies the statement I made when I came here. There is no indication of any desire on your part to assist the Allied cause. Good day!"

I marched out of the house and, for all I know, slammed the door. In any event, I got results. Immediately after luncheon, Admiral Fenard telephoned and asked me to meet again with Darlan. I found he had changed his mind, a fact which he tried to attribute to the receipt of information that German Marshal von Rundstedt and Marshal Pétain were at odds concerning the occupation of southern France by the Nazis. As a result, Darlan agreed to my demands.

That afternoon, he sent a message to Admiral de Laborde at Toulon, saying that the Germans had taken action which violated the armistice then existing in France and that "we have our liberty of action." Since Pétain was "no longer able to make free decisions," he added, "we can, while remaining personally loyal to him, make decisions favorable to French interests." Darlan then said it was impossible for the fleet to remain at Toulon and "invited" de Laborde as commander in chief to bring the warships to French Africa.

No one was optimistic that the fleet would come, but we had done all we could think of. I still didn't feel I understood the psychology of these men with whom I had to deal. I could not explain why French General A would condemn General B for having participated in the very venture that General A had eventually joined himself, yet the fact was that ex-Vichyites under Darlan, although they had come over to our side, still looked upon Giraud and de Gaulle as traitors.

The next problem was Tunisia. I told Darlan that the honor of every Frenchman could only dictate that he fight the Germans in every land. I pointed out that they had broken their pledged word and invaded southern France, and that even Pétain had been compelled to protest Hitler's actions.

"I want you to call Esteva and order him to fight the Germans," I said, handing him the telephone. With the alacrity of a cashiered marshal who has suddenly been restored his army, he seized the instrument and put through the order. I understood enough French to know he pulled no punches. Darlan was nervously puffing his pipe when I left the house, but I felt far better. Later I had Juin telephone other commanders in Tunisia, directing them to resist the Germans; they indicated that they would do so where the means of resistance were available.

By nightfall it seemed to me we had made some progress, but we were by no means out of the woods. The situation generally was shaky and I seriously considered removing Darlan from the Fenard villa and putting him in custody on a warship in the harbor. There was, however, the important question of his prestige, and finally I decided on the opposite course. I called Colonel Slocum and ordered him to remove the guard from around Darlan. I thought that ought to bolster his prestige; also, if he had really decided to cooperate, he was probably the only man who could hold the French together. I certainly could not overlook the possibility that fighting might break out among the French if some of the important commanders tried to string along with Pétain.

A few hours later I discovered my mistake. I was awakened at five o'clock in the morning to learn that the French order to resist the Germans had been revoked. I was boiling by the time—an hour later—I had both Darlan and Juin at the hotel.

"Why, in the name of all that is decent, honorable, and intelligent, have you revoked your order to oppose Axis movement into Tunisia?" I demanded.

Darlan remained silent. Juin, a small man with a close-cropped mustache, wrung his hands while he said that the order had not been rescinded.

"It has only been suspended until General Noguès arrives," he explained.

Noguès, whom Pétain had named to succeed Darlan, was due to arrive in Algiers that afternoon.

"Not once," I continued, "have you shown me that you were working for our interests."

Juin continued his pleading for time, looking across the room at the silent Darlan, who was twisting and creasing little strips of paper and looking somewhat like a punished schoolboy.

"We don't recognize Noguès," I told him. "Those whom we recognize must guarantee that they will fight on our side against the Germans."

"I am willing to fight the Germans," said Juin.

"It isn't enough to say that you are willing; you must prove by your actions that you actually are fighting," I said.

"But," General Juin replied, "you must understand my difficulty. I am subject to the orders of Noguès and honor requires that I obey him."

"And while you are delaying," I asserted, "the German troops are moving in! I want that order reissued now!"

Admiral Fenard, who had accompanied Darlan and who spoke English, came up to me at this point and, while Darlan, Juin, and Murphy were engaged in an animated conversation, said that he believed I was making a mistake.

"You are getting what you want if you will only be a little more patient and wait," he whispered. "Don't spoil everything. You almost have a solution, a victory in your hand."

I just shook my head. "I think they're stalling," I said. Fenard stepped back, letting his hands fall in a gesture of despair.

"That's not true," he exclaimed. "You are blind. You are blind."

Darlan had hardly contributed a word to the general conversation until I turned to him and exclaimed, "Anyone who is going to be accepted by us must concretely show his willingness to fight against the Germans. I asked you for two simple things to prove you want to save France: one, order the French fleet to North Africa; and two, resistance to the Germans in Tunisia. Neither of these things has materialized."

Darlan finally said, "I know that the fleet has received my message and I have received indications that it will be willing to come here if the Germans enter Toulon. I know that the fleet is prepared to go to sea."

"The orders to the commanders in Tunisia were revoked without reference to me," I told him. "That, to me, is almost treachery. Because of your promises certain military moves are being made, in the belief that you were acting in good faith. You could be executed for this treachery, if treachery it is."

Darlan and Juin began to talk simultaneously. Their hands were tied. They must talk to Noguès as a matter of military command, honor, and discipline; the order had not been revoked, it had merely been suspended; they really wanted to fight the Germans; just give them time to see Noguès. Darlan volunteered the information that Noguès would arrive by four o'clock. In answer to my question as to whether Giraud would be in the conference with Noguès, he said that the first meeting "will be held by the people in power. We will notify you of the results," he pleaded. The conversation then proceeded as follows:

Clark: Who is in power and who will be in power will be decided by the Allied forces.

Darlan: Who is going to command?

Clark: The supreme commander will be American. We will settle the French commands later.

Juin: I suggest that Giraud be the military commander from Dakar to Bizerte, and that I command Algiers.

Clark: That is satisfactory to me provided the necessary orders go forth to Tunisia.

Juin: Now or after the meeting?

Clark: I mean now! The Germans are preparing to land in Constantine and Setif [in Tunisia]. Your future depends on whether you do this or not.

Juin: This puts me in a bad position.

Clark: It is a spot of your own choosing.

The orders were reinstated and I took time out from tangling with the French to inspect our 39th Infantry Combat Team in the field. When I returned to Headquarters, Noguès had arrived. He came to my office to say that, as commander in chief by Pétain's orders, he was entitled to a private conference before the general session. I looked at him steadily for a moment and then said, "I do not recognize either you or Pétain."

Noguès blinked and passed into the general conference room to join my staff officers, Mr. Murphy, Admiral Darlan, General Mast, and practically every other important officer or official of either side on hand in Algiers at that time.

I started a whole hour of general discussion by outlining the objectives we were striving for and the specific results I expected. I told our people that if the French did not come to a decision I was prepared to arrest them all and lock them up aboard one of the ships in the harbor. There was an hour of fruitless talk and then I insisted that they admit Giraud, who had been in the hotel lobby when the conference began, but was ignored by the other French officials. I had told Giraud I was not going to let him down, but he was nervous about this first meeting with Darlan and Noguès, and with good reason. When he entered the conference room, they more or less turned their backs on him. I went over to them and persuaded Darlan and Noguès to shake hands with Giraud. They did, but they were cold toward the tall general.

Giraud, however, entered into the conversation, and after a few minutes I left them to battle it out among themselves. They were all arguing hotly. Having been told they had to compose their differences, Darlan was trying to persuade Noguès to accept Giraud as a part of the military picture. I figured he could do a better job of it than I.

When I returned to the conference room later, the outlook seemed more hopeful. I had suggested that Darlan assume political leadership for the time being and that the present governors of Morocco, Algiers, and Tunisia be retained with Giraud authorized to organize a volunteer French army to fight with the Allies. We would equip only those French units that fought with us; the rest of the army would before long stagnate or would be available for the defense of North Africa in the event of trouble by way of Spain. The French conferees suggested that I give them until the next day to work out a final agreement, and I agreed.

That night I took a quick look at the military developments. There still was some fighting at Casablanca, but elsewhere it was generally quiet. General Anderson's army, starting the drive eastward to meet the Germans in Tunisia, had occupied Bône, Bougie, and Philippeville, and more troops, including the 39th U.S. Regiment, were ordered up to join him. The Germans had moved some tanks into Tunisia and had two hundred airplanes on the Tunisian airdromes. The battle in Egypt was still going well, with Alexander's force pushing steadily westward. There also was a message from Ike, saying he would visit Algiers the next day, Friday the thirteenth. It would be some relief to me to have him on hand and to get some appraisal of how our actions were being taken in London and Washington.

The day started off pleasantly. The Algerian newspapers had a front-page story saying I had been made a lieutenant general. No official confirmation had reached me, however. Otherwise, the day didn't promise much. In my brief acquaintance with the French officials, I had decided—quite mistakenly, I discovered later—that Juin was a weakling and that Noguès was less desirable as a comrade than even Darlan. I didn't like any of them that morning and I certainly wasn't prepared to accept any further delay in settling their differences. The situation was becoming critical, and the measure of my anger at some of the men with whom we had to deal was indicated by the occasional appearances in my message to Ike of the word YBSAS. This was a private code word that we had invented sometime earlier for use only between ourselves because it often saved a paragraph or two of description when we wanted to explain "what kind of person we were dealing with. Decoded it meant Yellow Bellied So and So.

Reports came in soon after breakfast that Vichy, apparently desperate at seeing the North African situation getting away from them, had sent Admiral Platon to Tunis to give personal instructions to Admiral Esteva to cooperate with the Germans and resist the Allies. The situation seemed further mixed up by the fact that General Emile Béthouart had been jailed in Morocco for helping us.

In Algiers, at the telephone exchange, an obviously hostile group of French Senegalese had suddenly moved in opposite our American guard. Similar moves were being made all around the city. I directed General Ryder to do what he could to smooth out individual situations. All American troops in the Algiers area were alerted for possible fighting in case the negotiations with Darlan and his people failed completely.

When I finally reached the conference room, Darlan, Giraud, Juin, and Noguès were as far apart as ever, each sulking around the table and feeling thoroughly irreconciled to the others. I minced no words in telling them that they would have to agree or I would put them in immediate custody and establish a military government.

I had to leave the meeting long enough to go to the Maison Blanche Airport to meet General Eisenhower and Admiral Cunningham, who flew in together from Gibraltar in a B-17. On the jeep ride to Algiers, I told the Commander in Chief briefly what had been going on. We decided that I would continue my talks with the Frenchmen and that General Eisenhower would assume a rather distant position, being called into the conference only after agreement had been reached.

I was lunching with Ike and Admiral Cunningham when word was brought that the French officials were ready to report agreement.

In outline the agreement was that Darlan would head the civil and political government of all French North Africa; the present governors, Noguès of French Morocco, and Chatel of Algeria, would remain at their posts. Giraud would head the French armed forces, organizing a reinforced army to fight at our side. Giraud was to be allowed to recruit freely volunteers from the Regular French Army, but, for the time being, Giraud's appointment would be kept quiet for political amity.

I thanked them for subordinating their personal differences in this agreement and brought General Eisenhower into the room. The Commander in Chief shook hands all around, apologized for the briefness of his visit, and endorsed all that we had done.

Ike and I then left for the airport, for he had to fly back to Gibraltar at once. We left the French officials at the hotel to work out details of cooperative action with our liaison people. Reporters and news photographers were awaiting at the airfield, but there wasn't time for Ike to tell them anything. He did, however, make one of the friendly and thoughtful gestures that are so typical of him. When the reporters and cameramen were crowding around, he said he had time for just one thing. Then he fished a star out of his pocket and pinned it on my shoulder.

"I've been waiting for a long time to pin on this third star, Wayne," he said. "I hope I pin on the fourth."

As soon as I returned to the St. George, I held a press conference and announced that we thought we had French North African politics at least temporarily ironed out. I was feeling more hopeful about the French fleet, with Darlan still putting pressure on the admiral at Toulon to come to Africa. I explained that we had to bring Giraud slowly into the foreground in order to avoid any further antagonisms.

Now I was able to turn my attention completely to the military situation, which was both complicated and hopeful. The immediate job was to integrate all available French units into our joint action and to prepare the way for equipping, training, and integrating additional units as quickly as possible.

"The past four days have been difficult," I told the reporters, "because we have had to disperse our troops to give an appearance of strength. We have had to keep looking back over our shoulder instead of to the front in Tunisia. Now we can proceed in a business-like way.

"General Anderson already is moving troops eastward at Bougie and Bône. There has been heavy Axis air bombardment, but the British fighter pilots are doing a wonderful job and the enemy has had heavy air losses. British and American paratroopers are being dropped in the east and their operations are successful. Things look good."

When the reporters had gone, the owner of the hotel brought in some champagne. I invited a few people in and we had a small party. By 8 p.m. I was in bed and sound asleep.

As it turned out, we had passed the crisis in our political turmoil in North Africa, although not by any means in Washington and London where the clamor against dealing with Darlan was building up a big head of steam. Fortunately, at the time I didn't know how big or how dangerous it was. I still had hopes that we might do something about the French fleet and I worked hard on that angle in the next few days. I remember that on November 15 I went to the Holy Trinity Church of Algiers (Church of England) with Captain Wright, Colonel Holmes, Major Meacham, Major Billingslea, Captain Boys, and Lieutenant Beardwood. Holmes and I, unarmed, sat up in front, but the rest of the party all carried concealed pieces. When prayer time came, I just kept repeating one phrase: "Oh, God, let me get the fleet from Darlan; let me get the fleet from Darlan."

Later, when the collection plate was passed, I remembered that I had in my pocket some French bills of large denomination which had been seized when our troops raided the German consulate and found the safe stuffed with huge bundles of francs. I pulled a ten-thousand franc note from my pocket and dropped it in the collection plate, murmuring, "compliments of the German consul." I'll never forget the expression on the face of the old fellow who was passing the plate. He almost fainted.

In order to keep Darlan's spirits bucked up, I showed him a copy of a telegram to General Eisenhower in which I praised his efforts. I warned him that he was not out of the woods as far as British and American public opinion was concerned, but promised him his position would be materially improved if he could deliver the fleet. I assured him we would supply air cover and even a naval task force to help protect the fleet if it moved out of Toulon. Entirely on my own hook, I held out the bait of a trip to the United States for his son, who was suffering from infantile paralysis, saying arrangements could be made to have the boy treated at the Georgia Warm Springs Foundation. The best the admiral could do was assure me that he would continue to try to get the fleet and to promise again that under no circumstances would his ships be turned over to the Germans. He said that any movement on the part of the Nazis actually to seize the ships would be countered by a scuttling action. "I pledge my head that the swastika will never fly over a single French ship!" the admiral reiterated.

General Carl "Tooey" Spaatz flew in from Gibraltar on November 18 with a secret message from General Eisenhower confirming that he and I were seriously on the spot, particularly in England, over our relationship with Darlan. He warned me that the case was becoming the subject of a vast amount of newspaper comment and closed with "I am desperately anxious to come down there, but until this pressure from the rear stops I don't see how I can do it. Again I say that I approve of everything you have done.

"I am sticking firmly by what we have done as the only possible solution in the circumstances," Ike wrote, "but I quite agree that we must do nothing to embarrass our governments in the future from a political angle. Therefore, we must (a) have no needless publicity about any dealing with Darlan, and (b) we must deal firmly with Darlan to get those obvious advantages that will convince the politicians of the wisdom of our action. . . . Please keep me informed of anything that I can use as ammunition in keeping the bosses at home from upsetting the applecart. . . . The case is apparently becoming one of a great deal of newspaper comment and of incessant correspondence between the Prime Minister and the President."

I was nothing less than amazed that our use of a man who had collaborated with the Nazis had resulted in such tremendous political pressure, in view of the results that we had already obtained. I cabled Ike that "if we had this to do over again, we would be forced to deal with Darlan as a military expedient in order to be free to move our troops to the east unhindered by strife and disturbances in our rear area." A short time later I received a cable from Washington to withhold all publicity on the Darlan case. Naturally, I tried thereafter to avoid publicity and promptly got myself accused of exercising political censorship. I was immensely grateful for Ike's presence in Gibraltar, where he absorbed all the heat and left me to do the job with the feeling that I would be backed to the hilt no matter whose feelings might be hurt. In hindsight, the fact that we won takes away a lot of onus, whatever one might wish to say about the ethics of doing business with people of Darlan's stamp. At the time there was only one objective, winning the war; we had little time to think of ethics.

From that time on, I had a lot of cooperation from Admiral Darlan. Once having committed himself, it was, of course, to his advantage to give us all the help he could. After all, he would have been in the soup along with the Allies had we eventually failed.

While continuing pressure on the French fleet on one hand, we turned Darlan's attention to French West Africa, where we wanted not only to get control of the vital port of Dakar on the peak of the South Atlantic bulge, but also to get what French naval units were there, particularly the uncompleted but entirely modern battleship *Richelieu*. Darlan, in fairly short order, put over an agreement with General Boisson of French West Africa which put Dakar in our pockets, including such choice additional plums as several cruisers, destroyers, and submarines and 75,000 trained troops including six air groups.

On November 20, General Eisenhower was able to say in a cable to Washington that "the French are now making a real contribution. We would have been badly handicapped without the assistance rendered us now by French military, naval, and civilian groups."

All went quite smoothly with the "Little Fellow," as I had taken to referring to Admiral Darlan, until President Roosevelt, in order to quiet the uproar at home, issued a statement that Darlan's position was only a temporary expedient. This brought a letter to me from Admiral Darlan that ran as follows:

November 23, 1942

My dear General:

Information coming from various ports tend to give credit to the opinion that "I am but a lemon which the Americans will drop after it is crushed."

In the line of conduct I have taken, out of pure French patriotic sense, in spite of the heavy inconveniences that are to result for me from it, though it would have been extremely easy for me to let events develop without my intervention, I, as a person, do not count.

I did what I did only because the American government took the solemn engagement to restore French sovereignty in its integrity as it existed in 1939, and because the armistice between Axis powers and France was broken by the occupation of the whole of French Metropolitan territory, against which Marshal Pétain has solemnly protested.

I have acted neither through pride, nor ambition, nor intrigue, but because the place I held in my country made it my duty to act.

When French sovereignty in its integrity is an accomplished fact—and I hope it will be in the least possible time—I firmly intend to go back to civilian life and to retire to end a life during which I have eagerly served my country. If this is the way I can interpret the declaration attributed to President Roosevelt, according to which an agreement with me can be but a temporary one, I completely agree. But I have the perhaps excessive pretension of thinking that under present circumstances it is around an association with such men as General Giraud, General Noguès, Governor-General Boisson, Admiral Michelier, that Africans can unite for a loyal and confident cooperation with the armies, allies of French forces and the people, a union which forms an essential part of the United States' success in Africa.

Things being thus, the work of reuniting all Frenchmen, which I am undertaking for a common aim, would be very difficult for me if France's allies were themselves to spread doubts among Frenchmen concerning the interest and scope of that work.

I hope I can trust the United States government to realize that, and, were it only in view of the results to be expected in the struggle into which French Africa is entering, that it will not give Frenchmen the impression that the authority of the Chief who makes it struggle again is a diminished one.

With kind regards, I am, very sincerely yours,

(signed) F. DARLAN

I showed this letter to General Eisenhower, and when he next came to Algiers, he said to Darlan, "Because of your former position in the Vichy government, you are, naturally, unpopular in the United States. Nevertheless, I have asked our government to let us alone. If you had an enlightened liberal government in action, the antipathy toward you would change." Darlan was more definitely than ever working for us.

More and more French leaders were piling on board the French-American bandwagon as it became apparent that we were in North Africa to stay. German agents in our own territory whom we closely watched reported to Hitler that all of French North and West Africa was solidly arrayed against the Axis. General Eisenhower moved his headquarters to Algiers from Gibraltar on November 23.

More and more I was able to get away from the demand of political negotiations and concentrate on purely military activities. We worked out what was called the "Clark-Darlan agreement," a protocol between the French and the Allied forces, which was approved of in advance by our two governments. Our relationship with Darlan was stabilized and went along smoothly until the events of the days just before Christmas of 1942 suddenly rocketed Darlan's name back into the headlines.

On December 23 I had a long conference with General Giraud, discussing the Tunisian operation and the technical details of French cooperation and French command. General Giraud was to meet General Eisenhower in a forward area two days later. Admiral Darlan gave a formal luncheon that day for American, British, and French officials. Relationships in general had grown fairly cordial and I had had a number of very confidential and personal talks with the Little Fellow. At the luncheon, Admiral Darlan turned to me and said, "Tomorrow the Axis press will say I gave this luncheon because a gun was pointed at my head."

"If the rest of the luncheons were as good as this," I replied, "I would get my gun out every week." Darlan chuckled.

A few minutes later, while I was talking to Mme. Darlan about the possibility of taking their stricken son to Warm Springs for treatment, I said (with the ulterior hope of getting a reaction from Darlan on his removal from the North African political scene), "I think it could be arranged for Admiral Darlan to go, too, if he chooses."

I watched Darlan narrowly for a reaction. He nodded and said, "I would like to turn this thing over to General Giraud; he likes it here and I don't."

On Christmas Eve I alone of the American command had remained in Algiers. General Eisenhower was at the front in Tunisia. I had fallen in with the plan of several old friends to cut work short for a change and leave the office about six o'clock for dinner. It was late in the afternoon when Bob Murphy came rushing in.

"They've shot the Little Fellow," were his first words.

"You mean Darlan?" I asked. "Where is he?"

"He's on the way to the hospital," said Murphy.

"Let's go," I said, heading immediately for a car. Bob Murphy had no details at the time. All he knew was that the admiral had been shot.

At the hospital there was a tense and excited group of Frenchmen, volubly accusing each other, the Axis, and the Allies of all sorts of provocations. There were plenty of hostile questions and suspicious glances directed at Bob Murphy and me as we pushed our way through to the operating room. Darlan was already dead, shot through the face and chest. The Little Fellow looked calm and quiet; I couldn't help thinking that maybe this was a relief to him after the terrible "hot seat" he had been occupying for the last month and a half.

My next thought was to get in touch with Ike and with General Giraud, who were together or about to meet somewhere in Tunisia. I found that Giraud had been called back by his own people before my message got to

General Eisenhower. He was at the St. George almost as soon as I returned there. Before he arrived, I heard from our intelligence people some of the details of the assassination.

Darlan had been on his way into the Summer Palace following a late luncheon when a twenty-two-year-old university student yelled some unintelligible phrase while firing four shots point blank at the admiral. One of Darlan's aides grappled with the assassin and succeeded in holding him; not, however, before he himself had received two leg wounds.

I didn't know what this might mean politically. I issued immediate orders alerting all our troops.

Two big problems loomed immediately: first, whom to put in charge of the French, and second, how to handle the announcement so that the Axis might make the least profit and French politics be disturbed as little as possible.

The French officers on hand at the St. George were clamoring for me to send for General Noguès. What I wanted was Giraud, and I wanted him fast. I warned everyone concerned that for the present General Noguès was not even to be informed of Darlan's death. In General Eisenhower's absence, I cabled General Marshall: "Darlan dead, we have imposed rigid censorship, request all possible restrictions to prevent leak from London or Washington; all alerted here and in task forces but no immediate trouble expected."

The reason for this was that I felt it urgent that we have an acceptable substitute commander to offer the world in general, and the French in particular, before the news of Darlan's death became generally known. I told Giraud that General Eisenhower felt it necessary for him to take over immediately as High Commissioner for French Africa, a title we had given Darlan. Giraud still wanted a military command, but quickly came around to our point of view and said he would go along with the plan.

I never personally saw Darlan's assassin, nor do I to this day know much about his background or the motivation of his deed. The best information our people could give me indicated that the attack had no complex background, but was merely the act of an unbalanced de Gaullist. The French gave the youth, Bonnier de la Chappelle, a quick trial on Christmas Day and executed him early the following morning. Naturally, the Axis tried to make all capital of Darlan's death; because we knew that there were Axis agents around, it became unwise to try to hold the news much longer. We didn't want Berlin or Rome to sound off first. I therefore ordered a formal announcement of the incident to be made by the French over Radio Algiers and Radio Morocco on Christmas Eve. We framed the announcements to give the affair an Axis tinge. We had received an urgent cable from London saying, "Prime Minister hopes that blame will be placed on Germans and their agents." Therefore, the announcement ended, "The examination of the murderer is now taking place. It is not yet known from preliminary investigation of the assassin whether the assassination was of German or Italian inspiration."

General Eisenhower, General Giraud, and I, as well as French officers of all political convictions, attended the Darlan funeral. There were elaborate precautions against incidents, but apparently neither Axis agents nor anti-Allied-elements of the population of French North Africa were able to stir up enough popular support for any overthrow of our cooperative setup with the French under General Giraud.

Admiral Darlan's death was, to me, an act of Providence. It is too bad that he went that way, but, strategically speaking, his removal from the scene was like the lancing of a troublesome boil. He had served his purpose, and his death solved what could have been the very difficult problem of what to do with him in the future.

Darlan was a political investment forced upon us by circumstances, but we made a sensational profit in lives and time through using him.

I do not think history will discount that usefulness, although I suppose there were those in London and Washington who were never reconciled to the fact that we dealt with a man who had collaborated with the Nazis. Part of this bitter feeling against our course was political, I believe, and part of it was due to failure to understand the circumstances. In concluding the Darlan chapter, I should mention that sometime later during the January Casablanca Conference I discussed the case with President Roosevelt and was surprised at the number of times he said, in reference to some phase of the negotiations, "I didn't know that" or "I had never understood that."

The President said, for instance, that he never knew that Darlan had been placed in protective custody at one time and his house surrounded by a guard, and he indicated that he had been led to believe that the French collaborator had been dealt with timidly.

Because the entire political phase of the invasion of North Africa became the subject of so much controversy, I might add here—as the unhappy soldier who had to sit in the middle of it—my own feelings about what happened and what it meant in the conduct of war.

In the first place, General Mast and his associates at grave risk of their own lives rendered a valuable service to the Allied forces. It was of great importance to our military command to be able to check our plans and our preparations with such military figures as Mast in advance of the invasion. It is true that he could not prevent resistance in all of North Africa, but he did greatly minimize the French resistance in Algeria and contributed immensely to our success by assisting our forces in many small but important ways during and after the landings. I consider him a great French patriot: one who could see that he was contributing to the defeat of the enemy and the liberation of France, and who was willing to risk everything for that end.

As for Giraud, I believe that he was then a symbol of French resistance, and an important one. We thought that he would have more influence at the time of the invasion than he had, but he later became an inspiration to French troops because of his burning, never-slackening desire to fight the enemy anywhere and at any time. History may judge that we picked the wrong man politically, but I shall always feel that he was a military asset of utmost importance, a symbol of the offensive spirit that was so desperately needed then among the French.

Darlan's role was the result of circumstances that are peculiarly French, as I have tried to bring out in the complicated maneuvering of the French officials. It is a situation that Americans cannot easily understand, but in effect it was true that in this confused period Darlan was the one man whose authority was recognized by *all* the French armed forces in North Africa. Military expediency dictated that we do business with Darlan to minimize bloodshed and get on with the war against the Germans who were pouring into Tunisia. Once he was committed to our service, he never deviated. He did the job. If I had it to do over again, I would choose again to deal with the man who could do the job—whether it turned out to be Darlan or the Devil himself.

7.

The Drive for Tunisia:

December 1942–January 1943

The campaign in North Africa was probably the most important time of testing for the Allied war effort, but in another way it was the dreariest chapter in the history of Allied collaboration. In Algiers, we were mired hip-deep in politics involving many unpredictable French factions, and on the fighting front we were sunk up to our knees in mud throughout a great part of that confused winter of 1942–43.

I often felt during the first two months in Algiers that I would never get back to soldiering. Occasionally, when I was completely fed up with the political wrangling and with the bombardment of criticism from home, I would go out in the hills and walk hard until I had reduced the head of steam under which I seemed to be working most of the time. Then I'd take a look at the military developments and sometimes I'd have to go for another walk to cool off.

There was—always—the problem of coordinating British and American operations in an effort to speed up the Tunisian campaign. As I mentioned earlier, there had been all along a fundamental difference between the American method of putting direct responsibility on a commander to plan and execute an operation, subject to higher direction and approval, and the British conference method of threshing out problems in roundtable talk fests, a custom which, incidentally, has become popular since the war in our own military establishment at the sacrifice of speed and efficiency. In the African campaign, not only did we have to add the task of integrating the French forces with our Army, but we had to deal with the day-to-day problem of the distribution of men and equipment under commanders of three different nationalities.

General Anderson, commanding the Tunisian push, had only one British division initially, but he had nevertheless set up an Army Headquarters in Africa, which meant that all of the forces operating in the offensive would normally come under his command because there was no American Army Headquarters. As soon as I could, after American strength justified it, I raised objections to the Anderson setup, recommending that American forces should be withdrawn from his command and organized in a separate sector of the front under their own commander. Not only did I feel that American-trained commanders knew better how to get the best out of our men and their equipment, but I felt that Anderson was using them piecemeal, interspersed with British forces, and that they were suffering as a result.

General Eisenhower, of course, had a tremendously difficult job in coordinating the Allied commands and keeping them working as a team. It often seemed to me that he leaned over backward to avoid showing any partiality toward the Americans in his desire to be objective and promote harmony. But Allied success, he knew, depended on eliminating friction between the different parts of the team. He, too, wanted to get U.S. formations under one command, but was willing to defer this action in order to capture Tunis before the bad weather set in. He was willing to gamble on the piecemeal employment of American troops under British command, if, in that way, time would be saved and all of Tunisia could be occupied.

Still another difficulty in this connection was the reluctance of the French to serve under British command. Giraud brought up this problem on several occasions and eventually suggested that it would work out better if an American sector were formed and the French became a part of it.

These were all major problems, but the biggest headache of the campaign from my viewpoint was in tactical concept. We had been unquestionably timid (although far less than Washington) in the scope of our original invasion of Africa. Had we struck out boldly and landed forces far to the east, even in Tunisia, as British Admiral Lyster had urged when I saw him in London, we would almost certainly have been successful and would have been spared much of the long, awkward overland transportation problem that now confronted us.

Briefly, the situation was this: We had established ourselves in North Africa and advanced early in December as far eastward as Tunisia. Anderson's main force had pushed to within twenty or twenty-five miles of Bizerte and Tunis, the two big towns into which the Axis was pouring reinforcements. Then the torrential rains and deep mud, plus enemy resistance, caused our advance to grind to a halt. To the south, Colonel Raff's paratroopers had joined up with local French forces and were active in the Pichon-Feriana area where the weather was better. In general, however, we were short of our goal in the race to seize Tunisia.

Meanwhile, Alexander and Montgomery had been advancing from Egypt and through Libya toward Tunisia as Rommel's Afrika Korps retreated. The British advance was sensationally rapid, arousing great enthusiasm in Allied capitals. There had been no more spectacular figure in the war up to that time than Rommel, and his downfall coincident with our North African invasion was the shot in the arm that the Allied nations needed. The British victory in Egypt unquestionably had prevented a disaster in the Middle East and had turned near-defeat into a brilliant success. Without detracting from that success, I want to point out that following the shattering British victory at El Alamein in Egypt, the Germans, faced with long and difficult lines of communication, were making a rapid strategic withdrawal to Tunisia to join up with the German forces already moved into Tunisia and with additional troops en route there.

As a result of this situation, the town of Sfax on the Tunisian coast became a key point. If we could take Sfax and hold it we would not only break the enemy's communication line but we would prevent the Rommel army from joining up with the rapidly increasing German army in the Tunis-Bizerte sector. Continual rains, deep mud and limited lines of supply, however, slowed down our entire advance eastward, particularly on the northern front opposite Bizerte, and we had been forced to go on the defensive in the face of increasingly strong enemy counterattacks. The Germans were thus able to build up their Tunisian forces about as rapidly as we did, and, except for some secondary paratrooper activity, circumstances prevented a major effort to seize the key city of Sfax by pushing forward the southern wing of our front. Consequently we had to slug it out in many weeks of hard fighting before we captured the entire North African coast and eliminated the Axis grip on the Mediterranean route.

The problem was largely a struggle to make the most of a difficult geographical situation in which our air support was far back of the front and often sunk in the mud, and our communications lines were extended until they were in danger of breaking. Let me outline briefly the military history of that dreary December when I still was deeply involved in the Darlan affair.

At the beginning of the month, Ike decided, because of increasing Axis subversive activity in the Spanish Morocco area, to form the U.S. Fifth Army. This Army would prepare for emergency action if our rear areas were threatened by way of Spanish territory, and also prepare for a future invasion of the European Continent

Ike named me commander of the Fifth Army, and planned to have my headquarters somewhere in the vicinity of Oran, but I wanted to see the Tunisian plans of campaign well under way, if possible, before I stepped out as Ike's deputy. On December 3, Anderson came back to Algiers for a conference, at which it was decided to halt our operations until we could build up air support and ground strength for a new offensive starting about December 9. One of our big troubles was that the Germans had fixed air bases close to the front while ours were almost five hundred miles back.

The front line was anchored to the north on the Mediterranean nine miles west of Cape Serrat; running southeast it crossed the Medjerda River nine miles northeast of Medjez-El-Bab, forming a salient in the direction of Tunis and only twenty-five miles away; then it ran due south through the mountains just east of Faid which had been captured by Colonel Raff. From Faid the line ran southwest to Gafsa, which was also held by Colonel Raff on a logical route, it seemed to me, to Sfax.

On December 8, with a jeep escort, I drove through a hard rain to First British Army headquarters at Ain Seynour. The water came down in torrents all day and at night it became so misty that we were forced to stop until I got out and walked ahead, the driver managing to keep the car on the road only by watching the dim blackout headlights reflecting on my leggings. I found Anderson extremely pessimistic. Some tanks and trucks were mired deep in mudholes and could not be moved. The weather had stopped all air activity. The Germans were believed to have some 32,000 troops in Tunisia compared to our 40,000. There seemed to be confirmation of reports we had already heard that friction was developing between American and British forces under Anderson's command. Anderson had sent out orders to withdraw to a new defense line, but I insisted that he cancel them until the next day at least.

Driving up to the front the next morning with Anderson, we discussed possible plans of action, and I became more and more impressed with how important it was to bring up without delay the subject of getting American troops assembled under American command. I expected Anderson to oppose the idea and so I put it off until late in the day, meanwhile doing my best to get everybody in a friendly mood in order to smooth the way for my proposal.

When, after various conferences at the front, I brought up the subject, I took pains to explain diplomatically my belief that "American troops being sent to the Tunisian area in both large and small units should be grouped under American commanders as far as possible to assure their employment in accordance with their training." Much to my surprise, Anderson immediately and happily agreed.

"You tell General Eisenhower," he said, "that hereafter American units coming up will be grouped, as far as the tactical situation will permit, under American commanders."

Having made the point—for the time being at least—with such ease and harmony, I was eager to get back to Headquarters and see that it was put into effect. The weather was as disagreeable as ever, and perhaps for that reason it seemed to me that on the return trip the towns and villages we passed through showed less enthusiasm for the Allied troops than on previous occasions. The trip was tiresome and slow, and about 175 miles from Algiers I couldn't stand it any longer. I told the driver to move over and drove the rest of the way myself, making better time but, I suspect, keeping my driver sitting on the edge of the seat all the way.

I reported to Ike and, calling in Gruenther, Lemnitzer, Rooks, Gale, Spaatz, Doolittle, Craig, and Whitely, began laying plans at once to get American units at the front on an all-American basis with their own supply lines and air support.

General Patton made a four-day trip to the front and then joined in recommending that we form an American sector fighting alongside the British First Army.

We were now trying to open offensive operations on December 20, but elements of our Armored Combat Command B, 1st Armored Division, commanded by Major General Lunsford E. Oliver and at that moment under Anderson's command, had become bogged down in deep mud in the Medjerda River Valley during the night of 10–11 December after the troops tried to withdraw to Medjez-El-Bab. Finding the only hard road out under fire, and being mired in the mud, the local commander of the troops became panicky and ordered approximately two medium tanks, twenty-five light tanks and fifty half tracks abandoned nine miles northeast of Medjez-El-Bab. There was no real reason for this loss. The outfit had been placed in the front line in the first place, and when it tried to withdraw it made the mistake of not making a determined effort to extricate its vehicles and of abandoning them prematurely. This loss, in addition to previous combat losses, weakened the combat command to the point where it no longer was immediately capable of offensive action.

Patton reported that part of our difficulties was due to the tactics being used by the British command. "They seem," he said, "to favor holding low ground, leaving high ground to the enemy. Frequently their positions are in front rather than behind rivers. They conceive of the tank as a defensive weapon and employ it in the front line as an antitank gun. They still believe that one should fight tanks with tanks." (This remark reflected our use of the antitank gun at the time, although eventually we too decided that the best way to fight a tank was with a better tank.) "They do not support the tanks with armored infantry." Patton also said that lines of communication to the front were "not being used to more than ten percent of capacity."

As the date for the December 20 offensive approached, Anderson began bucking the plan to have Americans under American command, despite his earlier agreement. A few days later he reported that he could not get the offensive started on the twentieth—the rain continued to make everything difficult—and the date was postponed. This gave us additional time to work on establishing an American sector.

Just before Christmas and just before the assassination of Darlan, I began planning with Giraud an American-French operation against Sfax to separate the Axis forces on the coast of Tunisia and to cut off the Rommel army, which was now retreating rapidly before the British and seemed certain to enter Tunisia for a final stand unless we acted quickly. Giraud agreed enthusiastically and worked energetically toward this end. Heavy rains had continued to stall Anderson's operation in the north and, although Ike was worried about causing a crisis with the British, we were able on December 27 to send out orders to several American units to leave Anderson's command and proceed southward. These included Combat Command B, General Oliver's mechanized force that had had so many difficulties and seen a great deal of action. I proposed to put Major General Orlando (Pinky) Ward, commander of the 1st Armored Division, in command of American troops in the southern sector and eventually to bring up II Corps.

Both Giraud and I were in a hurry to get the operation started before it was too late to cut off the Afrika Korps, and Giraud was interested in avoiding British command over French troops. When Anderson conferred with us on December 28, I purposely set up a situation that would lead the conversation around to this question.

"I must take cognizance," Giraud said to Anderson, "of the frame of mind of my troops and some of my officers. You must remember that not long ago the French fought the British in Syria. Many of my men have not forgotten what the British did to the French Navy at Mers-El-Kebir and Dakar. It is not desirable to put French troops under British command at this time. I do not share this sentiment but you must recognize that it exists. Some solution, such as an American command, must be found."

Anderson replied that it was the first time he had been told of this feeling, but that he realized there was "some slight drawback to our relations" although he had not known why. "I feel it is deplorable," he added, "now that we are allies."

Although I had been doubtful that it would work out that way, the command of the southern Tunisian front was given to me the next day with instructions that I would command all troops, American and French, south of a line running generally east and west through Sousse, on the Tunisian coast. This put my command right in the rear of Rommel's Afrika Korps and right where I wanted to be in order to deliver a healthy kick to that rear. It was a fine idea, but it didn't last long. On the afternoon of December 31, a cable from Marshall concurred in my appointment to the field command and then knocked it all over by suggesting that either General Patton or General Fredendall should command the southern sector as my subordinate, leaving me free to concentrate on organizing the Fifth Army and planning a possible operation against Spanish Morocco if such action became necessary.

I had to agree that the Washington decision was correct, but I regretted that I again was missing the battle command that I wanted so desperately. I consoled myself with the thought that the organization of the Fifth Army would be a job of vital importance if anything developed in regard to Spain and, in any event, would be the training ground for forces that would play the major role in later operations.

The important thing was that we had successfully put through the idea of having American troops under American command on a separate sector of the front. I completed the directive for the southern Tunisia offensive against Sfax on New Year's Day and delivered it to Fredendall, who was in command. The weather was satisfactory in the Tebessa-Feriana region in the south and it was decided to open the drive on Sfax and Gabès by January 20, or earlier, with the 1st Armored Division under Ward as the backbone of the assault. I felt pretty good about the way things were stacking up at the time and believed there was a fine opportunity to cut off the Afrika Korps. But, of course, we never did deliver that projected kick to Rommel's rear. Events just interfered. The Germans began their unrelenting counterattacks, which slowed down the shifting of U.S. units to the new American sector. Ike also insisted that his south flank be firmly protected before undertaking the attack on Sfax, and there simply were not enough troops to do both jobs. Thus we missed the opportunity we sought. In any event, the Germans were the ones who got to Sfax and Gabès and from then on it was a long, hard pull to clear the enemy's consolidated armies out of Tunisia. Not until early May was the stubborn German resistance ended.

President Roosevelt awarding the Distinguished Service Cross to General Mark W. Clark.

U.S. Army Photo

Going ashore in Algiers.

The rendezvous near Algiers where General Clark conferred secretly with
the Free French prior to the Allied invasion of North Africa.

left
"We climbed quickly up a steep and stony path over the bluff to the house . . ."

below
"Our party hid in an empty . . . wine cellar while an argument ensued with the police . . . "

General Clark and Admiral Jean François Darlan concluding the protocol governing French-American relations in French North Africa, November 1942.—*"If I had to do over again, I would choose again to deal with the man who could do the job . . . "*

General Clark and the Sultan of Morocco *(center)* at a *diffa* given by the Pasha of Oujda.—
"We exchanged the usual compliments in the most diplomatic language . . . "

General Marshall, General Clark, and General Patton at Mostaganem shortly before the landing at Salerno.

General Clark and Prime Minister Winston Churchill at a Guard of Honor during one of Churchill's visits to Italy.

General Alphonse Juin, commander of the French Expeditionary Corps, and General Clark at Fifth Army Headquarters.—*"There never was a finer soldier . . ."*

General Eisenhower and General Clark during a tour of the Mignano front in October 1943.—
*"At that time we hoped we would soon hold the mountain ridges overlooking the Liri Valley and
be well along the road to Rome . . . "*

Five Generals conferring at a forward outpost looking toward Venafro, November 1943. *Left to right:* Maj. Gen. Lucian K. Truscott, C. G. 3rd Division; General Sir Harold Alexander, C. G. 15th Army Group; General Mark W. Clark, C. G. Fifth Army; Brig. Gen. Lyman L. Lemnitzer, Operations 15th Army Group; and Maj. Gen. J. P. Lucas, C. G. VI Corps.

Brazilian generals visiting General Clark's Fifth Army Headquarters at Florence. *Left to right:* Brig. Gen. Euclideo Zenobio Da Costa; Maj. Gen. Joao Batista Mascarenhas, C. G. of B. E. F.; General Clark; and Maj. Gen. Gaspar Dutra, Brazilian Minister of War.— *"An atmosphere of strong friendship existed . . ."*

An American soldier discovering a relative in Italy.

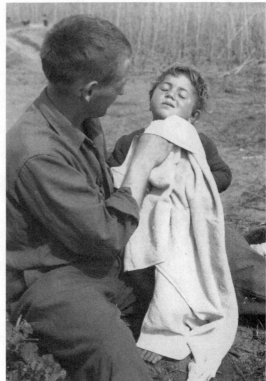

right

An American corporal, using his helmet as a basin, washes the face of a young Italian friend.

below

View from the German lines looking south through the Mignano Gap, showing Route No. 6 *(left)*, Mt. Lungo *(foreground)*, Mt. Rotondo, and Mt. Camino *(right).*—"We had to seize this gap—sometimes known to the soldiers as Death Valley—in order to reach the Liri River Valley."

above

View from the German Gustav Line just above Cassino looking along Route No. 6 past Mt. Trocchio *(foreground)*, down Purple Heart Valley to Mt. Lungo and Mt. Camino. The Rapido River is at the lower right.— *"In that winter of 1944 there was plenty of opportunity to die in the hills around Cassino and in Purple Heart Valley . . ."*

below

Bologna, Italy, April 22, 1945. Gen. Mark Clark, Commander in Chief of the 15th Army Group, riding in a jeep through the streets of the liberated city of Bologna with Gen. Wladyslaw Anders, Commanding General of the Polish II Corps *(saluting and seated behind Gen. Clark)* and Lt. Gen. Lucian Truscott, Jr., Commanding General of Fifth Army.— *"Bologna . . . was sweet revenge for the Poles . . ."*

right

Left to right: General Clark; General Wladyslaw Anders, Commanding General of the Polish Armed Forces; and General Henry Arnold.

below

Troops of the 88th Division moving on the double past open places to give the many snipers in Vicenza a difficult target.—*"Tired, dirty, but gaining momentum as they advanced . . . "*

A soldier of the 88th Division running past still-burning German equipment on the streets of Vicenza, April 1945.— *"It was bitter fighting every step of the way . . . "*

above

The ruined Abbey of Monte Cassino.— *"I say that the bombing of the Abbey was a mistake . . . "*

left

Vehicles of the Fifth Army rolling up the steep passes of the Italian Alps in over three feet of snow, May 1945.— *"Snow in the mountains added to our problems . . . "*

above

The Mt. Serrasiccia tramway, loaded with supplies, starting its trip to a point 1,600 feet up the mountain. Built by the engineers of the 10th Mountain Division in nine hours, it carried up to 350 pounds. Casualties could be evacuated in four minutes, whereas it had previously taken litter bearers six to ten hours.—*"The 10th Mountain Division was ideally suited for the high Apennines . . . "*

upper right

The "snake," a remarkable device used to clear a path through a mine field.

lower right

The battle sled, with infantrymen in position, being pulled by an M-3 tank.—*" . . . ingenious affairs, devised by men who discovered that necessity is the mother of invention . . . "*

The Anzio Express, a 280 mm. rifle mounted on a railroad truck.—*"I'll never forget how much noise it made at the receiving end on the Anzio beachhead . . . "*

A GI of the 34th Division washing and shaving in the snow in front of his dugout.

Gen. Clark driving through a street in Rome, June 5, 1944, the day after the Fifth Army took the city. Driving the jeep is Tech. Sgt. Robert R. Holden; in the rear seat are Maj. Gen. Alfred M. Gruenther, Clark's chief-of-staff *(left),* and Maj. Gen. Harry H. Johnson, Rome area commander. — *"Our little group of jeeps wandered around the streets... and eventually we found ourselves in St. Peter's Square . . . "*

An Indian mule convoy passing engineers of the 85th Division working on a trail ruined by rain and melting snow.— *"It was difficult to imagine the hardships under which our advance was made in mud and rain and snow and biting winds . . . "*

General Henry "Hap" Arnold *(left)* and General George C. Marshall.

IMPORTANT NOTICE

In case you are taken prisoner, you will very likely wish to have your relatives informed with as little delay as possible that you are alive and out of danger.

JERRY'S FRONT RADIO

has arranged to announce the names and addresses of prisoners of war and their serial numbers. The announcements will be made three times daily.

You will understand how *valuable* this service is when you consider that your relatives are spared the dreadful feeling of anxious suspense concerning your fate.

Be prepared and fill in this blank. It will be useful to you if you should be captured.

German propaganda leaflet dropped on Fifth Army troops in Italy.

above

General Clark, as commander of the 15th Army Group, receiving the surrender of German troops in Italy and western Austria from the representative of General von Vietinghoff, German commander in chief, southwest. With General Clark are *(left to right)* Maj. Gen. Benjamin W. Chidlaw, A.C.; General Sir Richard L. McCreery, Eighth Army; and Lt. Gen. Lucian Truscott, Fifth Army.— *"I suddenly realized there was something wrong with this picture . . . "*

below

General Clark receiving the Order of Suvorov from Maj. Gen. Souslaparov, the Soviet representative in Italy.— *"The medal was accompanied by a lifetime pass for travel on all Russian railroads . . . "*

above

The four Allied High Commissioners for Austria. *Left to right:* General Sir Richard L. McCreery (Gt. Br.), Marshal I. S. Konev (U.S.S.R.), General Clark (U.S.), and Lt. Gen. M. E. Béthouart (Fr.).— *"In the beginning we got along fairly well . . . "*

8.

The Fifth Army, the Arabs, and Some VIPs:

January 1943–September 1943

In writing this story, I have made reference to occasions on which I felt that the Allied powers and their armed forces failed to take full advantage of the opportunities, which is just a polite way of saying that, in looking back on the war, it is easy to see that at times we blundered or were stupid. This custom of second-guessing, or "Monday morning quarterbacking," which is an occupational hazard for sports writers and the occasional prerogative of generals, has the advantage of helping to avoid future errors. It also gives us a chance to take a clearer and more reasoned look at the actions of the enemy, and it has always seemed to me that first prize for stupidity in the Mediterranean Theater went to a man named Adolf Hitler.

In the long range of history we see events, and particularly military events, in a perspective very different from the light in which they appear at the time they are in progress. But even now I can recall only with a shudder the anxiety we felt just before and throughout the TORCH operation and much of the Tunisian fighting in regard to our vulnerable line of supply through the Straits of Gibraltar. Concern over an attack on our rear through Spain built up steadily as we progressed eastward from the narrow straits through which the bulk of our supplies must come. Spanish Morocco, on the African side of the straits, was overrun by Axis agents and pro-German officers of the Franco army. We were highly doubtful of the attitude of such powerful figures as General Noguès in French Morocco, and there was always fear that a military reverse for our forces in the Mediterranean area might touch off trouble in French Africa or open the way for a thrust from Spanish territory.

We were rather like a deep-sea diver moving farther and farther from his ship and maintaining only a slim lifeline connection with his air pumps, which might be severed by a single, sudden, and fatal blow. It is true that there were grave obstacles in the way of a German thrust to cut that life line, but throughout the Tunisian campaign it seemed to me and to many others that Hitler was muffing a great opportunity as he permitted himself to become entangled in a situation that prevented him from striking at our rear, where success would virtually have wrecked our entire Mediterranean operation. It was such a logical move from the Nazi viewpoint that I can only presume it was not undertaken because the Germans were in grave trouble in Russia. And, as we progressed in Tunisia, it became obvious that the Spaniards had decided they would fight any invader, including the Germans. It was a long time, however, before I could feel that the danger had been dissipated, because after the Fifth Army was formed the job of protecting our rear lines became my responsibility, among other things.

As I think back on it, it seems that there were quite a few "other things" and that I had a hard time getting down to work at my new headquarters at Oujda (French Morocco). On several occasions I was about to branch off on some other mission, such as the Tunisian southern front, and once I was tapped to return to London and act as a sort of official handholder for Churchill.

The Prime Minister was always up to something, always wanting to get on with the job. This was usually a great thing for us, but in the midst of the African tangle we had a terrific time trying to keep up with his demands for information. Marshall was worried and felt that somebody ought to be in London to keep a sort of checkrein on the Prime Minister. He nominated me for the job, saying I could be a politico-military liaison with Churchill and still command the Fifth Army. I knew it would be nothing but grief and I talked fast enough to persuade Ike to get me out of it. Ike convinced Marshall that Bedell Smith, as his new chief of staff, could do the job by making regular trips to London.

When it was decided that the Fifth Army would be formed, I had flown to Oran with Doolittle, Gruenther, Zanuck, Slocum, and others to meet British Lieutenant General Sir Frederick Morgan and go over plans for possible emergency action against Spanish Morocco. The 1st Battalion of the 19th Engineers was already at key points on the railroad and highway in the Fez region, and part of the 30th Infantry was occupying vital airfields adjacent to Spanish territory.

Upon arrival at Oran, I found Morgan had been delayed, so I went out to Oujda. There we inspected a girl's school at the edge of town, which was to be used as Fifth Army Headquarters. I remember that one of my officers, after a quick look around, said he voted in favor of using the school buildings if one of the instructors, who was an unusually attractive girl, remained as interpreter. It turned out that she did. Her name was Miss Raymonde Isoré and she worked for us as long as we were there and then married Major Robert Jaccard, who later became my aide. She was teaching English in the school as a cover for the job of being a Free French agent.

Later that afternoon, I flew back to Oran and met General Morgan, who was accompanied by Brigadier General Robert C. Candee of the U.S. Air Corps. The British had a plan, called BACKBONE, for counteraction if the Germans moved through Spain to close the Straits of Gibraltar, or if the Spaniards acted to close the straits in support of the Axis. It was a slow and cumbersome movement from England, however, and could not become effective for probably two months after trouble started. They wanted to abandon BACKBONE now in favor of an American operation from North Africa which could move quickly against Spanish Morocco if necessary.

Morgan and I, however, felt that both plans should be in effect. He had originally planned to land one division in the Tetuan area and another at Tangier (although it was doubtful whether the Tetuan force could reach its goal if the straits were closed), but both of us agreed that the main effort should be overland from French Morocco. We finally decided that, in the event of trouble, the U.S. 1st Division from Oran would move overland toward Melilla while the Western Task Force near Casablanca, under General Patton, would start moving up from the southwest toward Tangier. Our air bases for such an operation were already established and we believed that the overland attack would draw Spanish troops southward and facilitate General Morgan's landings on the coast from England. Doolittle reported that about four hundred aircraft were available for such an operation. The French appeared to be eager for a chance to take a whack at Spanish Morocco, but in view of the circumstances we decided not to incorporate them in our plans at that time.

"The best news I've had is that you are organizing the Fifth American Army and that the center of gravity of the Spanish Moroccan affair has shifted from the United Kingdom to your army," Morgan told me.

Our conference with Morgan was in mid-December, but because of the Tunisian developments I didn't get back to Oujda until after the first of the year, except for a brief trip to confer with Patton, who flew up from Casablanca. The Fifth Army was activated on January 4, with the Western Task Force under Patton and the Center Task Force under Fredendall. We had the 1st Armored Corps in French Morocco; the II Army Corps in Algeria; and the XII Air Support Command. Our territorial responsibility was initially the area of French Morocco and Algeria west of the north-south line through Orléansville. Our initial mission was to prepare a striking force for amphibious operations, insure the integrity of all territory of French Morocco and Algeria within our area, cooperate with French civil and military authorities, and prepare plans and execute special operations. On the evening of January 5, Ike had a farewell party for me at the villa we had shared in Algiers, and on the sixth I proceeded to Oran and thence to Oujda. I selected as my chief of staff Major General Alfred M. Gruenther; and the War Department had replied favorably to my request for two of my old friends and associates to be sent from the United States. They were Colonels Don Brann and Joseph Pescia Sullivan.

I had been at the Command and General Staff School and War College with Don Brann, liked him, and knew of his great ability and charm. I assigned him as G-3 in charge of operations and training. "Sully" Sullivan was a classmate of mine at West Point, doughboy with me in the 5th Division in France in World War I, and had later transferred to the Quartermaster Corps. He was a real friend, tireless and a successful operator. I knew my Fifth Army men would not lack chow or clothing with him around, so I made him the Army Quartermaster.

Ike let me pick the key members of my staff from officers then on duty at Allied Headquarters. They were a fine bunch and worked into a successful team. Principal appointments were named in Fifth Army orders on January 5, 1943.*

---

* Chief of Staff	Brig. Gen. Alfred M. Gruenther
Secretary General Staff	Maj. Ira W. Porter
Asst. Chief of Staff, G-1	Lt. Col. Francis A. Markoe
Asst. Chief of Staff, G-2	Col. Edwin B. Howard
Asst. Chief of Staff, G-3	Brig. Gen. Arthur S. Nevins
Asst. Chief of Staff, G-4	Col. Clarence L. Adcock
Adjutant General	Col. Cheney L. Bertholf
Air Officer	Col. Guy H. Gale
Artillery Officer	Col. Thomas E. Lewis
Chemical Officer	Col. Maurice E. Barker
Civil Affairs	Col. Charles E. Saltzman
Engineer Officer	Col. Frank O. Bowman
Headquarters Commandant	Lt. Col. C. Coburn Smith, Jr.
Provost Marshal	Col. Charles R. Johnson
Public Relations	Major Kenneth W. Clark
Quartermaster	Col. Joseph P. Sullivan
Signal Officer	Brig. Gen. Richard B. Moran
Surgeon	Brig. Gen. Frederick A. Blesse

Colonel Sullivan rode with me in the lead car on our trip to Oujda, where in a steady, cold rain we followed a twisting road over the mountains. I conferred later at the little house in the corner of the headquarters-school grounds, which I had taken for my living quarters, with Brigadier General Georges Beucler, French commander of the Oujda region,* and others, and then made a tour of the offices and grounds, introducing myself to the newly arrived officers and enlisted men as I went along. It was my idea that we would be called upon to develop the Fifth Army with considerable speed, because I felt that since its formation had been announced there would be a desire to get it into action somewhere within a few months.

"Some of you may wonder why I selected Oujda for our headquarters," I told my officers. "I did it from a map. It is centrally located, with a good air-field, good roads and railroads, and signal communications. There also is another reason that influenced me strongly. There are no politicians here." It turned out that Oujda was a most hospitable town—long afterward it honored our sojourn there by naming a square in my honor and changing the name of the principal street through the Medina (red-light district) to Avenue Cinquième Armée (Avenue of the Fifth Army). But all that came later. When we first arrived we got down to work with considerable speed, but, as usual, there were interruptions. The first one was the arrival of President Roosevelt and Prime Minister Churchill for the Casablanca Conference on the establishment of the French governmental and military leadership in Africa, and the future conduct of the war against the Axis. I had the overall responsibility for the preparations because it was held in the area that had just come under the Fifth Army command. Starting January 10, I spent more than a week checking security plans, housing arrangements, construction of a special air-raid shelter for the President, and building of ramps at key points so that it would be easier for him to enter or leave his airplane and to reach the quarters that had been set aside for him. I told no one at Fifth Army Head-quarters what was going on and I flew alone to and from Casablanca in order to take no chances on word of the impending conference leaking out. This greatly complicated my schedule and I found that I was working sixteen or eighteen hours a day by the time I had taken care of both jobs.

I had returned briefly to Oujda on January 15, but was almost immediately called back to Casablanca by General Marshall because the President wanted to discuss the North African political situation. As I have related earlier, he seemed surprised when I told him of various developments

---

* Beucler later became French liaison officer with Fifth Army Headquarters throughout the Italian campaign.

regarding Darlan, but he expressed satisfaction that I had dealt firmly with the French admiral. He then asked my opinion regarding Giraud, saying that he had heard Giraud was not too strong in Africa and that he was sometimes difficult to deal with.

I said I didn't agree. Giraud, I said, was a kind of symbol for France, when he was dealt with firmly he was cooperative, and I believed he was head and shoulders above other Frenchmen who were seeking power in North Africa. I asked Mr. Roosevelt to talk to Giraud, and later I brought the French general to his quarters. The President didn't like to make use of an interpreter and tried to conduct the conversation in French. This was a dismal failure since Giraud merely became more and more puzzled as the President rattled along in his rusty French. Finally, we had to get an interpreter to try to end the confusion. Mr. Roosevelt told Giraud he was hopeful that he would head the military setup with General de Gaulle as second in command and some third person as political head of French North Africa.

"Maybe we could get someone else out of France or someone who has taken refuge in Switzerland," he said. Then looking up at me with a smile, he asked, "Do you want to make another secret submarine trip, General?" Giraud was delighted with the conversation generally, and it was suggested that I escort him to his conference with Churchill—and that I stick around to see what the British thought in view of their recent efforts to build up de Gaulle. I accompanied him to the Prime Minister's quarters, but that was as far as I got. Churchill's aides took Giraud in tow and politely showed me to the door. Next day, when I told Mr. Roosevelt I was diplomatically kicked out, he grinned and said that was what he had expected.

Mr. Roosevelt wanted to inspect American troops and suggested going as far east as Algiers, but the Secret Service vetoed that as too hazardous, so I arranged for him to tour the Port Lyautey district in a jeep. We talked for a while, and later the President signed my short snorter bill, but said to keep it a secret lest he be "pestered" by persons wanting signatures.

Although detailed and specific orders had been issued about preparations for the Presidential inspection tour, I suppose it is typical that I could not be satisfied until I had personally checked on the arrangements. On January 20, I flew to Port Lyautey and drove over the route. I was glad that I did, because, despite our precautions, there were a lot of loose ends to be buttoned up. Among other things, I realized that we had made no provision for the Negro troops who had participated in our landings to be represented in the review, and I quickly got hold of Patton. He, of course, got the troops there. Georgie was the kind of soldier who could be counted on in both large and small affairs. When I took command of the Fifth Army, it occurred to me that the dashing Patton, who had known me when I was in knee pants and he was a young officer just out of West Point, would be under my command. I had a high regard for him, but I entertained some fears that he might resent being in a subordinate position to me. My fears were completely groundless. He not only accepted the situation pleasantly but went out of his way to be helpful on every possible occasion, and my feeling of admiration and friendship for him increased instead of suffering any strain.

I also was needlessly concerned about how I would get through a long day of close contact with Mr. Roosevelt on the inspection trip on January 21. We set out at 9:20 a.m. with two motorcycles leading the way, followed by a jeep. The Daimler in which the President and I rode was surrounded by a flock of jeeps, most of them carrying Secret Service men. In all there were fifteen cars and an air-cover umbrella as we drove northward.

The President started out asking questions and I don't believe he stopped all day. He transferred to a jeep at Rabat, where Major General E. N. Harmon, commanding the 2nd Armored Division, was introduced and joined us for that part of the trip. The President was driven within a few feet of the front rank of the troops, which were lined up with their vehicles. When the end of the line was reached, General Harmon got out and Major General Jonathan W. Anderson, commander of the 3rd Infantry Division, took his place. And so went on and on, with bands playing, past the 7th Infantry Regiment, the 15th Infantry Regiment, the 3rd Infantry Division Artillery, the 10th Engineer Battalion, the 756th Tank Battalion, the 3rd Medical Battalion, the 3rd Quartermaster Battalion, two platoons of 3rd Reconnaissance troops, and the division artillery band. It was a good day for a review. A stiff wind made the flags and banners stand out smartly and the outfits were polished and alert, so the President had a fine time, seemed pleased with what he saw, and showed his pride for what they had accomplished.

We crossed the Lyautey highway where the President was to have noon mess. We had a table set up in the open, and as he waited there the heroes of the Western Task Force, men who had received citations for bravery in the invasion, came by to shake hands with him. When the meal was over, the President called me to one side.

"I wonder," he said, "if I could have the mess kit I just ate from as a souvenir of this day?"

I said certainly, but I was looking at the table in a slight panic. The mess kits already had been removed. I dashed around to the kitchen and found they not only had been mixed up, but had all been washed. There was only one thing to do.

"Give me a mess kit—any mess kit," I said. "And make it fast."

I returned to Mr. Roosevelt with a mess kit, a canteen cup and service, and presented them to him with our compliments.

He was delighted. "I'll have them put in the Smithsonian Institution," he said with a broad grin.

We continued the review after lunch. I had been worried that Patton would be unable to get the Negro troops there in time, but before long I saw them and, as we approached, I invited the President's attention to them. He gave them special attention, having his jeep pass between their ranks and behind them. Later the 60th Regimental Combat Team of the 9th Division, which played a big role in the invasion, was reviewed and Major General Manton Eddy, its commander, was introduced. They were a good-looking outfit. They passed in review, with bands playing and flags snapping; then the President rode over the battlefield and visited the cemetery where the American and French dead were buried side by side. Mr. Roosevelt asked me and his aide to place large wreaths at both the American and French sections of the cemetery, which is on a high bluff overlooking the Atlantic Ocean.

We completed the tour about dusk, with the President in high spirits. I was feeling pretty good, too, because everything had gone smoothly. We had blocked off the whole area and troops guarded all the roads over which we passed, keeping everybody back at least a hundred yards. This action, of course, aroused curiosity among the Arabs, and we had to make up various excuses in order to avoid disclosing the meeting of the heads of state. Usually our excuse was that a special review was being held in my honor, which might have amused me if I had not been too busy working and worrying that something would go wrong. I was happy to get it over with and return to Oujda.

By the end of January, with Rommel's Afrika Korps backing into Tunisia, the enemy was consolidating his forces there, and the strength of the Fifth Army was lessened in order to move units to the Tunisian front. I noted on January 30 that if that trend continued, we would have only truck drivers, cooks, nurses, my two aides and my German police dog left for emergency action against Spanish Morocco. We worried about it, but there was some compensation in the knowledge that a more harmonious relationship was being built up with the French in Morocco.

In the next few months to help build up good will in that country I traveled many thousands of miles to pay official visits and to supervise our training. For my tours of the training area I secured a little Piper Cub "puddle jumper," which was piloted by Captain Eugene P. Gillespie, a fine lad and an expert who could set the craft down almost anywhere, and usually did. I know one day, when we sighted some soldiers playing baseball, the captain put our puddle jumper down alongside the diamond and the GIs let me get my daily exercise by playing first base for a couple of innings.

I had the plane equipped with a loudspeaker, primarily for the purpose of shouting instructions to the ground when we flew low over troops engaged in training exercises. But sometimes we used the speaker for less serious purposes. When we landed in Africa, each soldier was given a card on which were written words and phrases in French and Arabic for use in his contacts with the natives. I carried the card in my pocket, and one day when we flew low over a little Arab village I got it out and tried out the phrases over the loudspeaker. The people rushed out of their houses and stared in amazement into the sky from which came the booming Arabic words that might well have been their idea of the voice of Allah. On another occasion, when I was returning to Oujda, we flew over my headquarters and I shouted over the loudspeaker for a car to meet me at the airport. There was a fine flurry of activity around our offices, and by the time I got to the airfield there were three cars there to meet me. Three different officers within the range of the loudspeaker, which was considerable, had each decided the order was for him.

Our training program at this time was huge and intensive. There was an Invasion Training Center near Arzew and an Artillery Observation Training Center at Sidi-Bel-Abbès, the home of the famous French Foreign Legion; the 13th Field Artillery Brigade was at work around Chanzy; while at Arzew we organized a two-weeks course of training for amphibious landings that put the men through countless tough experiences and prepared the teams that later made possible our thrusts against the European Continent. The Arzew training was headed up by our amphibious expert, Brigadier General "Mike" O'Daniel. There also were centers for airborne troops, tank destroyers, engineers and battle training.

The North African Theater of Operations, United States Army, was organized the first week in February with General Eisenhower in command. A few days later he was given the supreme command of all Allied troops in Africa in an effort to coordinate the drive of two British armies and the American and French forces into Tunisia. The second British army was the Eighth, which had pushed the Afrika Korps back across Libya and into Tunisia. General Sir Harold R. L. G. Alexander was made Ike's deputy commander in chief.

About a week later, on February 17, the Axis forces in Tunisia, combined with the Afrika Korps, launched an offensive which changed the entire situation at the front. Since I have discussed earlier our efforts to organize a drive against Sfax, which, if successful, would have prevented the enemy from joining up his forces in Tunisia, I will quote here from my diary a résumé of developments on the 17th and 18th:

The Axis drive in the southern sector continues on a large scale and we have lost Sbeitla, Feriana, with its splendid natural airport, and Kasserine. We have lost 100 tanks and the only compensation is that the British Eighth Army is moving forward over the Tunisian-Tripolitanian border, approaching Medinine. Rommel apparently is getting elbow room in southern Tunisia for a probable stand against the Eighth Army in the Gabès Corridor, a 15-mile-wide area flanked by the sea on the east and a tremendous marsh area on the west.

I had predicted that Rommel would attempt to make a juncture with Axis forces in Tunisia as early as last December. It was constantly and habitually assumed by G-2 at Allied Force Headquarters in Algiers that Rommel was incapable of making such a long retreat and an effective fusing of his forces with those in Tunisia. I couldn't understand why Brigadier Mockler-Ferryman [G-2, AFHQ] figured this was impossible, but he said Rommel lacked sufficient transportation and gasoline. Nevertheless, Rommel has joined his forces and the fight now is going to be long and hard.

I waged a long campaign to get American troops out of the northern sector, where they were intermixed with British units, and into the southern sector under a consolidated American command. This finally was done and I proposed that our units be gathered under one command to drive a wedge into the Gabès-Sfax area to prevent just the thing that has happened.

Logistic experts said the road and railroad in the southern region wouldn't support the plan we had in mind. They said all that could be supported was the 1st Armored Division and one regimental combat team, plus service units. I know we can put five times that number of troops in there and support them. I have studied the region and know it can be done.

The force assembled under II Army Corps was to have started a drive on Gabès by January 20. [That was the plan when I left Algiers for Oujda.] Then it was called off. This decision, I understand, was reached by Eisenhower after Alexander urged that the attack be delayed so a drive by the American force and the Eighth Army could be coordinated.*

Eventually, of course, we drove them out, but we had to go through many anxious and difficult days.

In this period of uncertainty, I received a letter from Ike in reply to one that I had written him when he became Commander in Chief of Allied Forces in Africa. It was of special interest to me because he knew our strength was being depleted and that I was getting worried about it and

---

* I later learned the attack on Gabès was called off primarily because of German counterattacks.

becoming restless to get into action and not "sit on a dead fish" in Morocco. He thought this letter would buck me up, in case I began to feel too sorry for myself so far from the scene of fighting in Tunisia.

> There are things I have told you several times verbally [the letter said] and which I now want to put in writing in an effort to make sure that you can never let any doubt enter your mind on this particular score. It is that never for one second have you lost an atom of the great confidence I have always placed in you, nor has there ever been any diminution of the deep feeling of friendship I have held for you for so many years.
>
> You will never know how close I came within the past few days when the pressure on me was very, very drastic indeed to call upon you once more to come and help out when I found it impossible to be in three distinct places at once. There is no one on whom I depend more nor to whom I look with greater confidence to render great services to our cause in this war.
>
> I earnestly hope that you will take this letter literally and without any mental reservations. Nothing would be a greater tragedy to me than to come to believe that the close feeling of partnership with you, that I have so long depended upon, could be weakened in any slightest respect.
>
> As ever,
IKE

I appreciated Ike's letter—coming as it did from one I admired so deeply—and I felt that I knew him well enough to know how he felt. At that time he was again and again being forced to draw on Fifth Army troops for the Tunisian fighting, taking a necessary chance on weakening our precautions against an emergency at Gibraltar. He was right in doing this, but it didn't make me sleep any better at night.

Our relations with the French at this time were improved, but there were many new rear-area problems. The natives had become restless and were resentful of the French. They probably had always been resentful, but it didn't show through plainly until the Americans arrived and not only gave them cigarettes and chocolates (which the French didn't have to give) but mistakenly created a belief in some quarters that the United States might help them get out from under French territorial rule. Some of the native chieftains began flirting with high American officers; the French became nervous and remained nervous as long as we were in North Africa. A typical example of French fears was a letter from the United States consul general at Casablanca, H. Earle Russell, containing a report made to him as follows:

> Rear-Admiral Jacques Marie Missoffe, French liaison officer with our Navy, expressed his fear that the friendly relations of American military authorities

with the Arabs in Morocco were breaking down French influence in the Protectorate and that when the American forces eventually left the country, serious trouble could be expected. Missoffe appreciated our position here as tending to obtain the maximum for the war effort from the Arabs, but believes that as they are a feudal people, unaccustomed to liberty as it is known in the United States, they will not understand the reason for the difference between French control intended to maintain peaceable conditions and the equality now accorded them by the Americans.

American-Arab policy here seems to be one of the moment and its possible effects after American troops have left apparently do not weigh greatly in the scale. Admiral Missoffe said that we are probably unaware of the future troubles we are building up for the French in Morocco.

As a result of their fears, I had constantly to reassure the French about the intentions of the United States, and I had to be careful on my visits to native chieftains not to give them the false impression that the United States was going to help them get rid of the French. Since some chieftains were always looking for encouragement along that line, I was under some strain during these visits, which introduced us to all of the ancient and elaborate customs of the region and required that we take part in magnificent *diffas,* or feasts.

One of these visits, on February 23, was to Rabat and Casablanca, to call on General Noguès and the Sultan of Morocco. General Patton and General Noguès and other officers met me at the Salé airport with the usual American and French military flourishes, and we drove to Noguès' residence in Rabat, picking up a guard of mounted Spahis in bright red, white and blue uniforms that added a brilliant flash of color to our procession of drably painted armored scout cars. A Moroccan drum and bugle corps greeted us at the broad stairs of the main entrance, where we passed between lines of native troops in flowing red uniforms, turbans and bright sashes. They stood stiffly with muskets at present arms.

With Noguès we drove through the city of ancient ruins, timeworn edifices, and strikingly modern buildings to the Sultan's palace where troops were drawn up in splendid array. There was first a guard of native troops leading up to the gateway in the high wall. Inside was a large quadrangle, an open field about half a mile square, with the slave quarters on one side and a private mosque where the Sultan prays each Friday on the other. Nearby was a private school for his children and in the background the palace rose impressively to dominate the scene.

Our way was flanked by mounted Spahis riding Arabian horses that were grouped according to color, ranging from brown to black and dapple gray.

Most colorful of all were the Black Lancers, the Sultan's own guard, which rode the handsomest horses and carried lances decorated with red, white and green streamers. The entire guard were either slaves or descendants of slaves of the Sultan and each wore a silver ring in his right ear.

With the guard stood Si Mammeri, *chef de protocol* to the Sultan, in a long white robe. As we saluted, the guard's band played the national anthems of America, France and Morocco. Or rather they believed they were playing the national anthems. They did fine with the "Marseillaise" and their own anthem, but when it came to the United States, either they had been misinformed or the "Star-Spangled Banner" was too much for them—they played "Yankee Doodle." I saluted stiffly, just the same.

We entered, with Si Mammeri, a palace of Oriental splendor, filled with beautiful carpets, elaborate furniture, and countless servants, splendidly dressed in the manner of *The Arabian Nights*. The throne room was not large, but it was a remarkable example of Moroccan architecture, with lovely columns, Moorish arches and mosaics that were like illustrations from some long-forgotten dream of Aladdin. The Sultan, Sidi Mohamed Ben Moulay Youssef, stood in front of the throne to receive us—a small, half-smiling and almost timid man of about thirty-five. A dozen of us were invited to be seated on gilt chairs at the left of the throne. After the ranking officers were seated, our subordinates stood behind our chairs.

Across the room, facing us, were members of the Sultan's cabinet. The viziers, the counselors and other dignitaries were all on hand and all barefoot, for they are forbidden to wear shoes in the presence of the Sultan. Si Mammeri, standing before the Sultan, acted as interpreter. We exchanged the usual compliments in the most diplomatic language, the Sultan, smiling faintly, clasping and unclasping his hands slowly. He spoke of his high esteem for the Americans and the French and his confidence that the three peoples would be firmly bound together in the future. In fact, he became so enthusiastic about the Americans that, I learned later, old Si Mammeri was careful not to translate in front of Noguès all that he said. At the end of the ceremony, he stepped down from the throne and motioned for a decoration—the Grand Croix Ouissam Alaouite—that he had decided to confer on me. As I stepped before him, I realized that the Sultan was going to have to make quite a stretch to get the sash over my head. I leaned forward as far as I could without falling on my face, and he made it with dignity, everything considered. I was informed that I had become a member of the Sultan's highest order before whose members "lions quake and foxes crawl into their holes."

We shook hands with the Sultan and backed from the room, stopping as we reached the door, standing at attention and then bowing stiffly. As we left the palace we could hear the Sultan's own guard band playing "The Yanks Are Coming." They did it up fine.

After luncheon at Noguès' residence we toured the old city, which dates back to the eleventh century, and I returned to Casablanca. The following day I toured the Atlantic Base Section and inspected the French battleship *Jean Bart,* which was commanded by Admiral Ronarch and took part in the fighting against our forces when Casablanca was invaded. The ship was struck by six shells and three or four bombs in the engagement.

"Did you fire back during the battle?" I asked Admiral Ronarch.

"Yes," he replied, "with everything I had."

I wasn't sure just what I should say next, but finally I asked, "Did you hit anything?"

The admiral shook his head. "Nothing."

"That is too bad," I said. "You have my sympathy."

He smiled wistfully and expressed his thanks. Everything was friendly enough, but it wasn't the kind of conversation that runs along easily.

When we landed at Marrakech Airport in the afternoon, there was a large reception awaiting us. The celebration was somewhat the same as at Rabat, but one difference attracted my attention. At various places along the crowded streets were numbers of large "dolls." These were merely fine dresses, brilliant shawls and other articles of women's apparel suspended on bamboo poles and roughly shaped to resemble a human figure. Some of them had faces painted on cloth and all of them were held high in the air by slaves of the wealthy Arab families. In this way the rich Arabs had their wives, who are never permitted to appear in public, represented at the celebration. The richer the clothing, the more powerful and influential the Arab husband was supposed to be.

Later we visited the Pasha of Marrakech,[*] where we were served cocktails from an American bar but sat on the floor for dinner at low, beautifully carved tables. Black slaves in lavishly embroidered white costumes served mutton, vegetables, fowl, fish and pastries, all of which had to be eaten with three fingers of the right hand alone. After the dinner, the Pasha's dancing girls, in heavy, elaborately decorated robes, and bedecked with bracelets and rings, danced and sang their native songs—one group from the hills around Marrakech and the other from the Arabian plains. The performance was fascinating, although quite strange to American ears. The singing and music sounded a bit like a combination of female tobacco auctioneers with a background of fire engines. The dancing was a melding of palsy, St. Vitus' dance,

---

[*] Usually called the Glaoui of Marrakech.

and a mild form of jitterbugging. We had a wonderful but strange time.

I might mention here that I wanted to do something later to repay the Sultan for the fine reception he had given us, but it developed that it was contrary to protocol for the ruler to accept the hospitality of anyone while he was in his own country. I fretted about this for a while, until old Si Mammeri gave me an idea.

"The Sultan," he said, "is very much interested in American battleships."

I said thank you, and the next time a battleship showed up in Casablanca Harbor I went into action. It happened to be the *New York,* and when I explained my plan to its skipper he agreed that they would do anything, including an impressive salute by the big guns, in order to impress the Sultan. I then sent the ruler an invitation to inspect the ship.

Because of various complications, the Sultan could not arrive at the harbor until late in the day. It is not customary for warships to render the usual honors after dark, but on this occasion the custom was ignored and we shot off the guns for the little man in the flowing white robes. We had laid white canvas down the steps of the dock to the Captain's gig, which took him aboard the *New York,* where the skipper gave him the works in the way of honors. The Sultan took the honors in his stride, but he was tremendously excited by the mechanics of the warship and went over it from stem to stern, giving the machinery a careful once-over and crawling enthusiastically into the gun turrets. We had dinner with him later and got him back ashore about ten o'clock at night.

As we parted on the dock, the interpreter said to me, "His Majesty wants me to tell you that this has been one of the happiest moments of his life."

I grinned and said, "Tell him that for a fellow who has a hundred and twenty wives that is saying something."

My tour went on for several days, involving quite a few other visits of a similar nature and many conferences with local officials, before I got back to Oujda on February 28, where an urgent message from Ike was awaiting me. I flew up to Algiers the next day and discovered that I was to launch a much bigger training program for new forces coming from the United States. It would include schools for mountain warfare and air-support training. Although Tunisia was far from conquered, we were starting the preparations for invasion of Sicily, which was to be handled by the Seventh Army—later to be created—under command of Major General George Patton.

One development in this connection that I didn't like was a message on March 8 informing me that the Navy would be responsible for all amphibious training. The Army had trained the necessary amphibious crews for TORCH because the Navy was unable then to provide sufficient boat crews within the necessary time. Now the Navy "desires to resume its responsibility for training all amphibious boat crews and operation and maintenance of all amphibious equipment necessary to carry out planned Army operations," the message said.

I knew that the Navy took pride in their feeling that anything afloat should be run by them, but it seemed to me there was no reason why they should want this responsibility now, when we already had it thoroughly organized and in operation. There was, however, nothing that I could do about it at that point and we were forced to accept the decision, until a later date when we achieved a compromise more or less along the lines I desired.

Another problem came up about this time in connection with the air-ground cooperation, and it was discussed at great length when Spaatz and Tedder came to Oujda to see me on March 10. I had strongly stated in a letter to Ike that if I was to be successful in training for air-ground cooperation we must have air units attached to the troops practicing at Arzew. We had had an Air Support Command at my headquarters until recently, but it had been disbanded just when I felt that by living and working together the ground and air forces were achieving the teamwork and cooperation so necessary to success in battle. Both Spaatz and Tedder to some extent agreed with me, but I was far from satisfied and felt that they were not wholly in sympathy with the War Department view (which was also my view) on close air support of ground troops and the command setup involved.

The Royal Air Force was separate from the British Army and Navy, while our Air Force was still an integral part of our Army. The British thinking ran more to strategic missions than to close support of the ground forces. I noticed from Tedder's comments that this British theory was growing among the American air officers and I began to wonder whether the ground troops would be able to get the air support they would need in action if that viewpoint prevailed. I also resolved to take up the question with Ike the first time I had an opportunity. It was a question that plagued us on many occasions throughout the war, and one that still does.

I do not mean to imply by these observations that later in the fighting in Italy we were not given splendid air support of all kinds by both British and American planes. Nevertheless, the command setup was never satisfactory from my point of view and it still is not satisfactory at the present time, almost five years after the end of the war. I believed then, and my experiences in Italy did not change my view, that ground troops cannot be successful in battle unless adequately supported by combat aviation, and that such planes as are used for this purpose are necessarily auxiliary weapons, as is the artillery, and that they should come under the direct orders of the ground commander. That, in a sentence, is still my belief today.

In mid-March, United States Consul J. Rives Childs drove down from Tangier, in Spanish Morocco, to discuss possible Spanish intervention. It had seemed less likely to us in recent weeks, but it could be more dangerous than ever as we extended our communications lines eastward, or if we suffered a military reverse in the Mediterranean. Childs felt that the head man in Spanish Morocco, Lieutenant General Luis Orgaz Yoldi "genuinely desires neutrality," but he pointed out that General Yaqui at Melilla was pro-German. He suggested that I should meet secretly with Orgaz somewhere near the Spanish Morocco border, and we agreed that he would try to arrange a meeting.

Less than two weeks later, we received from diplomatic sources in Madrid a copy of plans which Spain had decided to put into effect if the Germans invaded their country. They anticipated a mechanized-tank-air attack through the lower northwestern end of the Pyrenees and believed that they could hold the Germans for ten days.

"After ten days they would need Allied aviation to help," Colonel Ed Howard, my G-2, told me after studying the plans.

"They wouldn't want any of our troops?" I asked, surprised.

"No," Howard went on, "but at the end of twenty days they would need additional help in the form of antitank mines and anti-aircraft equipment."

"How about troops?" I persisted. "Won't they want our troops?"

"No," Howard said. "According to this plan they don't *ever* want any of our troops."

It would have been an amusing conversation, I suppose, except that I wasn't amused at the time. It would have been a hopeless situation if the Spaniards, under attack by the Axis, failed to invite us in, because we would have had to move in anyway to protect Gibraltar and the result would have been a muddle.

Meanwhile, General Orgaz proposed that I have a private meeting with him on April 2 at Taouima, about twenty-five miles inside the Spanish Moroccan border. This was fine with me because it would give me my first chance to look over terrain that we would have to move over if the emergency ever arose. At that time, too, we couldn't be too sure that we would not be forced to face Spanish as well as German opposition in such an operation.

Major General Gruenther, Colonel Saltzman, Colonel Howard, and Lieutenant Beardwood of the Fifth Army staff accompanied me in my meeting with Orgaz, which was kept very secret. I wanted, however, to give the trip a broader character, so I arranged for two colonels from Noguès' staff to go along and also took Brigadier General Eduardo Gomez of Brazil, who later became a Presidential candidate, and his aide, Captain Horta. Gomez was then on a visit to Fifth Army Headquarters in anticipation of Brazilian participation in the war.

Accompanied by two representatives of Orgaz, we proceeded in five automobiles across the sluggish, muddy Moulouya River at the International Bridge, where Orgaz, a short, stubby man, awaited us with a group of about twenty officers. We reviewed a mounted troop of native soldiers and then I rode with the general to Taouima. In the automobile I presented him with an American carbine, which had been mounted with a silver plate saying "To Lieutenant General Luis Orgaz Yoldi from Lieutenant General Mark W. Clark."

We drove along a paved road that wound up a fairly wide valley through almost barren countryside. I carried on a conversation with the general through an interpreter, but I also kept my eyes on the terrain, observing to myself that it definitely was tank country.

Orgaz kept his eyes on me and finally asked abruptly, "How old are you?"

"Forty-seven," I replied. There was a moment's silence and then I asked, "How old are you?"

"Sixty-one," he said. "How long have you been a general?"

This seemed to me a strange conversation, but the stubby little general spoke in friendly fashion. I answered that I'd been a general for a couple of years.

"How long," I asked, "have you been a general?"

"Twenty years."

I kept looking out the window and thinking that this would be one route to be followed in any invasion of Spanish Morocco.

"I see," Orgaz said finally, "that you are studying my terrain."

"Yes," I said bluntly. "I didn't realize it was so good for tanks."

I thought I might as well let him know that we had been thinking seriously about his terrain, although I had no doubt he was well aware of it.

"How many tanks do you have?" he asked.

I said we had something like eighteen thousand, which was more than a run-of-the-mill exaggeration.

"That many!" he exclaimed, and I said that of course I was speaking only in round numbers.

I still had my eyes on the terrain and the general, nodding toward a flat area I had been studying, asked me if I was thinking that it would make a good airfield.

"Oh, no," I replied carelessly, "I was just thinking what a good drop zone it would make for paratroopers."

"How many do you have?" he asked quickly.

I don't remember exactly what I replied, but I made the number a great deal larger than the truth. I may have made it too large, because I believe that was about the end of that unusual phase of our conversation. I think perhaps we had been feeling each other out, for we were thereafter on good terms. During the day's ceremonies I saw a great deal of stiff-armed Fascist saluting; and our intelligence reports suggested that most of the officers associated with Orgaz were pro-German, although Orgaz was usually described in vague terms as a monarchist. I thought it would be difficult to say whether he would be for or against us in a pinch, but by that time I was pretty well convinced that the Spanish Government would fight any German invasion of their territory. Although Franco was playing an opportunistic game, he was losing faith in the ability of the Axis to win the war. Later the Spaniards, in defiance of the rules of international warfare, rescued, aided and returned to us many hundreds of American fliers who were forced down on Spanish territory. They did as much, and more, I suppose, for the Axis.

My visit with Orgaz resulted in nothing concrete, but I believe he was convinced that the Spaniards could frustrate a German invasion. We witnessed the usual exhibitions and parades by native troops and I returned to Oujda before nightfall. Later General Orgaz sent me a Spanish-English dictionary inscribed with the notation "I hope this will improve your Spanish."

When Orgaz paid a return visit to Fifth Army Headquarters on June 3, we were far advanced in our training program for the invasion of Sicily and I was able to put on a show for him that, I feel sure, helped cement the Spanish determination to remain neutral. Generals Patton, Omar Bradley, Dawley, and Ridgway, and General Noguès attended the affair, as did a number of Spanish officers and three Mexican officers who were on a special mission to the Fifth Army.

We gave Orgaz the usual escort and military welcome and then took him to the Oujda Airport to review the 82nd Airborne Division, which was tough, tanned and impressive. Then dive bombers peeled off menacingly over a nearby field, laying a smoke screen, and a battalion of paratroopers plummeted to the earth from an altitude of about 400 feet, landing with their weapons directly on the objective. A moment later, a wave of transports parachuted supplies on the same target; and, as the men gathered up the equipment and began a simulated attack, a big glider soared across the field, landed smoothly, and disgorged armed infantrymen who charged out almost into our laps.

The Spanish general was obviously wide-eyed, and that was my idea. I hoped he would take the word back, particularly to his pro-German friends. When the party was over, we served him and his aides cool bottles of Coca-Cola on the hot and dusty airfield. The drink seemed to surprise him almost as much as had the paratroopers.

Ike had earlier asked me to attempt through Orgaz to counteract any unfavorable Spanish ideas about the extensive movements of Allied troops in Morocco and Algiers at that time in order to quiet any suspicions regarding our next move. I told Orgaz that these movements were solely the result of reorganization and refitting following the Tunisian campaign, and he said that he was not in the least worried that such movements were directed against his territory.

However, I am getting a bit ahead of my story. That spring, while the battle of Tunisia was grinding slowly to an end, our training program was directed toward future operations. Except for the decision to invade Sicily, however, we were never sure just what these operations would involve and we were forced to plan for various contingencies while our governments tried to make up their minds on an overall course of action. My own hope was that we would go back to the United Kingdom and prepare for the invasion of France across the Channel, and we all made a great many speeches and announcements that spring about how the Fifth Army would soon join with other Allied forces in freeing France from the Nazis.

My attitude toward the planning of future operations at that time was reflected in notations that I made in my diary on April 28, as follows:

> It is inexcusable that high planning, on an overall scale, is not taking definite form. Planners should project themselves forward and set up a grand-scale strategic plan for the Allied forces. We can't win a war by capturing islands [a reference to plans regarding Sicily and Sardinia]. This coming move [Sicily] in the Mediterranean will be no great move. In reality, we will get no place by doing it and the result will not be commensurate with the effort and the losses involved.
>
> We are going to have to attack the Continent proper and we should decide now how we are going to do it. We are losing time to plan and train for a specific goal.

But when the Tunisian campaign ended in mid-May, there was still no decision on anything except the Sicilian campaign. At the end of the month, Marshall and Churchill, after conferences in Washington, flew to Algiers to reach an agreement with Ike. The British thought that the Mediterranean should be further exploited, while the Americans in general wanted to return to England and strike across the Channel.

The conferences in Washington had been held "in an atmosphere of mutual suspicion," according to some of the military men who attended them, and we believed that Churchill had gone to Algiers in order to persuade Ike to come around to his point of view. Nothing definite was settled at the time, but in the end Churchill's views prevailed and we struck into Europe by way of Sicily and Italy.

I suppose this situation caused me still greater concern because at Oujda I was more or less remote from the center of action and from the headquarters where the decisions were being made. I kept abreast of developments, of course, and had occasional chances to visit Algiers or to go to the Tunisian front, and twice Ike visited Fifth Army Headquarters. Patton had taken over command of II Corps at the front during the drive to capture Sfax, but because we had to prepare for his role in the Sicilian invasion he turned the corps over to General Omar Bradley on April 14 and returned west to reassume command of the I Armored Corps. At that time the Germans had fallen back to Enfidaville, and I made a tour of several days around the front, visiting Bradley, Alexander, and Montgomery and getting my first look at the victorious British Eighth Army.

I thought the Eighth Army was a real fighting outfit. They showed a cocky confidence in their own abilities that was impressive, but I was surprised at their careless dress. Many officers wore sweaters, and discipline was not particularly tight, but they displayed a tremendous fighting spirit. They also showed great confidence—too much, I thought—in their air cover. Outside Enfidaville, their vehicles were lined up in three rows and standing bumper to bumper over a long stretch of road; they would have been duck soup for enemy air attack. The transport was of all types and well worn, and I was surprised that it was still painted for desert camouflage, which was completely ineffective in Tunisia. In other words, this was a high-spirited army that disregarded many of the basic rules on which Americans placed a good deal of emphasis, but nobody could doubt that it was an effective fighting force.

The men were well-informed and alert too, and whenever I stopped to ask directions or to get information almost any one I spoke to could tell me what I wanted to know. Their confidence was impressed on me when I drove up on a ridge overlooking the valley at Enfidaville.

"Where are the front lines?" I asked the first man I met.

"This is our front line," was the laconic reply. "The German front line is right down there."

In regard to the American forces, I felt that II Corps was doing a good job in Tunisia, and the 1st Division, which had lost some 1,800 men, had made a reputation for itself as a fighting outfit, but there was evidence in some areas of the front of lack of discipline and a lack of fighting spirit. Part of this, I felt, was due to the way in which our outfits had been mixed in with the British and French and in some cases to the lack of experienced American officers.

A few days after my return from the front, General McNair, chief of the Ground Forces in Washington, on a similar tour, was wounded by fragments from artillery fire, when, as usual, he insisted on seeing everything at first hand. Later in April, I eagerly took advantage of an opportunity to visit my old boss, whom I considered one of our greatest soldiers, at the Oran hospital, and I was much interested in his view of conditions at the front.

McNair felt very strongly that "American soldiers are not fighting" in Tunisia. He attributed this situation to lack of discipline in training and said that discipline would be heavily stressed in the United States when he returned there. He also deplored the mixing of British and American units, insisting that each should be under its own commanders.

His remarks on discipline impressed me because they reflected my own views, and I was fortunately able to tell him of extensive measures we had taken in the training of the Fifth Army to remedy the situation. I had been as tough as I knew how to be in punishments for offenses in Fifth Army territory and repeatedly insisted that we crack down on disciplinary matters involving both officers and men, particularly the former, taking the attitude that the men should be only too willing to learn rules and discipline on the training ground since in action their lives would depend on how well they had absorbed the lesson. We took as our slogan the sentence, "An alert soldier is an alive soldier," and we never lost an opportunity to din it into their ears.

I remember one day in Oujda I stopped my automobile in the middle of town because I saw a sergeant standing on the corner, obviously very drunk, with a large police dog on a leash. I got out and asked his name and to which outfit he belonged. He straightened up and seemed alarmed when I tore into him for his disgraceful conduct. He was a good-looking, big man and I felt that perhaps I was being a bit too rough with him.

"Can you get back to your quarters?" I asked, having by that time become more concerned over his ability to navigate than anything else.

"Yes, sir," he said.

"Will you promise me to go immediately to your quarters and remain there until you're sober?" I asked sternly.

"Yes, sir."

"And never permit yourself to appear in public again in this disgraceful state?"

"Yes, sir," he said with such sincerity that I felt he'd probably learned his lesson.

"Very well," I said, motioning my aide to follow him to be sure he got back to quarters. "Go along at once."

"Yes, sir," he said. Then turning to his fine dog, he added, "Don't bite the General, doggie."

I obviously hadn't impressed him as much as I had believed, but there was not much I could do other than beat a dignified retreat, which I did. I checked up on him later and found he had a fine record, and not long afterward I was given one of the pups which "doggie" had produced. We called the pup Mike, in spite of the fact it was a bitch, and she stayed with me from then until the end of the war, acquiring a blanket with a fine array of battle stripes on it. I took her to Austria later; when I finally came home, I gave her to one of my sergeants.

I was caught under an increasing burden of work throughout the spring, but I wasn't so busy that I forgot my birthday, which falls on the first day of May. I had always meticulously remembered the birthdays of the members of my staff, and I arrived at the office that morning in a pleasant frame of mind, prepared to accept good wishes on my anniversary and perhaps even take time out for a small party. Nobody, however, remembered the occasion. Gruenther greeted me about as usual and even Sergeant Chaney, who was pretty good about remembering such things, said nothing about my birthday.

In fact, instead of having a party, it looked as if I were going to have more work than ever. I had never seen so many papers as were piled up on my desk awaiting my attention. Colonel Joseph I. Martin, Fifth Army Surgeon,* came in shortly after I arrived and launched into a long and not very important discussion of his problems. Sullivan showed up as Martin was leaving and insisted on taking up a dozen minor matters concerned with the Quartermaster Corps and then gave out with a time-consuming talk about how the British did things as compared to how we did things. At 10:30 a.m., Gruenther had arranged some sort of meeting that sounded highly unimportant. I was in a rather sour mood, so when I finally broke away from Sullivan I left word with my secretary to call me out of the conference room at ten minutes past eleven.

Gruenther presided at the conference, but he had hardly started to explain its purpose when there was some sort of rumpus at the door. Gruenther finally broke off and asked Lieutenant Lemaux what the trouble was.

---

* He had replaced General Blesse, who had moved up to become Ike's chief surgeon.

"There's a message for General Clark," he replied.

Gruenther brushed him aside and said to tell them to deliver it later, but he had hardly gotten back to business when the disorder broke out again and became so persistent that I was halfway out of my chair, rather grimly determined to settle it myself, when the door was pushed open and two Red Cross girls, wearing Western Union signs, marched in and began singing "Happy Birthday to You." Even then it took me a moment to catch on, although I should have been suspicious because Gruenther is a notorious practical joker. He had issued orders to the whole staff the day before to avoid any mention of my birthday until the framed-up conference started and had sent both Martin and Sullivan around to take up my time until 10:30 a.m. in order to keep me from getting suspicious.

I was completely fooled and I had also been definitely piqued during the several hours in which nobody mentioned my anniversary. I even had told Gruenther at midmorning that I thought I would take a plane and fly down to the beach, but he explained, regretful and untruthful, that my pilot had a bad cold and that the weather was too bad to make the flight anyway.

The program included a ceremony in the courtyard, where a guard of honor drawn from C Company of the 101st Military Police Battalion greeted me and all of the headquarters personnel were lined up in formation. The band played ruffles and flourishes and interpolated the strains of "Happy Birthday," and later a Red Cross wagon brought up doughnuts and coffee for the entire assemblage. That evening there was a buffet dinner with a big cake in the center of the table. It had been prepared on instructions from Mrs. Clark and was inscribed "Happy Birthday—Wayne from Renie."

The spring wore on into summer with our training program progressing as rapidly as possible in view of the fact that we didn't know exactly what we were training for. The French situation settled down a little, with Noguès resigning—much to our satisfaction—and Giraud and de Gaulle getting together after a fashion. I learned to take off and land an airplane, making a complete flight in a C-47 from Fez to Oujda with only a couple of bounces when I got off the ground and a few skids that brought the right wing to within a foot of the ground as I landed. I received encouraging news from General Gomez of Brazil, who was promoting the idea of having a Brazilian detachment of 5,000 men attached to the Fifth Army. We designed a new insignia for the Fifth Army—a red background, with a blue Moslem mosque imposed and inside it a white capital A and the Arabic figure five. Finally, I should note that I received a letter reading as follows:

DEAR GENERAL:

Venerated, glorious and distinguished one, let benediction and grace be upon you, greetings: I have the honor to request you to accord me, out of your high consideration, the authorization of B.M.C. [*Bordel Militaire de Campagne*, i.e., accompanying brothel for troops on campaign], whether in Oujda or Tafaralt. My conduct is good, never convicted, and I have always been correct toward my chiefs and conformed to the law.

Please accept, General, the homage of my most profound respect.

Your obedient servant,

SADDIKI FATMA

P.S. The patroness Saidia of Tafaralt has been sentenced several times, but I never have.

I later was told that the writer was a woman who ran most of the brothels in the Oujda district. Colonel Arthur Sutherland of my staff answered her in eleven words—"It has been decided that the authorization sought cannot be granted."

Meantime, we received on June 2 instructions to prepare for a possible invasion of Sardinia, an operation known by the code word BRIMSTONE. We were doubtful from the first that it would ever be executed, unless the impending invasion of Sicily failed, but at least it gave us something specific to work on. I should like to give one illustration of the training methods we had developed by the middle of June, when we were ordered to prepare for a demonstration of our work in honor of the British War Minister, Sir James Griggs, and a special visitor.

The special visitor turned out to be King George VI, who arrived in a four-motored York bomber with an escort of fighter planes. In addition to the usual ceremonies on such an occasion, we took His Majesty to the Arzew area to witness an exercise scheduled to start about one o'clock in the afternoon. The King had asked the name of the hotel at which we would eat and apparently was surprised when I told him that we would have luncheon in the open. We had made arrangements at a shady spot; it was not unpleasant except for the flies, a discomfort that I tried to overcome by having a man swinging a large towel stationed behind the King's place at the table. We had small tables, and Sir James Griggs and Patton joined His Majesty and myself at one of them, where lunch was served in GI mess kits. Just as President Roosevelt earlier had done, the King expressed interest in the kits and I presented him with one. Then Sir James, who had found the kit a bit awkward and spilled a little stew on his suit, asked for one too. I sent for another, and when it arrived I noticed that Sir James put it on his lap. Watching him, I had a hunch something was wrong; finally I walked over and lifted the lid of his kit. Inside was a brimming portion of fresh beef stew on the verge of running out on Sir James' already-stained trousers.

This catastrophe was averted, but I can't say that the luncheon was a great success. Even when it was over, I was dogged by bad luck. The photographers crowded around for pictures, and when the party lined up I was standing at the King's left. Under any circumstances I would be a good deal taller than the King, but on this occasion it developed that I had taken my place on a hump that made me tower still more definitely over His Majesty, who was standing in a little depression.

"Would you," he asked before the picture was taken, "mind trading places with me. You're so tall that I'd like to stand on the hump. You can take the rut."

I took the rut and everything was fine. The show that we put on for him was pretty good, too. Near Arzew we had constructed a village with streets and mock-up houses and stores, to train troops in street fighting. Live ammunition was used as the soldiers raced up the streets, keeping a few inches under the bullets only by crouching and then hugging the walls in order to remain a hands-breadth out of the line of live fire. Hand grenades were exploded within close range and demolition charges knocked down buildings, hurling debris that the men could avoid only by carefully following the training rules. It was as close to battle as a soldier could get without graduating into the real thing, and the King was deeply impressed by the rigorous methods of training and by the splendid way in which the men were performing. He departed in a pleasant mood, and I felt that perhaps the afternoon's exercises had made up for the difficulties we had at luncheon.

Ike came down a few days later and inspected our whole setup, where practically all the troops that Patton was to use in Sicily had received their battle training. "Any soldier who goes through Fifth Army training is going to be much better prepared to meet the initial shocks of actual battle," he told the correspondents later. "The training is comprehensive, thorough, and efficient. I have found the leadership to be excellent."

He had, of course, seen a great deal more than King George had time to witness. I had two Cub planes in which we flew over the whole area. The men were doing everything from climbing ropes while wearing full packs to dropping paratroopers within ten feet of the reviewing stand, and Ike agreed with me that the Fifth Army appeared ready for any job. Unhappily, he couldn't say just yet what the job would be because he didn't know. However, he had repeatedly told me that I would have a battle command and I knew he would see that I got it.

The invasion of Sicily by the British Eighth Army and Patton's forces, including the I Armored Corps, was launched on July 10, and it was immediately announced that the United States Seventh Army had been formed under Patton's leadership. The assault ran into many difficulties; but by mid-July began to pick up speed, and its success was pretty well assured despite the hard fighting ahead. As a result, we knew that Operation BRIMSTONE would be abandoned; on July 16 we were given a new plan, called GANGWAY, which would involve the seizure of Naples. A week later, we received still another plan, Operation MUSKET, calling for a landing on the heel of Italy. The British, meanwhile, were working on two other plans, GOBLET and BUTTRESS, which were landings on the instep of Italy.

All these projects were in the planning stage when news came that Premier Benito Mussolini had resigned and that King Victor Emmanuel had appointed Marshal Badoglio as head of the Italian Government. This and subsequent developments indicating that the Italians desired to make a separate peace brought political instead of military considerations to the fore again and kept us in a state of uncertainty and change up to the time of our invasion of the Italian mainland. On July 28, however, we received still another project, which called for an amphibious assault in the vicinity of Naples, probably at the Bay of Salerno in order to take full advantage of the Italian political and military collapse. From the first, this operation—known as AVALANCHE—looked good to me, and we went to work on it enthusiastically.

The date of AVALANCHE would depend on the conclusion of the Sicilian campaign and the possibility of Italian surrender negotiations, the latter being of tremendous importance because we hoped we could catch the Germans off guard and time our attack to take advantage of the end of Italian resistance. The Nazis obviously were going to fight for Italy regardless of the action of the Italian Government, but there was always the possibility that we could seize Naples with Italian assistance before the Germans could act.

Alexander, in command of the overall operation, planned to use Montgomery's Eighth Army for the GOBLET or BUTTRESS operation on the instep of the Italian boot, while the Fifth Army executed AVALANCHE a hundred and fifty miles up the west coast. Under my command, making up the Fifth Army, were the American VI Corps, consisting of the 84th and 36th Infantry Divisions, the 1st Armored Division, and the 82nd Airborne Division; and the British X Corps, which included the 46th and 56th Infantry Divisions, the 7th Armored Division, and the 1st Airborne Division. Our mission was to capture the city of Naples and to join up with Montgomery's forces coming up from the south.

In view of later developments, I might explain here how I happened to select the 36th Division for the main landing thrust at Salerno. I had available for the landing either the 36th or the 34th Division, the latter alone having had battle experience. But upon considering all factors involved, I selected the 36th for the initial attack because I felt that it had good leadership and high caliber personnel. I had known Major General Fred Walker, the commander, for years at the War College, at Fort Lewis and elsewhere. During the prewar maneuvers in Louisiana a vacancy had occurred in the command of the 36th National Guard Division, and I had told General McNair that I believed Walker was the man for the job. All of these factors entered into my decision on use of the division at Salerno. The other divisions would be available to follow up.

Since the Salerno operation called for use of a corps, the War Department had asked Ike if he would accept VI Corps, which was under command of Major General Ernest J. Dawley. I was not well acquainted with Dawley, but I did know that McNair thought very highly of him and I placed a great deal of confidence in McNair's sound judgment. I talked to Ike about Dawley and he was far from enthusiastic, although he reluctantly concurred when I said I recommended replying affirmatively to the War Department.

Admiral Hewitt was to be in command of the two naval task forces—one supporting my forces, and one supporting Montgomery's thrust into southern Italy. Hewitt himself was to accompany the Fifth Army on his flagship U.S.S. *Ancon,* on which I would make my headquarters until I could get ashore. The assault was to begin early in September, the exact date to be set by Alexander.

On August 3, I moved my headquarters to Mostaganem—between Oran and Algiers—to be nearer final training activities. Both Alexander and Montgomery were urging Eisenhower to make BUTTRESS or GOBLET, which were exclusively British operations, the main assault on Italy; whereas it was my belief that these thrusts the Italian toe were not tactically as sound as AVALANCHE, which would put us much farther up the coast, give us possession of Naples and the nearby airfields, and avoid some rugged terrain. I bolstered my argument by pointing out that Lieutenant General Sir Brian G. Horrocks, commanding the British X Corps in AVALANCHE, agreed with me. As it finally worked out, we reached the usual compromise, but the Fifth Army attack was the main operation.

There was a great deal of rivalry during the preparations between the British and the Americans, even in the Fifth Army. I had planned to put Horrock's X Corps on the right flank of our assault, which was closest to the area where the British Eighth Army would be operating. He protested mildly against this, saying that they were thus farther from Naples than the Americans. As it turned out, I later had to shift the line-up and Horrocks was told he would be on the left flank, with a brighter outlook for making a triumphant British entry into Naples. Unhappily, he was wounded in an air raid on Bizerte before D-day and we missed his excellent services in the invasion. We studied the possibility of landing north of Naples instead of in the Bay of Salerno. There were good reasons for this because the country was open and flat and lent itself to the type of warfare that Montgomery had developed in Africa. The area also offered an opportunity to drop airborne troops along the Volturno River and block German reinforcements from the north. I hoped we could land north of Naples, particularly in view of the absence of mountainous country like that adjacent to Salerno, and I flew twice to Algiers to discuss it. The Navy was opposed to the project because the waters off Gaeta were less protected than at Salerno. When I checked the American air experts, they said that as good air support could be given at Gaeta as at Salerno but the British experts disagreed. Air Marshal Sir Arthur Tedder, who was air commander in chief in the Mediterranean, was away from Algiers, but when I finally got in touch with him he said the proper support could not be given at Gaeta. After that we concentrated on Salerno.

General Juin arrived at Mostaganem and prepared to take part in the Italian campaign with the 2nd Moroccan Infantry Division and the 3rd Algerian Infantry Division, in addition to a force of Goumiers, the famous French Moroccan fighters.

The eagerness of the French to fight in the Italian campaign was illustrated by a story that arose when I was looking for some good fighters to undertake a hazardous mission during the AVALANCHE operations. There was a small town north of Salerno where we knew a big ammunition dump was located, and I thought that a band of parachute troops could be dropped there to destroy it. I asked Colonel A. L. Guillaume, now a general in command of the French forces in Germany, if he could recommend a group for the mission, and he suggested the Goumiers, native soldiers who are exceedingly clever at knife work.

He offered to investigate and a few days later said that he had fifty volunteers for the job, but that he had had a little trouble explaining to them about their transportation because none of them had ever been in an airplane.

"They wanted to be sure the plane would fly close to the ground and that it would slow down when they jumped," he said.

"Tell them," I replied, "that on such an operation the plane can slow down to about a hundred miles an hour, but it can't fly less than four hundred feet from the ground or their parachutes won't have time to open."

"Yes," said Guillaume. "I told them that. And that's where the confusion began. When I explained about the parachutes, their leader said, 'Praise Allah! Do we get parachutes, too?'"

General Giraud was extremely enthusiastic about the coming campaign and kept urging that D-day be advanced in order to give the Germans as little time as possible to prepare. He also told me that he was going to hold a French mountain division in readiness to invade Sardinia if anything should go wrong in Italy.

"But what would you use for ships in such an invasion?" I asked him.

"I would extemporize," he said. "I would use any ships I could lay my hands on, commercial or naval. I wouldn't need fancy landing craft. If a ship would float, I would use it."

There were times when I impatiently wished I had some of the same spirit at work in the Fifth Army preparations, especially when we ran into complications regarding use of airborne troops. Originally I wanted to land paratroops on a plain northwest of Salerno and southeast of Mount Vesuvius, where they could delay any enemy reinforcements moving down from Naples and Rome and, most important, could seize two rugged passes through which we would have to move from Salerno toward Naples. If those passes could be taken without serious opposition, we would be far on our way to our immediate goal.

This plan was vetoed by the air experts. They said that it would be extremely difficult if not impossible to land paratroopers effectively in that area because of treacherous air currents sweeping around Mount Vesuvius, the limited space in which transport planes could be brought to a low altitude, and the intense enemy antiaircraft concentrations nearby. My next plan was to drop paratroopers of the 82nd Division northwest of Naples along the Volturno River, particularly around Capua, as a diversionary effort and to blow bridges and otherwise delay enemy reinforcements from the north. Major General Matthew B. Ridgway, commander of the 82nd, had been through a bad experience in the invasion of Sicily, when his paratroopers were badly scattered in landing, and he was lukewarm at first toward my Volturno plan, which meant his men would be about forty miles away from our Salerno bridgehead. Both Spaatz and Tedder, however, welcomed the plan enthusiastically, and Ridgway, after further study, joined in wholeheartedly. I mention this plan here because later there will be a good deal to say about the use of airborne troops at Salerno.

In mid-August I went to General Alexander's 15th Army Group headquarters near Syracuse, and he approved our planning for AVALANCHE, especially the airborne phase. A radio was sent to Tedder giving Alexander's approval of our contemplated use of the 82nd Airborne Division. All of these details were wrapped up at a conference August 23 in Algiers, where Eisenhower, Alexander, Cunningham, Tedder, Spaatz, Montgomery, and I met to complete our plans. At this meeting, it was agreed by all, including Montgomery, that the Eighth Army thrust into the Italian toe would be diversionary and that our main effort would be made by the Fifth Army in the Naples area.

At this time I also was able to create a floating reserve, previously not in existence, to back up my assault at the Bay of Salerno. I arranged, after fighting down a good many objections, to have nine LSTs, six LCIs, and forty-eight DUKWs (GIs called them "Ducks")* at Palermo two days before the assault. I told General Middleton, the 45th Division commander, to load them with the maximum striking power and send them to Salerno as a D-day reserve to be called upon when and where needed.

On August 31, Ike flew to Mostaganem and we went over the final details again. As a complete surprise to me, he pinned the Legion of Merit on my battle jacket. Everything was all set; D-day at Salerno would be September 9. Well, everything was almost set. It turned out that there were quite a few last-minute alterations, owing in large part to the eagerness of the Italians to get out from under before we hit the beaches.

When I flew to Alexander's headquarters in Sicily, on September 3, both Ike and Bob Murphy, who had become American chief civil administrator in North Africa, were there. I noticed an air of excitement as soon as I arrived; it developed that the Italians, trying to negotiate for surrender, were even offering to give us material aid in getting into Italy. Representatives of Eisenhower and Badoglio were even then meeting secretly in Lisbon, trying to work out details of an armistice.

When I met Ike in a tent shortly after I arrived at Alexander's headquarters, he brought me up to date on late developments and said that the Italians were greatly concerned about what the Germans would do in Rome when they learned of the armistice. As a result of this situation Brigadier General Maxwell D. Taylor, assistant division commander to Ridgway and one of the Army's outstanding young officers, made a daring secret trip to the Italian capital, where he conferred with leaders of the armistice movement and got safely out again. The Italians had urged that we drop a division of paratroopers on Rome in order to seize it with Italian aid and hold it until our forces could land and take over. This was strictly a political idea, rather than a military plan, but at that point in the surrender negotiations political considerations were again outweighing military tactics.

---

* LST—Landing Ship, Tank; LCI—Landing Craft, Infantry; DUKW—Amphibious 2½-ton truck.

"It will be a shock to you," Ike said, "but it has been decided that we'll make the drop on Rome."

I didn't know exactly why it should shock me, but I soon found out.

"Where," I asked, "are you going to get an airborne division to do it?"

"The Eighty-second."

"No!" I protested. "That's my division! You know I am going to drop much of it along the Volturno River. The Germans have several panzer divisions south of Rome ready to rush down and block the passes through which we have to go from Salerno to Naples. Taking away the Eighty-second just as the fighting starts is like cutting off my left arm."

"Now, Wayne," he said, "keep your shirt on."

"Okay," I answered, "but after you drop the Eighty-second on Rome, what happens to it then?"

"Then it will pass to your command."

"Thanks," I said, permitting myself the luxury of a little bitterness. "That will be a great help! It will be two hundred miles away from me. Sort of like having a half interest in a wife."

By that time I felt that the shirt that Ike was continually urging me to keep on was becoming, figuratively, a little tattered from excessive handling, but at the same time I knew that Ike understood my position and, as an old friend, would not take offense because I was blowing off steam. The Rome operation seemed futile to me because I couldn't see how the paratroops were going to be successful in view of the strong German concentrations near the capital. Nor did I see how they were going to withdraw or how we were going to get help to them from the sea; but politically there were reasons, I suppose, for agreeing to the operation, and I knew my situation was subordinate to those considerations.

I was discouraged by this development, but it proved possible to arrange for the 179th Regimental Combat Team from the 45th Division to replace the airborne troops I had planned to use in my floating reserve. I was left without any paratroops to blow up the Volturno bridges, but our attack might be made less rugged than we had expected if the Italians refused to resist.

That same day, Montgomery's Eighth Army crossed the Straits of Messina and began taking over the toe of the Italian boot without much opposition. I returned to Mostaganem and on September 5 went aboard the *Ancon* at Algiers with thirty of my staff. Admiral Hewitt greeted us and gave me a cabin that I could also use as an office. I had had a tough day and decided to turn in. According to a long-standing custom, each day I read from a little book called *Daily Word,* a Unity publication. The prayer for

September 5, 1943, seemed to have been prepared especially for this occasion. It read, in part, as follows:

> Father, in Thy name I pray, let me know Thy will today. With Thee I am unafraid, for on Thee my mind is stayed. Though, a thousand foes surround, safe in Thee I shall be found.
>
> I have faith that Thou wilt be always guarding and directing me. In the air, on sea or land, Thy sure protection is at hand. Momently Thy love I share, Thy grace, and Thy protecting care.
>
> Spirit of the Lord Most High, gracious Spirit that is I, in Thy word my needs are filled, in Thy love my fears are stilled. In Thee I am stanch and strong. Thou art with me all day long, showing me the way to go, helping me always to know Thou art justice, peace, and life, healer of the nations' strife.

I slept better that night.

We sailed early on September 6, with a convoy of about seventy ships escorted by the cruisers *Boise, Savannah,* and *Philadelphia,* and fourteen destroyers. Other convoys sailed from Bizerte and Tripoli and Palermo for our rendezvous off the Bay of Salerno.

Not until three hours after we had sailed did I call in key staff officers and tell them the latest news of the armistice negotiations. The terms, which would be broadcast the day before we landed at Salerno, provided that the Italians would offer passive resistance to the Germans and would not maintain rail traffic or communications, nor would they permit the Germans to take over coastal defenses. I emphasized that these were merely the terms of the agreement; that enforcing them was something else again. I doubted that they would be effectively enforced, but we would soon find out. At best, we could steam into Naples Harbor unopposed. At worst, we could have a hell of a fight.

Anyway, we were on our way and, at last, I had my first battle command.

9.

Salerno: A Near Disaster:

September 1943

The Tyrrhenian Sea, rolling softly against the sun-browned shores of Italy, is generally regarded as one of the loveliest sights in the world, and for all I know it may be exactly that. When first I saw it, late on the afternoon of September 8, it merely was the meeting place for four hundred and fifty ships of all sizes and shapes, and my only immediate reaction was, Thank God, I don't have the job of getting them assembled and in to shore.

That was the task of Vice Admiral Henry Kent Hewitt, U.S.N., from whose flagship *Ancon* I watched the arrival at our rendezvous of the American and British forces that were to make the first assault against Hitler's "impregnable" Fortress Europa by landing at Salerno Bay, south of Naples. It is true that the British Eighth Army under Montgomery was already on Italian soil, 150 miles to the south, having hopped the three miles from Sicily to the toe of the Italian boot, but the enemy had opposed them only with delaying tactics. Kesselring chose to make the assault by the Fifth Army—which threatened the great port of Naples—the real test of strength in a struggle that would demonstrate to the world the power of Germany on the European Continent.

We had been for three days in the capable hands of the American and British naval forces, which transported the Fifth Army from Oran, Algiers, Palermo, Bizerte, and Tripoli to the assembly area off Salerno. They had been quiet days for me because in that brief period the conduct of the invasion was out of my hands. Until we reached the beaches, there was nothing I could do except take a last look at what we were up against. Despite the Italian armistice arrangements, there were many discouraging factors.

There was no question in our minds that the Germans would try to react strongly and that there was plenty of enemy strength available regardless of the Italian action. There were about eight Nazi divisions available to meet an attack in Italy, and we knew that some of their strongest forces were in the south. The 16th Panzer Division (armored) was in the Eboli-Battipaglia area, adjacent to Salerno; when the Nazis got wind of the Italian armistice negotiations, this division was ordered to assume defense of the entire coastal area where we were planning to land. We discovered later that artillery, tanks, and mortars were assembled in a semicircle covering the coast, and a concentration of heavy antiaircraft guns was stationed at Salerno and near Battipaglia. Mines were laid on the beaches, barbed-wire obstacles were erected, and many machine guns were aimed to cover the best landing spots. In addition, the Hermann Göring Division was near Naples and the 15th Panzer Grenadier Division of armored infantry was close by in the neighborhood of Gaeta. Other units were waiting near Rome to determine where we would land.

Furthermore, we knew that in command of these forces was Field Marshal Albert Kesselring, one of the ablest officers in the Hitler armies. He had served with distinction in the German artillery, the air force, and had been on the General Staff prior to the war. Kesselring was well qualified, both as a commander and an administrator, and he conducted the Axis operations in Italy with great skill for two years, after which he was transferred to command of the Western Front in Germany. I was glad to see him go. He was quick to reorganize his forces and shift reserves to meet our attacks, and he had the advantage of a homogeneous army in which he could move large or small units without restriction, in contrast to the Allied difficulties in handling men and equipment of many different nationalities.

To breach the enemy defenses we had the British 46th and 56th Divisions under Lieutenant General Sir Richard L. McCreery's X Corps, and the 36th Division under Major General Ernest J. Dawley's VI Corps, plus American Rangers, British Commandos, and part of the American 45th Division as a floating reserve. In all, we had about 30,000 British troops and 25,000 Americans to storm defenses that were mounted by some 20,000 German troops in the Salerno area, with 100,000 others able to converge on us in short order.

One thing that bothered me as we approached D-day was the theory on which our command setup was based. In practice, at Salerno it worked out well, except for one incident, but that does not lessen my objections to the basic system. General Eisenhower was the supreme authority and he had not only complete unity of command at the top but the authority to enforce it at AFHQ (Allied Forces Headquarters). My idea was—and still is—that at Salerno one commander might well have been given the complete authority over all services during various phases of the battle. Alexander had command of the 15th Army Group, which included the Fifth Army and the Eighth Army, and he was my immediate superior, but his headquarters was in Sicily and he was in no position to influence actions at Salerno; and anyway the air and naval commands participating in that operation were responsible to the Supreme Commander rather than to Alexander.

Three commanders were designated at Salerno: Tedder for air, Hewitt for the Navy, and myself for the ground forces. I accepted Hewitt as being in command until we had landed and established a toehold on the beaches. Until that time, Hewitt would have to depend on cooperation with Tedder for air cover; after we landed I would have to do the same in order to get air support for ground operations. Such a system, it seemed to me, could lead to grave difficulties. This was impressed on me after we were at sea, when I asked Major General Edwin J. House, A.C., our very able air liaison officer, what provision had been made to guard our convoy against air attack, and he said that he didn't know because that was in the hands of the Coastal Air Command; his own duties did not begin until we had landed and needed fighter-plane support from Sicily. Another example arose after the landing, when I went ashore to determine where I wanted to bring in my floating reserve. When I returned to the *Ancon,* I discovered that Hewitt had received orders from his superiors to land the reserve immediately because their landing craft were needed to bring up reinforcements, so he had put them ashore—in the wrong place, of course.

My belief is that a single command should be established over all three arms, in somewhat the same way the Russian air forces are usually employed under the operational command of the army-group commander. The Soviet air support, for instance, is normally subordinated under the operational control of a ground army or corps, or even a division commander, as the situation requires. For our purposes in an operation such as Salerno, the Navy commander should be in control of air support and everything else during the period required to get the assault forces to their destination and established with a firm toehold ashore. Then the ground-force commander should assume a similar role, having control over air support and such naval support as is necessary or as can be allotted to him. Thus, responsibility for the overall operation would be firmly designated and the possibility of confusion, conflicting orders, or an error such as landing the reserve at the wrong place would be reduced to a minimum.

The actual transfer of command from the Navy commander to the Army commander might seem to raise difficulties in the midst of a battle, but in practice Salerno demonstrated that it was feasible. Hewitt, under stiff bombing attack and with countless problems to solve regarding naval operations didn't delay in asking me, "When can you take over?" I had been only too happy to be a passenger while Hewitt wrestled so ably with the problem of getting us ashore; but when the land fighting started, I have no doubt he was just as happy to hand the job over to me while he lent powerful and much-needed support from the sea. My purpose here, however, is merely to point out that the situation which existed throughout the war, wherein unity of command did not exist on the field of battle in some echelons actually doing the fighting, was and still is an important question. It is the question of who commands whom when the Army, Navy, and Air Force are fighting together. Of course, there may be some situations where special circumstances would prevent complete unity of command, but in general, wherever the three services fight together, regardless of the size of the forces involved, we should strive to have but one head man.

The 1949 squabble over unification was intensified by this issue. We must accept the principle of unity of command in peacetime if we are to have it in war—where lack of it may prove disastrous. Otherwise, we will have extra echelons of command existing side by side, as we had in Italy, with the result that never were so few commanded by so many.

Problems of this nature were very much in my mind on that circuitous route across the Mediterranean to Salerno. I suppose that I was making mental preparations for the worst that could happen; but I recall that I also discussed with my staff such pleasant possibilities as a direct move into Naples Harbor if the Italian surrender cleared our path to a greater extent than we actually anticipated.

It is interesting to recall that as we approached Italian shores we entertained a number of theories that were going to be knocked sky-high when the fighting got under way. One of these, which was particularly held by the British, was that if we struck Italy with sufficient force and secured suitable ports and airfields for big-scale operations, the Germans would soon decide not to give battle but to pull back to north Italy. This theory, which originated in high intelligence sources in London and was reflected throughout the British intelligence in the Mediterranean, was based on the argument that the enemy would be unable to maintain his strength in Italy because of poor transportation facilities through mountainous territory and because of our air superiority. We gave the theory a good try. Allied bombers worked over the enemy communication lines for many weeks and, finally, for months and even years. The Brenner Pass, the tunnels, the bridges, were battered steadily, but the theory was a complete flop. The Germans kept right on increasing their strength in Italy until the very end and were able to battle us for every foot of Italian soil.

On September 8, we sat in Hewitt's cabin and listened to the radio broadcasts of the unconditional surrender of the Italian government. Before sundown that evening our transports and warships were in three lines approaching a designated area off Salerno, where minesweepers moved in to clear a path to the beaches. The sea was smooth, the sky was clear, and at ten minutes to midnight we lay, with engines stopped, only a few miles from the shore. I joined Hewitt on the bridge of the *Ancon*. I have already said that this naval phase of the assault was out of my hands, but I had not realized how helpless I would feel as everywhere in the darkness around us the officers and men of the Fifth Army started that last dash toward the beaches. There was nothing we could do but wait.

Our landings were on a strip of coast about thirty-six miles long, extending from Maiori, just west of the town of Salerno, southward to Paestum and Agropoli. As the men clambered into landing craft and the small boats maneuvered noisily into position all around us, I could see flashes of gunfire on the north sector of the assault zone where British warships were laying down a barrage in front of the British X Corps' first wave. On the south sector the American VI Corps was attempting to land quietly without previous bombardment, but there were ominous hints that the enemy was alerted. Flares and the flames of demolition fires could be seen in that area as the 142nd Regimental Combat Team, led by Colonel John D. Forsythe, and the 141st Regimental Combat Team under Colonel Richard J. Werner—both of the 36th Division—felt their landing crafts touch bottom on the shore at 3:30 a.m.

Then, to end any doubt about surprise, a loudspeaker voice on the shore roared out in English, "Come on in and give up. You're covered." Flares shot high into the air to illuminate the beaches, and German guns previously sited on the beaches opened up with a roar. The assault forces came on in, but not to give up. There was resistance on every beach, and within a short time the defenders were strengthened by artillery and planes so that our opposition increased steadily as dawn approached. Some boats in the first assault wave were unable to reach their designated beaches and had to shift to other sectors, especially Red Beach, where opposition was lighter; while many of the second-wave boats were badly damaged or had to turn back on their first attempt to get ashore. Men were separated from weapons in the confusion or when their boats sank. Radio communication was difficult in most instances because of loss of equipment and the intense enemy fire.

But, owing to sound basic training and countless instances of personal bravery, the assault forces not only held on but slowly advanced inland. Men squirmed through barbed wire, around mines, and behind enemy machine guns and the tanks that soon made their appearance, working their way inland and knocking out German strong-points wherever possible as they headed for their assembly point on a railroad that roughly paralleled the beach about two miles away. Singly and in small groups, they reached their first objective by devious means. Private J. C. Jones collected fifty stragglers, guided them off the beach through heavy fire, and destroyed several enemy machine-gun posts. Sergeant Manuel S. Gonzales wriggled on his belly through heavy rifle fire and grenade bursts and, with his own grenades, killed an 88-mm. gun crew. Private James M. Logan killed three Germans who rushed at him, firing rifles, from a wall, shot nearby machine gunners, and turned the weapon on the rest of the gun crew as they fled. Lieutenant Clair F. Carpenter and Corporal Edgar L. Blackburn, manning a 75-mm. self-propelled howitzer, in a defile swept by enemy fire from both flanks, knocked out a machine-gun nest and a tank before they were cut down by a heavy burst of fire. There were countless other acts of heroism.

Under great difficulties, heavy weapons were being landed by dawn. Ducks brought in 105-mm. howitzers of the 133rd Field Artillery Battalion, and the 151st Field Artillery Battalion landed at 6 a.m., just in time to beat off a dangerous German tank assault on the beachhead. The veteran 531st Shore Engineers began organizing the communication and supply lines, and bull-dozer men, ignoring a steady fire which inflicted many casualties among them, built exit routes for vehicles to move from the beaches through the sand dunes.

In this manner our toehold on Fortress Europa was gained, and no soldiers ever fought more bravely than the men of the 36th Division. I have spoken of their landing in detail both because it was the most difficult, since they were untested troops, and because they were among the first Americans to put foot on Hitler-held Continental Europe; but I do not want to seem to overlook the tremendous job that the rest of the Fifth Army was doing at the same time. The British veterans performed in splendid fashion.

On the bridge of the *Ancon,* it was a long time before we could begin to put together a picture that told us much, or that would give me an affirmative answer to Admiral Hewitt's question, "Are you ready to take over?" In an assault from the sea the first problem is to win elbow room so that enemy fire can be reduced on the beaches, supplies unloaded, and command posts and communications set up. During that difficult period, the beachmaster is a key man. A good beachmaster must be the symbol of authority, the traffic cop and the brains of early landing operations, and at Salerno I had one of the best in Brigadier General Mike O'Daniel. Out of the chaos he slowly molded a traffic system that could handle the incoming boats while the first assault fanned out to widen our grip ashore and knock out the artillery and tanks that kept the beach under fire. Signs went up to identify landing spots, radio contacts were established with the *Ancon* and other ships, naval fire was directed against enemy positions, guns and supplies began to roll, and wounded were collected and evacuated to ships.

At this point the first serious crisis was about over, but since then I have frequently wondered what would have happened if the Germans had possessed an atomic bomb which they could have dropped on our beachhead just as our operations emerged from the chaotic first phase of disorganization. Certainly the crowded, busy beachhead, as well as the adjacent waters, would have been a perfect target for such a blow; the result might well have been disastrous to our attack.

In any event, our assault progressed slowly, and by nightfall of the first day, with air cover from our Sicily bases, I felt that we had achieved as much as could be expected. On our north sector, British Commandos and American Rangers under Lieutenant Colonel William O. Darby, an outstanding battle leader, had been highly successful in surprising the enemy and seizing high ground near Maiori as the anchor of our left flank. This was of the greatest importance because it provided us with a vantage point for observation and artillery fire, and denied it to the enemy. The Germans counterattacked there repeatedly in the following days, but Darby's fine leadership and the determination of his men turned back all assaults; with later reinforcements, they held their ground and played a vital role in the battle, and later in the capture of Naples.

On the right flank of the Commandos, the British 46th and 56th Divisions landed at two points flanking Montecorvino Airfield. McCreery sent combat teams toward the town of Salerno in coordination with a Commando attack on the town and directed the remainder of his forces toward Montecorvino, three miles inland, and on toward the town of Battipaglia. They encountered heavy enemy fire on the beaches and had to fight, with the aid of naval gunfire, almost all the way against very stubborn resistance by the 64th Panzer Grenadier Regiment. The British veterans were up to the job, however, and by nightfall our forces were in Salerno and patrols were in Montecorvino and Battipaglia.

There was a ten-mile gap between the British X Corps and the American VI Corps at the end of the day's struggle, but that did not seem too serious.

The 36th Division, in its first test in battle, had won control of the plain south of the Sele River and had pushed on into high ground for an average penetration of about five miles. Only on the American extreme right flank, in the direction of Agropoli, had we failed to make much progress, but even there vicious enemy counterattacks had been successfully repulsed. By nightfall, I could feel that we had secured the beaches and were in a position to close the gap between X and VI Corps and to start the drive for the dominated mountain heights which we must seize and through which we must pass toward Naples.

On the following day, September 10, it became clear that the main German strength was massed on our left, against the British X Corps, which met strong opposition as it attempted to press inland from Salerno on the most direct route toward Naples. The Americans, on the other hand, were able to push farther inland and occupy an important range of hills from Altavilla to Ogliastro. The enemy, having failed in his tank attacks in that sector on D-day, had withdrawn except in a corridor formed by the Sele and Calore rivers. In that corridor, the main objective of the 45th Division was to seize an important bridge known as the Ponte Sele, about thirteen miles inland on a good highway. Its 179th Regimental Combat Team was ordered to advance northeastward and seize the Ponte Sele and the nearby hills, while the 142nd pushed into the town of Altavilla. The 179th, which had landed in the morning, moved out late on the evening of the tenth, dividing into two columns, one of which (the 2nd Battalion) advanced south of the Calore River, while the other (led by the 3rd Battalion) crossed the Calore and proceeded via Persano on a more direct northerly route toward the Ponte Sele.

The 2nd Battalion, after a four-mile march at night, forded the Calore River about three miles south of the Ponte Sele, but was counterattacked so viciously by tanks and infantry of the 29th Pioneer Battalion, plus artillery fire, that by noon it had been forced to withdraw to the south side of the Calore.

The 3rd Battalion, supported by the 1st Battalion, meanwhile had moved northward toward Persano, delayed only by a flaming bridge across the Calore, which became known thereafter as the Burned Bridge. Bypassing this obstacle, the battalions continued on to Persano and swung to the right toward the Ponte Sele without stopping to occupy the high ground at Persano. They passed many wrecked and burned German vehicles, tanks, and guns, and after a brief clash with the enemy reached the river bluffs overlooking the Ponte Sele. At this point a German tank attack turned them back.

I mention these details because they are essential to an understanding of what happened at Salerno, where it was difficult even after the battle had been fully reported for anyone except the men engaged to know how gravely disaster threatened the first Allied assault on European soil. And, even in the course of battle, we did not fully realize how great was the advantage of the Germans in holding all the high hills surrounding our beachhead, from which they continually were looking down our throats. Not until months later, when I had occasion to fly low over the German positions at Salerno, did I wholly realize how well the enemy had been able to observe our movements and thus shift his strength and artillery to oppose our thrusts. In this respect the German advantage was nothing less than appalling.

It was under such circumstances that the 45th Division had extended two fingers out from our beachhead toward the Ponte Sele, and it was there that the Germans hit the ends of those fingers and turned them back. At the same time the enemy struck at the British in a fight for control of Montecorvino Airport and the town of Battipaglia, and at the American 142nd Regiment at Altavilla. The first phase of our success was over by the afternoon of September 11, and the bitter struggle had begun between the main Allied and German forces.

I had gone ashore on September 10, the day after the initial landings, principally to select a place to land the 157th Regimental Combat Team, which was in my floating reserve. General Walker, in command of the 36th, had been reporting directly to me on the *Ancon,* rather than to General Dawley in order to avoid delaying decisions until Dawley got his headquarters with its communications ashore. I found Walker's situation favorable and morale appeared to be high.

On the beach I also found Mike, the German police dog, which had been presented to me at Oujda. There was a strict rule against taking dogs on the transports, but, unknown to me, Sergeant Chaney had put a tag on Mike's collar and turned her over to some soldiers before they went aboard ship. The tag said, "This is General Clark's dog. She is going to Salerno." Mike got there all right and on D-day was leaping up and down the beach so happily that she got in the way and had to be tied up.

Later, I visited General McCreery's X Corps headquarters and we decided to reinforce the Rangers under Darby on his left flank and to land the 157th Regimental Combat Team on the British right flank in order to start closing the gap between the British and American forces. The situation looked so good that I sent a message to General Alexander saying that we soon should be ready to make the attack northward through Vietri Pass toward Naples. This proved to be an optimistic outlook because from then on things began to happen.

The first thing that happened was that, upon my return to the *Ancon,* I ordered the 157th RCT landed on the British right flank, only to be told that it already was being unloaded in the American sector south of the Sele River. As I related earlier, Hewitt had been forced to order it ashore in my absence because his superiors in Algiers wanted the barges sent back at once. Consequently, I had to delay other units in order to get the 157th shifted to its proper position.

On the following day, as I was preparing to go ashore again, the cruiser *Savannah* passed within about two hundred yards of the *Ancon*. I was on the *Ancon* bridge, and had paused to watch the cruiser, when we heard a terrific screeching noise that indicated the approach of a new type of German bomb. Although we could see no planes, we had heard these bombs the previous day and believed, correctly, that they were radio controlled. On this occasion, as the noise grew louder, it seemed to be heading directly toward the *Ancon*. I have no doubt that it actually was aimed at our easily identified flagship, but there was nothing much we could do except wait. Then, at the last moment, it hit the *Savannah,* just forward of her bridge, with a tremendous crash. The missile went through the cruiser's deck and exploded below, shooting flames high into the air and causing several hundred casualties on the warship.

General Dawley had moved his headquarters ashore by the time I reached the beach again and reports were coming in concerning difficulty with the 45th Division's thrusts toward the Ponte Sele. The British also were meeting stiff counterattacks and their patrols had been forced out of Battipaglia. I instructed McCreery to reduce the area he was assigned, in order to mass his strength, and arranged with Dawley to shift troops from the south to meet the increased enemy strength in the northern sector along the Sele River.

When I returned to the *Ancon*—it was still not feasible to set up my headquarters ashore—I received a message from Alexander that added another chapter to the story of the 82nd Airborne Division, which had been taken away from me at the last minute to drop on Rome. We frequently had wondered how that venture came out, and it was something of a surprise when Alexander said he wanted me to know that I could "use the 82nd in any manner you deem advisable. All combatant elements of the 82nd are now concentrated at Sicilian airfields."

This was the first word I had received that the Rome drop had been called off. I found out later that Taylor's conference with Marshal Badoglio and others in Rome had convinced him that the Italian Government could not in any way produce the assistance that it had previously promised to the 82nd Airborne Division if it were dropped in the vicinity of Rome. Since the German counterattacks were becoming steadily stronger, I was only too happy to have the paratroops available. We arranged for some of them to drop near the town of Avellino on the evening of the thirteenth, in order to strike at the enemy rear lines.

The following morning, which was September 12, I moved my headquarters ashore. A large mansion that stuck up like a sore thumb had been selected, but I decided it would be better to use my trailer and picked out a spot in a wood a little farther to the south. I spent much of the day on the road in a jeep, moving from sector to sector, through clouds of dust that were churned up by the bursting of bombs and shells and by the heavy traffic of vehicles over narrow and unpaved roads. Although we were only a step from the clear, cool Mediterranean, the dust hung over us like a fog. We breathed dust and ate dust. Our clothes and bodies were covered with it. Some of the vehicle drivers invented a sort of mask that they strapped over their faces to protect themselves. I found that it frequently was necessary to tie a handkerchief over my face in order to breathe as I traveled about. I sometimes must have given the impression of a tall and dirty western bandit on the prowl.

The dust was uncomfortable, but nothing compared to the discomfort that the enemy was causing. The two fingers which the 45th Division had stuck out toward the Ponte Sele were being badly bruised, and it appeared they might be cut off. The 157th RCT, under Colonel Charles Ankcorn, which had been shifted to the British flank after being landed in the wrong sector, was instructed to advance along the Sele River to a tobacco factory on high ground near Persano, where it would be able to protect the flank of the northerly finger which the 45th Division had exposed.

Ankcorn soon discovered that the Germans had infiltrated across the river and occupied Persano and had tanks and machine guns concealed in and around the tobacco factory, where our tanks fell into a trap and were caught in a devastating fire that knocked out five of the seven involved. Thus, the high ground near Persano, which the 179th RCT was unable to occupy as it struck toward the Ponte Sele, was now held by the enemy and served as a kind of spear thrust into the center of our entire beachhead. If the Germans could push that spear forward to the sea, they would divide the American VI Corps from the British X Corps and gain ground from which to try to turn both flanks.

Kesselring, having gathered reinforcements, immediately set out to exploit this possibility. He sent elements of the 26th Panzer Division, the 29th Panzer Grenadier Division, and the 16th Panzer Division southward against the north flank of VI Corps, while the Hermann Göring Division and units of the 15th Panzer Grenadier Division and the 3rd Panzer Grenadier Division attempted to drive the British X Corps from the Montecorvino area. Fighting on September 12 was approaching a new peak all along the front. A strong enemy attack drove the 1st Battalion of the 142nd Infantry out of Altavilla, a vital high point in the American sector. A similar thrust on the British front forced us to abandon Battipaglia. In the center of the beachhead heavy fighting swung back and forth around the tobacco factory, and elements of the 45th Division which had been pushed back from the Ponte Sele were in danger of being isolated. It was becoming obvious that General Dawley had not been fully aware of the strength of the enemy on his left flank and had not taken steps or been able to take steps to protect himself from counterattack in that sector after the failure of our thrusts toward Ponte Sele and Battipaglia. Furthermore, as the counterattacks developed, it was disclosed that all the troops had been committed in a cordon defense, leaving none in reserve to meet an enemy breakthrough. We were getting into a very tight place.

I recall that about this time I had to consider the possibility that we would be driven back to the sea. A commander always is supposed to have an alternate plan, and I felt that if it came to a point where we had to abandon part of the beachhead, we should be able to evacuate some troops by sea to the British sector and continue the fight from there. It was routine in such circumstances as we then faced to issue orders for the destruction, if necessary, of all supplies and equipment on the beaches. I went down to look over the vast piles of supplies on the beach and to recall the stern admonitions that had been drilled into us in school about taking precautions to prevent stores from falling into the hands of the enemy. I knew that if I were involved in a theoretical problem at the War College, I would at this point get hell from some instructor if I failed to issue orders to be prepared for possible destruction of those supplies; but this wasn't a theoretical problem, and I couldn't see how I'd do anything but damage morale if I issued such orders at Salerno. I thought it over carefully as I walked along the beach. I was dirty and tired and worried, and finally I said to hell with the theory. I'm not going to issue any such orders. Furthermore, I decided, the only way they're going to get us off this beach is to push us, step by step, into the water.

The next day, I thought for a while that they were going to do exactly that. I began the day by sending a message to Alexander telling him to call off plans we had made to drop elements of the 82nd Airborne at Avellino that night. Then I wrote a letter to Major General Ridgway, commanding the 82nd Division, saying that the fight for the Salerno beachhead had taken a turn for the worse and that it was a touch-and-go affair. I said I had learned only the day before that the 82nd had not dropped on Rome and that it now was available to me.

"I want you to accept this letter as an order," I wrote, knowing that Matt Ridgway was the kind of a commander you could count on. "I realize the time normally needed to prepare for a drop, but this is an exception. I want you to make a drop within our lines on the beachhead and I want you to make it tonight. This is a must."

I added a few other details in order to be sure Ridgway would understand why I asked the impossible: that he make a drop within a few hours after he had received the letter. Then I sent someone out to find a fighter pilot. A number of pilots—part of the crew that gave us good support throughout the Salerno operation—had landed from time to time on a hastily prepared strip south of the Sele River. One of them on that day was Captain Jacob R. Hamilton, who was on a tactical reconnaissance flight. He volunteered to carry my letter to Sicily and was given maps which would show Ridgway exactly where to drop his men. Hamilton took off immediately for Licata in Sicily.

Meanwhile, I got busy with messages and orders designed to relieve the situation at the front, where the enemy attacks continued on an increasingly strong scale. Ironically, we heard a broadcast over the British Broadcasting Company that suggested that General Montgomery's Eighth Army was dashing up the Italian boot to our rescue. The BBC was about all our men on the Salerno beachhead could get on their radios, and such broadcasts, naturally, I suppose, presented the news with a strong British slant. This eventually proved pretty irritating at times, particularly as the Eighth Army was making a slow advance toward Salerno, despite Alexander's almost daily efforts to prod it into greater speed.

Later General Dawley telephoned me and reported that the Germans had broken through the Persano sector and were fanning out in our rear areas. It was the first word I had had that such a critical situation had developed at that point.

"What are you doing about it?" I asked. "What can you do?"

"Nothing," he replied. "I have no reserves. All I've got is a prayer."

That was the beginning of a couple of days of real nightmare for me and a lot of other people. What had happened was that Kesselring had sent a strong attack, led by tanks, against both flanks of the 1st Battalion, 157th Infantry, at Persano, where our line ran along the Sele River. In midafternoon German tanks hit the battalion on the left flank and others, followed by elements of the 79th Panzer Grenadier Regiment and supported by towed artillery, hit the right flank. The fighting was intense for a couple of hours, after which German tanks slipped down a draw, caught our men by surprise, temporarily trapped the battalion headquarters, and eventually forced our lines back enough to let the main German force across the Sele River.

The enemy column divided at Persano, one part of it striking northeast against the 2nd Battalion, 143rd Infantry, which simultaneously was hit by a German attack from the opposite flank and soon became completely isolated. The main enemy thrust from Persano, however, was due south about two miles toward the Burned Bridge. In effect, Kesselring was now pushing forward the spear which had been thrust into the center of our beachhead perimeter, and he might well drive it clear to the sea, splitting the American and British sectors. He had, furthermore, picked the sector where we were least able to meet such an attack.

Late in the afternoon the Germans pressed steadily along the dusty road toward the Burned Bridge, while their artillery moved into Persano to support the advance, and their infantry made heavy attacks on both sides of the gap to preclude any hope of closing it in time to cut them off. At six-thirty o'clock, fifteen Nazi tanks reached the heavy underbrush on the north side of the Calore River, where its juncture with the Sele formed the bottom of the Sele-Calore corridor adjacent to the Burned Bridge.

At this point we were almost certainly at the mercy of Kesselring, provided he massed his strength and threw it at us relentlessly. It is possible he never realized his opportunity, or that he feared a trap, but, considering merely the logic of the situation, it would have been agreed by any military expert that we didn't have much with which to stop him. Well, that's not quite true. There were some military men in the path of the German tank spearhead who would not have agreed. They were the men of the 189th Field Artillery Battalion, under Lieutenant Colonel Hal L. Muldrow, Jr., and the 158th Field Artillery Battalion, under Lieutenant Colonel Russell D. Funk, both from the 45th Division.

The two battalions were on the south bank of the Calore, where a gentle slope runs down to the Burned Bridge. They stripped their gun crews to a minimum and sent men down that slope with rifles and machine guns to dig in. They posted six 37 mm. guns to support the men. They went out on the nearby roads and began stopping trucks, jeeps and everything else that came along. Every soldier who got out of the vehicles was given a gun and put in the line. They collected an emergency reserve of mechanics and truck drivers to go into action at any point where a break was threatened.

There was a hill on their flank that might have offered the enemy a vantage point; but by the time I had discovered the immediate situation there were no troops left to take it over, so I ordered a regimental band armed and sent there immediately. The hill didn't have any name and there was some confusion about designating it until I pointed it out and told them to call it Piccolo Peak, because there was nobody there but the musicians.

By this time, the German tanks were firing on the positions of the 189th

Field Artillery Battalion in preparation for crossing the Calore near the Burned Bridge; and by this time, too, the sweating, dust-coated men of the two battalions were ready. They opened up with everything they had.

The ford beside the bridge and the road leading to it simply went up in dust. The fields and the woods in which the enemy tanks took cover were pulverized. When the Germans tried to fight their way across the ford, the fire laid down by everybody from the artillerymen to the piccolo player knocked them back on their heels. At one time the two battalions were firing eight rounds per minute per gun, and they acted as if they could keep it up all night if necessary and someone passed the ammunition.

After several unsuccessful thrusts, the enemy column wavered and began to fall back. By sunset the two battalions had fired 3,650 rounds and seven guns of Battery B, 27th Armored Field Artillery, had arrived in time to fire another 300 rounds. A few minutes later, the Germans were in full retreat from the Burned Bridge and the artillery was feeling fine. I was feeling somewhat better myself, although I knew that we were far from being out of the woods.

When I got back to my headquarters, it was obvious that we had narrowly escaped disaster that day and that we were still in a difficult position all around the front. On the north, or British sector, the enemy had infiltrated in the direction of Maiori and the situation was critical around Vietri Pass, with reinforcements needed at once. But it was on the American sector that we had suffered most and were most urgently in need of reorganization before we could withstand another attack. Elements of the 142nd and 143 RCTs had been thrown back from Altavilla; Company K, 143rd, was cut off; the 1st Battalion of the 142nd had lost all but sixty of its men; the 2nd Battalion, 143rd, had been beaten up in the Sele-Calore corridor and lost 508 officers and men; and the 157th's 1st Battalion had been badly bruised west of Persano, where the Germans had seized the key tobacco factory buildings on high ground.

We spent the night reorganizing and pulled back our lines to tighten our defenses. There was only one encouraging factor. Hamilton had returned from his trip to Licata, where he had delivered my message to Ridgway. Actually, Ridgway had left the field in a C-47 just before Hamilton arrived, but the pilot dashed up to the tower and got them to call the general's plane, explaining he had an important message from me. Ridgway came back at once and after a couple of hours' study sent Hamilton back to Salerno with the message I had expected—"Can do." Hamilton landed on our makeshift strip and caught a jeep ride to my headquarters, but when eight strafing enemy planes flew along the road he was forced to dive out of the jeep and dislocated his shoulder. He flew his own plane back to Sicily, however, after delivering Ridgway's message.

About the same time I received urgent messages from Ridgway and Alexander saying that not only would the 82nd Airborne troops be landed inside our lines, but that the drop previously scheduled for Avellino would also be carried out the next night in order to harass the enemy's rear.

"Vitally important," Ridgway emphasized, "that all ground and naval forces in your zone and in Gulf of Salerno, respectively, be directed to hold fire tonight. Rigid control of antiaircraft fire is absolutely essential for success."

I replied that orders had been issued, but just to be sure I sent staff officers to every battery to be certain that all fire was halted at midnight, the hour set for the drop. I knew Ridgway's men had been fired on by Allied gunners and had suffered losses during the invasion of Sicily, and I didn't want it to happen again. At the scheduled hour, every gun on the beachhead was silent. Then we could hear the roar of planes coming—but it was the wrong kind of a roar, and coming from the wrong direction! Just at that moment the Germans had chosen to make a raid! For five minutes, they roared up and down the beach, strafing and bombing; not a gun fired on them. We just sat there and took it.

Five minutes later—just ten minutes behind schedule—the American transports came over the beaches and the men of the 504th Paratroop Regiment, under Colonel Ruben Tucker, a real fighting soldier, plummeted down through the darkness to join our badly battered defense lines. By the next morning they were in action on the Altavilla sector, where they lived up to their fine reputation.

The next day was September 14, and all day the German attacks continued in strength against our new defense lines, which had been drastically shortened and reorganized during the night. The 36th Division was subjected to new enemy onslaughts and the 45th Division, holding a line west of the Sele River, was under heavy attack along the sector where, by our realignment, we had closed the gap between the American and British forces. On the British sector, the 46th Division dug in on the hills around the town of Salerno; the 56th Division was in an open plain southeast of Battipaglia, where the enemy had excellent observation of its movements and was able to send repeated tank thrusts against the Coldstream Guards of the 201st Guards Brigade and the 9th Royal Fusiliers of the 167th Infantry Brigade.

Early in the day, following a conference with General Dawley at 7 a.m., Sergeant Holden drove me by jeep, with my aide, Captain Warren Thrasher, to the front sectors. We drove along the highway to a small road that paralleled the south bank of the Sele and thence followed the front line eastward at the critical point where the German breakthrough of the day before had been finally halted. We stopped at points where small units had been posted on the shortened front line; it was evident that officers and men had taken a severe drubbing and were tired. Everywhere we stopped I talked to as many of the men as possible, telling them that the situation was improved, reinforcements were arriving, and that this was where we quit giving ground.

"There mustn't be any doubt in your minds," I said. "We don't give another inch. This is it. Don't yield anything. We're here to stay."

There was plenty of spirit left in the men when they understood the situation, and I felt that they would be equal to the order of the day, to hang on, which I had issued earlier.

At one point we went forward to a hill near the spot where our most-forward elements were dug in. Climbing to the top of the hill, I studied the rough terrain ahead of us in the hope of finding some of our forces still hanging on in that sector. There were no such hopeful signs, but I did see eighteen tanks beginning to infiltrate our lines. For a moment I hoped they were ours, but studying them through binoculars I soon discovered they were German. It also was obvious that they had found a weak spot in our lines and that if they were merely the spearhead of a big tank attack, we were again in the utmost danger of being split apart and crushed. Anxiously I searched the rear area for indications of other tank columns. I couldn't see any—but that didn't mean they were not there. I could not imagine that Kesselring would fail to exploit this opportunity to rush up powerful armor and break through to the sea.

We hurried back to our own lines and called up an antitank unit that I previously had seen there and an engineer unit that was not far away. They were able to get into favorable positions quickly, and laid down a heavy fire that turned back the eighteen tanks. I still can't understand why such an able general as Kesselring failed to carry through on that occasion with a stronger attack force, or why he used his plentiful armor—he originally had probably six hundred tanks at Salerno—in piecemeal fashion at critical stages of the battle. I can't understand it, but I can be thankful for it. Looking back, I often feel that this lapse on the part of Kesselring was all that saved us from disaster.

At another point on the day's journey, I passed a line of trucks coming back from the front sector and noticed that the men were wearing gas masks. At first I thought that some of the drivers were wearing their masks because of the extreme dustiness, but when I saw all of them had on masks I stopped the first truck and asked the driver why.

"Gas!" he exclaimed, motioning back toward the front. It flashed through my mind that there had been a long argument before the Italian invasion over whether the men should take their gas masks ashore, since it usually happened that in action they threw them away or "lost" them in order to lighten their packs.

"Where's the gas?" I asked. "Who said so?"

"Somewhere up front," he said. "I don't know who said so."

Since there obviously wasn't any gas around us at the time, I made them take off their masks, and later discovered that it was, as I had expected, a false alarm. Since everybody was on edge at the time, it was the kind of rumor that easily could spread and cause serious trouble.

My tour of the front ended with the 157th and 179th Regimental Combat Teams of the 45th Division. These troops had been in the Sicilian campaign and were doing a fine job. They were well led by Major General Troy Middleton, the division commander. They had good liaison with their artillery and in the period of an hour that morning had knocked out thirteen enemy tanks. We were under artillery and small-arms fire most of the time we were talking to the men of these two regiments; but they went about their jobs in workmanlike fashion, and I had every confidence that they would stand their ground. They did. And so did other outfits all along the front, where the enemy had been turned back time after time in desperate fighting.

We were getting excellent air support throughout the day, with big-scale attacks against German formations and heavy bombing of their supply lines, troop concentrations, and dumps. British warships also moved up close to fire their big 15-inch rifles at enemy positions, with devastating effect. On the night of the fourteenth, reinforcements arrived by air and by sea, and the 509th Parachute Battalion dropped near Avellino, under command of Lieutenant Colonel Doyle R. Yardley, to strike at the German rear lines. Yardley was wounded, but the outfit did a wonderful job. Since it was not possible for us to advance immediately to make contact with them, I was criticized for carrying out such a hazardous operation as the Avellino drop, which was the first one made behind the enemy lines. It was true that it appeared for a while that the 509th suffered heavy losses. Very few of the men got through to our lines; but they turned out to be capable soldiers and hid in the hills in small groups, often with the aid of Italian families. They made many raids that seriously disrupted the German communications, and within two months 80 percent of the battalion was safely back within the American lines. Considering the hazards of merely existing on the Salerno beachhead at that time, the mission of the 509th paid off in big dividends.

That night, after about forty-eight hours in which I hadn't taken off my clothes, I began to feel that we would pull out of the hole into which we had fallen. It was a help, too, to get a letter from Eisenhower, in which he said:

> We know you are having a sticky time, but you may be sure that everybody is working at full speed to provide the reinforcements you need. ... In the meantime, don't forget that we have an Air Force that is more than anxious to do its full part in your support. I hope that your bombline* will be drawn as accurately as possible along your front so that our Air Force can continue to disrupt the forces trying to concentrate against you.
>
> You and your people have done a magnificent job. We are all proud of you and since the success of the whole operation depends upon you and your forces, you need have no fear that anything will be neglected in providing you all possible assistance.

It is difficult now to describe how important it was at that time to receive such a message and to know that we could count on the unqualified support of all that it was possible for Ike to throw into the battle. We were in a pinch, but in the pinch the Allied forces didn't let any ordinary considerations or differences of opinion stand in the way of unlimited cooperative action. Ike stated it well in his letter; Alexander made the same idea clear in his messages to me; and all branches of the armed services—British and American—made it evident in their contributions to the battle of Salerno.

Alexander, accompanied by Air Marshal Sir Arthur Coningham, arrived from Bizerte on a destroyer on September 15 and came to my headquarters for breakfast. I had set up a mess for my staff and for the British and French officers attached to it, but shortly afterward I decided that the arrangement was not satisfactory from my point of view. It gave me little time to myself and little chance to get away from the heavy pressure of work, so I arranged for Sergeant Chaney to prepare my meals at my trailer office. This system I continued throughout the Italian campaign. Chaney was a good cook and I could invite a friend or two whenever I chose, or be alone when I felt like it. Or we could, when necessary, serve a meal for Churchill, Ike, or the King of England—and Chaney did it for those distinguished people.

Alexander appeared to be satisfied that we had overcome the crisis created by Kesselring's counterattacks and that we could soon take the offensive toward Naples. We visited Dawley's headquarters and later went by PT boat to McCreery's sector, where we visited parts of the front and got a good look at the rugged area in which the British 46th Division, under Major General John L. I. Hawkesworth, was still engaged in bitter fighting southeast of Salerno.

---

* Line designated to avoid bombing of our own troops.

Now I had time to give attention to a matter that had bothered me during the Salerno battle. It concerned Dawley. After consultation with Alexander, we were in accord that a change in command of VI Corps was necessary. I had taken steps to put General Ridgway in as deputy to Dawley in order to be of the maximum possible assistance. When Ike came to Salerno a couple of days later, I reported the situation to him. He concurred with my views that a change would be to the best interest of all concerned and said he would arrange for Major General John P. Lucas to replace Dawley. By that time the immediate crisis on the beachhead was resolved, and on September 20 I informed Dawley of the situation, relieved him of command and directed him to report to Eisenhower.

Meantime, I had received several letters by courier from General Montgomery detailing his progress up the coast toward our beachhead and suggesting, on September 15, that "perhaps you could push out a reconnaissance along the road from Agropoli to meet my people, who have already started from Sapri. . . . It looks as if you may be having not too good a time and I do hope that all will go well with you. We are on the way to lend a hand and it will be a great day when we actually join hands."

I replied that "it will be a pleasure to see you again at an early date. Situation here well in hand." But in view of the fact that we had narrowly escaped being pushed into the sea, I didn't mention his optimistic idea of sending out a reconnaissance party.

On September 16, I radioed to Ike, giving him some details of the rapidly changing situation and explaining how the force of the German counterattack had hit the 36th Division. I added, "We are in good shape now. We are here to stay. This morning we have restored the salient between the Sele River and the Calore. I am reinforcing Darby's force [on our left flank in the Sorrento region]. Darby has done his usual grand job and I recommend that he be promoted to the grade of colonel. . . . I am prepared to attack Naples. We have made mistakes and we have learned the hard way, but we will improve every day and am sure we will not disappoint you."

I then reported the first totaling of casualties in approximately a week of fighting. It showed that the British X Corps, which had performed so well against the hardest blows Kesselring could strike, had suffered 531 killed, 1,915 wounded and 1,561 missing. The American VI Corps, with a little greater than half as many men engaged as the British, had lost 225 killed, 853 wounded and 589 missing. Most of those listed as missing in both corps later turned up safe.

Alexander returned to my headquarters on September 21, when he outlined future plans for the 15th Army Group. Running his finger along the map of Italy, he indicated a boundary between my Fifth Army and Montgomery's Eighth Army. The Fifth Army was to seize Naples and without pause cross the Volturno River and work up the western side of the mountainous peninsula while Montgomery advanced along the eastern side. Polish, French, Italian, and other units were to join our offensive; it appeared that we would have about fourteen divisions, which probably would be slightly more than the number of German divisions opposing us.

By the following day, it was apparent that the Germans were withdrawing and that we would be opposed principally by strong delaying tactics in the advance through the mountain passes to Naples. On that day we also received the first of the censorship-guidance instructions, which henceforth came daily from Fifteenth Army Group Headquarters. These instructions laid down the broad outline for our daily communiqués, specifying which towns might be mentioned and indicating the general line to be followed for security reasons. They often reflected political factors, too, particularly in reference to the units of various nationalities that were being collected in our army group. On this occasion, Lieutenant Colonel Kenneth Clark, the Fifth Army public relations officer, showed me a guidance cable that said: "First, play up the Eighth Army progress henceforth. Second, the Fifth Army is pushing the enemy back on his right flank. Americans may be mentioned. There should be no suggestion that the enemy has made good his getaway."

When men have just been through a bruising battle such as the Fifth Army had experienced, it is difficult for them to understand the reasons, if there are any, for instructions to play down their activities and play up the operations of someone else. It wasn't easy for me to understand either, particularly when we were all set to resume our drive into rugged terrain, where we were certain to have difficult going regardless of the enemy withdrawal. Such instructions, however, became a regular part of the campaign, and on many occasions we had a hard time writing a communiqué within the limitations laid down for security or other reasons.

Our thirty-mile advance to Naples was anything but easy. Cold rains made progress slow. Kesselring was a master of delaying tactics. His use of artillery was highly effective in the mountainous region through which we had to pass. Small rear-guard detachments of motorized German infantry dug in their machine guns on important hillsides while their riflemen on higher ground forced us to make wide, time-consuming envelopments almost every mile of the way. As we did so, the enemy artillery harassed our columns. Often one 88-mm. gun, properly placed, could deliver fire along an entire valley floor and might not be knocked out for many hours. Mud added to our woes, and with trucks mired down soldiers and pack mules had to move supplies over rugged hills. Blown bridges and mines were constant problems; each hillside became a small but difficult military problem that could be solved only by careful preparation and almost inevitably by the spilling of blood.

While this advance was in progress, General Montgomery paid his first visit to my headquarters and we discussed future operations. The Eighth Army commander said that his forces were greatly extended and that their build-up of supplies was not sufficient to enable him to give any direct support to the Fifth Army as it swung westward toward Naples. He therefore planned to establish a supply base near Bari, but could not get moving before about October 1 toward the important Foggia airfields.

The British general was rather formal in his explanation, but when he had finished I said, "The Fifth Army is just a young outfit trying to get along, while your Eighth Army is a battle-tried veteran. We would appreciate having you teach us some of your tricks."

This apparently pleased Monty, and his visit went along after that on a very friendly and cooperative basis. When the newspapermen and photographers came around later, he was in a good mood.

"We are going up Italy side by side," he said. "Where we shall spend Christmas, I don't know. A war correspondent wanted, however, to bet me five shillings that the war would be over by Christmas. I have taken his bet. He didn't say what year."

Just as he was ready to leave, Montgomery spoke to me confidentially.

"Do you know Alexander well?" he asked.

"No," I said.

"Well, I do. From time to time you will get instructions from Alex that you won't understand. When you do, just tell him to go to hell."

I thought this over for a moment and replied, "I've got a better idea, General. If I have that trouble, I'll tell you about it and let you tell Alex for me."

"I'll be delighted," Montgomery beamed as he climbed into a jeep and waved goodbye.

A day or two later, Brigadier General Fred A. Blesse, chief surgeon of the North African Theater of Operations, visited my headquarters and I had an opportunity to express my appreciation for the admirable manner in which the medical services performed at Salerno. Prior to the invasion there had been a difference of opinion between the British and the Americans over whether nurses should be landed on the beachhead. The British were opposed, but I decided that when the American hospitals went in the nurses should go along. They did and under the most difficult conditions they carried out their jobs like veterans. The hospital units were landed, set up and receiving patients in a minimum time, and the presence of the nurses and their Red Cross colleagues was an invaluable morale booster throughout the Italian campaign.

By September 28, our preparations for the final thrust into Naples had been completed. Colonel Darby, on the Sorrento-Salerno ridge, was heavily reinforced by elements of the 82nd Airborne, and under the leadership of Ridgway the whole force broke out into the plain of Naples. The British X Corps at the same time drove into Castellammare, on the south coast of the Bay of Naples, and the following day worked their way around Mount Vesuvius.

On that day, Colonel Frank Knox, Secretary of the Navy, visited our headquarters. I was pleased to see him, for he was the first visitor we had received from the States after our grueling initiation into battle. He brought a message of encouragement from President Roosevelt and told us the people at home realized the difficulty of our mission and were proud of our accomplishments to date. This word helped a lot. Soon thereafter we received General Juin, in command of the French Expeditionary Corps that was to join the Fifth Army. On October 1, Juin and I drove up toward the front, working our way slowly toward Naples in the hope of seeing something of the action near the outskirts. We were surprised that we took so long to get to the forward elements, and eventually I discovered that we were in San Giovanni, on the southern outskirts of the city. There we met the British 23rd Armored Brigade and General Ridgway, who told me that our leading elements had entered Naples.

Strangely enough, I found this was embarrassing to me at the moment because I wanted to enter the city, but did not feel that it would be politic to enter with General Juin at my side, in view of the fact that the French troops had not yet participated in the battle. I therefore had to leave Juin. Then I climbed into an armored car and, with General Ridgway and an escort from the 82nd Airborne, drove into the city.

After we captured the dominant peaks overlooking Naples, our final swoop down from the hills on to the plains had been rapid; and although the enemy had carried out tremendous destruction, he had been denied a chance to complete his work. Fortunately, from my viewpoint, we had prepared ahead of time for the occupation. Some days earlier we had been advised of a serious shortage of food and medical supplies in the city, and had made arrangements not only to cope with any trouble that might arise among the civilian population, but to alleviate their hardships as rapidly as possible.

It must be remembered that Naples was not only a great port, which we vitally needed, but the first large city on the Continent, with a population of three quarters of a million, to be wrested from the grip of the Germans. It was therefore particularly important that the Allied occupation should make a good impression and that word of what was done should be spread to other cities still in enemy hands. Brigadier General Edgar Erskine Hume, U.S.A., was made chief of the Allied Military Government in the city. Hume was a medical officer by profession and an extremely energetic and able administrator, eminently well qualified to deal with the Italian authorities in the handling of the multitudinous duties involved in the rehabilitation of the great city. He established a hygiene department and a fire-fighter crew, particularly trained for emergencies such as enemy aerial bombardment. I recall that even before we left Africa we got the fire marshal of London to come down to Algiers to discuss the methods the British had developed for fighting Nazi incendiary bombs, so that we would be prepared for such emergencies when we occupied Naples. In addition we had ships loaded with food, medical supplies and all sorts of construction supplies and equipment waiting outside Naples Harbor to move into port as soon as the city was in our hands.

All these elaborate preparations were in my mind when I climbed into the armored car at San Giovanni and started for the center of the city. I had long looked forward to that trip. Certainly it was a hard-won victory, but there was little that was triumphant about our journey. There had been a German air raid just as we approached the city, and I was especially conscious of the wreckage as we moved along the streets. The port area could be described only as a mess. There was utter destruction of ships, docks, and warehouses, such as not even ancient Pompeii, through which we passed earlier in the day, had ever seen.

But after our first glimpse of the city, I became aware that there was something besides the wreckage that impressed me. I felt that I was riding through ghostly streets in a city of ghosts. We didn't see a soul. There were piles of debris in the street; there were wrecked vehicles and burned-out houses; but there simply was nobody in the streets, with the exception of a few *carabinieri.*

We drove almost directly to Place Garibaldi. The King's Dragoon Guards of the British X Corps had been the first to enter Naples about 9:30 in the morning, and the 82nd Airborne already was taking over police duties, but they had so far had very little contact with the population.

I made a quick survey of the area around Place Garibaldi and still saw almost no Italians, but I was becoming conscious of the eyes that peeked out on us from behind the closed shutters of every house and every building. It was still that way as we drove out of Naples; I had a feeling that I had been seen by millions of persons, although I hardly glimpsed a civilian during the entire trip. It was an eerie sensation.

Before we left the city, I stopped long enough to send a message over the field radio that settled a small bet I had made with General Gruenther about the date we would capture Naples. It said, "Am in center of Naples. Ten bucks please."

I drove on back to my headquarters in a less-happy mood than I had expected to be in on the day we entered Naples. We had come along a rough road to get there from Salerno and we had paid a heavy price for the short progress we had made into the soft underbelly of the Axis—a price that was only partly discounted by the knowledge that the enemy had paid even more dearly. In my mind I could see the familiar map of Italy stretching northward to the Volturno River and on through the mountainous masses to Rome. It was a rough road all the way.

Rain drifting against the windshield of the jeep didn't make the picture I had in my mind any more pleasant. It would be a muddy road, too.

PARATROOPER

10.

From the Volturno to Cassino—in Mud:

October 1943–November 1943

All the way into Naples the next afternoon, October 2, the rain hammered against my jeep. Water glistened on the pale road, dripped from the walls of the smashed buildings, and formed a misty curtain over the towering sides of Mount Vesuvius. A cold wind blew the rain against the faces of the men of the 82nd Airborne Division as they patrolled the streets of the city, and spattered the civilians, who now were beginning to swarm out of their houses in search of food.

I went directly to Ridgway's headquarters and immediately went into a huddle with him, Brigadier General Hume, and Brigadier General Arthur W. Pence. Pence was an engineer officer who had gained valuable and practical experience in command of the advance section supporting American combat troops in Tunisia; he had been selected to head up the Peninsular Base Section that was to support me throughout the Italian campaign.

After we had had a chance to take a good look at Naples, we felt that the damage done by the Germans, although tremendous, was less than we had expected. They had destroyed all key rail facilities serving the city, blocked the critical rail and highway tunnels through the surrounding bluffs, and made away with practically all automotive transportation; but it was quite obvious that they had spent most of their time wrecking the port. At first glance it seemed that we might be denied use of this valuable harbor for many weeks. Ships had been scuttled at piers and at places where they blocked entry to the inner port. Warehouses, loading and unloading facilities, and utilities had been systematically demolished. To complicate matters further, the city itself was without water and electric power and its sewage system had largely been destroyed by Allied bombings.

Now, however, General Pence and his Base Section troops entered the picture to perform a miracle of reconstruction, in which the leading role was played by our engineer troops. A substantial number of engineer officers, fortunately, had had experience in the large civil works projects for which their corps has been responsible in the United States during the last 125 years. They thus were accustomed to dealing with big problems, and in this case they had no intention of being cowed, or even held up long, by the task of clearing the Port of Naples. As soon as the city was in our hands, they moved in with a complete organization of general and special construction battalions, dump truck companies, cranes, steam shovels, bulldozers, and all the vast and complicated machinery needed for the work.

Almost overnight, bulldozers began pushing roads through tons of rubble from wrecked buildings. Sunken ships were ingeniously left on the bottom of the harbor and converted in place to foundations for emergency piers. It was incredible that by October 3, some seventy-two hours after our entry into Naples, the first landing points for lighters had been provided and exit routes cleared for hauling supplies from port to dumps. On the following day the first berth for a Liberty ship was ready, and from that time on additional berths were added day by day. Within a week supplies were coming in steadily, and soon the port of Naples was handling over 20,000 tons daily.

In the following weeks we had a tremendous struggle against disease and hazards such as the time bombs planted by the Germans to destroy important buildings in the heart of the city. Thanks to Hume, who got the Italians to cooperate actively, and to Pence, whose service units quickly restored water, power, sewage, and telephone facilities, we rapidly overcame most of the obstacles in our rear area and avoided delays that would have been invaluable to the enemy.

In the rehabilitation of the port of Naples, we had the assistance of a few British Army engineers and of Rear Admiral J. Anthony V. Morse of the Royal Navy and Commodore W. A. Sullivan of the U.S. Navy, who did wonderful jobs in removing magnetic mines from the approach waters and in salvaging operations at the port. The Naples job was only one of the many achievements of the U.S. and British Army engineers in the Mediterranean Theater, although perhaps it was the most spectacular and contributed most to our efforts quickly to follow up the retreating enemy.

For several days I remained at my headquarters near Pontecagnano, although I went into Naples each day. On October 4, I flew in a Cub plane with Captain Gillespie, landing on the Boulevard Carragiola, which runs along the edge of the Bay of Naples in the heart of the city. The regular airport had not yet been cleared of mines and communications were so disrupted that Ridgway had not received notice of my arrival, so I had to commandeer a jeep to get to his headquarters. The progress of the Fifth Army beyond Naples was continuing slowly but steadily, however, and on that day I was able to send two messages that gave me a certain satisfaction. The first one was to Eisenhower saying that progress was sufficient to permit me to start moving my headquarters to Naples. The other one was to my wife in the United States saying that I'd not had any time for shopping, but that I'd give her Naples for a birthday present.

On our first Sunday in Naples, General McCreery and I and many of our staff and thousands of Fifth Army British and American soldiers, of all creeds and denominations, attended church in the great Cathedral of Naples. All of us wanted to thank God for the divine direction He had given us during our first month of desperate fighting on the Continent of Europe.

Right after church, the first German time bomb exploded in the artillery barracks occupied by the Engineer Battalion of the 82nd Airborne Division in the heart of the city. One end of the building was completely demolished. I immediately went to the scene of the blast and assisted in removing the living and dead from the ruins. I counted fourteen bodies and over fifty wounded and many more pinned beneath the wreckage. This was the first of several such incidents that occurred in Naples during the next few weeks. The seizure of Naples actually provided no pause in our drive toward Rome. Although the main enemy forces fell back to the strong defense line formed by the twisting Volturno River, this did not permit us to avoid strong delaying tactics up to that point. To continue the offensive, I still had the British X Corps and the American VI Corps, now commanded by Lucas.[*] In all, that meant about 100,000 combat troops.

Our plans called for McCreery's X Corps to advance about thirty miles northward along the fertile coastal plain to the Volturno, facing the Mount Massico ridge, with his right flank extending some fifteen or twenty miles inland. The VI Corps was to move through mountainous terrain parallel to the British and on a front of about thirty miles. This would bring it to the Volturno adjacent to the X Corps, with its front extending from the Triflisco Gap (the most logical river crossing) eastward to where the river makes a

---

[*] The X Corps included three veteran divisions: the 46th under Major General John L. I. Hawkesworth, the 56th under Major General Gerald W. R. Templer, and the 7th Armored under Major General George W. E. J. Erskine. The VI Corps included the 3rd Division under Major General Lucian K. Truscott, Jr., the 34th under Major General Charles W. Ryder, and the 45th under Major General Troy H. Middleton.

junction with the Calore River. (This, incidentally, is not the same as the small Calore River near Salerno.) The most easterly American outfit was Middleton's 45th Division, which was ordered to advance beyond the Calore in an effort to press the enemy's left flank at a point where the Volturno turns abruptly northward. Middleton ran into stiff opposition, and the 3rd Division, advancing in the center, also had a bitter struggle to drive the German rear guard across the Volturno.

In addition, winter rains, whipped by a chill wind, made all the advancing troops miserable. The 34th Division moved forward with slight opposition, but in such heavy rainstorms that its equipment was mired in the muddy mountain trails and it was impossible for it to keep to schedule.

I should mention here that a bright spot in this period was the performance of the 100th Battalion, which had recently been assigned to the 34th Division. This battalion was made up of Japanese-Americans and was to become one of the most valuable units in the Fifth Army. As the first Japanese-American unit in the United States Army, the 100th Infantry Battalion was organized in the vicinity of Pearl Harbor. Composed largely of Hawaiians of Japanese descent, the battalion was activated in June 1942, and joined the Fifth Army at Salerno on September 22, 1943. Except for several months in southern France, the 100th Battalion fought magnificently throughout the Italian campaign. It won the Presidential Citation for the destruction of a German SS Battalion on Mount Belvedere, north of Piombino, in June, 1944. It participated in many other engagements, had heavy casualties, and earned fourteen Distinguished Service Crosses and seventy-five Silver Stars. These Nisei troops seemed to be very conscious of the fact that they had an opportunity to prove the loyalty of many thousands of Americans of Japanese ancestry and they willingly paid a high price to achieve that goal. I was proud to have them in the Fifth Army.

On the march to the Volturno, which was their first time in combat, they acted as an advance guard for a regimental combat team and covered a distance of almost twenty miles in twenty-four hours, despite the extreme difficulties of the mountain road. I sent a cable to Eisenhower on October 8, stating that they had seized their objective and that they were quick to react whenever the enemy offered opposition.

The difficult road and weather conditions under which the Japanese-Americans received their baptism of fire were responsible for the delay which our main units experienced as they struggled to get set for the Volturno crossing. The crack 30th Infantry of the 3rd Division, which was to be relieved after having cleared the path to the river, reported on October 9 that all its transportation, including signal equipment, was immovable in the mud, with the exception of eight jeeps. One of its battalions had many casualties from enemy artillery fire, and the wounded had to be carried out on stretchers. In addition, the men had not yet received their barracks bags, owing to shipping delays, and they suffered severely from the cold because they were not yet clothed for wintry weather.

So serious were these difficulties with the mud and rain that I postponed the date of attack on the Volturno three days to the night of October 12–13, in order to give us an opportunity to be fully prepared. The German defense line was about as good as could be imagined for the defense of a river, even after the 45th Division had successfully taken the high hills to protect our right flank. The approach to the river on our side was flat and provided little cover. On the German side of the river, however, there were a number of high mountainous sectors where the enemy had perfect observation and where his heavy guns could command the entire front, particularly in the vicinity of the Triflisco Gap, near which one of the main American crossings had to be made in order to get passage for heavy weapons and equipment. As long as the enemy held the Triflisco ridge, he could knock out any effort to erect a bridge. Therefore, the first assault faced not only the job of crossing the swollen, swift-running river, which in some places was 200 to 300 feet wide, but of clearing the Germans off the high peaks on the opposite side, without even a pause for breath. This same situation existed eastward of the Triflisco Gap, where the Germans were entrenched on Mount Monticello and, farther back from the river, on the Mount Caruso hill mass. And westward from Triflisco, the British, after fording the river, would be required to cross an exposed plain in order to attack the German guns on Mount Massico. Any way we looked at it, our men had to ford a treacherous river and then scale high hills, with the German guns looking right down our throats.

For several nights, patrols had been sent out along the riverbank to find the best places to cross. In one sense these men were the real heroes of the Volturno, because they had to fight German patrols and outposts in pitch blackness while they probed along the slippery river banks and waded waist deep in the freezing water. One patrol that was typical of many made several unsuccessful attempts to cross, and on a final effort managed to wade through the swift current almost to the steep, brush-covered bank on which the Germans were hidden. There they drew enemy fire and had to retire, slipping and stumbling through the darkness to the south shore. That patrol lost three men and had four others wounded, but reported that a crossing could be made.

Information gathered by these men was pieced together at headquarters and the troops were informed of the conditions they would face. About a thousand Italian kapok life-preserver jackets were found in a warehouse and distributed among the 3rd Division. Assault boats and rubber pneumatic floats were provided for some units; others improvised rafts to carry their weapons and equipment across.

On October 12, I completed arrangements with General House concerning air support for the attack and then made a tour along the British sector, stopping at the X Corps Headquarters to confer with McCreery. He was in a pessimistic mood, and after a brief talk I suggested that we walk out across the fields, primarily in order to speak frankly out of hearing of members of his staff. I should explain that it is customary to make an attack on a river line along a wide front in order to deceive the enemy as much as possible in regard to the main assault and thus prevent him from concentrating his defenses at the critical point. Following this practice, the attacker would have several plans: a primary plan and several alternate plans to be put into effect if a thrust at some point made it apparent that an easy crossing could be achieved there. At the Volturno we had gone into the merits of various plans and especially the question of whether to attack simultaneously all along the line.

At that time McCreery had pointed out that his British forces were on flat ground and would, after crossing the river, be on a plain in front of strong German mountain defenses. He felt that VI Corps was in a better position and should attack first, permitting the British to cross a day later when the enemy presumably would be outflanked by the Americans and less able to pour his fire down on the X Corps. All these considerations were carefully weighed before my order was given for a simultaneous attack on the entire front. I realized when I reached his headquarters that McCreery still had misgivings and, knowing that he was not a man to shrink from plain talk, I asked him what was on his mind as soon as we had walked out across the field.

"I want to make it plain as the commander responsible for British troops," he said, "and with my experience against Rommel in Egypt, that this is the most difficult job I've faced. You know how I feel about a simultaneous attack. I was opposed to it. We accept your order, of course, and we will go all out, but I have to say that I am embarrassed when an American gives British troops orders that we don't like."

We talked a while longer. He felt that it would be difficult in the extreme to get tanks across the river until a bridge was built, and he estimated it would take three days for him to get in a bridge at Grazzanise, which was a river town near the center of the British sector. And there was not much that could be done on the flat ground opposite his sector until the tanks were across.

"Well, Dick," I said. "I considered the possibility of having the VI Corps make the first attack in order to turn the enemy's flank, but in the end it seemed much better to have everybody attack at once to prevent concentration of forces against our crossing. That is my decision and it can't be changed now. All units have their orders and they will carry them out, and I know you will. I am glad you have been frank about it and I know you realize the difficult position I am in when I give you orders that you don't like." We felt better after getting that off our chests.

We talked over air support and I agreed to provide the extra planes that he felt he needed. That evening McCreery moved the 46th Division up along the river adjacent to the seacoast, put the 7th Armored in his center, and the 56th on his right. The VI Corps lined up with the 3rd Infantry Division next to the British, the 34th in the center, and the 45th on the right. There was a full moon beaming peacefully over the valley at midnight when six hundred artillery pieces fired their first blast at the Germans at the same instant. Along the river bank, mortars, machine guns, and small arms opened up simultaneously and smoke shells were laid on the heights from which the enemy looked down on our positions.

Near the Triflisco Gap, the 1st Battalion of the 15th Infantry, supported by heavy weapons of the 30th Infantry, poured the greatest concentration of fire across the river at a point where the Germans had made extensive preparations to protect the most suitable crossing. While this diversion was in progress, the 7th Infantry led the 3rd Division's main attack at a point farther eastward where the river formed a hairpin loop. The 1st, 2nd, and 3rd Battalions were involved.

At five minutes to one, they pushed their boats and heavy rafts down the bank, waded out into the icy river, and began feeling their way along guide ropes which were quickly strung from bank to bank. The Germans laid down a heavy fire with small arms, but fortunately the high bank on which the enemy was entrenched made it difficult for him to sight down toward the river and in the confusion much of his fire was over the heads of the attackers. On the other hand, the improvised rafts proved hard to handle; most of them broke up in the swift current, and many of the trees that anchored guide ropes were pulled out, forcing the men to swim and flounder toward the hostile shore.

Most of the 1st Battalion men reached a sand bar under cover of the north, or German, bank of the river and then moved upstream to a small creek, through which they deployed into the fields and protected the flanks of the 2d and 3d Battalions which headed for their main objective—towering Mount Majulo, almost two miles away. The 15th Infantry, meanwhile, had crossed the river on the right flank of the 7th and, in severe hand-to-hand fighting, had driven the enemy back from the banks and seized Mount Monticello. At the same time, the 30th Infantry, after creating its earlier diversion, attempted to cross the river near the Triflisco Gap and seize the high ridge there. This attack was to be in coordination with a crossing by the British 56th Division, which would attempt to flank the enemy ridge from a point near Capua. The diversionary tactics employed earlier, however, had drawn so much enemy strength to the Triflisco Gap that both attacks were beaten back; and although the 30th made several other attempts during the day, it was not until the advance of the 7th Infantry, making the Germans vulnerable to flank attack, that the strong point of Triflisco fell into our hands.

On the British sector, the 7th Armored crossed after meeting severe opposition, and the 46th Division made good progress at the mouth of the Volturno, but the 56th at Capua was thrown back and could not cross. As a result I later shifted the boundary between the corps to include in the British sector a thirty-ton bridge that had been thrown up hurriedly at the Triflisco Gap by the 3rd Division engineers, and it was there that the 56th made its crossing.

In any event, by nightfall of the first day the Fifth Army as a whole had made safe its bridgeheads and had forced the enemy back so rapidly in some places that he did not have time to complete demolition work or mine the roads. When Alexander visited my headquarters that afternoon, he expressed great satisfaction with our progress and, I was happy to note, fully approved my decision for a simultaneous attack all along the river front.

Although the breaking of the German line on the Volturno was achieved by mid-October, we were confronted during the following month with some of the most difficult terrain and the worst weather of the campaign. The rain came down in torrents, vehicles were mired above the hubcaps, the lowlands became seas of mud, and the German rear guard was cleverly entrenched on the hills to delay our progress. We knew from questioning prisoners that the main enemy force had retired to a *Winterstellungen,* or "Winter Line," a strong outpost to the Gustav Line, which guarded the Liri and Rapido valleys from the south. But from mid-October to mid-November, the tired and muddy and freezing men of the Fifth Army felt they were going up against a major defense position every day as they inched their way over rugged terrain toward the Winter Line.

The 34th Division moved forward astride the twisting Volturno River, crossing and recrossing the stream as it advanced, while the 45th Division got a brief rest after having captured Piedemonte d'Alife and San Gregorio in hard fighting. The British X Corps moved over a shorter route past Mount Massico and to the Garigliano. In these operations we received strong air support, and I was fortunate to have General House always at my side to arrange for bombardment of enemy positions.

Our transportation problem became serious almost from the time we crossed the Volturno, and especially in the days immediately thereafter when it was difficult to erect enough bridges because of enemy artillery fire from the hills ahead of us. For some days it was necessary to ferry water, rations, and all other supplies across the river in order to supply the advancing units. Later, as we began to get the railroads into operation in order to lessen the difficult traffic of trucks over the narrow mountain roads, we had the able assistance of Brigadier General Carl R. Gray, director general of the Military Railway Service, who had arrived in Naples soon after we captured the city. The Germans had invented a remarkable device for destruction of railroads as they retreated. This was a huge iron claw that was attached to the bottom of a flatcar, on which a heavy load of rocks was placed to add to the effectiveness of the claw. When this device was pulled along the tracks, it not only tore up the roadbed, but broke the ties in two as well. It was responsible for one of the worst headaches of the Italian campaign, but the railroaders did a fine job of restoring traffic. Carl Gray, with his railway service outfits, knew his business. His vast railroad experience and cooperative attitude helped us continually as we struggled up the boot of Italy.

On October 24, we moved Fifth Army Headquarters from Naples to Caserta, about twenty miles to the north. Here was located a magnificent palace, built to compete in grandeur with Versailles, erected by King Charles III of Naples for his wife. I did not use this great establishment for my command post, partly because I knew that before long 15th Army Group (Alexander's headquarters) would be moving to Italy and would probably want the palace; partly because I had decided to keep my headquarters out of buildings, preferring to set them up in woods, using tentage and trailers so we could pick up and move forward on short notice.

There was a large forest behind the palace with a series of ponds at various levels and a number of waterfalls. I had my trailer set up there where I could use the nearby road as a landing place for my Cub plane. Later, when we landed at Anzio and daily overwater flights were necessary, we improvised pontoons for the Cub plane and used the long pond as a take-off and landing field.

My staff immediately began advancing plans for making amphibious "end runs" up the Italian coast in order to cut in behind the German strong points and avoid some of the bitter fighting in the mountains. These proposals involved many difficulties, and I was convinced that it would be unwise to land behind the enemy lines unless we could feel assured of joining up the amphibious attackers with our main elements within a few days. Although we discussed and worked over a number of such "end runs," we always decided against them for one reason or another—generally because the naval experts felt the operation was not feasible, since the beaches were unsuitable and small and usually dominated by defended mountains.

At the end of October, General Giraud came to Naples in connection with the preparations for putting French troops into the field as part of the Fifth Army. We were steadily adding units of different nationalities to our polyglot army, which in the end represented a score of countries. The French general was a welcome guest and I arranged for him to occupy a van next to mine in the Caserta woods. With Lieutenant Colonel Arthur Sutherland as his guide and interpreter, Giraud visited VI Corps Headquarters and pushed his way up to an observation post where he could witness an attack by the 3rd and 34th Divisions. He was the kind of officer who always wanted to know what was going on at the front and usually felt he had to see it with his own eyes.

This was evident when he returned to my quarters and agreed to talk to the correspondents who had assembled there. We went out under the trees and stood before a map showing the front lines while photographers crowded around. Giraud asked me to point out on the map the front positions that he had visited. When I had done so, he said, "May I make an observation?"

"Certainly," I replied.

"Your headquarters is too far back from the front lines. I'll give you some historical examples of what I mean. In the First World War, when I commanded a regiment, my headquarters was only one-half kilometer back of the front lines. In the beginning of this war, in 1940, I commanded an army in France and my headquarters was only two kilometers back of the front."

While he was talking I suppose I was a bit openmouthed, and I noted the newspaper boys were scribbling notes furiously and waiting to see how I would take Giraud's remarks. I had to think fast—and suddenly it came to me. I merely nodded in agreement when he had finished.

"Yes, General," I said, "and as I recall, you were taken prisoner by the Germans on both of those occasions."

Giraud's handlebar mustache bristled, and the press conference ended rather abruptly. I enjoyed having him visit my headquarters and it was usually a pleasure to greet other distinguished persons who came there; but at that time the most active theater of war was in Italy, and it sometimes seemed to me that we were overrun with visitors, many of them in the V.I.P. (Very Important Person) classification. They included high government officials of various Allied nationalities, who for some reason or other (I wasn't always sure of the reason) were making a tour of the war zones, and, of course, they included a large number of Army, Navy, and Air Force officers who were preparing for action in other theaters and, reasonably enough, wanted to get a look at what we were doing in Italy. All of this took up a great deal of our time, and I sometimes felt we were being pushed into the tourist business.

In this period, when the foul November weather and the German delaying tactics made the going tough, we continually were reviewing the situation in an effort to find ways to speed up our advance. Lieutenant General Alec Richardson, Alexander's chief of staff, and I discussed the situation in great detail on November 4. Richardson said that according to intelligence at Fifteenth Army Group Headquarters, the German Winter Line was so rugged that we might have to hold our present positions unless we could get strong naval support for an amphibious operation farther up the coast. I said that there was no doubt in my mind that somehow the Fifth Army could continue its advance and take Rome, regardless of amphibious support.

I suppose there was a general feeling of discouragement in the final months of 1943 as the Fifth Army took one strong point after another, only to see, through the rain and the mud, still another mountainside on which the enemy was entrenched in pillboxes and well-protected artillery emplacements. In any event, the problem of morale arose. The Air Force during most of the war had a system of rotation of pilots and crews under which a man flew a certain number of missions and then was eligible for a rest back in the United States. How this method of rotation worked out for the Air Force I am not in a position to say, but I was certain that it could not work for ground forces on the basis of rotation for individual soldiers. It would be desirable to rotate large combat units; but in the Italian campaign any kind of rotation would have meant the end of our forward progress, for we had so few divisions.

In any event, there arose a good deal of talk during the early winter about whether or not men should be shipped home after so many months of combat service. I was disturbed by this talk because I considered that it represented a lack of effective leadership in the units involved.

I wrote a letter to all subordinate commanders calling upon them to "give particularly careful attention" to the welfare of the troops because of the hardships they faced and to take positive action to keep personnel informed of the progress of our operations and those going on in the Pacific in order to improve morale and correct unfounded rumors.

"I realize," I wrote, "that the soldier considers that he has an inherent right to gripe. Nevertheless, all such complaints must be carefully examined. Where legitimate cause of complaint is found, it must be removed wherever possible by constructive action and good leadership."

I reminded them that a rest-area program had been started for troops withdrawn temporarily from combat, with accommodations for enlisted men in Naples. There were recreation rooms run by Red Cross personnel, dances, motion pictures, stage shows, and other forms of entertainment, including sightseeing trips to such towns as Pompeii. We also had provided accommodations for officers at Sorrento. Two of my military government officials and some correspondents, including Mark Watson of the *Baltimore Sun,* had been in Sorrento before the war and remembered that the Albergo Vittoria was a large and handsome hotel on the Bay of Naples. At the first opportunity they drove down there for lunch and found that it was practically unchanged in appearance, but that it was housing many ardent Fascists who were as insulting as they dared be under the circumstances. I later sent General Hume to investigate the hotel and he made a similar report, adding that the hotel would make a fine convalescent center. We didn't need any further encouragement. We kicked out the Fascists and from then on it was run for the Fifth Army.

I mention these things primarily to make it clear that everybody was aware of the necessity for alleviating as far as possible the hardships which the men—and the officers too—of the Fifth Army suffered in the grueling push toward the enemy's Winter Line. I think I might add here that the *Stars and Stripes,* which was published primarily for the men, and sympathized with their viewpoint, tried to be as objective as possible about the rotation problem. It regularly published many letters from men who thought there should be some system of rotation, which kept the controversy stirred up, but it also understood the problem from the command side and presented its point of view, too. The discussion continued, and early in December I again wrote to subordinate commanders, urging them to counteract the home leave idea.

"Unfortunately," I said, "our *Stars and Stripes* has stirred up this subject. An editorial in that paper has provoked letters from enlisted men urging that veteran troops be returned to their homes and that new divisions from the United States be brought into overseas theaters to replace them. It is natural for many soldiers to wish to return home, without realizing the problems involved in such a program.

"I want you to take immediate steps to see that this subject is thoroughly explained to all individuals. Shipping is the most important factor. It will not permit exchange of divisions between the United States and the various theaters, even if they were available. Even now, we are struggling to build this theater up to the strength required. We can give no thought to troops going home at the present time."

It was a long time, however, before we heard the last of the rotation controversy. A few days later, for instance, about forty enlisted men of one division in the front line left their units without permission and went to Naples. Several were tried and convicted of misconduct in the presence of the enemy.

In the middle of November, the Fifth Army was pretty well into position facing the German Winter Line, running through Mount Camino, Mignano, Mount S. Croce, and north through the mountains, where our right flank made a junction with Montgomery's Eighth Army. The British X Corps, on a front extending from the coast about fifteen miles inland, had on its right flank a number of mountain masses which dominated the most direct road to Rome and from which we would have to drive the enemy before we could advance. Mount Camino was the most formidable of these peaks, although there were other rugged hills in the vicinity.

On November 12, with Captain Lampson, my British aide, I went to X Corps Headquarters to discuss McCreery's plans. He said that his 56th Division, which had suffered heavy casualties, was badly in need of rest after having been in combat since our landing at Salerno. He had lost a number of officers and noncommissioned officers, and for the time being there were no replacements for them in the Mediterranean Theater. His battalions were depleted and tired, and he expressed fear that the 56th would not be able to take the mountain defenses.

The Germans had flooded lowlands along the Garigliano to prevent the British from outflanking Camino, and the 56th Division had been forced to attack up the mountainside with almost no cover. The 201st Guards Brigade had fought its way up from Calabritto, at the foot of the mountain, against strong enemy defenses, mines and booby-trapped approaches to strong points. The weather became colder and rains intensified, and they were near exhaustion by November 10. Reinforcements had joined them at that time and they took the ridge known as Hill 819 (near Camino) at a cost of 60 percent casualties in the two lead companies. Most of their officers were killed or wounded, and for five nights and four days they had only a twenty-four-hour haversack ration, an emergency ration, and one water bottle per man. They were forced to leave their wounded lying on the ground without blankets despite the freezing temperature.

This situation, as outlined by McCreery, was a severe disappointment to me. I had hoped that the 56th could seize the high ground that overlooked the road to Rome—it was called Route No. 6—and thus achieve an immediate breakthrough in the enemy's Winter Line, but there was no question that the British division was tired and that reorganization was necessary. On November 12, their supply problem had become so impossible that I directed a withdrawal. This was almost as hazardous as the ascent, but, with remarkable skill, the British veterans pulled out at night so quietly that the Germans continued for forty-eight hours to shell positions they had vacated. This was one of the most courageous battles of the campaign, but the fact remained that the Germans still held Mount Camino. When I ordered the withdrawal, I considered switching the American 86th Division to attack Mount Camino; but since that would mean that I had committed the last of the Fifth Army reserves to battle, I decided to delay any decision for a day or so.

The next day I conferred with General Lucas, commanding VI Corps, and his divisional commanders. Lucas expressed doubt whether it would be possible to seize quickly other mountainous areas on their sector which joined the British near Mount Camino. Counterattacks by the enemy also were developing in the mountains around Venafro, and the terrain was so difficult that it was requiring three battalions to do the work normally assigned to one. At that time our information was that six German divisions were opposing our four divisions on the road to Rome, while only two enemy divisions were in front of Montgomery's Eighth Army. Alexander decided that the Eighth Army would launch a heavy attack on November 20, driving northward toward Pescara, and that the New Zealand Division and an armored force under Lieutenant General Bernard Freyberg, the famous British hero of two world wars, would swing to the north and thence southwestward in an effort to threaten Rome from that direction. Thus it appeared at the time that the Freyberg attack might cut in behind the German forces facing our Fifth Army.

As a result of this situation generally, I directed that the Fifth Army should pause for reorganization and regrouping until around the end of November, taking strong precautions against counterattacks. I advised Alexander that the 56th had been unable in several days' attack to secure Mount Camino; that it was necessary to give both the 56th and the 3rd Divisions a rest; and that the attack would be resumed after regrouping. This was bad news, of course, and a few days later when Alexander visited my headquarters, he remarked that it now would be harder than ever to get Mount Camino and Mount Maggiore, another large hill mass along Route No. 6. I agreed, but pointed out that three times X Corps had attempted to take Mount Camino and that there had been three failures.

I told Alexander that when our forces were regrouped we would take the hill masses, but he suggested that we would have a hard fight for them and it might be wise to wait a while.

In the latter part of November, the Fifth Army lost some of its finest fighting men when the 82nd Airborne Division departed for the United Kingdom, where preparations were being made for the 1944 cross-Channel invasion of France. General Ridgway came around on November 18 to say goodbye, and I promised to see that the 504th Regiment of his division, which was remaining for a while with the Fifth Army, rejoined him in due course. It was a sad day for me when Ridgway departed. He was an outstanding battle soldier, brilliant, fearless, and loyal, and he had trained and produced one of the finest Fifth Army outfits.

By the end of the month we had received reinforcements and were regrouped for the real beginning of the assault on the German Winter Line. On Thanksgiving Day, I made a tour of the American sector and found that morale was good despite the fact that the heavy rains continued, everything was coated with sticky mud, and the Germans were making frequent small counterattacks. I wanted to be sure that every outfit had turkey for Thanksgiving; and, so far as I could determine, they did, although at some mountainous front-line posts it had to be packed up to the men by mule train. I had Thanksgiving dinner with Brigadier General Raymond S. McLain, artillery commander of the 45th Division at Venafro.*

I was especially pleased at this time by the arrival in Italy of the 1st Special Service Force, made up of Canadians and Americans and commanded by Colonel Robert T. Frederick. This outfit, which was attached to the 36th Division, was trained to do anything from making a ski assault to dropping by parachute on the enemy's rear; in a long period of outstanding service, I don't believe they failed once to come up to the demands of a job. Frederick, who quickly rose to a divisional command, had worked early in the war with a British scientist who planned the descent of parachute "suicide" troops on the Norwegian center where the Germans were trying to develop heavy water as a tremendous new explosive element. Later, when the Special Service Force was organized and equipped with skis, snow weasels, parachutes, and various weapons for various jobs, Frederick had been put in command of the 5,000 men. I had learned about the organization and had asked General Marshall that it be sent to Italy to work in the difficult mountain terrain. Marshall agreed, and Frederick's outfit, ready to do anything at any time,

---

* Because of McLain's exemplary conduct in action, he later became a division commander and, still later, a corps commander.

arrived on November 23.

We also were given an Italian unit organized to fight with the Allied armies. It was the 1st Italian Motorized Brigade, commanded by Brigadier General Vincenzo Dapino. I promised them an important mission at an early date, and Dapino assured me that his alert and apparently eager men were ready for anything. Still another new unit was the 2nd French Moroccan Infantry Division, the first element of what was to become the French Expeditionary Corps, commanded by General Juin.

The attack that had been planned by General Montgomery's Eighth Army for November 20 was delayed by the rain and mud, but Fifth Army preparations were completed by the end of November and we were prepared to resume the offensive. The terrain that lay before us was well worth noting in some detail because it was studded with names that were to become familiar to Americans. As I explained previously, our left flank was anchored on the Gulf of Gaeta near the mouth of the Garigliano River, where an advance in force was impossible because of a deep series of mountains that extended from the coast some twelve miles inland. At that point the Garigliano twisted northward through a narrow gap, and then came Mount Camino. Eastward of Camino was Route No. 6, the road to Rome, and then the front ran northward into endless mountainous terrain.

There was only one sector on which we could move in strength; that was on either side of Mount Camino, beyond which lay the Liri River Valley leading to the Italian capital. To reach the Liri Valley, we first had to drive the Germans off the Camino hill mass, which included Mount Lungo, Mount La Difensa, Mount La Remetanea, Mount Maggiore, and a little town called San Pietro Infine. That would let us into the head of the valley where the Liri was joined by the Rapido River. It also would, unhappily, bring us under the guns of the Germans in high hills around a little town called Cassino. We would have to take Cassino and ford the Rapido River in order to advance down the Liri Valley toward Rome. Anyone who remembers the names of places associated with the bitter fighting in the Italian campaign will readily understand what we were up against when we set out to break the German Winter Line.

But only those who were there can ever realize how it rained, or appreciate why it was that we designated the attack on the Camino hills by the code name of Operation RAINCOAT.

"TOMMY"

11.

The Drive into the German Winter Line:

December 1943

Operation RAINCOAT coincided with what I usually think of as the Russian invasion of the Fifth Army front. It wasn't what I would call a large-scale invasion, nor did it last long, but it is one that sticks in my mind.

I had received a message asking if it would be possible for a Red Army mission that was then visiting the Mediterranean Theater to see something of the fighting on the Italian front. I didn't pay much attention to the request at the time, other than to reply that it was all right with me. We were swamped with visitors of all kinds during a great part of the Italian campaign, and a few heroes of the Soviet Union would make very little difference in our schedule.

Our attack on the enemy's Winter Line—starting with Operation RAIN-COAT—began, however, before the Russian mission arrived at my command post, and I was quickly involved in a multitude of decisions and orders. Perhaps I should make the picture clear by explaining first how the front lined up. It was a formidable picture, with the Germans entrenched on high peaks which we must puncture in the middle to gain entrance to the Liri Valley road to Rome.

General McCreery's X Corps, including the 46th and 56th Divisions, were on our left flank from the coast to Mount Camino. There, where Route No. 6 winds through the hills at Mignano Gap, the American II Corps under General Geoffrey Keyes took over and held a five-mile front curving northward toward Mount Lungo and thence northeastward beyond Cannavinelle Hill. II Corps included the 3rd and 36th Divisions. General Lucas' VI Corps held a front extending northeastward another fifteen miles over the mountains to a point near Castel San Vincenzo, with the 45th and 34th Divisions as Lucas' main elements.

Opposite the Fifth Army, which now included the U.S. 1st Armored Division in reserve, the Germans had the XIV Panzer Corps guarding the Liri Valley road to Rome. This corps included the equivalent of five and a half divisions, two Panzer Grenadier (motorized infantry) and two plus infantry divisions in the line, and the Hermann Göring Panzer Division (armored) in close reserve. We had little choice but to blast our way through the narrow Mignano Gap adjacent to Mount Camino, and Kesselring knew it despite our feints along the coast and elsewhere. At four-thirty on the afternoon of December 2, we fired the first round from 925 pieces of artillery into the Winter Line, with all but 105 of them aimed at the enemy position on Mount Camino's bald and rocky slopes.

For the next two days, tons of high explosives and phosphorus shells descended steadily on the hill mass that blocked our path. In all, the Fifth Army fired 206,929 rounds weighing 4,066 tons against the caves and deeply entrenched positions of the Germans as our troops moved forward against the rugged peaks.

The British 139th Brigade of the 46th Division, elements of the 40th Royal Tank Regiment and the 56th Division met strong resistance on the south side of the Camino sector; but on the northern ridge of the hill mass Colonel Frederick's Special Service Force climbed a steep razorback ridge at night, seized Mount La Difensa, and pushed on to a high peak of the Camino mass known as Hill 960. After repulsing or containing a number of German counterattacks, they fought their way to the top of Mount La Remetanea, while the British 169th Brigade sent the 2/5 Queen's Infantry Battalion[*] to the crest of Camino on December 6.

The American 142nd Infantry of the 36th Division, meantime, had attacked a ridge leading to Mount Maggiore, another strong point overlooking the gap through which we must reach the Liri Valley. Starting out in heavy rain on December 3, they made good progress over the steep mountainside where, as on Camino, the Germans had blasted machine-gun positions out of solid rock and had heavily mined every avenue of approach. Two enemy counterattacks were broken up, one by a ten-minute blast of 338 rounds of artillery fired by the 132nd Field Artillery Battalion. By December 9 the entire area south of Route No. 6 was in our hands, except for Mount Lungo.

It was while this fighting was in progress that I received the five Soviet

---

[*] Second Battalion of 5th Queen's Infantry Regiment.

Army officers who were visiting the Fifth Army front. The party, including General Vasiliev and General Solodovnek, came to my van in a jovial mood and expressed great interest in getting a close-up look at the fighting.

"We want to see what the Americans are like in action against the Huns," Vasiliev exclaimed, after discussing the valiant stand of the Red Army on the Eastern Front and the manner in which they were slaughtering the enemy. "We would like to get right up to the front."

I poured him another drink of vodka, which the Russians had brought, and said: "I'll make certain that you see some fighting."

The Russians were accompanied by three American officers, but I assigned a British officer attached to my staff, Major Renwick, who spoke Russian fluently, to see that the party got a good look at what was going on. In fact, I emphasized to Renwick that it would be unfortunate if our visitors were given any grounds for feeling that we didn't want them to see everything, because from their questions I was sure that they had been sent to our front to find out whether the Italian campaign had drawn off from the Russian front any appreciable German strength. We knew from questioning prisoners that it had, but the Russians had trouble believing it and were inclined to regard the Italian fighting as a picnic.

Renwick proved more than able to conduct the tour. He took them up toward the rugged 3,000-feet-high peaks of the Camino hill mass, where enemy artillery made travel more or less hazardous on any road. He put them astride some mules and led them up the twisting mountain paths where American troops were struggling to overcome mines, wired booby traps, machine-gun nests and mortar positions concealed deep in the rocky slopes. With the help of the elements, he saw that they were rained on most of the day and had to slither through sticky mud when they dismounted from the mules. Finally, to complete the picture, he got himself wounded by a shell fragment.

That night, when I saw the Soviet mission at dinnertime, they were considerably less jovial than when they started out. I might even say they were impressed by what they had seen. Later in the evening, when I questioned them about the day's trip, Vasiliev suggested that I had misunderstood his explanation of just what the mission wished to see.

"What we're most interested in," he said, "is logistics. We want to see how your rear elements are organized and how your supply problems are handled."

He took another gulp from his vodka glass. "After all," he added, "we can die for Mother Russia any day in Russia. Why should we die in Italy?"

I might mention here that later in December, Andrei Vishinsky visited

Italy in his capacity as Soviet member of the Allied Mediterranean Commission, a board formed to settle political issues arising from the Italian campaign. For the next few months, Vishinsky was a very active figure in Italy, with our government's full consent. The Allied attitude in this connection seemed naive in the light of later events. There was no question in my mind that, as we paid a high price to drive Germans out of Italian cities and towns, Vishinsky was busy organizing Communist activities in the liberated areas. I imagine he did a good job, because when he returned to Moscow he was decorated with the Order of Lenin for his "distinguished services" to the state.

During the first week of the drive into the German Winter Line, both the 2nd Moroccan Division and the Italian Motorized Brigade got into action on the American sector. The Italians had a difficult beginning because they were ordered northward on Route No. 6 to attack Mount Lungo. It was necessary for them to pass near the 142nd Infantry, which apparently didn't expect to see any strange Allied uniforms and quickly "captured" the brigade's first reconnaissance party. After this was straightened out, the Italians were moved in position to attack Mount Lungo. The night before the attack they crept through the darkness toward the German lines and shouted threats and insults, promising that they would punish the Nazis for "deserting" Italian troops in the African campaign. Unhappily, this tipped off the enemy to the impending attack. Next day the Italians stormed Mount Lungo and almost reached the top—only to be forced off by a strong German force that was waiting to counterattack from a favorable position. When I talked with General Dapino the next day, he said they had been caught in a heavy cross-fire and he feared they had lost at least 300 men. The brigade was badly shaken by this experience, but they remained in position and later participated in the final capture of Lungo.

On the night of December 7, I had been advised by radio that a distinguished visitor would be at Palermo in Sicily the following day and that I should appear there, if my absence from the battle permitted, with several of my men who were to receive the Distinguished Service Cross. We flew to Castelvetrano Airport the next day, where we were soon joined by General H. H. Arnold, chief of the Army Air Forces, and George Patton, then in command of Seventh Army and awaiting orders in Sicily, and other officers. At midafternoon a plane landed on the field carrying President Roosevelt, General Eisenhower, Admiral Leahy, Harry Hopkins, and others. We all assembled and the President awarded the Distinguished Service Crosses.

When he had finished the ceremony, he looked around and said, "General Clark!" I was as much surprised as anyone else when he motioned me over and pinned the D.S.C. on my battle jacket. In a jovial mood, he said that he hadn't really expected that I could come, so had written me a letter in case I did not see him. He handed it to me.

"I am very sorry to miss seeing you," it began, "but much as I wanted to come to Italy to see you at the front and to greet your fighting army there, I was told I just could not go! You and your Fifth Army are doing a magnificent job under the most trying conditions imaginable. Eyewitnesses have told me about the fighting, so I know how tough it is.

"I have also been told of your personal courage in leading your forces, and especially of your gallantry in those first desperate days after the landing, when by personal example and fine inspiration to your officers at the front line, there was averted a critical situation in which the enemy might have burst through with disastrous results.

"Keep on giving it all you have, and Rome will be ours and more beyond!

"I am grateful to have such a staunch, fighting general."

Upon my return to my headquarters, it appeared that while our first onslaught had taken the Camino-Maggiore peaks, progress had then slowed down and we were up against a series of mountains that had to be taken, one by one, slowly and painfully. The II and VI Corps went about this job in continuous days of hard fighting.

During the third week in December, I made a number of tours along this front, including one journey in the vicinity of Montaquila, where the 2nd Moroccan Division was operating on our extreme inland, or right, flank. I went to its command post and found General Dody directing an attack by five battalions and a force of Goums along the Colli-Cardito road. It was a daring and difficult attack, with the Germans holding two strong points along the route, but Dody was confident they would succeed.

"I'd like to go up to the command post of the 4th Moroccan Tirailleurs," I told Dody.

"That's at Scapoli," he said. "You can go as far Colli, but I doubt if you can get to Scapoli because of heavy fire."

He gave me a guide and we drove in jeeps a couple of miles beyond Colli, turning westward along the ridges above the River Acquoso toward Scapoli. We couldn't see any particular activity, so we proceeded on the road until, just below Scapoli, a shell whistled over the shoulder of the hill and exploded beside the road. The French guide spotted a German observation post that commanded the road, so we left the jeeps and walked to Scapoli. From the village we could get a good view of the appalling terrain through which the French were advancing. Their difficulties were emphasized when we were forced to hug the sides of buildings to avoid enemy shellfire as we worked our way back down to our jeeps.

I returned to the Mignano Gap sector in the center of the Fifth Army front, and a day or so later made a tour on which I had a chance to compare the terrain where American troops were making an attack with the mountainous front where I had visited the French. For almost a week, American infantry, with some tank support, had been attempting to break into the village of San Pietro Infine, which lay in the Mignano Gap on the north side of Route No. 6. We had to seize this gap—sometimes known to the soldiers as Death Valley—in order to reach the Liri River Valley. Repeated attacks had failed because the town was on a steep, terraced hillside and the Germans held towering Mount Sammucro behind the town as well as Mount Lungo across the gap on the south side of Route No. 6. From these two peaks they commanded every approach to San Pietro and repeatedly turned back our thrusts toward the town.

On the night of December 15–16, however, the 142nd Infantry had finally taken Lungo, and at the same time the 141st Infantry had launched a new attack on San Pietro, under the direction of Lieutenant Colonel Aaron W. Wyatt, Jr. The outcome was still uncertain when I drove north along No. 6 on December 16 to a point not far from Mignano Village, where a winding trail branched off into the hills.

Our jeeps turned off the highway on a muddy track leading, with a great deal of difficulty, to a high hill which we held and which was the last protection against enemy shelling from Sammucro. From there we proceeded on foot up a draw between the hills toward San Pietro. The sun was out, for a change, and the ground was drying somewhat as we came upon elements of the 141st near an olive grove, but it was obvious that the attack on San Pietro had failed again. Foxholes had been dug along the hillside and exhausted men lay in them, with their weapons at their sides. Twice we stopped to talk to wounded men who were being carried to the rear. We had difficulty in finding the command post and there was no sign of the commanding officers.

Both L Company, under Lieutenant Lewis, and G Company, under Lieutenant White, had suffered many casualties during the attack of the previous night, and the survivors had fallen back to the edge of flat ground extending along a depression adjacent to San Pietro. The two lieutenants were collecting stragglers and trying to organize their defenses. There was a good deal of firing going on up ahead toward the village, and I called White over to ask him how far our lines extended.

"Good morning, Lieutenant," I said. "What troops are in front of you?"

"German troops, sir," he answered.

He said that Major Hilton J. Landry and about fifty men of the 2nd Battalion were pinned down several yards ahead and that enemy snipers had infiltrated on our right. Mortars and machine pistols could be heard plainly, and three burned-out American tanks lay in ruins on the roadside ahead of us. White said that the attack had started up a small draw the evening before, but had run into heavy enemy fire. The men had huddled together in the draw until daylight, when they attempted another advance, but were badly cut up by small-arms and mortar fire. Part of them got back to the positions where we now were, but the others with Landry were cut off and still waiting a chance to withdraw.

I moved around as much as I could, talking to the men who had dug in. I was able to tell them that we had taken Lungo the night before and were overcoming strong enemy resistance on the heights of Mount Sammucro above us. The week-long battle for San Pietro was about to be won if we held our ground, for it was certain that the Germans could not remain long in the town after losing the two dominant peaks.

Just before we left the G Company positions, I saw a little infantryman with a heavy growth of beard on his face, sitting in a foxhole. I went over to speak to him; considering the circumstances, he was in surprisingly good spirits. Then I noticed that he was wearing overshoes.

"What's your name?" I asked.

"Private Gebhart," he replied.

"Why are you wearing overshoes?"

"Haven't any shoes, sir," he answered.

"Don't you want to wear shoes?"

"Yes, sir, but mine are worn out and my feet are so small that I couldn't get any others."

"What size?" I asked.

"I wear a 7A."

That was such a small size, as I discovered later, that out of every 100,000 pairs of Army shoes, only 67 are 7As; but I was on the spot, so I said, "I'll get you a pair of shoes if there is a pair that size anywhere in the Mediterranean Theater."

When I got back to headquarters, I asked Brigadier General Ralph H. Tate, my G-4, to see what he could do. Ralph could do anything, and fortunately, he found a pair of 7A shoes within a few hours. I sent my Cub plane to pick them up, and when they arrived I gave them to Captain Warren Thrasher, my aide, and drew a map for him showing exactly where I had talked to Gebhart in the foxhole outside San Pietro. Thrasher made his way there the next morning and found the soldier in the same foxhole.

"Your name Gebhart?" he asked, although he was sure he had recognized him from my description.

"Yes, sir."

"General Clark sent these shoes," Thrasher said, handing him the shoes. Gebhart took them without any change of expression.

"Thanks."

"Aren't you surprised?"

"No," Gebhart replied. "He told me he'd send them."

With the ousting of the Germans from Mount Lungo and the Sammucro heights, the enemy was in a box at San Pietro and, after making a strong counterattack to protect his lines of communication, he began a withdrawal at night. On December 17, our patrols entered the town without much opposition.

Although the fall of San Pietro and the surrounding heights opened a way for us into the Mignano Gap, the Germans continued to hold the towering peaks that extended all along the north side of Route No. 6 in the direction of Cassino, and it was necessary to clear this area before we would be free to advance into the Liri Valley. For the next month, II and VI Corps were engaged in heavy fighting on a fifteen-mile front through high hills north of No. 6 where the Germans could be driven from their advantageous positions only by constant pressure exerted under great difficulties.

While this agonizing progress continued, I had become involved in two planning projects of importance. The first was of a long-range nature and concerned the 1944 invasion of France, which was to be commanded by General Eisenhower, who was getting ready to shift back to England. General Sir Henry Maitland Wilson (nicknamed "Jumbo" because of his size) was named to take Ike's place as commander in chief in the Mediterranean. The reason this planning involved me was that Ike wanted to mount an attack across the Mediterranean on southern France shortly after he landed with the main Allied forces across the English Channel. The southern attack was to be called ANVIL and was designed to split the enemy defense in France and facilitate Ike's attack. The ANVIL army obviously would have to be formed in the Mediterranean, and Ike proposed that I should command it.

At the time this planning began, I had my hands more than full in Italy and I was able to devote very little time to it. Furthermore, as I will explain later, I was not enthusiastic about going into southern France. I could appreciate the fact that Ike wanted an assault in the south in order to increase his chances of success in the north, but southern France looked like a dead-end street to me, or at least a very roundabout way to get to Germany or the Balkans.

201

In addition, it was essential for various reasons—mostly political and psychological—that the Fifth Army capture Rome prior to the invasion of France. From where I stood, it was apparent that this was a large order for the Fifth, and I was busy trying to work out methods for speeding up our advance. One of the methods we settled on was Operation SHINGLE, which involved an amphibious landing in January at the Italian coastal town of Anzio in order to turn the enemy's flank at a point just below Rome.

When Eisenhower came to Naples on December 18, I went over with him both ANVIL and SHINGLE, which were closely linked because the Navy had said it could spare ships for our landing at Anzio only until January 15. After that date, they had to be withdrawn to get ready for the invasion of France. We agreed that our progress up the Italian boot had not been sufficient to guarantee that a January landing at Anzio could be linked up to the main Fifth Army advance within a reasonable time. In other words, the Anzio landing would be successful only if our main forces were in a position to attack through the Liri Valley and make a junction with the amphibious troops within a week or so. We definitely were not going to be in that position by the first week in January.

"I feel that I must recommend cancellation of Operation SHINGLE in January," I wired Alexander that afternoon. "The limiting date of January 15 makes it impracticable. I will continue planning SHINGLE in the hope that craft will be made available at a later date when it will be possible to execute the operation with proper preparation, supported by the main part of the Fifth Army. It is my urgent request that all efforts be made to get necessary craft for a later time."

Ike and I went over plans for ANVIL that had been discussed previously in Algiers, where General Gruenther had been my representative. Ike said it definitely was decided that I would command the southern France invasion, but that it would probably be necessary for me to remain in command of the Fifth Army for a while longer, possibly until Rome had been captured. That, we believed with high optimism, might mean that I could not begin detailed planning of ANVIL until sometime early in February. The next day I took Ike for a tour of the Mignano front. We took only two jeeps, leaving the rest of our party at a point a little beyond Mignano in order not to attract the attention of enemy artillery in the hills ahead of us. We drove around a loop on Route No. 6 where he could get a good view of the San Pietro positions and of the road leading on into the valley.

From the mountains to the north, the Rapido River rushed down to join the Garigliano below the little town of Cassino. We figured that once we drove the Germans back across the Rapido, we would be in a position to launch an amphibious attack on Anzio while the Fifth Army pressed an offensive up the Liri Valley to make a junction with the Anzio forces. On that day, December 19, we took a good look up the highway toward the peaks behind Cassino. They didn't seem far away when you looked across the valley, and nobody could imagine then that we would still be looking at those rugged hills when spring came around in the Apennines.

In the latter half of December, however, our problems increased, partly as a result of the intensifying preparations for the invasion of France, which limited replacements for battle-worn units in Italy and cut down on our reinforcements. The British X Corps had been in battle continuously from the time it landed at Salerno, and was not only badly in need of rest but seriously weakened by lack of replacements. The American II Corps was making slow progress, and the 34th Division had been withdrawn for reorganization and rest until the end of December. The Christmas season—not a happy one—was upon us and our breakthrough into the Liri Valley was by no means achieved.

I toured II and VI Corps areas all day on Christmas, decorating and promoting men who had distinguished themselves in battle and visiting the 8th Evacuation Hospital, which was filled largely with American and Canadian soldiers of the Special Service Force that had fought so well in the high hills northeast of San Pietro. I then called on General McCreery and returned late in the afternoon to Caserta. We had arranged dinner for fifteen of my staff officers in our mess tent, and I had given special instructions to Chaney about preparing it.

I also had decided that one of my Christmas gifts to Chaney would be the Good Conduct Medal. He more than deserved it. He had not only demonstrated his bravery on various occasions from Salerno onward, but had been unstintingly devoted to duty throughout the campaign. As I approached Caserta, I recalled some of the episodes in Chaney's career since he asked me to take him overseas. One occasion that stood out in my memory was when we first got settled in a flat in London and the fire warden called on us to inform us of our duties in case of an air raid. He explained about the fire bombs and the delayed-action explosives that fell with them on the rooftops, and told us how they should be handled when we were on duty. He asked me who would be our fire watcher and I said, "That's Sergeant Chaney."

Chaney's eyes rolled toward me. "As watcher," he said, "what do I do when a raid starts?"

"You," I replied, "go up on the roof."

Chaney went up on the roof when the occasion arose and he did whatever job came to him in line of duty. On my first night in Algiers, when we were preparing amid great confusion to negotiate with Darlan, he decided that there were too many unidentified Frenchmen dashing about the hotel, so he slept outside my door to be sure no one molested me. I felt that he would be pleased by the Good Conduct Medal as a Christmas gift and I held it concealed in my hand as I entered the tent with General Gruenther, General Brann, and several others.

The tent looked fine, with everything in shipshape order. The table was neatly decorated with evergreen branches. We were late in getting back, so we all sat down immediately. I looked around for Chaney. He wasn't there, and I had just started to call him when I heard a squeaky, off-key voice outside the tent, wavering uncertainly through a few bars of "Silent Night." Everybody paused to listen, and then I let the Good Conduct Medal clatter on the table. Chaney was drunk as a goat.[*]

I helped put him to bed and the corporal who was assisting him carried on. The dinner was excellent, having been prepared before Chaney decided to celebrate, and I think everybody had a good time. I was worried, however. At first I thought I would simply stick the Good Conduct Medal in my pocket and forget about it. Under the influence of a good meal, however, I began to debate with myself about whether or not I should relent and give it to Chaney. By the time we had finished dinner, everybody was in on the act. Some thought yes; some thought no. It seemed for a while that the most difficult if not the most important decision of the war was whether Chaney got the medal or didn't get the medal.

A couple of hours later, I looked around and found Chaney pretty much recovered. I propped him up in a corner of the tent, made a little speech, and pinned the Good Conduct Medal on his breast. After all, it was Christmas, wasn't it?

Sometime after this little ceremony, I received a message from Alexander that marked the beginning of one of the arduous phases of the Italian campaign. Just before Christmas, Prime Minister Churchill had gotten back into the Mediterranean picture as a sort of super commander in chief, a role that he loved to play when the going was tough—and he did it very well. Eisenhower, Wilson, and Alexander were summoned to Tunis to see Churchill, and on Christmas Day the situation in the Italian war was can-

---

[*] When I decided to tell of this incident in this book, I wrote to Chaney, who now lives in San Francisco and is retired as a master sergeant, telling him of my intentions and asking if he had any objection to the story's being told. He replied as follows: "Now about Caserta, Italy. I well remember the incident and time and I have no objections to your mentioning it in your book. The only difference is that it was not me that was put to bed, it was the corporal. I had been celebrating earlier, as you say, while preparing the dinner, and my big mistake that made me feel so small was when I spilled the apple pie into an officer's lap."

vassed in relation to plans for the 1944 European invasion. That night, Alexander sent me a message saying:

> Certain decisions were definitely reached today at a high level conference. Operation SHINGLE [Anzio] is to be strengthened and will be put into effect at end of January. We will have available 88 LSTs, which will permit mounting of an amphibious operation of more than two divisions. If you desire to use two American divisions I will replace them by transferring two Eighth Army divisions to X Corps of Fifth Army. Start planning straightaway.

On December 27, Alexander arrived from Tunis and gave me further details at a meeting attended by General Richardson, General Robertson, and General Gruenther. In the first place, he said, it had been decided that a British division definitely should take part in Operation SHINGLE at Anzio because it was a hazardous venture and heavy casualties might be expected. It was desired that British and American forces share the hazards in order to offset any undesirable reactions at home if things went unfavorably. Previous plans to withdraw the British X Corps from the Fifth Army were canceled, and in addition the British 5th Division would be put under my command.

SHINGLE would be commanded by the American VI Corps commander, Major General Lucas, who would have available the U.S. 3rd Division and the British 1st Division, plus other necessary troops.

"I am enthusiastic about carrying out this operation," I told Alexander, "and I'll see that the planning is thorough. We've got to put it across."

After discussing various details Alexander left, and I called a staff meeting to take up Fifth Army problems and begin the planning for Anzio. It was only later that it occurred to me that nothing had been said in Alexander's conversation about the January 15 deadline or any of the other deadlines that had previously been fixed by the Navy as a limit for the use of naval craft in Operation SHINGLE. I assumed that Churchill, in his usual vigorous fashion, had entirely abolished the deadline.

In a way, that was what had happened, but not quite. Churchill always had his eyes on the soft underbelly of the Axis, and that included the Balkans. He was not pleased when he saw that plans for the cross-Channel invasion of France were already sucking men, ships and matériel away from the Mediterranean and that the situation would be intensified later on. At that Christmas conference he overrode all objections, including Eisenhower's, who warned Churchill that the Germans probably would not withdraw but would fight it out, as they did. Ike emphasized that his role was as an advisor only, for he was imminently giving up command in the Mediterranean to return to England to prepare plans for the invasion of France. Thus the projected Anzio operation would not take place under his top command. As a result of this conference, we were committed to a landing at Anzio. If it was a great success, we would soon be in Rome. If it proved a hard nut to crack—and we had called it a hazardous venture—then we would have an amphibious force of Britons and Americans isolated on the Italian coast below Rome. Churchill knew that once we had a claw hold at Anzio the Allied high command would be forced to keep on pouring in strength to make that amphibious assault a success. A failure at Anzio on the eve of the invasion of France simply could not be accepted. Thus, however you looked at it, Churchill had again prodded everybody concerned until he had achieved his aim of keeping up the pressure in the Mediterranean. We were going to start it quickly; once started, there would be no question of going on the defensive in Italy, or even slackening our drive, until the politically important capital of Rome was in our hands.

I must add one more thought here, because it became an important problem later. In getting his own way, Churchill may or may not have made definite promises about how long the Navy would be called upon to support the troops at Anzio, but in any event the Navy experts got the definite impression that it would not be for more than a week or so. There was no question that we all hoped it would not be for long; but Churchill doubtless realized that if it turned out to be a lengthy period, the Navy couldn't do anything about it except beef—and it would beef, and did, not to Churchill but to me.

The Prime had again demonstrated his ability to force decisions, and it was a decision with which I fully agreed. On the other hand, I was concerned about being burdened with planning ANVIL at the same time that I was trying to fight a war in Italy. Eisenhower was about to leave Algiers for London to take up his new command, and I decided to send Gruenther to see him before he left in an effort to get straightened out on my own future plans. It had not yet been announced in orders that I was to command the Seventh Army, which would invade southern France, and I felt that that assignment might yet be abandoned.

I fixed up a simple code arrangement with Gruenther whereby he could inform me of the outcome of his talks with Ike by merely sending one word, such as ARIZONA or JITTERBUG, and he flew to Algiers on December 30. That night I got the code words that said, "Clark to command ANVIL. Your request to keep Fifth Army disapproved. Part of Seventh Army ordered to arrive Algiers soon but training center for ANVIL will be in Italy." I still was stuck with the whole works. Immediately following this, I received secret orders placing me in command of the Seventh Army in Sicily, in addition to my command of Fifth Army in Italy.

Meantime, General Montgomery was ordered to England to prepare for his part in the invasion of France, and Lieutenant General Sir Oliver W. H. Leese took over command of the Eighth Army. General Patton also was relieved of command of the Seventh Army (which was being turned over to me for ANVIL) to permit him to join Eisenhower in England in preparation for what was to be his last and perhaps his most brilliant campaign as America's foremost commander of fast, mobile armored forces. It is interesting to note, however, that Patton was doubtful about his future when he made a final call at my headquarters before departing for the United Kingdom in January.

He spoke highly of the fighting ability of the Seventh Army and said the staff officers were the best. Then, after we had gone over various details, he began talking about the coming invasion of northern France, an operation known by the code word of OVERLORD. He didn't know then just what his assignment would be in the invasion and he felt that he was handicapped as a result of the incident in Sicily when he had received unfavorable publicity because he slapped a soldier. In any event, he finally asked me what I thought his job was likely to be in the cross-Channel invasion.

"I would guess that you will command an army that will follow up the assault on the French beaches," I said.

"Well," he replied, "I think that would be a poor command for an officer who has had my experience. Anyway, unless I get some army command, I think that I'll retire."

As a result of Gruenther's conferences in Algiers, the plans for the SHINGLE assault on Anzio began to assume serious complications shortly after the first of the year. For one thing, I discovered that the Navy had never abandoned its idea of limiting the time in which it would make craft available for the Anzio landing and for supplying our troops thereafter. My first hint of this situation came in a message from Gruenther saying that it looked as if SHINGLE would be canceled and that some of the top officers there felt that Alexander was "badly off base" in regard to the operation.

"Admiral Cunningham [Sir John Cunningham, who is not to be confused with his cousin, Sir Andrew] understands that almost all LSTs to be used for Anzio will be released to proceed to United Kingdom by February 2nd at latest," Gruenther's message said. "According to information here, the Anzio force must land with eight days supplies, but with no expectation of further supplies by water."

He added that it was believed at Algiers that SHINGLE should be canceled unless Alexander and I could show that it would not interfere with the ANVIL invasion of southern France. This idea that Fifth Army forces could be landed at Anzio and then left out on a limb without naval supply or support was further emphasized by a long official message from AFHQ to Alexander saying that the Christmas Day conference at Tunis had agreed that the Anzio attack must not interfere with either ANVIL or OVERLORD and that, therefore, we would have to release all but six of the naval craft employed by February 3.

I felt that I had a pistol pointed at my head. I had been told to make an end run to Anzio, but now I was told that it would have to be done without sufficient craft and that virtually all those craft would be withdrawn a few days after we hit the beaches with two divisions. Since it would obviously take much longer than that for the beachhead troops to join up with the balance of the Fifth Army, I would have two divisions left high and dry at the end of a long limb. I immediately sent Alexander a long message explaining my point of view and urgently requesting him to see that adequate craft were provided for sufficient time to assure the success of the Anzio landing, which was to start the last week in January, if weather permitted.

The time for planning and rehearsing the Anzio assault was getting so short that we proceeded full steam with our staff work despite the fact that the outlook seemed to become more muddled every day. I explained the developments to my staff at a conference at Caserta on January 4, saying, "we are supposed to go up there, dump two divisions ashore without resupply or reinforcement, and wait for the rest of the Fifth Army to join up.

"I am trying to find ways to do it," I said, "and I am not looking for ways in which we cannot do it. We are going to do it successfully."

I must admit, however, that at the time I didn't know how. When Alexander arrived that afternoon, I told him that I had been completely surprised to learn about the limitation on shipping, since he had not previously hinted at such a deadline. I pointed out to him that I had known for several weeks that I would command ANVIL (something that Alexander hadn't known about until then) and that I naturally would not want to weaken that operation; nevertheless, I had been glad to undertake the hazardous Anzio assault on the understanding that necessary shipping would be available. I spoke out bluntly because I felt that the Tunis decision to stage SHINGLE had been made a bit carelessly and without the participants in the conference understanding the requisites for a successful operation, though they had been clearly stated in advance by my staff. The matter was made even more complex by the fact that Churchill, in his eagerness to capture Rome, had assumed that the Anzio attack could make use of a large number of American craft, which were not subject to his control.

Alexander undertook to draft a cable to Churchill explaining what we needed to put SHINGLE across and, after some struggle with the facts and figures involved, I supplied him with a copy of the message I had sent him two days earlier containing all the needed information. After he had cabled the Prime in support of these requirements, I mentioned that I understood the German 29th Panzer Grenadier Division had just been moved from the Fifth Army front to a position near Rome where it would be close to our proposed Anzio beachhead. I said I understood it was the function of Alexander's headquarters to determine the strength of the opposition we would encounter at Anzio and that I would leave that question up to him in connection with a final decision on whether to proceed with SHINGLE as scheduled.

By prearrangement we had agreed to refer to Churchill in future messages as "Colonel Warden," and on January 5 I received a message from Alexander saying that "Colonel Warden" was hopeful we would get the necessary naval craft for Anzio. Since "Colonel Warden" was then at Marrakech, Alexander asked me to send both Army and Navy experts to confer there on detailed requirements. I sent the group by airplane after explaining to them that President Roosevelt was anxious not to undertake any operation that would delay or damage the invasion of France, but that Churchill felt it was desirable to take Rome at almost any cost. With that in mind, I added, they must stick to the figures needed for the Anzio invasion and not permit the Prime to cajole them into retreating an inch as far as our shipping requirements were concerned.

We got the answer in a message on January 8. Churchill again had forced through an arrangement assuring us of enough craft for resupply and to bring in reinforcements. He had said he hoped the assault on Anzio would start on January 22. The next day, Alexander and my staff officers returned to Caserta and said that, depending upon agreement by Mr. Roosevelt, SHINGLE would go ahead full blast even if it weakened the coming invasion of southern France. Churchill had felt that the entire Allied position was prejudiced by the fact that the Germans were putting up such a successful defense of Rome. This, he believed, was having an unfavorable effect on both Turkey and Spain; it was, therefore, essential that the Italian capital be captured, and soon. It did not seem likely to me that we could land at Anzio by January 22, but Churchill believed we should try it.

"Your officers will tell you about the two searching discussions we have had," Churchill said in a letter to me regarding the decision.

I hope they will reassure you completely about the aquatic support our great operation [SHINGLE] will receive. It may even be possible to throw in the equivalent of a third division, which ought to clinch matters. I am deeply conscious of the importance of this battle, without which the campaign in Italy will be regarded as having petered out ingloriously.

One thing I beg you, namely, to do everything in your power to start off on the 22nd, if the weather is good. Every day gained increases the use you will have of these invaluable landing craft. . . . It would even be better to start with three-quarters on the 22nd than with full numbers on the 28th or later. . . .

I have been meaning to write to offer you my sincere congratulations on the signal honor paid you by the President in decorating you for your personal bravery in the great battle of Salerno. I have heard from British sources of the way in which you exposed yourself in the forward positions to sustain and animate your troops, and it is very likely that your personal intervention was decisive in a battle of which it might well be said, as the Duke of Wellington in after-life said of the Battle of Waterloo: "It was a damned close-run thing."

Before Alexander left Caserta, we talked over plans for the Fifth Army offensive which would be started a week or so prior to the Anzio landings in order to draw the Germans away from the beachhead area. I said that the French would start the attack on our right wing in the vicinity of Sant' Elia, General Juin's forces having taken over there from General Lucas' VI Corps, which was thus freed for the Anzio operation. Other attacks would be launched along the front in the following week, including attacks across the Garigliano River by the British X Corps and across the Rapido by the American II Corps.

Our forces were still engaged in bitter fighting to get into position for these attacks. Under heavy pressure to be ready for Anzio they made progress in the first part of January, and by the middle of the month had completed penetration of the German Winter Line with the seizure of a huge isolated hill called Mount Trocchio, about a mile from the Rapido River. This six-week drive into the Winter Line had represented an advance of only eight miles on the center sector of our front, but it brought the Fifth Army to the grim hills overlooking the Rapido River, the Gari River and the Garigliano River, which formed an unbroken water line from Sant' Elia, some thirty-five miles southward past Cassino, to the sea. It was difficult to imagine the hardships under which this advance had been made in rain, snow, and biting winds and against a powerfully entrenched enemy. Casualties had been high: 8,841 for the Americans, 3,132 for the British, 3,305 for the French, and 586 for the Italians—a total of 15,864. Yet, even as the 135th Infantry Regiment clambered up the rocky crest of Mount Trocchio, there loomed up before them still another German defense barrier, built along swift rivers and high hills, some ninety miles from Rome. It began in the mountains north of Sant' Elia and ran southward along the Rapido to Monastery Hill behind the town of Cassino, thence along the Rapido and Gari Rivers in the broad Liri Valley, on the south side of which it again entered steep mountains that rose behind the Garigliano River and extended to the sea. It was a line built by the famous Nazi Todt Organization on terrain that the Italian War College had used for many years to illustrate to students an area that was ideal for defense against almost anything. To the Germans it was known as the Gustav Line.

12.

The Rapido-Garigliano Front:

January 1944

The story of the breaking of the Gustav Line is not an easy one to tell for several reasons. It is a story studded with names—Cassino, Anzio, and the Rapido River—that made headlines around the world for many days and furnished fuel for many controversies. It is a story of bitter failures and brilliant successes, of outstanding bravery and fatal hesitation, of disagreements in the upper echelons, of international politics, and of grimly endless fighting by the men who took everything the enemy could throw at them and still kept on going.

So complex and controversial were some phases of the long struggle that, before I get into the story, I would like to pause long enough to explain one circumstance that often has been overlooked or forgotten by the public. I want to put special emphasis on it here because the reader will not get a true picture of the behind-the-scenes disagreements that arose, particularly in connection with the Battle of Cassino, unless this basic circumstance is kept in mind.

The British people and their Dominion armies had borne almost the full force of the Nazi attack in the period after the fall of France and until the German invasion of Russia; before and after that period they were almost constantly engaged in a great and exhausting struggle that cost the nation a tremendous price in men—their finest and strongest men—as well as in resources. The British Commonwealth paid that price while other Allied powers still were neutral, or while they were preparing themselves for military action—and their resistance vastly affected the course of the history of our time.

It also affected the way the war was fought after 1942. I have mentioned how, in the early days in London, it seemed to me that Churchill was constantly thinking of ways and means by which American forces could be gotten into the various theaters of war. I also referred, in connection with the crossing of the Volturno River, to General McCreery's reluctance to send his X Corps against such strong German positions until after the Americans had attacked and outflanked them, and to his request for additional air support. Furthermore, I have pointed out not only that the British divisions in the Fifth Army were tired from months and even years of constant fighting, but that few replacements were available, owing to their loss of officers and men.

I discussed this problem of replacements on November 16 with General Sir Ronald Adam, Adjutant General of the British Army, when he visited my headquarters at Caserta. Sir Ronald, who was the ultimate British authority on such problems, summed up the situation quite frankly. The British, he pointed out, were coming to the end of their manpower resources. They had to follow an extremely rigid national policy of manpower conservation, not only to last out the war, but to be able to hold their own after the war. Sir Ronald said, for instance, that at that time replacements were so lacking that he was breaking up divisions in the British Army at the rate of one division every two months in order to use the men as replacements for other units committed to action.

As a part of this policy of manpower conservation, it had become the usual practice for British commanders to depend largely on air bombardment and artillery fire expended lavishly against the Germans in an effort to minimize the necessity of making infantry attacks. Because of this procedure, numbers of Americans are quick to allege that General Montgomery's advances were often slow and cautious, illustrating the idea that the artillery and air force should carry the main burden of the attack.

Let me emphasize that I approve of such an attitude 100 percent if there is any chance it will work. But against an able and disciplined enemy it was seldom possible, and carried to extremes it is an idea that may well increase the final loss of manpower. Certainly, it is of vital importance that a commander use artillery and aerial bombardment and anything else he can lay his hands on to reduce the enemy position and to guard his soldiers as much as possible from the hazards of attack. But, in the end, it is necessary for the men of the infantry to attack and seize the objective immediately following its bombardment before the enemy has time to recover from the havoc wrought by the air force and artillery. The air force cannot take or hold ground. That's the job of the doughboy with his rifle and bayonet.

Having said these things, I want to add that nobody who has seen him in action can question the bravery or ability of the British soldier. I have seen many examples, and I have known many British Commonwealth officers and men who never so much as thought of hesitating in the face of danger—men like Major General H. K. Kippenberger, a New Zealander, who now walks on two artificial legs. Near Cassino, Kippenberger stepped on a mine, which blew off one leg. Looking around, he realized that he was in the middle of a minefield. Nevertheless, he stood up on one leg and began hopping out. He hopped on another mine and went down in a blast of explosives that was only slightly less noisy than the voice in which he roared, "Goddamit! There goes the other leg!"

Or men like Major Sandy McNab, who was a British officer attached to Eisenhower's staff in Algiers during the early stage of the invasion of Africa. He didn't like staff work and finally wangled himself a job on the Tunisian front, where he was under General Anderson. Sometime after his transfer, I visited the Tunisian front and inquired how Mac was getting along.

"He's dead," I was told.

I asked how it had happened.

"Oh, it was a lovely, a beautiful piece of work," my informant replied. "His men were pinned down on a hillside during an attack on a German position at the top. It seemed quite impossible that they could do anything about it, but at the same time it was tremendously important that they advance. Mac just got up on his feet, carrying nothing but his walking cane. He stood up straight and said, 'Follow me, men!' and started walking up the hill toward the Germans. Everybody followed him, and they made the top, too. Except for Mac. He was badly wounded. The stretcher bearers got him down later and were on the way to a hospital when their vehicle suffered a direct hit by enemy artillery."

As he talked, I could visualize exactly how Mac did it. It was the sort of thing that was perfectly natural for him, even in a war where most combatants necessarily spent a good deal of time with their faces pushed into the dirt—just as they were told to do. To me, Mac represented the willingness of the British to die when dying became necessary, and to do it well. There were countless others like him.

In that winter of 1944 there was plenty of opportunity to die in the hills around Cassino and in the Liri Valley, which became known to our soldiers as Purple Heart Valley. The Germans had moved reinforcements into the Gustav Line, including picked troops who were instructed to hold the road to Rome—or else. Their defensive positions were strengthened at Cassino by the diversion of the water of the Rapido to flat ground, which thus was made impassable for our armor. Huge emplacements were dug into the hills, some of them with living quarters for troops under steel and concrete fortifications that would withstand the heaviest artillery. Observation posts on peaks all along the river gave excellent views of our movements and permitted the enemy to gain the maximum benefit of interlocking fields of fire that he had cleared along the rocky slopes. Cassino was fortified as no other city that we had approached on the advance up the Italian boot. Heavy concrete and steel emplacements gave protection to enemy machine gunners, and snipers and self-propelled guns and tanks guarded the approaches. To the south of Cassino, overlooking the valley, artillery and the famed German Nebelwerfers were placed on high ground to cover almost every foot along the river and up Route No. 6, which skirted Cassino and ran over level ground toward Rome.

Opposed to the Gustav Line we had seven divisions in mid-January. The northern French sector included the 3rd Algerian and the 2nd Moroccan Divisions (commanded by Major Generals Goisland de Monsabert and A. Dody, respectively, both veteran and competent officers). The American II Corps, in the center of the front, had the 34th Division north of Route 6 and the 36th Division south of that highway; while the British X Corps had the 46th Division, the 23rd Armored Brigade and the 56th Division guarding our left flank to the sea. Actually, there should have been a pause for regrouping and reorganization before striking at the Gustav Line, but time was running short for the Anzio landing; so, with virtually no halt for some of the units, we resumed the offensive on January 17.

On that date, the British 5th Division having arrived as reinforcement, McCreery's X Corps successfully crossed the lower Garigliano and advanced on Minturno and Castelforte. The Germans counterattacked repeatedly, but in the next few days sufficient progress was made to protect the river crossings, except on the British right flank. There the swift current and a heavy fog coupled with strong enemy resistance frustrated the cross-river attack by the British 46th Division and created a critical situation by leaving open the left flank of the American II Corps in its scheduled new position near the village of Sant' Ambrogio. The Germans then stiffened along the rest of the British sector and progress was ended for the time being in that area, although McCreery held the ground he had gained. Great credit should be given to the British X Corps for the intensity of this attack. It constituted such a threat to the enemy that he reinforced that front by twenty battalions, including the Hermann Göring Panzer Division and the 90th Panzer Grenadier Division. The X Corps' losses during the period 17–31 January were 4,152.

On the afternoon of January 18, I talked to a group of war

correspondents who had arrived to accompany the amphibious landing to Anzio, although they did not yet know their destination. I explained to them that the French were attacking on our right flank in an effort to draw more German troops into that area, and that the British X Corps attack was also a flanking operation designed to draw the Germans' strength away from the center of the front, particularly around Cassino. The next move, I said, would be a II Corps assault in the center, supported by a continuation of the attacks by the French and British, in an effort to open the Liri Valley road and to draw enemy reserves away from the amphibious operation at Anzio, which I said would be the hardest blow struck at the Germans since Salerno.

When it came time for the correspondents to ask questions, most of them concerned the probable date of our entry into Rome and the date on which I expected the amphibious forces to line up with the main army. I said that depended upon the reaction of the enemy to our Anzio landing, but I hoped it would not take too long.

It was only with the greatest difficulty that we managed time for a rehearsal of the Anzio landing by the 3rd Division. The affair was staged on the Salerno beaches. I had insisted that a rehearsal was necessary even if it delayed the date of landing at Anzio. It was my contention that such "dry runs" usually are bad performances, like the dress rehearsal of an amateur play, but that they are vital in order to straighten out mistakes and encourage teamwork in the actual landing. In this case the rehearsal not only was bad— it was almost fatal. Everything went wrong.

First, the Navy switched the practice-landing place at the last minute to an unsuitable beach. Then it failed to provide the majority of the craft that were scheduled to be on hand. When General Truscott reported to me on the exercise, he listed what happened thereafter as follows:

> No single battalion landed on time or in formation. Transports were so far offshore that assault craft required up to four and a half hours to reach the beach. Four DUKWs, carrying antiaircraft guns, were swamped and it appears that at least five others, carrying howitzers, were lost. No single element was landed in hand and on its correct beach. Some beaches were missed by as much as 1,000 yards. No antitank weapons, artillery, or tank-destroyer guns were ashore by daylight. No tanks were landed. Ship-to-shore communications were defective if not totally lacking.

Truscott added that "to land this division on Anzio beaches as it was landed during this rehearsal would be to invite disaster if the enemy should counterattack at daylight with forty or fifty tanks. In my opinion, there is grave need for additional training."

The loss of matériel was serious. About forty-three DUKWs had been swamped, dumping a score of 105 mm. howitzers and a number of antitank guns into the sea. Communications equipment also was lost. I was appalled by the overwhelming mismanagement of the naval phase of the operation and embarrassed by the necessity of replacing the equipment. The loss meant that X Corps was deprived of many DUKWs needed in operations across the Garigliano and that a dozen others which were expected by the 36th Division for its coming attack on the Rapido would not be available.

Truscott was rightly upset by the whole performance. In a note that he sent along to my chief of staff, he said,

> I believe you know me well enough to know that I would not make such a point [re the mismanagement] unless I actually felt *strongly* about it. If this [Anzio] is to be a forlorn hope or a "suicide sashay," then all I want to know is that fact. If so, I'm positive that there is no outfit in the world that can do it better than we [the 3rd Division] even though I reserve the right (personally) to believe we might deserve a better fate.

There was not, of course, time for any more rehearsals, but I telephoned to Rear Admiral Frank J. Lowry, U.S.N., commander of Combined Naval Forces in the Anzio operation, and expressed my concern at the situation and arranged to get Truscott and Lucas together with the naval experts to do what they could to straighten out the landing routine. After their conference, Lucas said that he felt they had done everything possible to minimize the danger of confusion in the actual landing.

Meanwhile, the failure of the attack by the British 46th Division toward San Ambrogio, just south of the junction of the Liri and Gari Rivers, had aroused serious concern. This failure, which I felt was largely due to lack of strong aggressive leadership at the divisional level, caused the British front to swing back sharply several miles below San Ambrogio and thus greatly complicated the task of the adjacent II Corps, under General Keyes, which was to cross against very strong enemy positions along the Rapido north of the junction of the Liri and Gari. Nevertheless, it was imperative that the southern front of the Fifth Army should make its attack in order to facilitate the Anzio landing.

After I talked the situation over with Keyes, I sent General Gruenther to see General McCreery, to whom I sent a special directive. It said that in order to protect the left wing of the attack by II Corps on the Rapido River, the British should feint a crossing of the Garigliano on the night of January 20 and should make every effort to indicate to the enemy that it was a large-scale crossing in the same area where the 46th had earlier been repulsed. McCreery also was instructed to hold a battalion ready to protect the left flank of II Corps and, in any event, to aid the II Corps by supporting fire. In my diary on January 20 I wrote:

> I maintain that it is essential that I make that attack [across the Rapido], fully expecting heavy losses, in order to hold all the German troops on my front and draw more to it, thereby clearing the way for SHINGLE [Anzio landing].

Because of the controversy that later arose regarding the Rapido crossing, I believe I should here point out several factors that influenced my viewpoint. As has been made clear, we were under strong political pressure to capture Rome. The Germans, at the same time, were under pressure just as great. We later found an order to the German troops that said, "The Führer demands from each and every man to hold the Gustav Line to the very last. A complete success may have political repercussions. The Führer relies on the most stubborn defense of every meter of ground. This order will be read to all troops."

Now in these circumstances the Allied Commander in Chief had agreed at his Christmas Day conference with Churchill at Tunis that the Anzio landing was the best if not the only way we could drive the enemy from his immensely superior positions and capture Rome without gravely interfering with preparations for the invasion of France in the summer of 1944. Not only did we feel it was politically necessary to take Rome, but the basis of Allied overall strategy in Italy was to retain the initiative, thus preventing the enemy from withdrawing divisions from the Mediterranean Theater for use in the defense of France. Anzio consequently had become a vital part of that strategy; and to assure its success, it was essential that the Fifth Army exert the utmost pressure on the Gustav Line to prevent German divisions from being withdrawn and used to oppose the Anzio landings. Our mission was to attack incessantly, and that's what we did.

In Alexander's formal instructions, for instance, the Fifth Army was directed to "make as strong a thrust as possible towards Cassino and Frosinone shortly prior to the [Anzio] assault landing to draw in enemy reserves which might be employed against the landing forces, and then to create a breach in his front through which every opportunity would be taken to link up rapidly with the seaborne operation." We knew that the Germans had three divisions in reserve near Rome where they could attack the Anzio beachhead unless they were drawn to the Rapido-Garigliano front by our attacks there. As later developments showed, the enemy did move reserves down to meet our assault and left only two battalions in the Anzio area. There was no question in my mind that we were going to have to spill blood, either to break through the Gustav Line or to flank it at Anzio; and there was no question in my mind that, in the beginning, it was better for us to spill it where our main force was well established and on the offensive than on the hazardous and unorganized beachhead at a time when a powerful counterattack there might drive us into the sea and wreck our whole plan of campaign. Thus, on the day I recorded that I expected heavy losses on the Rapido-Gariglino front, it was our deliberate strategy to draw the Germans there in order to safeguard our landing at Anzio.

On that same day—January 20—the second phase of our main assault on the Gustav Line began to take shape in a struggle that became generally known as the Battle of Cassino, because the hills around that town dominated the Liri Valley and the enemy had to be driven from them before we could proceed toward Rome along Route No. 6. While General Lucas' American-British amphibious forces assembled to board naval craft for the voyage to the Anzio beaches, the Allied air force stepped up its battering attack on the enemy Gustav Line positions and on rear-area communications. The XII Air Support Command flew 124 sorties on the 20th in the area to be attacked by II Corps. Then twelve battalions of field artillery, two tank-destroyer battalions and the artillery of the 34th and 36th Divisions pounded away systematically at enemy positions south of Cassino. And in the evening of the 20th the 36th Division under Major General Fred L. Walker attacked across the Rapido River.

It was the plan of this attack to penetrate the Gustav Line south of Cassino, open up the Liri Valley, outflank the Cassino defensive bastion, and thus clear the way for a drive toward Anzio by elements of the 1st Armored division. The 36th Division was to cross the Rapido and the Gari rivers on either side of the village of Sant' Angelo and advance a mile or so to Pignataro in order to form a bridgehead for the 1st Armored to pass through south of Route No. 6. On this sector, where the two rivers form a continuous water barrier, the Rapido is from twenty-five to fifty feet wide and flows swiftly between vertical banks from three to six feet high. At that time of year the river is unfordable, with water as much as nine to twelve feet deep. The town of Sant' Angelo, on a forty-foot-high bluff, gave the Germans good observation of the opposite side of the river.

The attack, initiated in foggy weather, was led by the 1st Battalion of the 141st Infantry, which previously had moved boats and matériel to dumps near the river. Enemy artillery on high peaks from Monte Cassino southward to beyond the Liri River was able to fire on the Rapido front around Sant'

Angelo, and the 1st Battalion found that some of its boats and other equipment had been destroyed. The men had to cross a low, muddy area, heavily mined, to reach the steep river bank. Heavy enemy fire not only caused casualties, but destroyed the white tape that had been used to mark lanes previously cleared through the mine fields. Visibility was poor, considerable confusion developed, and it was nine o'clock in the evening by the time elements of A and B Companies of the 1st Battalion had forced a way across the Rapido under heavy small-arms fire from the enemy positions north of Sant' Angelo.

Under the most intense and steady resistance by hostile artillery, mortars and Nebelwerfers, as well as machine-gun and rifle fire, the 1st Battalion put up a tremendous fight to secure its position. Engineers struggled with footbridges, most of which were destroyed by mines or artillery as they were being erected. From remnants of four damaged and destroyed bridges, one was finally installed to permit the rest of Companies A and B to get across the river. The Company C attack put only a few men across despite the efforts of the other two companies to silence the enemy fire along the west bank. Men were swept down the icy river. Mines on the banks and in the water took a heavy toll. Rubber boats were sunk by small-arms fire. Assault boats were knocked out by mortar fire. On the hostile bank the men who had crossed successfully encountered barbed wire, mines, machine-gun fire, and a steady artillery barrage. Both A and B Companies suffered a severe loss of officers and noncommissioned officers. When daylight came on January 21, the two companies were dug in on the enemy side of the river, but Brigadier General William H. Wilbur, the assistant division commander, ordered C Company and other elements still on our side of the river to withdraw to their assembly areas in order to avoid destruction by enemy artillery during daylight hours.

South of Sant' Angelo, part of the 143rd Infantry had crossed the river through thick fog and darkness, getting three platoons of Company C across before enemy fire destroyed their boats. Two footbridges were installed before dawn, despite heavy casualties, and the rest of the 1st Battalion reached the German side. One bridge was soon knocked out and the other badly damaged, and Major David M. Frazior, the battalion commander, decided to withdraw after his men were driven into a pocket by powerful counterattacks. Only remnants of the battalion got back to the east bank. The 3rd Battalion of the 143rd encountered such heavy artillery fire that its assault was broken up, and by daybreak the battalion had retired to assembly positions. Thus, after a night of valiant effort, the 36th Division had only two companies across the river, both north of Sant' Angelo and both dug in under the most withering fire from all kinds of enemy weapons.

General Keyes, commander of II Corps, conferred with the 36th's commander, General Walker, in midmorning and ordered resumption of the attack by the 143rd south of Sant' Angelo as quickly as possible and reinforcement of the two companies of the 141st which were across the river north of the village. The 143rd attack did not begin until about four o'clock in the afternoon, by which time the Germans had moved up the 211th Grenadier Regiment, part of the 104th Panzer Grenadier Regiment, and the 115th Reconnaissance Battalion to reinforce their lines. This enemy shift doubled the odds against us.

Nevertheless, the 3rd Battalion of the 143rd Infantry ferried three companies across the Rapido about six o'clock and threw up a footbridge on which the rest of the battalion made the crossing. The 2nd Battalion followed then during the night and the two outfits advanced about five hundred yards, only to be met by such enemy onslaughts that their positions became untenable and they were forced to retire. An attack by the 1st Battalion during the same period was even less successful and only a few men got across the river. The battalion was seriously depleted and retired to its former assembly area.

Meantime, the 1st Battalion of the 141st Infantry had expanded its foothold on the German side of the river north of Sant' Angelo to a point about a thousand yards from the bank. During the daylight hours on the 21st, however, it proved impossible to reinforce them. It was not until two o'clock in the morning of January 22 that enemy machine-gun positions covering the crossing were eliminated and two bridges erected. By dawn the 2nd and 3rd Battalions had crossed to the German side after losing a number of men to enemy fire and the swiftly flowing river.

During the 21st, I had been occupied not only with the problem of the attack along the Rapido, but with the progress of Fifth Army forces on other sectors and en route to Anzio. My diary for that day shows only the following reference to the Rapido:

> As was anticipated, heavy resistance was encountered to the 36th Division crossing of the Rapido. Accurate enemy artillery fire destroyed bridges as they were erected. It became necessary, late in the day, to withdraw the 143rd, but the 141st, north of Sant' Angelo, maintained its position, and efforts to reinforce it were to take place this afternoon. The 143rd was to go across again at 1600. I have talked with Keyes and not only yesterday but today directed him to bend every effort to get tanks and tank destroyers across promptly.
>
> The Anzio convoys are at sea. We have no indications, as yet, that the enemy has discovered them. In fact, there are no indications of any kind that he knows of our SHINGLE landings.

On the 22nd, the day of the landing at Anzio, which I accompanied, the 141st fought in heavy fog on the German side of the Rapido, but enemy guns were zeroed in on our lines and crossings, and our toehold on the west bank became steadily less secure. No progress could be made in erecting Bailey bridges.* Communications between regimental command post and assault troops began to fail. The two battalions on the west bank—the 2nd and 3rd of 141st Regiment—asked for an order to withdraw and a smoke screen under which they might hope to get back across the river. This request got through by telephone to regimental headquarters, but the reply was that the regiment would hold its ground.

Keyes conferred again with Walker that morning, the 22nd, and directed that the 142nd Regiment, which had been held in reserve, should make a third attempt to establish a bridgehead across the river and relieve the pinned-down 141st.

In regard to this conversation, Keyes later said,

> General Walker informed me that the 141st was still holding its positions, but that the situation with the 143rd was not good [at 10 a.m.]. The Regiment apparently was disorganized, but inasmuch as an entire regiment in reserve [the 142nd] was available there was no reason to admit failure and defeat, especially as the 141st was still holding on. Actually, the maps and reports at the Division Command Post and as transmitted to my headquarters, showed nearly six battalions on the far side of the river. It was proper and sound to continue the attack without delay.

Meantime the isolated 141st was being smashed, despite one of the most valiant fights of the war against insurmountable odds.

At 4 p.m., 22 January, the Germans made a counterattack with two companies, but were repulsed with heavy losses. An hour later a second counterattack on each flank of the American position met with considerably less fire, suggesting that the remaining elements of the 141st were about out of ammunition. In the next three hours the fire from the American guns gradually died out and the German fire increased. By nine o'clock that evening about forty Americans returned to the east bank of the Rapido. All the rest had been killed, wounded, or captured.

I had talked with Keyes early in the evening, shortly after my return from Anzio, and questioned the advisability of continuing the attack, but he felt that it should be continued as long as the 141st was holding out on the

---

* A Bailey bridge is a portable steel truss bridge of sectional design capable of being erected in the field by relatively inexperienced personnel with the minimum of accessory construction equipment and in the minimum of time.

German side. When he later was advised by Walker that the 141st was practically wiped out, the scheduled attack by the 142nd was, of course, canceled.

Thus the three-day attack by the 36th Division failed to secure a crossing, despite a total of 1,681 casualties, including 143 killed, 663 wounded, and 875 missing. The missing comprised largely the men who had become separated from their units and who later turned up for duty. It was a high price to pay, but to suggest that the brave and able soldiers of the 36th made their sacrifice in vain would be to overlook the fundamental strategy of our drive toward Rome. The landing at Anzio was the key to that drive, and—as will be fully demonstrated—it was our assault along the Rapido, coordinated with the other thrusts by the Fifth Army against the Gustav Line, that made it possible for General Lucas to avoid a bloody battle and to secure the beaches at Anzio with only 236 casualties, including 56 dead, among the 3rd Division in the first-three days.

It has always seemed to me that the successful landing at Anzio, where we might have been driven into the sea had not the Germans been busily occupied on the Rapido, was more than sufficient justification for the task to which the 36th Division and others were assigned; but in view of the controversy that arose much later and was aired before a Congressional committee, I feel that I must call attention to some details that otherwise might better be forgotten.

The Rapido failure was a serious blow, but at the time I had no idea that it could become so controversial, for all our battles in Italy were tough ones. My reaction, when I visited Keyes and Walker on January 23 and received a full report on the failure, was that the 36th had tried magnificently and that its effort had paid off at Anzio. This I noted in my diary.

I heard no more about this attack until after the war, when I was stationed in Vienna. At that time, a meeting of former members of the 36th Division in Texas passed a resolution asking Congress to investigate the Rapido River failure, which was blamed entirely on me.

In brief, the charges in this resolution (and later in testimony before a Congressional committee in unsuccessfully opposing my nomination for promotion to the permanent rank of major general) were that I had blundered in ordering the Rapido River attack against what we knew to be very strong enemy defenses; that the divisional commander protested against making the assault in the Sant' Angelo sector; and that it was unnecessary to make the attack in which the division suffered "casualties amounting to 2,900 men."

When these charges were brought before Congress, I asked General Eisenhower, who then was Chief of Staff, to permit me to return home from

Vienna and answer them, but he felt it was not necessary. The Congressional committee asked the War Department for a report on the battle. After a thorough study of the action, a report was submitted to the Committee on Military Affairs, House of Representatives, by Mr. Robert P. Patterson, then Secretary of War, whose letter of transmittal summarized the findings of the War Department. His letter is quoted below:

HON. A. J. MAY,
  Chairman, Committee on Military Affairs,
    House of Representatives.

DEAR MR. MAY: Herewith is submitted, in response to your letter of January 29, 1946, a report of the circumstances under which the Thirty-sixth Division was engaged at the Rapido River in January 1944.

These activities were an element of a large-scale operation in which the United States Fifth and British Eighth Armies were directed to pin down enemy reserves by aggressive action and thus prevent them from imperiling our Sixth Corps as it made its hazardous landings on the beaches at Anzio. The Thirty-sixth Division attacked on the day that the Anzio expedition was definitely committed to making its landings. Preceding attacks on the southern front having met increasing difficulties, unremitting pressure at the Rapido now became essential.

The division reported its casualties for the period in which the attacks were made as 155 killed, 1,052 wounded, and 921 missing—a total of 2,128. [These figures are for period January 20–31.]

I have carefully examined the reports in this case and it is my conclusion that the action to which the Thirty-sixth Division was committed was a necessary one and that General Clark exercised sound judgment in planning it and in ordering it. While the casualties are to be greatly regretted, the heroic action and sacrifices of the Thirty-sixth Division undoubtedly drew the Germans away from our landings at Anzio during the critical hours of the first foothold, thus contributing in major degree to minimizing the casualties in that undertaking and to the firm establishment of the Anzio beachhead.

Sincerely yours,

ROBERT P. PATTERSON,
Secretary of War

My superiors in the Mediterranean Theater, General Wilson and General Alexander, both spoke out, saying that they had instructed me to order the attack and approving my course of action.

I do not, however, take refuge behind the fact that the operation was ordered by my superiors. The facts are enough for me. In the resolution and in testimony before the committees of Congress, for instance, the figure of

2,900 casualties was given. This was an exaggeration. There were actually 1,681 casualties, including 143 killed, according to official Fifth Army reports (for the period of the Rapido Crossing, January 20–22). Actually, during the entire month of January, the 36th Division suffered 2,255 casualties. The 34th Division suffered 2,066 casualties in the same period, during which it had most of the time an equally tough assignment alongside the 36th Division. Nothing, however, can minimize the losses of the 36th Division, which I selected for the tough, unglamorous job at the Rapido because I knew its men had the stuff to get across the river if anybody could.

General Walker testified that he could not recall ever having read of a successful frontal attack across an unfordable river in the face of organized positions on the opposite shore, and that he had suggested a much better place to cross the river at a point north of Cassino where the river was "easily fordable" and the German defenses weaker. In this connection, the British 56th Division had crossed the unfordable Garigliano River only a few days before, against a strongly organized position on the opposite shore. His other reference was to the locality where the 34th Division forced a crossing a few days later, after five days of bitter fighting. In that area the German defenses were also strong and thoroughly organized as at Sant' Angelo, and it was also difficult for tanks to follow the infantry there because the approaches to the river had been flooded by the enemy. Furthermore, it was necessary to assault the steep mountain slopes near Cassino in order to secure the bridgehead.

When the 34th Division, under General Ryder, launched its attack on January 25, it got three battalions of the 133rd Infantry across north of Cassino in an envelopment maneuver against that formidable mountainside, but strong enemy opposition developed before this bridgehead could be exploited and the battalions were forced back to our side of the river. The next day, the 1st Battalion of the 135th Infantry crossed just north of the town of Cassino, but ran into flooded ditches, wire, mines, and heavy machine-gun fire that forced them to retire. Another attack by the 100th Battalion also failed, and no armor could get across the river after six tanks became stuck on the most favorable route. Nevertheless, by continual probing the 133rd had a few men dug in across the river by the night of the 26th. Immediately following up this advantage, the 1st and 3rd Battalions of the 168th Infantry, assisted by the 756th Tank Battalion crossed the river against strong enemy opposition and held on throughout the 27th. At one time they were under such heavy attack that a withdrawal was started, but the battalion commander stopped them at the river's edge, reorganized his forces and saved the bridgehead until the engineers could build a corduroy route over which our tanks could move. With armored support, the infantry quickly made secure its crossing.

I cite all these circumstances in regard to the crossing of the Rapido only because I feel that the heroic men of the 36th Division are entitled to the complete record. They were a fine outfit and they performed a high service at the Rapido. Like the guards and tackles of a football team, the 36th was called upon to attack and attack hard in conjunction with other divisions of many nationalities on its right and left, while somebody else made a spectacular end run to Anzio that would have failed if the guards and tackles had not been up to their jobs.

I salute them for their charge and courage. As for myself, I can only say that under the same circumstances I would have to do it over again—and if I am to be accused of something, thank God I am accused of attacking instead of retreating.

NISEI

13.

The Agony of Anzio:

January 1944–February 1944

S ome fifteen miles southeast of Rome a high hill mass called Colli Laziali, but better known as the Alban Hills, stands like a rugged, broad-shouldered guardian of the two main approaches to the Italian capital. In January of 1944 these hills became a key by which we hoped to unlock the German defenses in the Gustav Line.

The two main highways by which the Gustav Line could be supplied were Routes No. 6 and No. 7. By the same token they were the main avenues of retreat—although there were several secondary roads available to the east—for enemy forces opposing the Fifth Army in the bitter battle for Cassino. No. 6 runs from Cassino along the Liri Valley, passing north of the Alban Hills; while No. 7 swings along the coast from Formia, near the Garigliano River mouth, to Terracina, and thence inland, passing south of the Alban Hills. The two roads then join at Rome. If we could seize the Alban Hills, we would threaten the Gustav Line defenders from the rear and might force the enemy to give up his powerful defense line in order to avoid entrapment.

Our end run from the Garigliano sector some sixty miles up the coast to Anzio was designed to provide just such a threat and to force the enemy to fall back beyond Rome. We would, in effect, stab a dagger into Kesselring's right flank at Anzio, with the blade directed at the Alban Hills. He would then have to decide whether to withdraw his strength from the Gustav Line, where the Fifth Army offensive had already begun, in order to oppose our

Anzio landings, or whether other forces could be rushed to the beachhead. What seemed most likely under the circumstances was that the Germans would be forced to divide their strength on both fronts, and that we would achieve a breakthrough in one place or the other. That would have been according to the schoolbooks; but in warfare, things very seldom happen according to the book.

In the case of Anzio, political rather than military considerations dominated the decision made at Tunis; hence it became necessary to shape the military scheme to fit the political decision. Our intelligence reports, for instance, would under normal military conditions have been a deciding factor in ordering the Anzio attack, but in this case they played a strictly secondary role. At the Tunis conference on Christmas Day, the decision already had been made at Churchill's insistence, as I understood it, before the Prime Minister turned to the chief of intelligence of Allied Force Headquarters and said, "Now, we'll hear the seamy side of the question." The G-2 of AFHQ, Brigadier Kenneth Strong, was skeptical of the advisability of the operation, because he knew the political importance of Rome to Hitler; he knew there were German divisions in France and Yugoslavia not too busily engaged during this winter period; and he also knew the enemy could move these divisions to Italy, if they were needed. All these factors added up to a dangerous undertaking. In spite of all this, Churchill was ready to accept the obvious hazards of the landing because the prize to be gained by seizing Rome justified a calculated risk.

I do not desire to give any impression that I am disagreeing with the decision. On the contrary, I approved it on condition that it was undertaken with sufficient strength. The Gustav Line certainly would be a tough nut to crack. We had excellent intelligence reports showing that the enemy had three divisions available in the Rome area to oppose the beachhead landings unless we could draw them south by our Cassino-Rapido River attacks, which we did. The estimate by 15th Army Group Headquarters, signed by Brigadier Terrence Airey, who was responsible for the production of enemy intelligence in Northern Italy and beyond the battle area, was that if the Anzio landings were successful, the Germans would make an attempt to seal off the beachhead and thereby would be maneuvered out of their strong defensive position at Cassino. Thus they could be expected to fight a delaying action northward, beyond Rome, where the several Nazi divisions then idle in southern France and Yugoslavia might be sent to help establish a new defense line.

It had been our experience that British intelligence was excellent, but that their estimates did not always reflect their true opinions. Sometimes they were overly optimistic about a difficult job to be done, in order to hearten the troops. Airey's report reflected this tendency. In the light of subsequent events, I felt that their estimate of the Anzio situation was deliberately made optimistic because it was shaped to fit the decision already made at Tunis. Our own Fifth Army estimate, prepared by Colonel Howard, was more conservative and suggested that the enemy would concentrate all the force possible in an effort to defeat the landing and prevent us from reaching the Alban Hills. Colonel Howard felt, in other words, that the Germans would not permit the Anzio threat to cause their withdrawal from the southern front, but would fight it out, and would pull back only if they were defeated on one of the two fronts. We were fully aware that German divisions outside of Italy might be dragged into our battle, but we hoped they would not be.

Another consideration of great importance in our plans was that the British Eighth Army, on the Adriatic side of Italy, would attack with sufficient force during this period to prevent movement of any Germans troops from that front to either the Gustav Line or the Anzio sector.

A final factor on which we counted was the belief of the Air Force that it could "isolate" the beachhead area. Their theory was that, by heavy and coordinated attacks, they could smash the enemy's communication lines both close to the Anzio sector and far in the rear, so that he would be unable to shift his reserves rapidly enough to counter our landings and our thrust inland. I might as well say right here that this didn't work. It is true that during the Anzio landings and for some days thereafter the weather interfered with air operations; but throughout the Italian campaign I saw this isolation theory tried out again and again, and repeatedly the enemy moved his forces by railroad and by highway, with some difficulty to be sure, but with a great deal of effectiveness as far as the progress of the war was concerned. On some occasions, our Air Force would knock out vital bridges, and produce aerial photographs to show that the German supply route was interrupted, but then at night the enemy engineers would uncover a floating bridge that had been hidden against the river bank and swing it into position, or hastily replace a bombed-out span of a bridge in a mountain defile. Then his traffic would roll again. Our Air Force blasted the mountain tunnels in northern Italy, bombed railroads through narrow passes, and performed other modern miracles of destruction. It hurt the enemy, without question, but it never kept him from reinforcing or supplying his Italian armies up to the very end of the war.

On January 21, the VI Corps embarked and set off for Anzio. The same day, we received the good news that weather conditions appeared favorable for Operation SHINGLE, and that the enemy, apparently unaware of our plans, was moving reinforcements southward from the Anzio-Rome region to strengthen the Cassino-Rapido-Garigliano line against our continued attacks there. On January 22 at three o'clock in the morning, General Lucas sent me a message from his ship that said, "PARIS-BORDEAUX-TURIN-TANGIERS-BARI-ALBANY." This was a code we had arranged, meaning, "Weather clear, sea calm, little wind, our presence not discovered. Landings in progress. No reports from landings yet."

Lucas had available for his landings the following forces: on the right was the 3rd Division under General Truscott, which went in about four miles east of the town of Anzio; a Ranger force of three battalions, the 83rd Chemical Battalion, and the 509th Parachute Infantry Battalion were landed on a small beach near Anzio harbor in an effort to get control of that port for a sort of superspeed unloading operation. We had arranged for combat-loaded trucks to be driven directly off the landing craft in order to speed up operations and increase the number of round trips that could be made by the craft in a limited time.

Six miles northwest of Anzio, the British 2nd Brigade of the 1st Division, under Major General W. R. C. Penney, landed with the 2nd Special Service Brigade of the 9th and 43rd Commandos, who were to set up a road block on the highway above Anzio. All of these forces were ordered to move inland, unite, and consolidate a beachhead seven miles deep with the port of Anzio as its hub. It was very much in our minds that the Anzio beachhead had to get off to a good start, so that before the Navy withdrew most of our craft a month hence the beachhead would be able to support itself indefinitely—or until the rest of the Fifth Army could drive forward to make contact. We planned to bring in a level of fifteen days' supplies and ten days of fire of ammunition as soon as possible. As time went on and the situation altered due to the heavy losses sustained in the supply dumps, levels were increased to thirty days' supply and fifteen days of fire. We expected, in all, to land a force of some 110,000 men at Anzio as rapidly as possible.

There was no further enlightening word from Lucas up to five o'clock in the morning, at which time I joined Alexander and other staff officers for a journey to Anzio by PT boat. En route up the coast, I received another encouraging message from Lucas: "NO ANGELS YET CUTIE CLAUDETTE." This, when properly decoded, meant "No tanks yet but the 3rd Division and 1st Division [British] attacks are going well." Other similar messages came in as we proceeded, showing that the landings had been opposed by only about a thousand enemy troops. Our strong Gustav Line assaults—including the Rapido attack by the 36th Division—had drawn southward the German Divisions which otherwise would have been immediately available to strike at

Lucas' force.

Some distance off the Anzio beaches, I went aboard the U.S.S. *Biscayne,* which was Lucas' command ship, and was informed that the landings had proceeded easily after our brief but heavy rocket barrage against the shore. Of the 50,000 men, with 5,200 vehicles, transported to Anzio on the first day, a large part was ashore on the broad and shallow beaches by midmorning. The Rangers had occupied Anzio under scattered shellfire and the harbor was filled with our craft. Steady files of soldiers waded ashore with rifles held high. There had been one enemy bombing raid and another occurred just after we went ashore, but neither was severe.

Major General William (Wild Bill) Donovan, who was head of the OSS, accompanied my party to the beachhead (he was always on hand when something was going on); after an hour or so ashore, we returned to the *Biscayne* for a talk with Lucas and Rear Admiral Lowry, U.S.N., and then made the return trip by PT boats in the afternoon, landing at the mouth of the Volturno River. That afternoon—January 22—everything seemed to be going far better than expected at Anzio, and I felt strongly the necessity for keeping up the attacks on the Cassino-Rapido front.

The next few days I was busy moving back and forth between the Anzio and Cassino fronts. On January 25, I flew to Anzio, with Major Walker piloting my Cub plane, and found the unloading proceeding well. German resistance had developed rather rapidly against the bridgehead troops, but satisfactory progress had been made toward the town of Cisterna. I alerted the 180th Regimental Combat Team (of the 45th Division) and the Special Service Force for movement to the Anzio sector to help out there.

A couple of days later I attended a conference at Caserta, where Alexander's 15th Army Group Headquarters had moved into the big palace. The subject of discussion was ANVIL, the invasion of southern France, which General Eisenhower was trying to build up into a strong force. I was surprised to find that virtually none of the British officers was in favor of the plan, because they desired to keep the Italian drive going full steam. Since I was still slated to command ANVIL, this development left me in a highly uncomfortable position. The next day, Jumbo Wilson* called me in to talk privately about ANVIL, and I said frankly that the Fifth Army had been engaged in a long and bloody battle up the Italian peninsula and that it was entitled to take Rome, regardless of interference with plans for ANVIL.

"When do you feel that you should leave the Fifth Army to give your full

---

* General Sir Henry Maitland Wilson, Commander in Chief in the Mediterranean, succeeding Eisenhower.

time to ANVIL?" Wilson asked.

"About March 15," I estimated. "But if we are still outside Rome on that date, I should not be pulled out under any circumstances."

Wilson assured me that it was his desire for me to remain with the Fifth Army and forget about ANVIL, and we left it about that way.

Meantime the situations at Anzio and Cassino were becoming more difficult. At Anzio, VI Corps had pushed inland along the narrow Roman coastal plain, but it was considered wise to make only limited advances the first few days in order to consolidate positions about seven miles deep and fifteen miles long around Anzio, pending the arrival of reinforcements. This schedule was designed to prevent the enemy from cutting off our forward elements, as he might have done. Later there was criticism of our failure to advance deeply inland at the beginning, but in my opinion we most certainly would have suffered far more heavily, if not fatally, had our lines been further extended against the reinforcements the enemy was able to move in rapidly.

The coastal plain around Anzio includes, near the town, a five-mile belt of low scrub timber, dotted by open fields. It was in this timber that our first positions and dumps were established with good screening from enemy observation. West of the Anzio-Albano road, which runs north and south, the plain is cut by many deep gullies, which provided grave obstacles to the armored forces on our left flank. East of the road, however, are rolling fields that extend northeastward to the town of Cisterna, a railroad point, and it was in that area that we planned to make our main advance.

This avenue of advance was about ten miles wide, from the Anzio-Albano road to the edge of the Pontine Marshes, which had been reclaimed and resettled as part of an elaborate project inaugurated by Mussolini. The gullies on our left flank and the low, flat marshland on our right, where there were many irrigation ditches and little cover, served to limit our exit from the beachhead to the rolling fields in the Cisterna direction.

By January 27, the 3rd Division had moved forward to a point within three miles of Cisterna, using the Mussolini Canal to protect its right flank near the Pontine Marshes. The British 1st Division, on our left flank, had pushed northward along the Albano road to a point a mile or so beyond the little center of Aprilia, which our troops called the Factory because it was built on modernistic lines in contrast to the little farmhouses in the area. At this point the increasing enemy resistance was aided by a period of bad weather and by heavy enemy bombing attacks on our lines whenever the planes could get through the rain, sleet, and strong winds.

"Unloading impossible," Lucas advised me. "Prevailing weather heavy rain, sleet, lightning and strong winds. Anzio harbor shelled by hostile long-range artillery."

The long-range shelling turned out to be powerful enemy guns mounted on railroad cars and moved up and down the rail lines in the vicinity of the Alban Hills. They were to become known in the following difficult days as the "Anzio Express."

On the next day, January 27, Alexander told me that he did not feel VI Corps was pushing forward rapidly enough. It happened that I knew at the time that he had received a personal telegram from Churchill, who wanted a rapid advance on Rome. I too felt, however, that the beachhead progress was lagging unnecessarily and I told Alexander I would go to Anzio the next day and remain until the attack got well started.

Before going to Anzio, I visited the northern and central sectors of the Fifth Army front. The 3rd Algerian Division was making progress in an effort to encircle Cassino from the north, and the 34th Division's attack across the Rapido, just north of Cassino, also was moving forward. I emphasized to both outfits that we were shooting our bolt in this attack and that we had to put everything into an attempt to break through.

The next morning, January 28, I went down to the mouth of the Volturno before dawn to embark by PT boat for Anzio. There were two boats for my party, and with me in PT *201* were General Brann, Colonel Howard, Colonel Bowman, Captain Beardwood, and Frank Gervasi, one of the American war correspondents who had covered many phases of the Mediterranean conflict. There was some tension as we went from shore to the PT boats. The waves were so high it was difficult to maneuver small boats. The operator of my boat hit a sandbar and shipped a great deal of water, getting all of us wet before we climbed aboard *201*. In addition, the situation at Anzio was becoming critical. The enemy air raids and shelling had caused heavy damage, and there were rumors that German torpedo boats were roaming along the coast to attack our shipping.

Everything went all right, however, until we were about seven miles south of Anzio, still traveling in semidarkness. There the *AM 120*, a U.S. minesweeper, challenged us. Lieutenant Patterson, commander of our PT, ordered green and yellow flares to be fired and we flashed the designated signal on the blinker to identify ourselves as friendly. Up until that time I had managed to get out of the wind by sitting on a stool beside the skipper where the bridge of the boat gave me some protection. However, just before the *AM 120* challenged us, I got up and moved slightly to one side. The captain of the minesweeper apparently misread our signal, or perhaps it was just that everybody along the coast that dark and windy morning was trigger-happy. Anyway, the minesweeper fired on us, cutting loose with 40 mm. and five-inch shells. Their marksmanship, unfortunately, was pretty good. A number of shells struck our PT boat and the second one went right through the stool on which I had been sitting.

The skipper was wounded in both legs and fell to the deck. I heard a shell explode below decks. There was confusion throughout the boat and several men were knocked from their feet, two of them fatally wounded.

I picked up a Very pistol, which someone had dropped and again fired the correct signal to identify ourselves as friendly, but the firing from the minesweeper continued. I fired it again, with no result. By that time I had had a chance to look around. I saw that all three naval officers on the boat and two naval ratings were casualties. There was no one at the wheel, but Ensign Benson got to his feet despite leg wounds and swung the boat around. I knelt down by the skipper, who couldn't get up from the deck, and said, "What do we do?"

"I don't know," he answered.

"Well, let's run for it," I said. Then I held him up so that he could see what was happening and direct the movements of the boat. We ran for it, with the shells still spattering around. So did the other PT boat accompanying us, although it escaped damage.

By the time we were clear, our deck seemed to be littered with casualties and running in blood. One of the figures that had been knocked to the deck turned out to be Gervasi, who was groggy and soaked with blood down the front of his uniform. I began helping him get his jacket unbuttoned; we had to dig clear down to his bare skin before either one of us realized that he wasn't wounded but merely covered with somebody else's blood.

While we sped southward for the next thirty minutes, an examination showed that Ensign Donald was in the most serious condition. One of his leg arteries was severed and he was losing blood rapidly. Patterson had wounds in both legs, one of which was fractured. Benson had shell fragments in both legs, an enlisted man had his kneecap blown away and was in great pain, and the fifth man, who had been below, had stomach wounds and a fractured pelvic bone.

There were some anxious moments while we approached the British minesweeper *Acute,* but the skipper, Commander Andrew Edward Doran, recognized our signals and said he had a doctor aboard. We transferred the wounded men to the *Acute* and I told the PT boat crews to head for Anzio again.

When we reached the point at which we had been shelled, we again approached the *AM 120;* this time our identification signals were recognized. Our new skipper, who had transferred from our second PT boat to No. *201,* pulled up alongside the *AM 120* and through a megaphone delivered an inspiring and profane lecture to the captain of the minesweeper, beginning with, "You just fired on General Clark!" and ending up with a great deal of strong but sensible advice. The flabbergasted captain said that the first rays of the morning sun had made it impossible for him to recognize our signals and that his crew had been quick to react because of reports of enemy torpedo boats in the vicinity.

A long time later, at a formal dinner in Los Angeles, my waiter was introduced as the gunner who had fired on my PT boat off Anzio. After the newspapers carried a story about the waiter, I received letters from two other former Navy men who insisted that the man was a liar and that they had the "honor" of damn near killing me.

The *AM 120* incident got the day off to a bad start and it went on from there on a downward slant. The third enemy air raid of the day was being made on Anzio harbor when we arrived, and we had to wait until it was over before landing. I went at once to Lucas' command post to look over late reports from the front. At that time we could not see the whole picture, but, as we discovered later, it was changing with amazing rapidity.

The enemy had not expected our Anzio landing, which accounted for the fact that there was very little resistance until the night of D-day, which was the 22nd. During the day, the Germans rushed to the beachhead all unengaged units that could be spared from the southern front and from the Rome area—about seven infantry battalions with supporting arms. At that time we might have advanced more rapidly, but the commanders knew that the real outcome of the struggle would depend on which side could increase his forces most quickly, and they could not afford to get out on a limb until they were strong enough to prevent it from being chopped off.

In the next few days, however, the Germans moved with extraordinary speed, and thereafter our advance became increasingly difficult. As I already have mentioned, bad weather helped cut down the effectiveness of the Air Force efforts to stop the enemy build-up. In addition, the Eighth Army's scheduled vigorous offensive on the Adriatic coast failed to develop enough steam to prevent the Germans from moving three divisions from that front to Anzio, a possibility that we had not seriously considered. We had estimated that on D-day the Germans would have perhaps 14,300 combat troops opposed to us at Anzio and that they could increase that number steadily until they would have about 31,000 by the end of the fourth day. After that, we couldn't guess.

Actually, their reinforcements on D-day brought their numbers up to only about 10,000 fighting men. On the second day they were able to move up seven additional infantry battalions, one engineering battalion and supporting troops that raised their overall total to 16,000 combatants, which was still 4,000 under what we expected. But thereafter the pattern began to change. Hitler personally ordered the destruction of our beachhead at any cost, and General Eberhard von Mackensen was sent from Verona to lead the German 14th Army against Anzio. Almost all the German reserve forces in northern Italy—one and one-half divisions from Yugoslavia, a division from France, and six infantry and two heavy-tank battalions from Germany—were dispatched at great speed by rail and motor toward Anzio. At the same time the three divisions from the Eighth Army front began to arrive, and at the end of the third day the enemy had almost 26,000 combat troops on the line as compared to an estimate of 22,300 on which we had counted. Furthermore, it was only in the initial phase that German troops were withdrawn from the Fifth Army southern front along the Rapido-Garigliano Rivers. Instead of weakening those defenses seriously, Hitler chose to send in divisions from distant areas. By the end of the fourth day, the German strength was up to 34,000 men, and the number grew steadily in the next two weeks until it reached about 70,000. Nor did the Germans devote all of their attention to Anzio. They were able in the first week in February to move the 90th Panzer Grenadier Division and elements of the 1st Parachute Division into the Cassino sector on the Fifth Army front in time to plug a hole that seemed certain to result in a breakthrough by the American II Corps.

This situation, of course, was not clear to us when I arrived at Anzio on January 28 and conferred with Lucas, but it was evident that bolder and more aggressive action was necessary in view of the enemy's strength. I urged Lucas to speed up his attack toward Cisterna, a town we wanted to include in our defensive line, and he fixed January 30 as the date for a major effort. About this time I set up a new Fifth Army advance command post in a pine grove on the grounds of the Prince Borghese palace near the town of Nettuna, northeast of Anzio; I also moved my regular command post on the southern front from the grounds at Caserta to a hillside south of Presenzano behind the Fifth Army front.

By the end of January operations on both fronts were indecisive. "The southern [Fifth Army] front," I noted in my diary on January 30,

> is like two boxers in the ring, both about to collapse. I have committed my last reserve and I am sure the Boche has done the same.
>
> I have been disappointed by the lack of aggressiveness on the part of VI Corps [at Anzio], although it would have been wrong in my opinion to attack to

capture our final objective [Alban Hills] on this front. [But] reconnaissance in force with tanks should have been more aggressive to capture Cisterna and Campoleone.

The next morning it developed that two battalions of the Rangers attacking Cisterna had been cut off and were considered entirely lost.[*] The 3rd Division reported meeting heavy resistance, and that afternoon Combat Command A of the 1st Armored Division, moving toward Campoleone, encountered many mines and very strong opposition. By nightfall of January 31 the whole front was up against powerful enemy forces and the going was sticky. So many veteran enemy outfits had been identified by then that I began to fear we soon would face a strong counterattack while we were in a more or less disorganized condition. I told Lucas that when Cisterna and Campoleone were captured, we should then take a position in readiness to minimize any enemy counterthrusts. We were still bringing in reinforcements, but we had about reached the point where additional forces would overtax the bridgehead supply system, at least until we had expanded our positions; too, I could not spare further replacements from the Cassino front. The 3rd Division was pretty well exhausted by three days of hard fighting which failed to take Cisterna from powerful enemy forces; the 15th Infantry suffered heavy losses in taking high ground overlooking Ponte Rotto, just to the southwest of Cisterna; and the 504th Parachute Infantry pushing north along the Mussolini Canal failed to reach Route No. 7. On the road to Albano, the British with American tank support inflicted heavy casualties on the Germans, but failed to break through toward the Alban Hills. General Lucas had no choice but to order our forces to dig in all along the front in expectation of a counterattack. There was no question in our minds by this time that the enemy had succeeded in rushing far greater strength than anticipated to the Anzio sector. He also had quickly converted every farmhouse and village into a fortress, with machinegun nests and rifle positions. Tanks and self-propelled guns bolstered his line, and artillery was massed on high ground with more effectiveness than we had encountered anywhere in the drive northward. All along our possible avenue of exit from the beachhead, from the Albano road to Cisterna, we were for the time being at least up against a stone wall. The question that now arose was whether we could hold the beachhead that had been pushed as much as eighteen miles inland to the Campoleone area on the Albano road and fifteen miles toward Cisterna on our right flank. For the first time since Salerno, part of the Fifth Army was

---

[*] Only six escaped; the majority of the others were taken prisoner.

going on the defensive behind hastily laid mine fields and barbed wire.

Meanwhile, other serious problems of reinforcing and regrouping the Fifth Army generally had arisen. Alexander had arranged for the New Zealand Corps under General Freyberg to be shifted to the Fifth Army southern front. A few days later, he asked me to come to Caserta; there I took up with him and Freyberg various problems connected with the transfer of the New Zealand Corps.

Freyberg had been directed by Alexander to prepare recommendations for employment of his reinforced New Zealanders on the Fifth Army front. This was a surprise to me because I had not been consulted about such recommendations. I got a definite impression that 15th Army Group and Freyberg were going to tell me what to do. I objected as diplomatically as possible, pointing out that their plans for using the New Zealanders and Indian troops in the Cassino-Mount Cairo mountain sector would not fit in well, and suggesting that the New Zealanders be sent in to exploit the Liri Valley road to Anzio as soon as the Cassino battle developments made that possible. After some argument, this was agreed to and Freyberg was placed under my command.

I knew that Alexander was in a difficult position in regard to Freyberg, a famous war hero who had won the Victoria Cross in World War I. The British were exceedingly careful in the handling of New Zealand forces because they were territorial troops responsible only to their home government and it was necessary to use tact to work harmoniously with them. I told Alexander that I appreciated this situation and that I was sure our relations with the New Zealanders would be harmonious. I was proud to have them come under my command, for they were experienced fighters with many glorious deeds to their credit.

Alexander brought up the Anzio situation and indicated that he did not agree with my order to Lucas on the previous day rescinding the instructions for the VI Corps to continue the attack on Cisterna. He urged me to be prepared to attack with the 3rd Division again in an all-out effort to get Cisterna and expressed the opinion that the enemy would not counterattack in force. I pointed out that the VI Corps already had 2,400 casualties at Anzio and that I could not further weaken the 3rd Division. Later that night, when Alexander's headquarters received additional intelligence reports, he communicated with me at midnight to warn me of the danger of a strong counterattack, and the next day he expressed great satisfaction that I had ordered defensive measures.

On February 4, Freyberg and his staff came to my command post for a conference with Fifth Army officers. The New Zealander immediately clashed with General Keyes by announcing the manner in which he intended to move his forces, his artillery, and other equipment. I told him to make sure that he coordinated all his movements with the other movements of the Fifth Army, and then turned the problem over to my staff. Keyes was a bit belligerent about the whole affair, having been through a difficult period of attack in which he got very little sleep. Because I felt it was necessary that all the American officers understand the special problem created by the arrival of the New Zealanders, I included my sentiments in a letter to Keyes:

"These are Dominion troops who are very jealous of their prerogatives," I explained. "They have always been given special consideration by the British and I intend to make their relations with the Fifth Army happy and successful. You must help me all you can."

Later in the day I noted in my diary that I now had five corps under my command, only two of which were American. Each of the others was of a different nationality—British, French, New Zealanders, and Indians—and I was about ready to agree with Napoleon's conclusion that it is better to fight Allies than be one of them.

In the next few days we began to get indications of the enemy intentions, which, we discovered later, were spurred by Hitler's direct order to eliminate the Anzio "abscess" in the German flank. There were several small but sharp counterthrusts, which were repulsed, and aerial and artillery bombardment of our positions was greatly increased. A number of shells fell in my command post, and the Anzio Express big guns heavily battered the harbor area. On February 7, the Germans bombed the 95th Evacuation Hospital on the beachhead, killing twenty-three persons, including an officer, three nurses, a Red Cross girl, and a number of Medical Corps men and patients. Sixty-eight were wounded, including Colonel George Sauer, who commanded the hospital. Although the tents were in an open space and plainly marked with red crosses, the hospital headquarters was destroyed with the loss of much valuable equipment.

I should say at this point that the work of Brigadier General Joseph I. Martin, our surgeon, and his Medical Corps, and particularly the nurses, was outstanding in the battle of Anzio. The nurses were tremendous builders of morale at a time when it badly needed building. They went about their work wearing helmets and facing danger as great as anyone else on the beachhead. They worked with the doctors and in the operating rooms through bombardment of all kinds, day and night. It seemed to me that they were among the real heroes of Anzio.

As the days wore on, the hospital tents southeast of Anzio took on a strange appearance. At first, the floors were level with the ground, but later, in order to get additional protection against shell fragments, they were dug a little below the ground level. Then, as the danger increased, they were dug still deeper almost every day until most of them were several feet below the ground. The main tents, of which there were a dozen or so, were sixteen by fifty feet, so that in time a major job of excavation had to be done to provide them all with cellars. It was an eerie sight, particularly at night, to make one's way down into these canvas-covered cellars where surgeons and nurses worked day and night without regard to air raids or artillery fire.

I should add that the Red Cross men and women also performed a tremendous service in Italy, much of which was due to the efforts of Bill Stevenson, now president of Oberlin College, and his wife, who was affectionately known as Bumpy. Stevenson was head of the Red Cross operation in the Mediterranean Theater and Mrs. Stevenson worked closely with him.

While we were awaiting the German counterattack at Anzio, our emphasis on the Fifth Army front was shifted to the drive to eliminate the powerful enemy positions around Cassino, in order to clear the way for an advance through the Liri Valley. As a result, I had to make many trips back and forth from Anzio to my Presenzano command post, usually by Cub plane. I believe it was sometime during this period that Lieutenant Colonel Jack Walker, my pilot, and I had one of our most memorable flights. We started out from the mouth of the Volturno and, following our usual route, flew twenty miles or so out to sea and then turned north to Anzio. We usually flew only half a dozen feet above the waves in order to escape detection by enemy planes, and at Anzio, where the landing field was regularly under artillery attack, we often landed on the water. Walker had constructed pontoons for the Cub, and we would land close to the beach, jump out and use ropes to pull the craft up on the sand.

On our return journey this day, the waves were a bit high when we left Anzio, and after getting several soldiers to give us a push we bounced roughly out to sea. It was necessary for Walker to bounce the plane from wave to wave in order to get it airborne, and the water whammed against the pontoons with every bounce. We hit one wave with a terrific thud, but a moment later were into the air and on our way. A few minutes later, Jack said:

"You see what happened?"

I looked over the side of the plane and saw that both pontoons had been broken off and were hanging to the craft by a single wire.

"I see," I replied.

"What," Jack asked, "do you want to do now?"

"Hell, you're the pilot," I said. "Don't ask me."

"The only reason," he said, "that I asked the question, sir, is that it is merely a matter of where the hell would you prefer to crash."

"In that event, make it Sorrento. It's a pretty place."

"Okay. It's Sorrento."

We flew for about two hours down the coast to the beach adjacent to the Albergo Vittoria, a hotel that had been made into a recreation and rest center for Fifth Army officers. There is a breakwater below the hotel, which stands on a high bluff with its spacious balconies facing the sea. The balconies were crowded with people, and as we circled unhappily over the beach they saw that the pontoons were broken and that we were in trouble. A crowd quickly collected at a point we indicated on the beach. Jack turned out to sea and then came in low over the water and as close to the beach as he could figure it. He put her down hard in about four feet of water and both of us got out as fast as possible. It was a good landing from my viewpoint, but as we waded to shore we could see that the plane was fit only for the salvage heap.

By the end of the first week of February, the German probing of our Anzio lines was increasing. However, we had strengthened our positions, including a second or final defense line along a road that ran parallel with the beaches about five to seven miles inland from Anzio. On February 7, a day when I took time out to present the Distinguished Service Cross to General Truscott for heroic conduct in Sicily, it seemed to me that our defenses were in fairly good shape, despite the fact that General Lucas lacked a mobile tank-destroyer unit that might be moved rapidly from place to place in an emergency. I urged him to use antiaircraft guns for that role. I didn't get any particular response to this suggestion, except that later he sent a message asking me to send him another antiaircraft gun battalion.

I also was worried about air support for the great battle I knew to be imminent. I was determined that we should demand strategic bombers be used in close battlefield support. Such use of them, I told Alexander, might do some good; whereas for the last six months strategic bombing of rear areas in Italy had not prevented the enemy from moving additional troops and supplies at will.

Another problem that arose at this time was a shortage of artillery ammunition. Brigadier General Thomas E. Lewis, my able artillery officer, pointing out that it had already been necessary to curtail the rate of fire of 155 mm. howitzers, said that the 105 mm. ammunition was running low and that he was worried about the 81 mm. mortar ammunition.

This was a particularly serious development because such ammunition is used by field artillery battalions and mortar units directly supporting the infantry. As far as the beachhead was concerned, the shortage was twofold: in the first place, theater stocks were at a low level; furthermore, we were seriously hampered in unloading what ammunition we could allocate to those forces. The theater shortages I couldn't do much about, but I felt that something could be done about getting to the gun positions all that we could ship to the beachhead.

On the 6th of February, when I established my advance command post, I had relieved the corps commander of all logistical responsibility; this left him unencumbered to handle the tactical problems. Fully recognizing the magnitude of the logistical support operations involved, I selected one of my most capable officers, Lieutenant Colonel Charles S. D'Orsa, who had proved himself in Africa and at the Salerno invasion, to take over complete operation of the port and supply functions. Now, with a counterattack likely as soon as the enemy could prepare for it, it was obvious that we would have to make a still greater effort to speed up supplies, particularly ammunition. That meant that the LSTs had to carry the maximum cargo each trip. It was when we initiated measures to achieve that goal that I ran afoul of Admiral Sir John Cunningham of the British Navy, who was not particularly happy about the Anzio operation anyway, because it forced him to keep in use craft that he wanted to withdraw in preparation for the coming cross-Channel invasion of Normandy.

Our idea of the best way to solve the Anzio ammunition problem was to load the ammunition on trucks and then load the trucks on the LSTs, so that when they hit the beach at Anzio the trucks could quickly go ashore, unload and return to the LSTs. We also placed ammunition loaded in trucks on the decks of the LSTs, which was contrary to the usual practice but permitted us to get more cargo aboard. Admiral Cunningham bitterly objected to this, saying that it was dangerous. From our viewpoint everything touching Anzio was dangerous in those days, but there was a long controversy over our loading methods, with Cunningham having the final say. It was one of those incidents that, in a grave emergency, merely strengthened my belief in the need for unity of command in such an operation.

On February 8 I discussed with General Alexander the problem of our repeated failures to take Cassino. We agreed that the 34th Division was weary and depleted as a result of its bitter fighting there and that it should be relieved by the 4th Indian Division under Freyberg. On the following day I made an all-out effort to get the Air Force to concentrate its efforts and all of its planes—everything—on the Mackensen forces, which obviously were getting ready to spring at Anzio.

"I know that concentrations of enemy troops and matériel are not traditional targets for the Strategic Air Force," I told Brigadier General Gordon

Saville, commanding XII Air Support Command, "but the fact is that ball-bearing factories and rail junctions in northern Italy are not going to have any effect on the battle of Anzio for a few days. The German troops are already at Anzio and their equipment is there, and I would like to hit them with everything that we can use."

Later in the day I received word from the XII Air Support Command that this would be done.

I also received a message from Lucas saying,

> Pressure is continuing against us. Necessary employ additional forces to maintain front. Request all available air and naval support and shipment of additional infantry division at earliest moment.

I didn't have another infantry division to send except those that were exhausted. I didn't have any shipping in which to send one, and I didn't have any way to maintain it on the crowded beachhead if I had had a division and a way of getting it there. I did the best I could and, after shopping around, decided to send the British 167th Brigade of the 56th Division in view of the fact that X Corps was in a position where it could make very little progress on the Fifth Army front until something happened at Cassino.

I informed Alexander of my decision and, although surprised, he agreed. A few minutes later, however, presumably after talking to General McCreery, he telephoned to say he presumed the 167th would be used to replace the most exhausted brigade of the British 1st Division, which already was at Anzio. The rest of the conversation, as I noted it in my diary, went as follows:

> I informed him [Alexander] that this was entirely contrary to my idea; that I was sending the additional brigade group up because I felt I needed that extra insurance; and that later, when the situation was in hand there, I would be glad to rotate personnel out of the beachhead. He insisted, and I strenuously objected and told him that if any of the British 1st Division was to come out of the bridgehead now it was over my strongest objection and that he would have to give me an order in writing. He said the British 1st Division was tired. I told him so was the 3rd Division, but that if the situation got more critical all would have to fight, whether they were tired or not.

In the end I agreed to talk it over the next day. At that time, however, Alexander merely listened to my argument and then concurred. He was fine that way, always extremely considerate of the other fellow's point of view. In fact, we agreed to send to Anzio all of the 56th Division not already there as soon as it could be moved and supported logistically without withdrawing any troops. We also agreed that if the current efforts of the 34th Division failed, the New Zealand Corps would be moved to the Cassino front in an effort to force a breakthrough.

The XII Air Support program for an all-out attack on the Germans at Anzio ran into unfavorable weather and only about one fourth of the scheduled tonnage was delivered, but reports from the beachhead showed that the men had been vastly encouraged by even that concentration of close support. Nor did the bombing come any too soon. On the morning of February 9, the Germans stepped up attacks that they had been pressing sporadically for several days against the British 1st Division along the Albano Road sector. In the new and stronger thrusts, they made a number of penetrations and seized the little village known as the Factory, which stood like a fortress above the road and now gave the enemy a good jumping-off place against our left flank. Our counterattacks failed, and, despite heavy Allied air attacks on German concentrations along the Albano Road, the enemy threw in additional forces on February 10 and captured the Carroceto railroad station. There then was a period of several days in which the Germans reorganized their forces and we had an opportunity to bolster our defenses and make such adjustments as were possible for the coming onslaught.

In this period my attention was more than ever divided between the Anzio and Cassino fronts because of developments I will explain later in regard to Monte Cassino, but it was apparent that the beachhead situation was not good. Alexander asked me to confer with him; the first thing he brought up was his concern about the way General Lucas was handling the command of VI Corps. I knew this was coming, for on several occasions Alexander had indicated his feelings. I also was inclined to agree with Alexander's viewpoint and had for some time been considering a change.

My own feeling was that Johnny Lucas was ill—tired physically and mentally—from the long responsibilities of command in battle (he died a few years later). I said that I would not under any circumstances do anything to hurt the man who had contributed so greatly to our successes since Salerno and our drive northward to Anzio.

I told Alexander that for the time being I would put General Truscott in as Lucas' deputy commander and later transfer Lucas to another job, making Truscott VI Corps commander. I also said I would give the 3rd Division to Brigadier General Mike O'Daniel and transfer Colonel Bill Darby from the Ranger force to command of the 179th Infantry Regiment in the 45th Division. That afternoon I dispatched these orders to the bridgehead and noted that they would become effective the next day, February 17. I selected

Truscott to become the new VI Corps commander because of all the division commanders available to me in the Anzio bridgehead who were familiar with the situation he was the most outstanding. A quiet, competent, and courageous officer with great battle experience through North Africa, Sicily, and Italy, he inspired confidence in all with whom he came in contact.

At six o'clock on the morning of February 16, even before my conversation with Alexander, the Germans opened up all along the beachhead with heavy artillery fire, followed quickly by attacks on a dozen different points. The enemy was using men and equipment lavishly in a frantic effort to push us into the sea. He also introduced a new weapon—a squat little tank (unmanned) called the Goliath, which was loaded with explosives and sent against such obstacles as minefields, barbed wire, and concrete walls in order to blast a path for the infantry. We had as much air support as possible switched to Anzio, but the weather interfered to some extent again, and the enemy long-range artillery knocked out airstrips and battered the port in an effort to handicap our unloading.

That afternoon I received a cable from the British naval liaison officer of VI Corps saying that the town and port were under such heavy enemy fire that if it continued the maintenance of the beachhead would decrease steadily. "The only remedy," he added, "is action by our own forces to silence these guns and prevent your vital line of supply being jeopardized." At that time we were not in a position likely to permit us to silence the Anzio Express or any other guns. Our troops had their hands full just holding on.

The German attack continued all day, with diversionary attacks against the 3rd Division guarding the road from Cisterna to Anzio, but the brunt of the attack was borne by the 45th Division,[*] which held a six-mile sector astride the Albano-Anzio road. Not much progress was made, but on the 17th the onslaught was renewed, with greater air support and with the main strength of Mackensen's forces thrown into the fight. In the early morning darkness, Germans infiltrated down the road from Albano and succeeded in driving a wedge into our lines. This was exploited in strength, and after bitter fighting our line was pressed back from a mile to two and one-half miles, dangerously close to our last line of defense. Repeated counterattacks were made that slowed down and then stopped the advance, but failed to regain lost ground. That same night, Mackensen worked furiously to regroup his troops, and at dawn the Germans came on again with everything they could muster. The advance continued, following for the most part the road

---

[*] This division reached the beachhead on January 30. It was under the command of Major General William W. Eagles, who had replaced General Middleton, transferred to the European Theater of Operations.

network, and by midmorning the beachhead troops were fighting desperately to hold the last line—the original D-day beachhead line about seven miles from the water.

I arrived at the beachhead about that hour, flying up in my Cub plane with a Spitfire escort. The airstrip was badly damaged and we had to land on a road. I met immediately with Lucas, Truscott, and other officers. The situation was tense. Lucas was very tired. He and Truscott both favored making a counterattack, but after discussion it was decided to hang on while readjustments were made to strengthen weakened sectors. It also was agreed that all the commanders would go among the front-line units, making certain every man understood that he must not give another foot of ground.

I will not go into details of the Anzio action here, but the situation was rather critical that afternoon. We had suffered heavy losses of men and matériel. We were back to a line that had nothing much behind it except the beaches and the sea. We were obviously going to take it on the chin with everything Mackensen could throw at us the next morning.

I told Truscott that he would take command of VI Corps as soon as the crisis was passed and that I would bring Lucas to my headquarters as deputy commander of the Fifth Army. All Truscott had to do was make sure he had a beachhead to command when the crisis was over.

On February 18, Mackensen made his expected attack. The men of VI Corps were in foxholes that became half filled with water before they were fully dug. Their tank-destroyer units in many cases were dug into the marshy ground. German artillery and German tanks, moving along the road network, were in a position to fire down their throats. All day the fighting went on along the entire front, and at several points a breakthrough seemed imminent. At Carroceto only a blown bridge stopped the rush of a dozen enemy tanks, which then laid down a withering fire under which enemy infantry attacked Company A, 180th Infantry. Company A held.

Small enemy units slipped into the heavy brush along the lateral road that was the spinal column of the defense line. They were wiped out before the advantage could be exploited. On the western, or left, flank the 1st Battalion, 179th Infantry, and the 1st Loyals (British) fought off waves of infantry for hours, inflicting huge losses on the Germans. Our tanks, patrolling the lateral road, shifted back and forth to threatened points and, since the Germans had to cross open ground in most places, piled up heavy casualties for the enemy. At a few points the German infantry reached our lines and there was hand-to-hand fighting, but even the highly touted Infantry Lehr Regiment failed to make a breakthrough. The heaviest onslaught came late in the day, but it fared no better than earlier attacks. Early in the evening the fighting began to slacken. Mackensen had used everything he had, but it wasn't enough. The VI Corps had stood fast.

That day I received the most stimulating and thoughtful message I believe I ever received. It came from Ike, then in London, just at the right time to give me the lift I needed after those last desperate days of clinging to the Anzio beachhead. It read:

> DEAR WAYNE:
>
> In all the years I have known you, I have never been prouder of you than during the past strenuous weeks. Despite every difficulty, you are obviously doing a grand job of leadership with your chin up. I read the fine message you recently sent to your troops. Together with men like Al [Gruenther] and Truscott, you are writing history that Americans will always read with pride.
>
> IKE

In the four-day battle, we had lost 404 killed, 1,982 wounded, and 1,025 captured or missing, plus 1,637 non-battle casualties due to exposure, exhaustion, and trench foot. But VI Corps had broken the back of the attack that Hitler had ordered. It had also battered the morale of some of the finest Nazi troops. They had been sent into the battle, we learned later, with promises of a quick and easy victory over inferior numbers of Americans and British. They were fed a number of lies about Allied willingness to surrender and were convinced that they had a pushover. Not only did they take a tremendous beating from Allied air attack, artillery bombardment, and our naval gunfire, but when the showdown came, they didn't have what it took to smash the beachhead defense line. They took big losses. They were discouraged. After a week of rest, they were able to renew the battle, but never again were they to achieve the peak of fighting strength that had been theirs up to the afternoon of February 18 on the Anzio beachhead.

14.

Cassino:

March 1944

The Battle of Cassino was the most grueling, the most harrowing, and in one aspect perhaps the most tragic, of any phase of the war in Italy. When I think back on the weeks and finally months of searing struggle, the biting cold, the torrents of rain and snow, the lakes of mud that sucked down machines and men, and, most of all, the deeply dug fortifications in which the Germans waited for us in the hills, it seems to me that no soldiers in history were ever given a more difficult assignment than the Fifth Army in that winter of 1944. And I am certain that no men in combat ever fought more gallantly against such incredible odds.

A whole book could be devoted to the vast job that the German Todt Organization had done in converting the mountains behind the enemy's river defense line into a bastion of reinforced steel and concrete, alternate layers of railroad ties, and stone and earth works and deep underground chambers; but perhaps one example will suffice. We found out later that during one of our most intense bombing and artillery attacks—an attack in which we threw all the great weight our forces could muster against a comparatively small target area—a group of German officers sat in an underground bunker in the mountainside playing cards. They didn't move from the table throughout the attack. Our greatest effort didn't even break up that card game.

The fact that these defenses were ever overcome, particularly in view of Graf von der Schulenburg's orders to the fanatical 4th Parachute Regiment that they were to die before moving from the positions at Cassino, was something of a miracle of stamina and courage on the part of men of many nationalities in the Fifth and Eighth Armies. And the fact that we made one tragic mistake, the bombing of the historic Benedictine Catholic Monastery, called the Monte Cassino Abbey, cannot detract from the accomplishments of the Allied soldiers and airmen.

I say that the bombing of the Abbey, which sat high on the hill southwest of Cassino, was a mistake—and I say it with full knowledge of the controversy that has raged around this episode. The official position was best summed up, I suppose, in a State Department communication to the Vatican's Undersecretary of State on October 13, 1945, saying that "there was unquestionable evidence in the possession of the Allied commanders in the field that the Abbey of Monte Cassino formed part of the German defensive system."

I was one of the Allied commanders in the field and the one in command at Cassino, and I said then that there was no evidence the Germans were using the Abbey for military purposes. I say now that there is irrefutable evidence that no German soldier, except emissaries, was ever inside the Monastery for purposes other than to take care of the sick or to sightsee—and after the battle started, they didn't have a chance for any sightseeing. Not only was the bombing of the Abbey an unnecessary psychological mistake in the propaganda field, but it was a tactical military mistake of the first magnitude. It only made our job more difficult, more costly in terms of men, machines, and time.

As I already have related, General Eisenhower and I had driven close enough to see Monte Cassino two months earlier when our forces were first fighting their way through the German Winter Line. At that time we hoped we would soon hold the mountain ridges overlooking the Liri Valley and be well along the road to Rome, but this was a hope long deferred. When the Anzio beachhead had to dig in to save itself from powerful enemy counterattacks, I realized that we would have a difficult time taking the Italian capital before Ike began his invasion across the English Channel into France. As a matter of fact, I didn't know then or later exactly when the invasion of France would begin, but I had a rough idea; and, although nobody said it officially or gave us orders, it was perfectly clear that the capture of Rome prior to that invasion would be of tremendous psychological importance to the Allied cause. Thus we were, in a rather definite way, engaged in a race against time to break the enemy's Gustav Line and reach Rome before the invasion of France.

Our effort to break through the Gustav Line and join up with the Anzio beachhead centered, of course, on Cassino, but we had made little progress by the beginning of February. The British X Corps had taken important ground across the Garigliano River barrier near the coast, on our left flank, but had then been stopped by strong German counterattacks and by rugged terrain. The 36th Division's efforts to outflank Cassino from the south at the Rapido River had been unsuccessful, but the 34th Division, later trying a flanking attack north of the town, made a small but important breach in the enemy line. Still farther north the French, with only two divisions on a wide front, had advanced and consolidated their positions on our extreme right flank in the mountains. Our real goal, however, was to capture the strong defensive bastion, consisting of the Monastery Hill, Hangman's Hill, and the other nearby peaks which furnished all-round observation for the conduct of the defensive battle. The town of Cassino, which was dominated by Monastery Hill, had been made an important part of the German defensive system, each building having been converted into a small defensive fortress guarding the approaches to the hills.

These positions were held by some of the most famous German units in Italy, including part of the 1st Parachute Division, which had been hurriedly moved from the Adriatic coast—where the British Eighth Army was making little progress—to Cassino. In the early days of February, heavy fighting carried the 34th Division under General Ryder to positions on the northern edge of the town of Cassino and along the northern approaches to Monastery Hill, forming a large blunt wedge in the Gustav Line on our right, or northern, flank. Twice—on February 2 and February 4—our infantry and tanks had battled their way into the outskirts of Cassino itself, and once a platoon of the 135th Infantry had fought up Monastery Hill to the very walls of the Abbey.

By the end of the first week of February, only Monastery Hill, Castle Hill, and the town of Cassino lay between the 34th Division, coming down from the north, and Route No. 6, running through the Liri Valley—our road to Anzio and to Rome. General Keyes kept II Corps pounding away at the enemy defenses until February 11, when only a few hundred yards separated it from the Abbey and only a mile from Route No. 6—but the Corps couldn't make it. Men were exhausted and numbed by days of desperate fighting in which they had practically eliminated the German 44th Grenadier Division and captured a regimental command post. The II Corps itself, however, had been reduced to about 25 percent of its fighting strength, and the final victory still eluded our grasp.

General Alexander, meantime, had secretly moved the New Zealand Corps from the Eighth Army front to Cassino, where it was placed under my command, as related earlier. This corps was formed especially for the Cassino battle and commanded by Freyberg. It included the 2nd New Zealand Division, the 4th Indian Division, and the British 78th Infantry Division. On February 11, the New Zealand Corps began the relief of the American II Corps in the battle for Cassino.

During this period, of course, my attention continued to be divided between Cassino and Anzio, where the Germans were building up their forces for their major counterattack. On February 9, Freyberg had come to my command post at Presenzano with several of his staff officers and had discussed the Cassino situation, expressing some apprehension that the Monastery buildings were being used by the Germans. He added that in his opinion they should be knocked down by artillery or aerial bombardment, if necessary. I did not, however, feel that it was necessary, nor did my staff or the generals who preceded General Freyberg in command at Cassino.

Two days later, on Alexander's orders, I directed that the 4th Indian Division should attack as quickly as possible to clear the high ground west of Cassino, extending our flanking operation around the town, and that a bridgehead should be established across the Rapido south of the town. Because the weather was bad, with occasional snow, this plan was slightly delayed. On February 12, Freyberg telephoned Gruenther, in my absence at Anzio, and asked for air support the next day for the Indian Division to soften the enemy position in the Cassino area.

"I'm not sure we can give you as much air support as you ask," Gruenther replied. "The Army commander [Clark] has directed the main air effort for tomorrow be concentrated on the Anzio battlefront. We will make every effort to give you what you want, however."

Gruenther checked up and later called Freyberg, saying that only one fighter-bomber squadron could be made available.

"Will you designate the targets you want attacked?" Gruenther asked.

"I want the convent attacked," Freyberg answered.

"You mean the Monastery?" Gruenther replied. "The Monastery is not on the list of targets." This referred to a list of bombing targets prepared at the Fifth Army headquarters based primarily on recommendations made by General Freyberg. It was to be modified only if the Fifth Army staff recommended substitution of more profitable targets, the bombing of which would be of greater assistance in helping the attacking forces. The list had been approved by me.

"I am quite sure that it is on my list of targets," Freyberg replied, according to a memorandum, which Gruenther wrote to me immediately afterward, "but in any event, I want it bombed. The other targets are unimportant, but this one is vital. The division commander making the attack feels that it is an essential target and I thoroughly agree with him."

Gruenther told Freyberg that because of restrictions in connection with this target (a strenuous effort was made throughout the war to avoid needless damage to historical and religious structures) he would have to check with me before doing anything further. I was not available at the moment, but Gruenther called General Harding, who was Alexander's chief of staff, and discussed Freyberg's request, recalling that I had consulted Keyes and Ryder about the necessity of bombing the Monastery and that both of them had made reports that convinced me it was unnecessary.

A short time later, Gruenther got in touch with me by radio, while I was inspecting units at Anzio, and advised me of Freyberg's position, which was that destruction of the Monastery was a military necessity and that it was unfair to assign to any commander the mission of taking the hill unless he also was given permission to bomb the Abbey. I replied that Freyberg's strong viewpoint on the subject had been evident previously and that it was putting me in a very difficult position, particularly in view of the British desire to handle the New Zealanders with great diplomacy and tact.

Gruenther talked again with Keyes, who said that bombing of the Abbey was not necessary; that it not only would fail to assist the attacking troops, but probably would make their job far more difficult by letting the Germans feel perfectly free to use the ruins of the buildings as defensive positions. Although it is often not understood, the knocking down of a building or a town by aerial bombardment frequently leaves great piles of rubble that are better defensive positions than were the original buildings. Keyes said that Ryder, Butler, and Boatner,[*] all of whom had had commands in the sector, were in unanimous agreement with him.

Gruenther also checked with Keyes' intelligence officer, who said that two civilian sources had disclosed that there were refugees—perhaps as many as 2,000—in the Monastery, but that he had no reports of any actual fire coming from the buildings. He did have several reports that appeared to show that the Monastery had been used as a German observation post and that there were enemy strong points close to the walls of the Monastery. At the same time, the Germans had many other equally satisfactory observation points on the mountain peaks in the vicinity of the Abbey.

In midafternoon Harding called back and told Gruenther substantially as follows:

---

[*] Colonel Mark M. Boatner, CE, commanded the 168th Infantry Regiment of the 34th Division in the attack on the Cassino position. Brigadier General Frederic B. Butler was assistant division commander of the 34th Division during the attack on Cassino.

General Alexander has decided that the Monastery should be bombed if General Freyberg considers it a military necessity. He regrets that the building should be destroyed, but he has faith in Freyberg's judgment. If there is any reasonable probability that the building is being used for military purposes General Alexander believes that its destruction is warranted.

Gruenther replied:

General Clark does not think that the building should be bombed. If the commander of the New Zealand Corps were an American commander, he would give specific orders that it should not be bombed. However, in view of the situation, which is a delicate one, General Clark hesitates to give him such an order without referring the matter to General Alexander. General Clark is still of the opinion that no military necessity exists for destruction of the Monastery.

He believes it will endanger the lives of many civilian refugees in the building, and that a bombing will not destroy its value as a fortification for the enemy. In fact, General Clark feels that the bombing will probably enhance its value.

"General Alexander has made his position quite clear on this point," Harding replied. "If General Clark desires to talk personally to General Alexander about the subject, I'm sure that General Alexander will be pleased to discuss it with him."

When Gruenther advised me of this conversation, I told him to let Freyberg know that I still did not consider it a military necessity and was reluctant to authorize the bombing unless Freyberg was certain that it could not be avoided. Freyberg replied that he had gone into the matter thoroughly and was convinced of the necessity. General Gruenther's memorandum on this conversation added:

He [Freyberg] stated that any higher commander who refused to authorize the bombing would have to be prepared to take the responsibility for failure of the attack.

Gruenther then told Freyberg that I would authorize the bombing if Freyberg said it was a military necessity. He replied that, in his considered opinion, it was. I never was able to discover on what he based his opinion.

"Very well," Gruenther said, acting on my instructions, "the air mission is authorized and you should arrange for removal of any of our troops which might be endangered and determine an hour when the area will be safe for bombing."

Gruenther then called General Brann and told him to arrange with the air for the bombing of the Monastery on the morning of February 13.

The matter did not rest there, because when I flew back late that evening from the beachhead, I discussed the whole situation with Alexander in a telephone conversation that covered almost exactly the same ground as recited above.

"If the Germans are not in the Monastery now," I added, "they certainly will be in the rubble after the bombing ends. If it were an American commander, I would refuse to give the authority; but in view of the circumstances, I am reluctant to cause a major issue. If you say to do it, we will, but not in a small manner. We'll put everything we've got in it."

The bombing was delayed beyond the 13th because of bad weather, and on the 14th Freyberg came to my command post and we went over the same ground again, with no change in the result.

The next morning I worked at my command post, poring over a big pile of administrative papers and studying reports from Anzio, where the German air raids on the port were becoming even more severe and where a number of ships had been damaged while unloading. I tried not to pay much attention to anything that wasn't on my desk, but I suppose I was unconsciously listening all the time; and when the clock got around to nine-thirty, I immediately heard the first hum of engines coming up from the south. I tried to judge their progress by the steadily increasing volume of sound, a mental chore that was interrupted by a sudden roaring explosion. Sixteen bombs had been released by mistake from the American planes; several of them hit near my command post, sending fragments flying all over the place, but fortunately injuring no one, except the feelings of my police dog, Mike, who at that time was the proud mother of six week-old pups.

Then the four groups of stately Flying Fortresses passed directly overhead and a few moments later released their bombs on Monastery Hill. I had seen the famous old Abbey, with its priceless and irreplaceable works of art, only from a distance, but with the thundering salvos that tore apart the hillside that morning, I knew there was no possibility that I ever would see it at any closer range. I remained at my command post all day and tried to work.

A total of 255 Allied bombers participated in the attack, dropping some 576 tons of explosives. Most of the bombardment was accurate, but, naturally, where so many planes were involved, a few explosives fell within our own lines, causing some casualties.

After the aerial bombardment, the entire area was shelled by our artillery. By nightfall, the whole sector was a mess of smoke and dust and ruins, through which an occasional figure could be seen in panicky flight through the artillery barrage. For the moment at least, the enemy was jarred off balance, and for the moment, there might have been the chance of a decisive success if Freyberg had hit him quickly.

His 4th Indian Division, designated for the assault, was unable to find a way to develop enough speed and force in its advance along a mountain ridge leading toward the Monastery. The attack was slow in getting underway and of a piecemeal character, so that the enemy was able to chop up the first thrusts and turn back the advance, piece by piece. That night, for instance, the first advance was made by a single company against a commanding hill overlooking the Monastery. By the time the company reached the hill, the Germans had been able to rally some forces and offer opposition. The company reached the hill, but was not followed up by forces strong enough to hold it, and by early morning a counterattack drove it off.

The next effort was made the following night, more than thirty-two hours after the start of the bombing attack. The 1st Battalion, Royal Sussex Regiment (British), valiantly attempted to clear Hill 593, but had to withdraw after losing 130 men and 13 officers. The final effort was made during the night 17–18th, when three Indian battalions of infantry attacked in the direction of Monastery Hill while a New Zealand battalion moved on the town of Cassino from the east. Some progress was made, but fierce counterattacks ended the effort before much ground had been covered.

There were many difficulties that accounted for this lack of success, including the incredible supply problem through the mountains where motor transport was virtually impossible and where it was necessary to use 800 mules and four companies of infantry to carry supplies. Such problems had been overcome in other sectors, but there was no question that Cassino was one of the Germans' strongest points. In the end, Freyberg became convinced that an attack strong enough to succeed was not practicable through the mountains, and he changed his plan in order to approach Cassino from the north. This plan of attack, however, required a period of several sunny days to make the ground suitable for tank operations, and as a result the New Zealand Division dug in to wait on the weather.

What had actually happened in the Monastery I found out months later from a variety of sources. One of them was Lieutenant General Fritz Wentzell, chief of staff of the Tenth German Army, conducting the defense of Cassino, which I cite for whatever it may be worth:

> The consequence [of destruction of the Abbey] was of no military disadvantage for the German troops, as up to this time the immediate area of the Monastery had not been occupied by troops. On the contrary, reasons for respecting the Monastery now ceased to exist and the ruins offered good possibilities for defense. The enemy ground attack met with no success.

Later, when I talked with Pope Pius and other Vatican officials in Rome, they gave me the results of an exhaustive investigation made by the Vatican. In brief, this information revealed that in October of 1943, when the Allied troops were nearing the Volturno River, a lieutenant colonel and a medical captain called on Monsignor Gregorio Diamare, titular Bishop of Costanza di Arabia and Abbot Ordinary of Monte Cassino, saying they had been sent to evacuate works of art and personnel from the Monastery. The Abbot refused the offer to evacuate personnel, except those who volunteered to leave.

Such works of art as could be moved—and by no means all could be—were later taken in German trucks to the north. The Vatican Secretariat of State then began a long series of negotiations with both the Germans and the Allies, as a result of which everybody promised to try to avoid damage to the Monastery, but nobody said specifically that it could be guaranteed. The Germans, however, stated they would not make the Abbey a part of their defenses.

There was so much confusion in the rear of the German armies that the Abbot later asked for two German soldiers to protect the Monastery grounds from raids by either German soldiers or Italian civilians. Four soldiers were provided, but after a short time they were replaced by three German military policemen.

In December, the Germans began building works of a military character near the Monastery. Caves were enlarged and observation posts and gun emplacements were built. Ammunition for mortars was stored in two caves a few yards from the enclosures of the kitchen garden of the Monastery. In mid-December, the Germans decided to establish a zone of protection, or a neutral zone, extending outward 300 meters from the Abbey enclosure, permitting no soldiers or military vehicles inside. They also insisted on moving the three military policemen outside this zone, although the Abbot protested that they should remain inside. Later, the military police did move back inside. The ammunition dumps remained inside the zone all this time and military works continued in the area. On December 17, a shell landed in the kitchen garden of the Monastery, and from then on shells frequently hit around the buildings, causing some damage.

On January 5, a German interpreter advised the Abbot that the neutral zone no longer existed and ordered all civilians evacuated from the Monastery. There were a couple of hundred, perhaps more, refugees in the buildings—not 2,000, as had been reported to the Allies. The Abbot expressed astonishment at this change in the German attitude and said that one day the whole world would hear the true story of what was happening. He and the monks refused to leave.

On January 13, a shell hit the Monastery entrance cloister. A week later, the German military police were withdrawn. German soldiers, but in reduced numbers, manned the positions in the area adjacent to the Abbey, particularly an observation post north of the Monastery and another in a cave not far from the kitchen garden enclosure. Early in February, when shelling was more intense, the Germans set up a mortar battery about 220 yards south of the Monastery and required civilians to carry ammunition there from the cave where it had been stored near the Monastery. Two German tanks were stationed on a road not far from the Abbey.

More refugees were coming into the Abbey at this time, but the exact number was not established. Early in February, an Allied patrol came within a dozen yards of the Monastery enclosure. On February 11, a German medical officer came into the Monastery to care for the wounded refugees.

On the afternoon of February 14, leaflets from a Fifth Army propaganda shell fell close to the enclosure; at considerable risk, one was recovered and brought inside. It read as follows:

> Italian friends, BEWARE! We have until now been especially careful to avoid shelling the Monte Cassino Monastery. The Germans have known how to benefit from this. But now the fighting has swept closer and closer to its sacred precincts. The time has come when we must train our guns on the Monastery itself.
>
> We give you warning so that you may save yourselves. We warn you urgently. Leave the Monastery. Leave it at once. Respect this warning. It is for your benefit.
>
> (Signed) THE FIFTH ARMY.

This caused panic among the civilians, but actually the danger of leaving the Abbey through an area that was being heavily shelled was so great that they could not get out. A German lieutenant finally was summoned, and he said that efforts would be made to open a passageway for the refugees on the night of February 15. On the morning of the 15th, the Abbot was in the thick-walled Museum of Natural Sciences when the aerial bombardment began. He and a number of the monks escaped, but a large number of refugees—estimated at from one to three hundred—were buried under the ruins of the Monastery.

After the bombing, the German lieutenant returned and asked the Abbot if he would state that there were no Germans inside at the time of the air attack. The Abbot signed the following:

I certify to be the truth that inside the enclosure of the sacred Monastery of Cassino there never were any German soldiers; that there were for a certain period only three military police for the sole purpose of enforcing respect for the neutral zone which was established around the monastery, but they were withdrawn about twenty days ago. Monte Cassino, February 15, 1944. (Signed) Gregorio Diamare, Abbot-Bishop of Monte Cassino. Dieber, Lieutenant.

On February 16, violent artillery action destroyed more of the buildings. Ceilings gave way or were about to give way. Holding aloft a large crucifix, the Abbot led those who remained alive out of the ruins of the old Monastery and down the shell-pocked mountainside where death had become so common. They found their way to a Red Cross station at Colloquio, while the German propaganda organization blared the Abbot's statement to the world and Hitler's fanatical, marked-for-death parachute troops crawled through the dusty rubble of the Monastery to fend off Freyberg's infantry attack. The dust soon was to be turned into mud by the heavy rains, which followed the termination of the attack.

Both Alexander and I were eager to keep up the pressure toward the Liri Valley, but circumstances, largely caused by bad weather, caused a lull in the Battle of Cassino, following failure of the infantry attack on the bombed-out Abbey. The Anzio beachhead, a bit later, was in something of a lull, too, although it would be a grave error to think of that sector as quiet. Following Mackensen's failure to drive us into the sea during his big offensive in mid-February, our forces were being constantly strengthened, and we made frequent counterthrusts that improved our positions. The latter part of February, as well as the first days of March, witnessed a final serious German attempt to crack our defenses, but this attempt broke down in the face of our powerful resistance. On March 4, the enemy definitely went on the defensive and even withdrew some of his crack units for reorganization, to lick their wounds, and to act as mobile reserves in the area north and south of Rome.

So the lull that occurred was merely comparative. In fact, I recall but one story, entirely imaginary, that suggested there was opportunity for anything but a struggle to exist throughout the duration of the beachhead. The men of Anzio got a much-needed laugh from this story of a baseball game alleged to have taken place at a relatively quiet spot within our lines. On the right flank of the beachhead, the Mussolini Canal formed a more or less static boundary where neither attack nor counterattack was likely because of the terrain. When there was any chance to give our men a rest they were moved over toward the canal where there was not as much activity as elsewhere. After a while, the Germans were inclined to do the same thing, contenting themselves with keeping an inactive force on the opposite bank of the canal. In the light of this situation, the story was hatched that some of our boys organized a baseball game one day on our side of the canal and had some fun for the first time in a long while. It was a mild, sunny day and all was quiet on the enemy side of the boundary. The game was closer than might have been expected, and in the late innings the score was tied with a man on second base and two out. The next batter connected with a hard drive over shortstop and the runner headed for home, coming in with a long slide in an effort to beat the throw from left field to the plate. It was a close play, but the umpire authoritatively jerked his thumb up over his shoulder and yelled, "You're out!"

There was a moment's silence on the part of both teams while the decision sank in. Then there came a tremendous shout, in pure Brooklynese, from across the canal where a German soldier holding a pair of field glasses and shaking his fist could be seen momentarily and heard clearly as he rendered a dissent:

"Whaddayuh mean—out? He vas safe a mile, ya bum!"

There weren't many times, however, when anybody got a laugh out of the Anzio beachhead. It was grim from beginning to end, partly because it was the first time VI Corps had really been forced into defensive fighting. We learned rapidly, but for weeks there was a shortage of engineer troops trained for such work as laying mines and stringing booby traps. The defense of our toehold required the use of engineers, tankers, artillerymen, and everybody else as infantrymen.

One of the most disturbing factors about life on the beachhead was the enemy's big railroad guns, which I have mentioned previously and which were called the Anzio Express and, sometimes, Anzio Annie. Everybody tried to joke about them, but it was no joking matter. We spent a great deal of time trying to knock out these guns, which continually interfered with landing of men and supplies in the harbor, but we never found them.

I recall that on one occasion, while at the beachhead, I took up the question with Brigadier General Urban Niblo, my ordnance expert, who said that the Anzio Express was a 280 mm. rifle mounted on a railroad truck so that it could be moved rapidly from place to place. A number of efforts to locate the gun had been made, but without success, either with radar or by air spotting. Brigadier General Aaron Bradshaw, the Fifth Army antiaircraft officer, who had done a fine job of organizing antiaircraft defenses at Anzio and elsewhere, worked out a method by which the night-flying Beaufighters would circle the area until they picked up the flash of the big gun. Then they would fly straight for the spot, and the radar would pick up the lines of flight where these intersected; that was where the gun was supposed to be. Bradshaw thought that with this system and the application of intelligence and mathematics we could locate and knock out the gun. We never did, but it was quite a while before we found out why.

The reason was that the Germans operated the guns most of the time near a railroad tunnel. At Anzio, the tunnel was not far from Castel Gandolfo, the Pope's summer palace. They would roll the gun out, sight it on the port or whatever target had been selected, fire it, and then trundle it back into the tunnel. This was done either at night or at a time when the weather prevented our aerial observation. We knew the tunnel was there, and suspected it was being used, but our attempts to destroy it by bombing were unsuccessful. We finally located one of the guns—many weeks later—at Civitavecchia, but the only reason we found it was that the enemy had been forced to leave it behind. It was thoroughly wrecked. Our experts said that it would shoot as far as fifty miles, with a rocket assist. It had done a lot of damage, and I'll never forget how much noise it made at the receiving end on the Anzio beachhead.

Enemy shelling and air attacks reached virtually every square foot of the beachhead; there was almost no spot and no hour of the day or night when anyone could be free from the tension of combat, with the possible exception of some essential centers which were dug deep underground. In fact, everybody lived underground as much and as far as possible, but the strain on nerves, greatly reducing the efficiency of personnel, continued throughout most of the Anzio period.

There were thousands of men crowded into a small, pie-shaped sector, which the Germans could clearly observe from their positions in the hills and on which they could fire with great accuracy. My own van was in a wood near a big house at the edge of the town of Anzio, probably a quarter of a mile from the port. The wood, like all other spots, was frequently under shellfire, and I remember that on one occasion I ducked behind a thin plyboard map stand for protection when shells came screaming by. The map stand, of course, didn't offer any protection, but I think there was some psychological comfort in having anything to put between oneself and the enemy's fire. In the same way, I often had seen Sergeant Chaney plaster himself against the side of his pup tent—which offered even less protection than my plyboard. We had a number of close ones during those days, but on the one occasion when my van was hit no one was there.

Both combat casualties and non-battle casualties were heavy, particularly during February when it was almost impossible to provide relief or replacements for men who were close to exhaustion. Later we were able to provide some relief, and our method of evacuating casualties by sea improved so that in all some 38,063 wounded were removed during the period from January to May.

On February 22, I went to Anzio by PT boat, approaching the harbor just as the German big guns cut loose on the docks. We stalled around outside until the firing ceased and then proceeded as rapidly as possible to VI Corps Headquarters, where I conferred with Lucas and Truscott. The situation generally seemed to be improved, although I had some personal misgivings about it when we drove over to another command post and were sighted by a German tank that laid four shells along the road in front of us.

In view of all the circumstances existing at that time, I decided that the day had come to carry out my earlier decision to make Lucas deputy commander of the Fifth Army and put Truscott in charge of the beachhead. Lucas had carried a tremendous load for some time and was obviously exhausted, so I arranged for him to go immediately to Sorrento for a much-needed rest.

In the next few days I continued to shuttle back and forth from Anzio to the Cassino front, but the weather prevented any real resumption of our offensive operations. Freyberg had shifted the focus of his attack from the Monastery sector to the town of Cassino, but he was unhappy about our inability to provide what he considered sufficient air support for seizure of the town. The attack had been scheduled for February 24, but was postponed because of weather.

As a matter of record, the plans for bombing the town of Cassino were extremely complicated because some of our troops were holding the northern edge of the town and it would be necessary to withdraw them at the last moment in order to avoid dropping bombs into our own lines. This called for some precise timing and some expert weather forecasting in order to make certain that the Germans would not, immediately after the bombing, seize the evacuated sector before the New Zealand Corps could reoccupy it. Complications of this sort, plus the continued bad weather, provided one headache after another during this period. I probably accurately expressed my feelings late in February when I received the following message from Rear Admiral J. Anthony V. Morse, flag officer of western Italy for the Royal Navy:

> Am so very sorry that the weather has broken to add to your worries. However, the Book says: "Whom the Lord loveth he chasteneth."

"Thanks for your kind thoughts," I replied. "Chastening is already ample. Surely the time has come to spare the rod."

Almost the only good news I can remember around this time was the word that because of my preoccupation with the Italian campaign I had been relieved of all further responsibility for the ANVIL invasion of southern France. This was a great relief to me because I had had no time to think of the operation and didn't see how I was going to get any time for it in the near future.

There were a lot of little disturbances as well as big ones as we waited for the weather to give us a break at Cassino. One of them, I note in my diary, was a message from the Public Relations Office at Alexander's headquarters saying that, on order of Prime Minister Churchill, the Allied troops in the Anzio bridgehead should henceforth be designated as "Allied Bridgehead Force" instead of Fifth Army forces. This didn't seem right to me, since all the troops at Anzio were in the Fifth Army, so I sent a message to Alexander protesting that the change would not help the morale of either British or American troops at Anzio. I suggested that the communiqués and other public announcements refer to the forces there as "The Fifth Army Allied Bridgehead Force." This was agreed upon.

Matters of this kind must have been on the Prime's mind at the time because a little later General Rooks told me about getting a message from British Administrative Headquarters saying that hereafter all dispatches sent personally to the Prime Minister should spell "theater" as "theatre" and should not spell "through" as "thru."

The continued delay in our offensive operations to link the Fifth Army on the Cassino front with the Anzio bridgehead was confusing to the public and resulted in criticism of our beachhead forces for failure to push further inland toward Rome immediately after landing at Anzio. This question came up during a press conference with some American correspondents at my headquarters early in March, and the following extract from my diary may help clarify the way I felt about it at the time:

> The correspondents brought up the matter of replacements and I said that the replacement problem, while bad enough for the American troops, was extremely difficult for both the British and the French. I said I hoped to get two more American divisions in Italy. . . .
>
> Jim Roper [a correspondent of the United Press] then brought up the question of why the Fifth Army bridgehead had not been exploited, and I pointed out that by dusk on D-day all that we had ashore was the 3rd Division and one brigade of the British 1st Division. Both organizations had only about one fifth of their vehicles ashore. The Germans, however, had land supply lines and had sixteen battalions, including supporting weapons, ranged around the bridgehead perimeter by the night of D-day. I said that Fifth Army forces could probably

have driven on to the high ground dominating the Anzio bridgehead, but that such a move would have greatly endangered the rear areas at Anzio and Nettuno and that our troops might have easily been cut off from all supplies had they moved too far forward and left their flanks and rear thinly held.

Another later excerpt continued:

Intelligence estimates of higher authorities had been furnished to the Fifth Army before we landed at Anzio to the effect that if a landing were made in that region it would oblige the enemy to withdraw a substantial force from the Cassino front, since the enemy would not be able to bring reinforcements from the north [because of our air interdictions of his routes of access]. Unfortunately, the estimate proved incorrect. The enemy did not withdraw any considerable forces from the Cassino front and, on the contrary, reinforced himself up to a strength of ten divisions on the Anzio front by bringing troops down from France, the Balkans, and northern Italy. So equipped, the enemy strongly attacked the bridgehead.

Various armchair strategists in the United States and elsewhere are now criticizing the Fifth Army for failure to seize the Alban Hills and take Rome immediately. Such a course would have been reckless in the extreme and would have resulted in cutting off and capture by increasing enemy forces of the troops which attempted such a long advance without a secure base.

On March 15, the attack on the town of Cassino began. I drove early in the morning with General Gruenther to the New Zealand Corps Headquarters near San Pietro and, with Alexander, Freyberg, Lieutenant General Ira Eaker, and others, proceeded to Cervaro, where a special observation post had been set up in an old stone house overlooking Cassino. From the second floor of the house we could see the besieged town, less than three miles away, shimmering in the sun.

At eight-thirty o'clock, standing on the balcony, I could hear the first bomber squadron coming toward Cassino. The planes accurately launched their explosives and the heart of Cassino seemed to go up in sharp, stabbing flames of orange, followed by a great eruption of smoke and debris. By the time the second wave of bombers arrived, it was impossible to see the town. We climbed up to the roof of our observation post, finding we could see better from there. Eaker and Gruenther and I had just settled ourselves on the ridgepole, our legs hanging down on the roof, when the second wave of Flying Fortresses let go their bombs with a convulsive reverberation that shook the old house on which we sat. It went on like that until almost noon.

One wave of bombers dropped a stick near San Michele, which was well within our lines, and another bomber unloaded near a New Zealand artillery battery, killing several men. The bombing was, in fact, so close to our own lines that 75 Allied soldiers were killed and 250 wounded by misdirected bombs. The planes, which encountered virtually no flak or other opposition, dumped about 1,320 tons of bombs on Cassino during the attack.

When the aerial bombardment ended at noon, the Fifth Army artillery opened up a tremendous attack, and infantry and engineers, waiting in the flatlands behind the Rapido River, began moving slowly toward Cassino. The 6th New Zealand Brigade, with the 19th New Zealand Armored Regiment, led the entry into the town. The streets were almost impassable for tanks because the vast tonnage of bombs and artillery shells—almost 200,000 rounds were fired in two hours—had knocked down such buildings as had not previously been reduced to rubble. The Germans caught in exposed positions had suffered high casualties, two companies of parachute troops being almost exterminated. Others had been jarred severely, and many weapons were destroyed; but, in general, the strongly protected cellars, the steel and concrete pillboxes, and the caves in which most of the Germans took refuge had come through the attack without too much damage. Nor was the morale of the veteran and well-trained enemy troops destroyed. By the time the New Zealanders had gotten into the town, they found the remnants of the German units reorganized and waiting for them behind endless barricades of rubble. They had beaten us to the draw. Heavy rains that night further slowed up the attack. However, in the next three days the New Zealanders succeeded in capturing about two-thirds of the town. At the same time the 4th Indian Division attacked southwest up the slope of Monastery Hill and succeeded thrusting as far as Hangman's Hill with the 1/9 Gurkha Rifles.[*] Here they were in a tenuous position and were still three hundred yards short of the Monastery, which was their objective. It was not encouraging.

The effect on our polyglot collection of infantry units was unfortunate. The effect on the Germans in Cassino, meanwhile, was less severe than we had expected. "It seems to me that the net effect of the attack was to confirm that aerial bombardment alone never has and never will drive a determined enemy from his position," I added in my diary. "Cassino has again proven this theory. The enemy has now held up our advance in severe fighting in the town for the last two days."

In the next week the attack was continued, but without any decisive results. The Germans fought from every pile of rubble in the town and on the hills, and their counterattacks frequently regained scattered key points that we had taken at high sacrifice. Our supply problem was difficult and we were only partly successful in trying to drop ammunition and supplies by air

---

[*] 1st Battalion of the 9th Gurkha Rifles Regiment.

to some of the Indian troops that were isolated on the ridges. In some instances more of the drop fell into German hands than into the pockets held by the Indians.

By March 20, Freyberg had made so little progress that Alexander decided to hold a conference that would decide whether to call off the operation or to make one more effort to break through. He had decided previously that the British Eighth Army soon would be shifted over toward the Liri Valley in order to take part in the push northward once the road to Rome was opened, and he felt that the time for this shift should be decided soon.

Before the meeting, on the following day, I set out for Freyberg's headquarters in a discouraged mood. Freyberg was up against an enemy that was skilled in this kind of fighting and ready to hold his ground until the last man was dead. The Germans had suffered very high casualties, but they hung on; and I saw little chance of a breakthrough at that time.

I talked to Freyberg and many of his officers that morning. They felt that success was so near it would yet be gained. It seemed that progress of only a few hundred yards, both in the town and on Monastery Hill, would mean the difference between success and failure.

"I think you and the Boche are both groggy," I remarked. Freyberg immediately objected that his troops were not groggy and expressed a belief that he could break through.

After listening to the New Zealanders, I felt better about the outlook, and admired their determination to keep up the attack. At Alexander's conference that afternoon, I was inclined to agree when Freyberg argued for continuation of the attack. In the end it was decided to keep going, and on March 22 the New Zealand Division made a final all-out effort to reduce the enemy strong points in the town. Heavy artillery support and a fresh infantry battalion were used in the assault, which made some progress, but not enough. By sundown it was obvious that a withdrawal for reorganization was necessary. I felt that the New Zealand Corps had failed because it placed too much reliance on the overpowering weight of bombing to reduce the enemy defenses. The enemy was too well protected and too determined. Maximum advantage of the powerful aerial and artillery support, which was provided, could be taken only by speedy, aggressive action by infantry and armor, using the maximum available force. Piecemeal action, committing a company or a battalion at a time, merely invited failure against the German veterans.

From March 15 to 23, the New Zealand Corps suffered 1,594 casualties. It had killed a great many Germans, but in terms of progress we still were looking at the battered ridges of Monte Cassino, and it still barred our road to Rome.

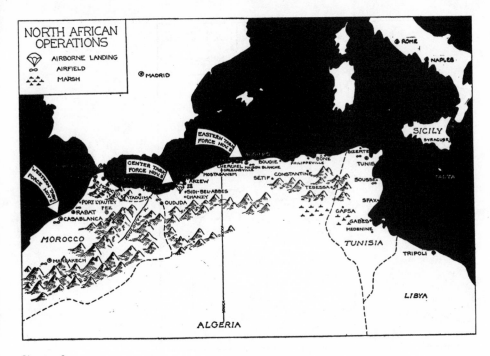

Chapter 6

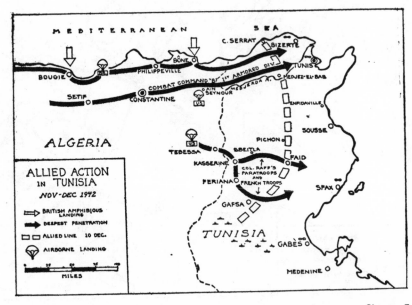

Chapter 7

Chapter 8

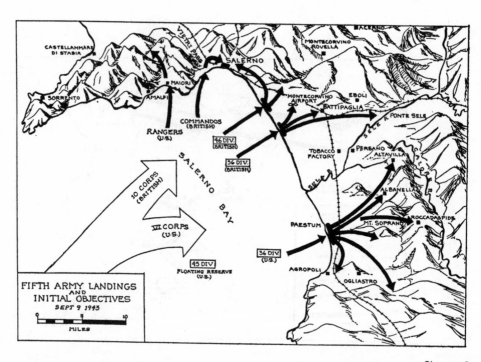

Chapter 9

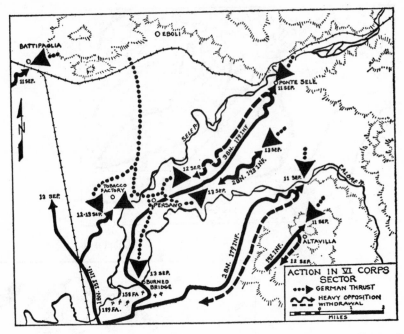

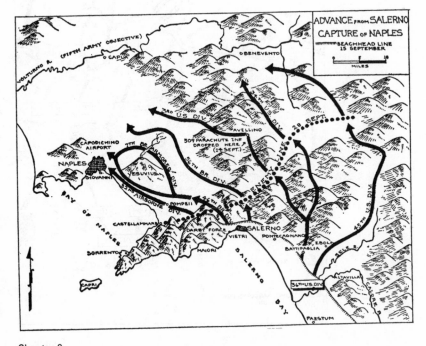

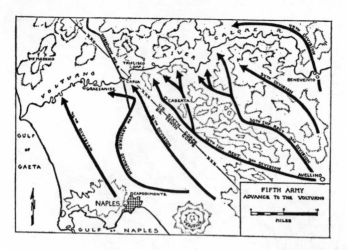

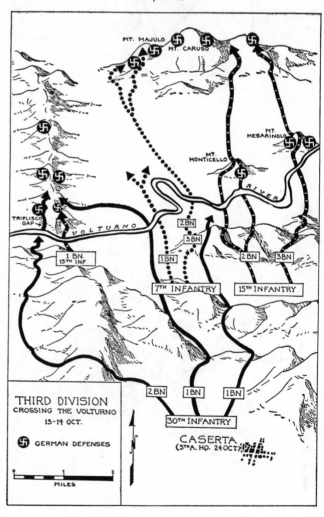

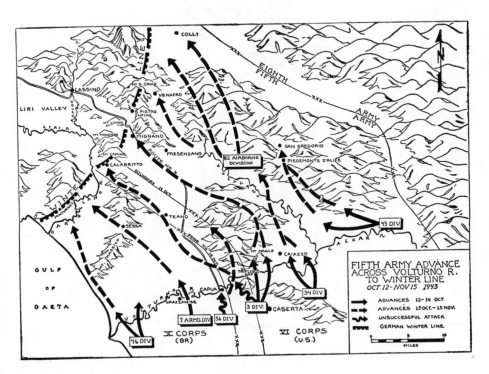

FIFTH ARMY ADVANCE
ACROSS VOLTURNO R.
TO WINTER LINE
OCT. 12 - NOV 15 1943

Chapter 11

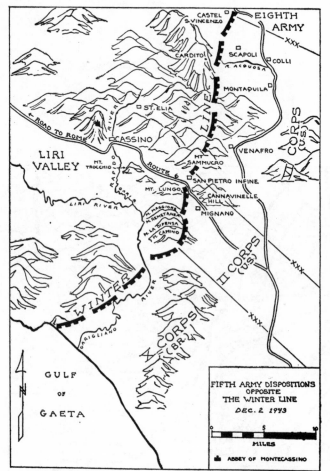

FIFTH ARMY DISPOSITIONS
OPPOSITE
THE WINTER LINE
DEC. 2 1943

MILES

ABBEY OF MONTECASSINO

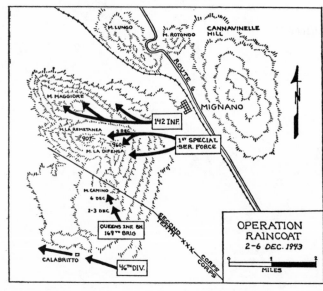

OPERATION
RAINCOAT
2-6 DEC. 1943

MILES

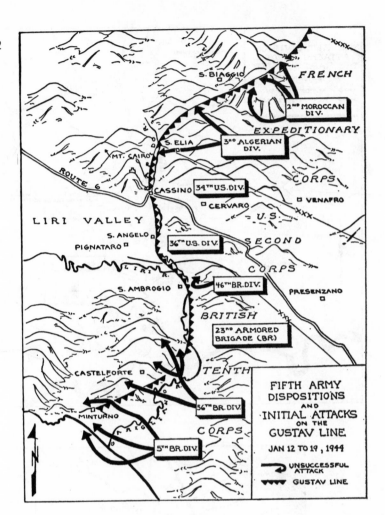

FIFTH ARMY
DISPOSITIONS
AND
INITIAL ATTACKS
ON THE
GUSTAV LINE

JAN 12 TO 19, 1944

⟲ UNSUCCESSFUL ATTACK
⋁⋁⋁⋁ GUSTAV LINE

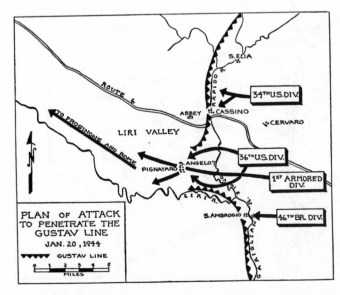

PLAN OF ATTACK
TO PENETRATE THE
GUSTAV LINE
JAN. 20, 1944

⋁⋁⋁⋁ GUSTAV LINE

MILES

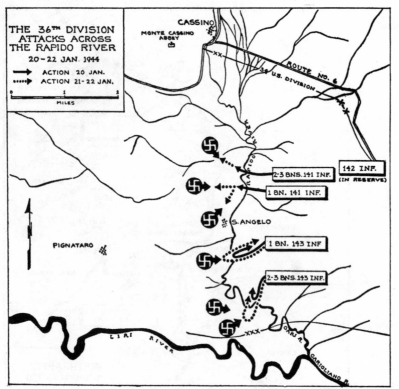

THE 36TH DIVISION
ATTACKS ACROSS
THE RAPIDO RIVER
20-22 JAN. 1944

→ ACTION 20 JAN.
••••▶ ACTION 21-22 JAN.

0   1   2
MILES

CASSINO
MONTE CASSINO ABBEY

ROUTE NO. 6
34
U.S. DIVISION
XX

142 INF.
(IN RESERVE)

2-3 BNS. 141 INF.

1 BN. 141 INF.

S. ANGELO

PIGNATARO

1 BN. 143 INF

2-3 BNS. 143 INF.

LIRI RIVER

XXX

GARI R.

CARIGLIANO R.

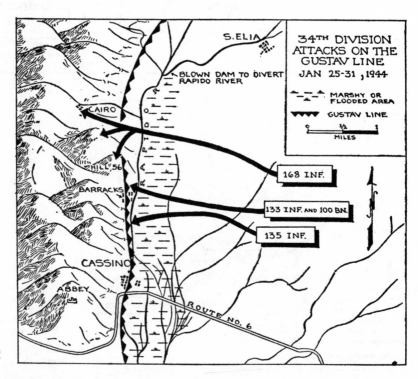

S. ELIA

BLOWN DAM TO DIVERT
RAPIDO RIVER

34TH DIVISION
ATTACKS ON THE
GUSTAV LINE
JAN 25-31, 1944

⟞⟝ MARSHY OR
FLOODED AREA

vvvv GUSTAV LINE

0   ½   1
MILES

CAIRO

HILL 56

BARRACKS

168 INF.

133 INF. AND 100 BN.

135 INF.

CASSINO

ABBEY

ROUTE NO. 6

RAPIDO

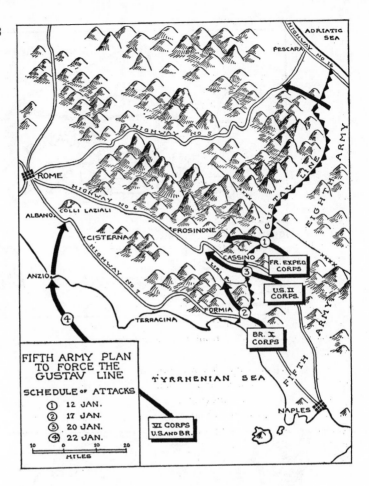

FIFTH ARMY PLAN
TO FORCE THE
GUSTAV LINE

SCHEDULE OF ATTACKS

① 12 JAN.
② 17 JAN.
③ 20 JAN.
④ 22 JAN.

VI CORPS
U.S. AND BR.

10   5   0   10   20
MILES

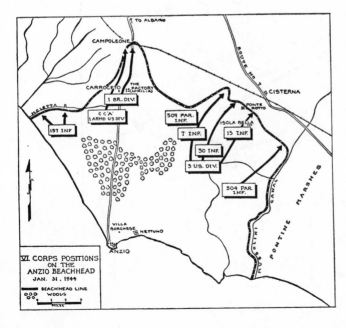

VI CORPS POSITIONS
ON THE
ANZIO BEACHHEAD
JAN. 31, 1944

■ BEACHHEAD LINE
○○○ WOODS
1   0   1   2
MILES

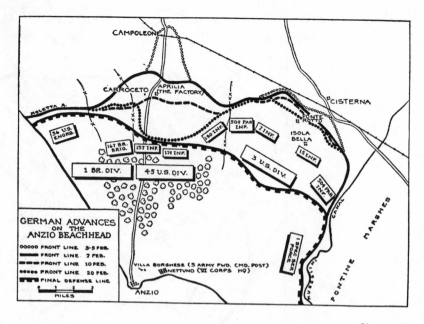

GERMAN ADVANCES
ON THE
ANZIO BEACHHEAD

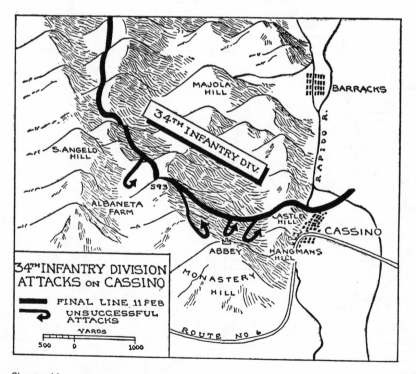

34TH INFANTRY DIVISION
ATTACKS ON CASSINO

FINAL LINE 11 FEB
UNSUCCESSFUL
ATTACKS

YARDS
500   0   1000

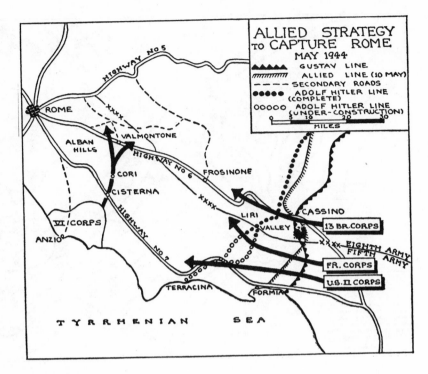

Chapter 15

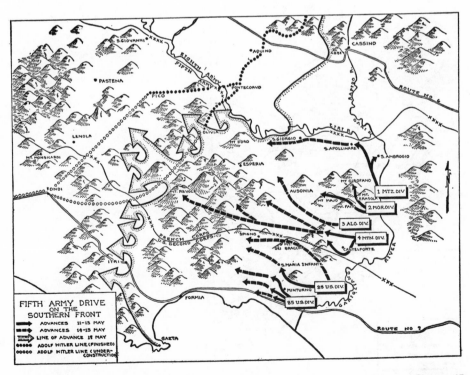

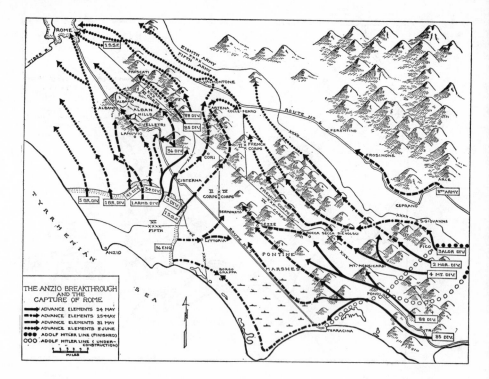

THE ANZIO BREAKTHROUGH
AND THE
CAPTURE OF ROME

ADVANCE ELEMENTS 24 MAY
ADVANCE ELEMENTS 25 MAY
ADVANCE ELEMENTS 31 MAY
ADVANCE ELEMENTS 3 JUNE
ADOLF HITLER LINE (FINISHED)
ADOLF HITLER LINE (UNDER-CONSTRUCTION)

MILES

Chapter 15

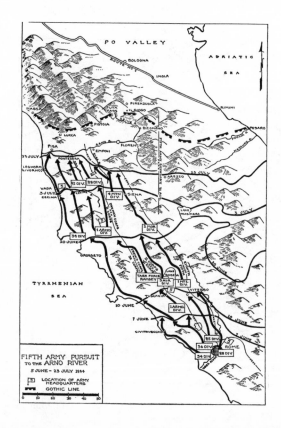

FIFTH ARMY PURSUIT
TO THE ARNO RIVER

5 JUNE - 25 JULY 1944

LOCATION OF ARMY HEADQUARTERS
GOTHIC LINE

Chapter 16

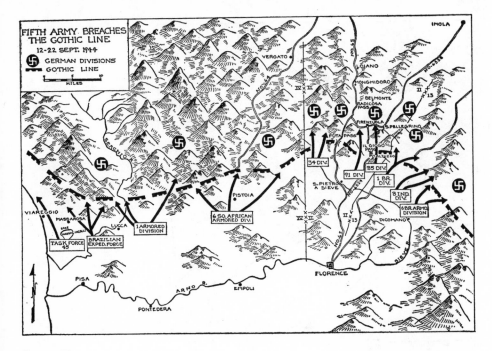

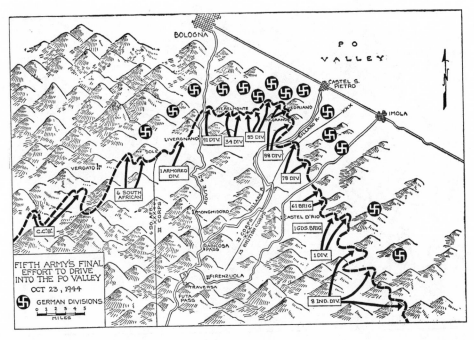

THE BALKAN
SPRINGBOARD

SCALE (MILES)

0   50   100

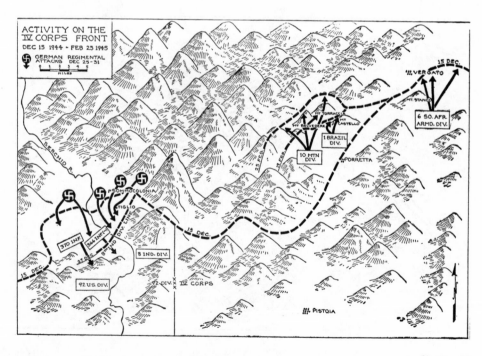

ACTIVITY ON THE
IV CORPS FRONT
DEC 15 1944 - FEB 23 1945

GERMAN REGIMENTAL
ATTACKS DEC 25-31

MILES
0   1   2   3   4   5

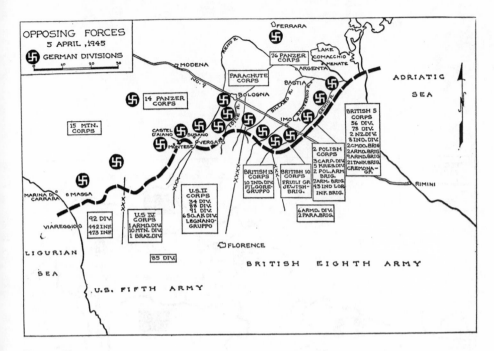

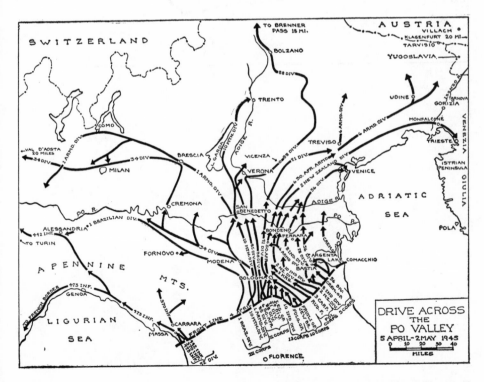

Chapter 19

15.

Rome, the Great Prize:

April 1944–June 1944

When Spring came round to Italy, after that gloomy winter of 1944, the Fifth Army had eliminated a great many Germans, but about all we had gained was experience and a new song. January, February, and March were, I believe, the most difficult months of the entire campaign and perhaps the most costly. We had won a foothold at Anzio and we had edged into the mountains above Cassino, and that was about all we got on the field of battle. Our casualty list for the period from January 16, when the offensive started, to March 31, when the New Zealanders had to stop the attack at Cassino, was 52,130 as compared to 37,773 for the drive from Salerno through the German Winter Line.[*]

I believe it is fair to say, however, that the arrival of warm sunshine on that bleak, mountainous landscape made a difference. We felt that the treacherous mud that had almost nullified the effectiveness of our armor would soon be gone. We practically halted operations in April in order to give the weary units a chance to rest and reorganize. The British Eighth Army in great part shifted over from the Adriatic coast to take over the Cassino

---

		16 Jan.–31 Mar.	Salerno-Winter Line
[*]	American	22,219	20,631
	British	22,092	13,251
	French	7,421	3,305
	Italian	398	586
		52,130	37,773

sector, while the Fifth Army moved west along the coast, thus massing greater strength for the day when our offensive would be renewed. And then, as I mentioned, we got a song.

I don't know why it was that in World War II the Allied nations couldn't produce a good war song. If the contest had been decided on musical merits, I feel no doubt that the Germans would have had a walkover with "Lili Marlene." Our men soon picked up the enemy song and it was often heard where they gathered. In fact, at a later date in the campaign, our arrival in Florence, where a considerable number of Americans or former American citizens had been in residence throughout the war, resulted in a touch of panic because the American soldiers were singing "Lili Marlene" as they marched along the street.

"What can this mean?" the American-born wife of an Italian asked me urgently. "We have been sitting here listening to the Germans sing that song for months, and now the Americans arrive and they are singing it too."

I suppose the reason was that, in the opinion of the soldiers, it was a good song. Our song wasn't that good, but I liked it because it was one that Irving Berlin dashed off on the spur of the moment when he brought his great performance of *This Is the Army* to the Fifth Army area. Lots of the men liked it, too, and I've heard them sing it many times. It went like this:

> I met her in America about a month ago,
> She asked me if I'd give her love to a certain GI Joe.
> She said when he returns, I'll be his bride.
> I asked her where he was and she replied:
>
> Not the First, not the Second, not the Third not the Fourth,
> But the Fifth Army's where my heart is.
>
> He's somewhere on a beachhead which must be lots of fun,
> I can see him in a bathing suit, basking in the sun.
> From a cute signorina, he's been learning to talk like a real native of Rome.
> She's a very tasty dish, but my baby "No capish," until the Fifth Army comes
>   home.[*]

Well, it went something like that, although now that I look at it in print, I have a suspicion that it doesn't look as good as Berlin made it sound. Anyway, we had a song.

In mid-April, General Marshall instructed me to return to Washington for a brief period of consultation before the renewal of our offensive, which we had decided could not start before the end of the first week in May. He

---

[*] Copyright 1944, by Irving Berlin.

wanted a firsthand report on our situation and to know what chance there was that we would reach Rome before the cross-channel invasion of France started. I figured that it would be necessary for me to have all the answers, so considerable time was spent before my departure in working out final details of the plan by which we intended to complete a breakthrough and join up with the bridgehead below Rome.

Marshall had emphasized that my trip home was to be strictly a military secret, but I was surprised at the lengths to which he went in concealing my presence in Washington. I landed in General Ira Eaker's plane at 3 a.m. on April 11 and was met at the airport by a representative of General Marshall, who hustled me quickly into a car where Mrs. Clark was waiting for me. I was told I could not go home, for security reasons, but that we would go to General Marshall's home at Fort Myer.

Next morning, in General Marshall's office, I discovered that not even my mother, who lived in Washington, had been told I was arriving. The general said that I could send her a letter by special messenger, telling her to put on her hat and meet me and Mrs. Clark and Ann at the airport. I sat down and wrote the letter, but I had to read it aloud to Marshall to make sure I hadn't revealed too much.

We all got together at the airport and were flown immediately to White Sulphur Springs in West Virginia, where the Army's Ashford General Hospital had taken over the beautiful Greenbrier Hotel. Because Marshall thought I needed a rest for a few days, I stayed at a guest cottage and had my meals served in. President Roosevelt at that time was at Bernard Baruch's estate in South Carolina, and after a few days I flew over there and gave him a full report on developments and battle plans in Italy. As usual, he showed a surprising knowledge of details and was quick to offer ideas as I explained our plans for reaching Rome.

After a few more days at White Sulphur Springs, I flew back to Washington and Marshall reluctantly said that I could spend the night in our apartment at the Kennedy-Warren. When I was driven there, however, they took me to the basement door in the rear and put me in an elevator on which a Secret Service man had taken the place of the regular operator. I guess I got into our apartment without being seen, but I felt a bit like a prisoner of some sort.

The next day Marshall sent word for me to be at a certain small restaurant in Washington at seven o'clock in the evening, and to be there on the dot. When I arrived, I discovered that he had taken over the entire place for the evening and that it was filled with specially invited guests, most of whom were Congressmen. We ate oysters and threw the shells in a bowl in the center of the table. Finally, Marshall said for me to tell everything. I did, even explaining exactly how we were going to capture Rome. Fortunately, it worked out about the way I forecast.

Before I left, Mrs. Marshall asked me if I could take a couple of packages and letters to her two sons, Captain Clifton Brown and Lieutenant Allen Tupper Brown, both of whom were serving in Italy. I was happy to do so because no one could have been more thoughtful of me or my family than General and Mrs. Marshall. One of the saddest duties of my life came a month later when I had to advise them of Allen's death in a tank engagement at Anzio. He was killed by a German grenade because he insisted on standing up in his tank, with the turret open, in order to have the advantage of better vision in directing action against the enemy. He was a fine soldier and a brave man.

Upon my return to Italy, we plunged into the final plans for the renewal of the offensive against the Gustav Line and the formidable Adolf Hitler Line, which the enemy had been constructing across the Liri Valley as still another obstacle in our drive on Rome. The removal of the Eighth Army units to the Cassino front permitted the Fifth Army to concentrate in a comparatively narrow sector running along the Garigliano River as far as the seacoast. Of course, our forces at Anzio were also under my command. Actually, in the realignment, I came out with seven American, four French, and two British divisions in the Fifth Army. Of these, both British divisions and three and one-half American divisions were at Anzio. On the Garigliano, or southern, front I had the 36th, 85th, and 88th Divisions and one-half of the 1st Armored Division (all American); and four French divisions, the 3rd Algerian, the 2nd Moroccan, 4th Mountain, and the 1st Motorized.

The problem of outflanking and seizing Cassino and breaking into the Liri Valley now was assigned to the British Eighth Army, while the Fifth Army's task was to drive up the coast toward Anzio. On our sector there was but one road, Route 7, which ran along the coast and was under the complete domination of deep and high mountain ridges. That road was like a little gutter at the edge of a steep roof, and going up it without control of the adjacent mountains was impossible. I decided, therefore, that the Fifth Army would do what nobody expected, particularly the Germans—strike out directly over the mountains with all the strength and speed that we could muster.

There were a number of reasons for this decision, in addition to the fact that going up Route No. 7 alone was suicidal. In the first place, although we had been amateurs at mountain fighting when we landed at Salerno, we learned a great deal since then. The French, perhaps, had learned the most of all, and I knew that I could count on Juin to give everything he had when the going was tough.* Furthermore, we knew that the Germans had built a powerful line (the Adolf Hitler Line) across the Liri Valley where they were expecting our attack if we ever got past Cassino. It would be an extremely difficult one to overcome, but they had not had time, or had not taken time, to complete the line through the mountains near the coast, which was the way we would go. The most important point in favor of our plan, however, was that the enemy would not be expecting us to try to cross the mountains. They were formidable barriers and they would be relatively lightly held if we could conceal our purpose until the moment when we were ready to thrust forward with all the surprise and strength we could manage.

"Surprise," our Camouflage Plan emphasized, "is the most powerful weapon in the hands of the assaulting units of the Fifth Army."

Everything was directed toward that end. Elaborate plans for deception were arranged. Detailed directions were issued to control our preliminary patrols and to avoid any hint that preparations were being made in that sector. Units were held in their training areas until the last possible hour. In the last week of April, we settled down to hard and secret work.

On the 27th, I had a chance to break the routine by presenting theater ribbons with battle stars to selected WACs serving with the Fifth Army, a pleasure which had long been delayed. The WACs had first joined us in North Africa, but they had been left behind when we invaded Italy and did not rejoin us until we reached Naples. In the following months they more than lived up to the job that was given them. They were efficient and hard working, and ready to face whatever dangers or hardships came their way. I know that my secretary, Sergeant Jerry Horne of Mississippi, did an excellent job, and I always felt that the mere presence of the WACs bucked up the Fifth Army's morale. I'm sure that it also resulted in greater attention to neatness and deportment.

There was another ceremony a couple of days later that pleased me too, but for an entirely different reason. General Alexander came to my headquarters at San Marco, where he decorated a number of Fifth Army officers and pinned on my blouse the ribbon of a Knight of the British Empire

On May 2, I made an inspection visit to the 85th division, which was commanded by Major General John B. Coulter; I was delighted with the way this new outfit had taken up its duties. I had special pride then, and later, in both the 85th and the 88th Divisions, which were the first to arrive in

---

* The French had been assigned to mountainous sectors since their arrival in Italy. Practically all their soldiers—although officered mainly by Frenchmen—were colonials who lived in the mountains of North Africa.

Europe of the new divisions trained entirely under the system I had helped General McNair inaugurate in the United States before we were in the war. I had long ago asked General Marshall to send me one or more of these divisions as soon as possible, and now I was able to see the finished product turned out by our training system. Both of them looked like good divisions, with capable leaders, ready to go at any time, and they later proved that they were.

I should point out here in advance that the sector in which I visited the 85th was across the Garigliano River, adjacent to the coast. This sector had been taken by the British X Corps the previous January when our generally unsuccessful offensive was started against the Gustav Line. Among the few gains of that offensive, the X Corps contribution stood out like a bright light. It gave the Fifth Army a jumping-off place toward the mountains and was of tremendous importance to us in carrying out our plans.

I made a similar inspection tour a day or so later to the 88th Division, when it was a pleasure to meet again my old friend Major General John E. Sloan, who had been an instructor of mine at Command and General Staff School at Fort Leavenworth, Kansas. Sloan mentioned this fact in introducing me to his men; and I replied that if any tactical mistakes were made in the forthcoming offensive, the blame should be placed on General Sloan because it would merely show that he had failed to give me the proper instruction.

One of the important decisions made in this period was in regard to timing. After considerable discussion, it was agreed that the Fifth and Eighth Army offensive on the southern front should start first; that, in effect, the attacks up the Liri Valley and across the coastal mountain ranges would be drives to join up with the beachhead. Then, as a climax, General Truscott would launch his VI Corps attack out from Anzio to seize the Alban Hills, cut Route No. 6, and cut off a large German force, if possible, but in any event to open the gates to Rome.

The exact design of Truscott's breakout was, however, the subject of considerable controversy, beginning when Alexander visited Truscott's command post at Anzio the first week in May. Truscott told him that we were working on four different plans for the most effective plan when the time came.

"The only worthwhile plan," Alexander said, "is attack on the Cisterna-Cori-Valmontone line."

This attack called for Truscott to push northeast from Anzio, through Cisterna and Cori, and move south of the Alban Hills to Valmontone, on Route No. 6. The result of such a drive, if timed properly with the British

Eighth Army's advance up the Liri Valley, would be to come in behind the main German forces defending the valley, threaten the rear of the Adolf Hitler Line, and thus simplify the Eighth Army's progress. If it succeeded, the Germans' main forces would either be caught in a pincers or, as was far more likely, would avoid capture by withdrawal northward along a number of suitable axial roads that ran east of Rome.

The trouble with this plan was that in order to get to Valmontone the beachhead forces would more or less bypass the Alban Hills, leaving the enemy holding high ground that was vital to us if we were to enter Rome.

"I told General Alexander," Truscott said in a message to me, "that timing of the attack from the bridgehead was my greatest concern and he informed me that he had reserved to himself the decision as to the time of launching the attack. In view of the above, please advise me if this meets with your approval."

This message made me fear that Alexander had decided to move in and run my army. I therefore called him on the telephone to say that I was surprised by Truscott's message, which indicated that Alexander had issued instructions contrary to mine (I had told Truscott to prepare the alternate plans), and that Truscott was confused and had asked me for clarification. I asked Alex to please issue orders through me instead of dealing directly with my subordinates. He understood and assured me that he had no intention of interfering.

I talked to him again when I saw him a couple of days later, and I believe he jumped to the conclusion that I was not all-out for the attack. One reason for this was that while he kept emphasizing that the Valmontone attack would result in the capture of a large number of German prisoners, I doubted it because there were other roads over which they could withdraw. I pointed out that I merely did not want to have to follow any rigid, preconceived ideas in the breakout, and that if we played our cards right we had a chance for a great victory.

In the final days of preparation I visited the beachhead to witness a demonstration of a number of new methods and machines that had been developed to facilitate our attack. These were ingenious affairs, for the most part, devised by men who had discovered the hard way that necessity is the mother of invention. Some of them were to prove of little use in battle, but others were practical devices that since have been or may become a part of our regular equipment.

One of the most interesting to me, in view of the Italian mud, was a tank retriever developed by the 1st Armored Division to pull broken-down or stalled tanks out of mine fields. The GIs had merely applied the experience of their hometown garage men to tanks. The retriever consisted of a tank with a front crane that dropped down and hooked on to a cable in the rear of the stalled tank. The operation was smooth and fast, and the stalled tank was yanked to safety in a very short time.

We next looked at a remarkable device that became well known as the "snake," which was used in clearing a path through minefields. A tank pushed forward what looked like a huge boa constrictor, but really was a long, segmented piece of metal tubing bolted in the center, with a space for packing TNT along each side. A ball-shaped runner out in front of the linked metal tube made it easy to push over the ground as the tank moved forward. The whole thing was about a hundred feet long. Once the tank had shoved it into the mine field, it was detonated by firing one of the tank machine guns into a target detonator at the rear end of the snake, the last twenty feet of the tube being packed with sand so that no damage was done to the tank when the TNT exploded. The blast was strong enough to explode mines as deep as five feet and over a space wide enough for a tank to pass through. As soon as one snake had been exploded that tank withdrew and another moved forward over the cleared path, pushing out another snake, and so on until the mine-field had been crossed.

When I visited the 3rd Division, which was then in a rest area, I saw a number of model pup tents that could be set up in foxholes in a manner that left only a small part of the top showing, thus providing maximum protection for the men, something that was desperately needed at a place like Anzio. Another demonstration was of battle sleds developed by the 3rd Division in preparation for the coming offensive. One of the difficult problems of this kind of warfare is the coordination of tank and infantry operations. The infantry needs the tanks to knock out enemy strong points and the tanks need infantry protection when they run into close fighting where a grenade or a rocket can put them out of order in a hurry. The practice of having infantrymen ride on tanks is a makeshift that sometimes works, but, obviously, it exposes the infantrymen while the tank is in motion.

The battle sled was designed to solve this problem. It looked like something made of an ordinary hot-water boiler or a big metal pipe, sliced in half. The result was a sort of shallow metal dish, about six feet long and three feet wide at the open top. It rested with its curved bottom on the ground, and a man lying prone inside it was fairly well protected from small-arms fire.

Six of these sleds were hooked together and then a tank attached two such tows, or a dozen sleds in all, to its rear and pulled them forward. This enabled each tank to carry with it a full squad of infantry which, from a distance or if moving through a field of grass, could hardly be seen by the enemy. The men, however, were ready on an instant's notice to leap out and seize a strong point that the tank had overrun or to provide protection for the tank if it was attacked by enemy infantry.

Still another device was known as the "mangle buggy." It looked something like an old farm hayrack axle on which a jeep motor had been mounted, with a trail guard in the back. This vehicle, if it could be called that, pulled a long strip of primer cord, which was a powerful enough explosive to blast out barbed wire and similar defensive obstacles. The mangle buggy did not carry any driver or other personnel. It was placed in position and aimed forward toward a barbed wire entanglement. As the driverless contraption smashed through the barbed wire, it towed its primer cord tail into position, where it was detonated by a time fuse and thereby cleared a passage through the barbed wire and knocked out any nearby antipersonnel mines as well.

In addition to these devices, the engineers had worked out a method of using tanks with cranes to put various types of treadway bridges across small streams or dry creek beds. Use of the tank crane and a system of rubber pontoons enabled the crews to install the bridges under heavy fire because they had far more protection than when working with the usual truck crane.

The final demonstration was of a 60 mm. mortar that fired a harpoon. The harpoon had attached to it a primer cord which, when it hit the ground, ignited and cleared away grass or other vegetation. It also exploded antipersonnel mines. When fired, the harpoon arched through the air for about fifty feet, something like the harpoons fired from a whaling vessel. By successive shots with these mortars, the men could clear a trail for a column of men through either minefields or thick vegetation. The same idea was applied to an 81 mm. mortar mounted on a tank, which fired a lanced harpoon attached to a cable. This cable, however, was released from sprockets on the front part of the tank and its end remained fastened to the tank. The idea was that the harpoon would be fired into a barbed-wire entanglement, where it would hook itself on to the wire. Then, when the tank reversed, it could drag out a big section of the entanglement to open a path for infantry. A somewhat similar purpose was served by a tank rigged with a three-pronged, anchor-type hook. The tank negotiated close to the wire, dropped the hook over the wire, and then turned away, pulling the wire with it.

In the first part of May we completed a period of vigorous training for mountain warfare with special attention to the French Expeditionary Corps, which, with the addition of scattered elements, had approximately four and one-half divisions available. The Fifth Army's American representation on the southern front was the II Corps, consisting of the 85th and 88th Divisions, both untried in battle. The 86th Division was in reserve, with the idea that it probably would be moved to Anzio to join in the breakout there.

On our right flank, heading for the Liri Valley, was the British Eighth Army with eleven divisions of various nationalities.* Its Polish Corps had taken over the Cassino sector. It was this Liri Valley force on which the Germans centered their attention, apparently certain that even if a breakthrough finally was achieved at Cassino, the Allied offensive could not penetrate the Adolf Hitler Line farther up the valley.

The evening of May 11 was misty after a little rain, but by the time darkness settled over the Fifth Army front the sky was clear and the stars were out. Our right flank began at the junction of the Liri River and the Garigliano, with the French facing the necessity of crossing the Garigliano in that sector, although farther south their line already was across that barrier and joined with the American II Corps line near Castelforte, where we had occupied the Minturno sector taken by the British in January.

As soon as it was dark, a steady movement of troops began behind the Fifth Army lines as well as behind the British Eighth Army lines to the north. Everything else went on in as near the normal routine as possible. Patrols were out. There was occasional artillery fire. It was just as it had been on the previous evening and for many evenings before. On the German side everything went on as usual, too, except that they were in earnest about it. We weren't. We were waiting and preparing for the hour before midnight.

At 11 o'clock about a thousand big guns from Cassino to the sea fired at approximately the same moment, their shells aimed with great care at enemy headquarters, communications centers, command posts, and other vital targets that had been quietly located by air reconnaissance during the previous month. The ridges in front of the Fifth Army seemed to stand out momentarily in a great blaze of light, sink again into darkness, and then tremble under the next salvo. It was perhaps the most effective artillery bombardment of the campaign. It simply smashed into dust a great number of enemy batteries and vital centers; so that for hours after the Germans had overcome

---

*   In the line: 2nd New Zealand Infantry Division
                    4th Infantry Division (British)
                    3rd Carpathian Infantry Division (Polish)
                    5th Kresowa Infantry Division (Polish)
                    8th Indian Infantry Division
                    1 Italian Motorized Group

    In reserve:

                    78th Infantry Division (British)
                    6th Armored Division (British)
                    5th Canadian Armored Division
                    1st Canadian Infantry Division
                    6th South African Armored Division

the initial shock of an attack where they least expected it, they were still confused and unable to establish good centralized direction of their defense lines.

Just for statistical purposes: our artillery fired 173,941 rounds in the first twenty-four hours of the attack. At dawn our Air Force began flying what turned out to be approximately 1,500 sorties that did a workmanlike job of knocking out enemy positions, battering the inadequate mountain communications routes over which he could move up reinforcements, and smashing both the German Tenth Army Headquarters and Kesselring's headquarters with heavy loads of high explosives. Not only had we surprised the enemy, but we were able to get in quick artillery and aerial blows that jarred him to the bottom of his feet.

Meantime, the French forces had crossed the Garigliano and moved forward into the mountainous terrain lying south of the Liri River. It was not easy. As always, the German veterans reacted strongly and there was bitter fighting. The French surprised the enemy and quickly seized key terrain including Mounts Faito, Cerasola, and high ground near Castelforte. The 1st Motorized Division helped the 2nd Moroccan Division take key Mount Girofano and then advanced rapidly north to S. Apollinare and S. Ambrogio. In spite of stiffening enemy resistance, the 2nd Moroccan Division penetrated the Gustav Line in less than two days' fighting.

The next forty-eight hours on the French front were decisive. The knife-wielding Goumiers swarmed over the hills, particularly at night, and General Juin's entire force showed an aggressiveness hour after hour that the Germans could not withstand. Cerasola, San Giorgio, Mt. D'Oro, Ausonia, and Esperia were seized in one of the most brilliant and daring advances of the war in Italy, and by May 16 the French Expeditionary Corps had thrust forward some ten miles on their left flank to Mount Revole, with the remainder of their front slanting back somewhat to keep contact with the British Eighth Army.

Only the most careful preparations and the utmost determination made this attack possible, but Juin was that kind of fighter. Mule pack trains, skilled mountain fighters, and men with the strength to make long night marches through treacherous terrain were needed to succeed in the all-but-impregnable mountain ranges. The French displayed that ability during their sensational advance which Lieutenant General Siegfried Westphal, the chief of staff to Kesselring, later described as a major surprise both in timing and in aggressiveness. For this performance, which was to be a key to the success of the entire drive on Rome, I shall always be a grateful admirer of General Juin and his magnificent FEC.

The American II Corps, as well as the British Eighth Army, began its attacks in coordination with the French. On the II Corps front, commanded by General Keyes, the 85th and 88th Divisions did not get off to as good a start as the veteran French units. This was to be expected in view of their lack of battle training and in the face of more organized opposition. One main objective was the town of Itri, but first it was necessary to smash through the mountain defense line north of Minturno to Mt. dei Bracchi and to Santa Maria Infante. General Sloan was in a disappointed mood when I conferred with him late on May 12. He promised stronger efforts, however, and we soon got them, in a big way. The rapid advance of the French in the next few days seemed to spur the II Corps, and it began pressing forward despite stiffened resistance and the many ruses that the German veterans pulled on our untried troops.

One of the German tricks usually was tried at dusk, when several of their men would rise up and rush forward yelling *"Kamerad!"* as if they wished to surrender. Company F of the 2nd Battalion, 351st Infantry, had advanced a couple of miles from the Minturno cemetery at the beginning of the attack and had lost touch with units on its flanks. It was pinned down and isolated by the enemy for many hours. On the evening of the 12th, the Germans pulled the *"Kamerad!"* trick on Company F. When the Americans scrambled out of their foxholes to take the supposed prisoners, the enemy closed in on them from all sides and captured all but a few.

At the end of two days of fighting, II Corps had, despite heavy casualties, penetrated most of the German defense positions and was nearing the road junction at Spigno behind the Gustav Line. At the same time, the French advance had badly crushed the German units defending the Gustav Line and, penetrating it, had caused them to withdraw in an effort to rally and defend the Hitler Line. The French and Americans pursued rapidly in order to attack the enemy's new line before he could get set.

In the next day or so it became clear that the offensive had broken the back of the German resistance in the Ausonia Valley, wiping out the 71st Grenadier Division and battering the 94th Grenadier Division severely.

Actually, neither II Corps nor the French ever ceased their powerful forward movement from that time on, but the British Eighth Army was forced to proceed against the best-prepared enemy positions and thus lagged behind in the Liri Valley. Cassino was as difficult as ever, and it was a week after the offensive started before the Polish Corps seized the battered, besieged, and outflanked town of ruins. The Eighth Army's delay made Juin's task more difficult because he was moving forward so rapidly that his right flank—adjacent to the British—constantly was exposed to counterattacks.

It should be emphasized that the Eighth Army was going up against prepared defenses. The Polish Corps fought with utter bravery and disregard for casualties, and the XIII Corps (British) advanced two miles in four days at a cost of 4,056 casualties in order to outflank Cassino on the south. The Abbey fell to the 3rd Carpathian Division (Polish) on May 18, and the way into the Liri Valley was opened.

While the drive was under way, on May 17, Alexander came to my headquarters, accompanied by Lieutenant General John Harding, his chief of staff. Harding, by the way, was a fighting soldier and was an outstanding commander later in the campaign. I detailed the progress the Fifth Army had made and Alexander was elated. Not only were we close to Itri, but we had taken some 3,000 prisoners up to that time.

Alexander asked about the 36th Division and I told him it was ready to load for movement to Anzio whenever we decided the time was right. He felt that the time would come when Cassino fell. He also said that he did not believe the Germans would make a serious stand on the Adolf Hitler Line, and I agreed.

I then brought up the question of which way VI Corps would attack out of the Anzio bridgehead. Alexander remained adamant that the attack should be toward Cori and Valmontone, regardless of the enemy situation at the time. I got a map and drew a circle around the high ground that Truscott would occupy when and if he reached Valmontone.

I asked him, "Where will Truscott go from there?" Alexander replied that fast, mobile patrols could operate to cut the German routes to the east and make it possible for us to trap a huge number of Germans between VI Corps and the Eighth Army.

I said it couldn't be done. "In getting to Valmontone," I said, "we will have gone over the mountains. There will be no roads and only footpaths over which to move from there, and the enemy still will hold the Alban Hill and its dominant observation. It seems to me that we should keep ourselves in a position to evaluate the situation when the time comes, and it may prove then that the Cori-Valmontone direction is the wrong one."

We left it that way, with Alexander still feeling that it would be best to cut Route No. 6 at Valmontone in an effort to trap the Germans opposing the Eighth Army.

That night I wrote to Marshall about the splendid performance of the 85th and 88th Divisions, saying that "their morale is high."

"In one instance," I continued, "an infantry regiment of the 85th was driven off its objective three times. Each time it counterattacked and finally retook the hill with heavy losses to the enemy. The tenacious, determined sort of fighting which these divisions have shown speaks well of their training at home. I knew you and General McNair would be interested, as I am, to see the result of the War Department's effort to build new divisions for battle. They have met their final test in combat with complete success.

"I am delighted with the five-day results of our Fifth Army attack. We have broken the Gustav Line in several places by attacking over the Mountains. We have penetrated to a distance of fourteen miles on both the II Corps and French Corps fronts."

Progress continued in the next few days, after the Polish Corps, a splendid fighting outfit under Lieutenant General Wladyslaw Anders, had finally done what the rest of us had failed to do—take Cassino, with the help of the British flanking thrust to the south. The Eighth Army front then began to move forward in the Liri Valley and German resistance seemed to be less effective along the entire front. I directed the 36th Division to embark for Anzio.

On May 20, I received a message from Major General Lyman L. Lemnitzer, the American general on Alexander's staff, saying that Alexander had directed the attack from Anzio to be launched on the night of May 21 in the direction of Cori and Valmontone

I was shocked that Alexander had made this decision without reference to me. I should point out at this time that the Fifth Army had had an extremely difficult time throughout the winter campaign and that we were now trying to make up for our earlier slow progress. We had massed all of our strength to take Rome. We were keyed up, and in the heat of battle there were almost certain to be clashes of personalities and ideas over this all-out drive. We not only wanted the honor of capturing Rome, but we felt that we more than deserved it; that it would to a certain extent make up for the buffeting and the frustration we had undergone in keeping up the winter pressure against the Germans. My own feeling was that nothing was going to stop us on our push toward the Italian capital. Not only did we intend to become the first army in fifteen centuries to seize Rome from the south,[*] but we intended to see that the people back home knew that it was the Fifth Army that did the job and knew the price that had been paid for it. I think that these considerations are important to an understanding of the behind-scenes differences of opinion that occurred in this period. Such controversies as arose were conceived in good faith as a result of honest differences of opinions about the best way to do the job. There is no exact science for conducting a battle; there usually is more than one way that will produce satisfactory results.

---

[*] See footnote, page 10.

General Lemnitzer told me later that Alexander's decision regarding the start of the Anzio offensive was made after a report was received that the British had broken the Hitler Line at Aquino. I was sure at the time that this was erroneous, and it was. I told him that we could not possibly attack out of the bridgehead before the night of May 22, and I felt that I should not commit myself about the date until the time had actually come. I certainly did not want to send Truscott forward until the enemy had been driven into a position from which we were certain we could force him to fall back beyond Rome.

Soon after this situation arose, Alexander came to my headquarters and said that Lieutenant General Oliver Leese did not believe the Eighth Army could renew its attack until the night of May 23 and then with only one Canadian division. He asked me whether the Fifth Army could outflank the German positions, making it unnecessary for the Eighth Army to attack. He said that he hoped in that manner to conserve losses. I replied that if we conserved losses in the Eighth Army, we were going to have to take them elsewhere, namely the Fifth Army. I said that both armies should attack with maximum effort at the same time.

"I believe," I told Alexander, "that it will be necessary to delay the attack from Anzio at least twenty-four hours and possibly forty-eight hours because we must have strong air support and the weather forecast at present is not good. I am directing the II Corps to break through the Hitler Line north of Fondi, and when it does I am going all out to join up with the bridgehead."

Alexander agreed with the plan in general. He had in the past been dubious of the Fifth Army's ability to drive through the mountains, but on this occasion he said he had never dreamed that we could make the progress that had been made and that he was enthusiastic about the outlook.

"I believe," I noted in my diary that night, "that if the Eighth Army will attack in the Pontecorvo region in the next two days [actually it did attack, but with only one division] and if we hit the Hitler Line north from Pico in an all-out blow, with the Anzio offensive starting the next day, we will fold up the German army in Italy."

The next day I visited forward elements and saw evidence to support my belief that success was near. With General Juin, I made a short trip beyond Esperia, where elements of the German 90th Panzer Grenadier Regiment had been caught on the road by our artillery fire. Dead Germans, trucks, tanks, guns and personnel carriers were demolished and scattered everywhere. Successive artillery concentrations apparently had caught the enemy force while it was moving in close order down the road; the result was so disastrous that the French had to bulldoze vehicles and bodies over the side of the hill in order to permit their troops to pass along the road.

On May 22, I moved permanently into the forward echelon of my head-quarters at Anzio in preparation for the breakout. Still having in mind the necessity for flexibility in our plans, I had decided that all units would attack at the same time to breach the German defense line, with the principal attack headed initially toward Cisterna-Cori-Valmontone. VI Corps was to be pre-pared to switch its main effort to the north to capture the Alban Hills. The Fifth Army was still hopping the mountains in an aggressive fashion and there were signs that the Germans were pulling out of the Hitler Line under almost panicky conditions in some sectors. Our air was supporting us up to the hilt. Almost every inch of space at Anzio was crowded with men, guns, and ammunition in preparation for the attack. Any time the enemy fired a shell in our direction it was almost certain to hit something, but we had taken what precautions were possible and most of our supplies were protected by mounds of earth.

On that day the 88th Division on the southern front smashed northwest-ward across the mountains above the Fondi Plain to Mount Monsicardi and thus sealed the fate of the Hitler Line. While elements of the 85th Division were pushing across the Fondi Plain toward Terracina on the coast, the 350th Infantry of the 88th Division made a bold thrust from the center, deep behind the enemy positions toward the village of Roccasecca dei Volsci.

Before dawn on the morning of May 23 I went with Truscott to a forward observation post on the Anzio front, where just before six o'clock some 500 pieces of artillery opened up on the enemy, whose positions were concealed by a morning haze. The smoke and haze hid our movements, but in the next hour or so we could hear our tanks moving forward to the attack and there was a dull rumble of aircraft overhead as bombers began to pour it on the German positions. The beleaguered Anzio garrison was about to break out, with the town of Cisterna their first objective.

The timing of the attack from Anzio again caught the enemy off guard. As the artillery fire suddenly ended, our tanks drove through the smoke, followed by swarms of infantry that caught the enemy outposts unprepared. Some of the Germans in dugouts had to be dragged out with only part of their clothes on, completely unready for battle. Our artillery had previously been aimed at specific enemy centers, which were heavily shelled, but the morning haze interfered with the German artillery observation and gave us an opportunity to make considerable progress before meeting firm resistance. The Germans never were able to recover from this initial setback and their later counterattacks were weak and poorly organized.

The 1st Armored Division, the 3rd Division, and the 1st special Service

Force fought their way toward Cisterna or on either side of the town, and by the night of May 24 they had all but isolated that center of enemy resistance. On the following day the 3rd Division's 7th Infantry drove into the town to wipe out remnants of the 362nd Grenadier Division while the rest of our offensive strength surged on toward Cori or swung northwestward toward the Alban Hills before the gates of Rome.

On that day, May 25, the German defenses were beginning to crumble on both fronts. On the southern front, elements of the 85th Division, after meeting veteran German reinforcements at Terracina, rallied and crashed into that coastal town and pushed on up the coast. The French 3rd Algerian Division entered San Giovanni on our right flank; thereafter the Germans fought a delaying action on that front. The climax was approaching and we hoped it would not be long delayed.

I talked over with Truscott the possibility of directing the attack by the 45th, the 34th, and the 36th Divisions in the direction of Velletri, which was on the edge of the Alban Hills, and at the same time pushing other elements forward on the Cori-Valmontone line on which Alexander had insisted. I had felt, as I said, that it was essential to maintain flexibility of movement at this period of the battle, and as it turned out, it was possible to pursue both objectives. We had taken 9,018 prisoners at this point and I felt that it would not be long before General Keyes' vigorous advance through Terracina would put his forces in contact with the bridgehead.

This meeting took place even sooner than I had expected. Shortly before ten o'clock that morning, when I was in my jeep, our radio picked up word that elements of the 48th Engineer Regiment and the 91st Reconnaissance Squadron were close to a junction with a task force from Anzio. The task force was from the 36th Engineer Regiment and included American tank-destroyer elements and members of a reconnaissance unit of the 1st British Division. I drove hurriedly to the sector, arriving as the two groups were meeting on the Anzio-Terracina road about a mile northwest of Borga Grappa, a little village that had been beaten almost into rubble by air attacks. The juncture was a triumph as far as I was concerned because of the difficulties of the previous five months, although it was not of any great importance in the battle that was raging to the northwest. The men were tired but grinning, as they joined hands, and that was about all there was to it. Thanks largely to the great aggressiveness of Keyes and II Corps, which had come sixty miles through the mountains in fourteen days, the beachhead had at last been liberated; but in the moment of liberation, everybody's thoughts were turned to Rome.

With Keyes' II Corps joined to the beachhead forces, our strength was greatly increased in the next few days, and our entry into Rome became mostly a matter of time and the choosing of the exact direction of our approach. Yet this period posed some extremely troublesome problems for me, almost all of them more of a political than a military nature. There were three considerations always in our minds. First, we wanted Rome prior to the beginning of Eisenhower's invasion of France, and that time was getting very close. Second, we wanted, if possible, to avoid fighting in the Eternal City, not only because of its position in the eyes of the Italian people, whose aid we sought, but because of its historical and religious significance throughout the world. Lastly, and of equal importance, we wanted to destroy as much of the German Army as possible in doing all this.

On the other hand, as I have pointed out, I was determined that the Fifth Army was going to capture Rome and I probably was overly sensitive to indications that practically everybody else was trying to get into the act. These indications mounted rapidly in the next few days and I had my hands full.

On May 26, Alexander conferred with Gruenther at my rear headquarters, and they discussed the direction of the attack we were making out of the bridgehead, which actually was swinging more to the northwest into the Alban Hills than toward Valmontone, as Alexander had hoped.

"Alexander agreed that your plan is a good one," Gruenther advised me later. "He said he was for any line of action you believed would offer a chance to continue the present success. Then about five minutes later, he said, 'I am sure that the army commander will continue to push toward Valmontone, won't he?' I assured him that you had that situation thoroughly in mind and that he could depend upon you to execute a vigorous plan with all the push in the world."

As a matter of record, we were pushing toward Valmontone at the time with a strong force and it was highly important to do so; but at the same time, we turned the 34th and 45th Divisions west below the Alban Hills and sent the 1st Armored Division against Velletri in the center of the hills barrier. The 3rd Division and the 1st Special Service Force swung eastward around the Alban Hills to cut Route No. 6 in the Valmontone sector. There they encountered strong enemy forces which had been committed to holding out on high ground for the few additional days needed for the main German army to retreat northward out of the Allied pincers.

As a result of this maneuvering, our main strength was thrown against the Alban Hills at the gateway to Rome, with the Germans fighting very stubbornly in a delaying action along the railroad that ran from Velletri to Lanuvio and Albano. It soon became evident that strong pressure would be necessary to smash our way through.

At this time, in the last days of May, our Anzio front, strengthened by part of II Corps, was being extended northeastward to a point where it would intersect the line of advance of the British Eighth Army up the Liri Valley. The immediate result of this movement was that the French Expeditionary Corps, which actually had sparked the whole drive toward Rome, was being squeezed out of our front and more or less left dangling in the mountains south of the Liri.

"In a very short while," General Juin advised me on May 28, "should we continue on the same axes, a large number of divisions will find themselves massed in front of Rome, or, in other words, on an extremely narrow front with poor communications. Therefore, it is important that from now on everyone's mission be clearly determined within the framework of the Army and the Army group's overall maneuver. Otherwise, there would be the risk of a terrible congestion of itineraries which would cause a complete lack of power against an enemy whose only aim is to gain time."

This problem came up the next day at the conference with Alexander when I proposed that the French advance on Ferentino and then move northwestward along Route No. 6 toward Valmontone. This maneuver would take them into the zone previously specified as the area of the Eighth Army, which at this time was still many miles behind the Fifth Army forward elements. This was agreed to, but later General Harding called and said that Alexander wanted to be certain that Route No. 6 from Ferentino to Valmontone was kept open for the Eighth Army.

Gruenther told Harding that such an order nullified our earlier agreement.

"No," Harding replied, "that is not true. He [Alexander] will be glad to have the French advance on Ferentino, which would have the effect of helping the Eighth Army along. But he insists that the road to Valmontone must remain clear for the Eighth Army. Otherwise, it might be impossible to bring the Eighth Army to bear in the battle for Rome."

There was quite an argument, but the only effect on Alexander was that he authorized the Fifth Army, if it captured Valmontone, to use Route No. 6 in continuation of its attack on Rome. In that case, he would then divert the Eighth Army northward from Valmontone and bypass Rome.

Juin was gravely disappointed by this decision, and we decided that the Ferentino attack would not work under such conditions. Instead, Juin agreed to push straight on through the mountains toward Valmontone. I told him that from there on I would, by hook or crook, arrange to have his forces assist in the II Corps attack toward Rome. This was a hazardous route for the French to follow, but Juin was willing, as always.

I summed up my feelings at this time in an entry in my diary on the evening of Memorial Day, following a brief ceremony at Nettuno Cemetery.

My French corps is being pinched out. A more gallant fighting organization never existed; yet my offer to have it attack Ferentino was promptly turned down, unless the French then agreed to withdraw to the south over the roads they had come forward on.

I am throwing everything I have into the battle [for the Alban Hills], hoping to crack this key position, which will make it necessary for Kesselring to withdraw both his armies to the north of Rome. [This was almost an understatement. Actually, I was committing all of my reserves, every single man, including a new regiment of the 91st Division that had just arrived from the States.] If I do not crack this position in three or four days I may have to reorganize, wait for the Eighth Army, and go at it with a coordinated attack by both armies.

Progress on May 31 was slight, partly because the great efforts of the previous week had exhausted most of the Fifth Army, and partly because the French encountered very strong resistance in attempting to reach Valmontone. The Eighth Army, at this time, spurted forward to Frosinone. The next day a liaison officer from the Eighth Army arrived at my forward command post, having been sent by General Leese to explain that if the Fifth Army was able to take Rome without assistance from the Eighth Army, the Eighth Army would continue its attacks in a direction north of Rome. This I agreed to.

We were preparing for an all-out attack, and I emphasized to all subordinate commanders that we had to crack through this time if the Fifth Army was going to do the job. We had been moving our forces forward from the now-collapsed southern front as rapidly as possible to join with the beachhead forces; by May 30, General Keyes had turned over mopping-up operations in the former II Corps zone to the newly formed IV Corps under Major General Willis Crittenberger, while Keyes took over the Artena sector between Alban Hills and Valmontone. We figured that when the French reached the Valmontone sector our right flank would be secure and we would have considerable superiority over the Germans for the final thrust.

On June 2, when our final attack actually had started but results were still uncertain, Alexander came to see me about a dispute that had arisen over the boundary between the Eighth Army and the French on the approaches to Rome along Route No. 6. I wanted to switch the French over into Eighth Army territory there because I needed that high ground for protection and the Eighth Army was not yet close to it. I rather expected an argument, but Alexander said that I shouldn't worry; if my attack didn't go through, he would bring in the whole Eighth Army to assure success. I replied that our attack was going through.

I went on to explain why we had to cross over Route No. 6 in Eighth Army territory, and Alexander said to go right ahead. I added that we would clear out just as soon as the British got there and could take over. Everybody agreed on the plan, and we also got together on the text of a communiqué to be released when Rome fell, making it clear that "Fifth Army troops" entered Rome. This was more important to the men of the Fifth Army—and to me—than it might seem, and the agreement gave me a good deal of satisfaction. Now all we had to do was go out and get Rome.

On May 27, the 36th Division had relieved the 1st Armored Division below Velletri and, in a daring night advance, made its way up the north end of Mount Artemisio in the Alban Hills behind Velletri, where it seized a German artillery observation post at dawn on May 31 without firing a shot. So complete was the surprise that one of the Germans surrendered in a bathtub where he had been taking his early morning dip.

From there the 36th fought its way deeply into the rear of Velletri, which fell on June 2, and pushed on close to Lago Albano. At the same time, the II Corps, now composed of the 3rd Division, Special Service Force and the 85th and 88th Divisions, made an attack to the northwest, where it cut Route No. 6 and broke the German defenses at Valmontone, establishing contact with the French at Colle Ferro.

All day on June 3, I went from command post to command post urging that "this is the day" for the kill. The dusty roads were alive with traffic and many prisoners were pouring into our cages. There were countless wrecked German vehicles along the roadsides and everywhere there was evidence of the enemy's breakup. Even the vaunted Hermann Göring Panzer Parachute Division was cracking under the intense force we were concentrating on a narrow front. Keyes had begun wheeling his II Corps to the west, the French pushed up to protect his right flank, and with a series of stiff tank and infantry blows against the German rear guard he advanced to within four miles of Rome by the night of June 4.

While this advance was in progress, I had, on June 3, received a message from Alexander's headquarters saying that the Polish commander in chief in London had requested that a detachment of the II Polish Corps participate in the entry into Rome. Apparently the idea had spread around that we were going to have a formal parade into the capital.

"Please politely tell everybody, including the Swedes, if necessary, that I am not framing the tactical entrance of troops into Rome," I said in a message to Gruenther. "God and the Boche are dictating that. I wouldn't know where to put anybody anyway and I concur in Alexander's idea of having a parade later, if necessary. . . . So let everybody know that there will be no detachments of Greeks, Poles, Indians, or anybody else entering Rome until the formal parade is held. Also try to keep visiting firemen from running up here as soon as the capture of Rome is imminent."

I was especially insistent that visitors be kept out of our way; nevertheless, I got some the same day. Five Yugoslav officers arrived at my headquarters with an American lieutenant as their guide and with instructions from the 15th Army Group that they were to tour the front. We were having enough troubles of our own at the time without having to look out for visitors for whom there were absolutely no facilities, and I probably was not very cooperative. It happened that I had just been informed that telephone communications had been established for the first time between the beach-head area and my southern-front headquarters, and I had been waiting to get a call through to Gruenther.

"Can I get him now?" I asked.

"Yes, we just got through," I was told. The connection, however, was poor and I could barely hear Gruenther's voice. I tried to shout a message to him about keeping visitors away. Finally, somebody at a relay point along the line said he could hear us both and would relay my message.

"All right," I said. "Tell him that I've got five Yugoslavs here."

There was a mumbling on the line.

"What did he say to that?" I asked angrily. "What's he doing about my instructions?"

"General Gruenther," answered the voice, "says that he's a bit puzzled, but he guesses you want him to send you five Yugoslavs and he will try."

I yelled, "Don't do that! I've got five I can't use now!"

I threw down the telephone in disgust, but I discovered later that I had been shouting so loudly in order to be heard that the five Yugoslavs, who were in a nearby room, had listened to most of the conversation. They were huffed and, when I said they could visit the beachhead but not the forward area, they decided to leave.

"Please make it clear to everybody," I told Gruenther, "that this was a most inappropriate time for them to come here. The first thing you know the claim will be that the Yugoslavs were the first to enter Rome."

On June 4, I jeeped by way of Velletri, Artena, Valmontone, and thence along Route No. 6 to a point about five miles from Rome, where I met General Keyes and General Frederick, who told me that some elements of the Special Service Force were already on the western edge of Rome. Other flying spearheads also were entering the city, but all were meeting resistance. I had told my pilot, Major Jack Walker, to fly along Route No. 6 at about the time I expected to be there and to try to locate my party so that he could land nearby to pick me up if conditions permitted. I saw him flying low over the highway as we got into the outskirts of the capital, but there was considerable firing going on not far away and no good place to land. Finally he picked out a schoolyard near the side of the road and brought the little Cub plane down inside a kind of courtyard formed by the buildings and an eight-foot brick fence. It was a good spot for protection from the occasional shells falling in the area, but not what I would call an ideal landing field. It definitely was short on runway space.

After Jack had landed, we went to the foot of a hill leading up to the gates of the city, where, at the top of the hill, we could see a large sign labeled ROMA. I must say that sign had a great appeal for me; my only regret at the moment was that there was so much firing in the vicinity that we hesitated to approach it. The firing died down about an hour later and Frederick and I walked up toward the sign. About halfway up the hill Keyes joined us, and we all crawled along a ditch to get to the top.

At that time things seemed safe enough and we stood up. Some of the newspaper photographers had followed us, and they asked us to move over beside the ROMA sign because it would make a good news picture. We did, and they quickly snapped the camera shutters, just as a German sniper cut loose at us. The first bullet went through the sign with a bang. I doubt that anybody ever saw so many generals duck so rapidly. We crawled back down the ditch to safer ground, but later Frederick had someone get the sign and eventually brought it to me as a souvenir.

Jack Walker and I waited around the school buildings for several hours until it became definite that I could not feasibly drive into Rome until the next day. With some hesitation, I got into the Cub plane while Jack figured out whether he had runway enough to clear the schoolyard fence. I was inclined to doubt it. He argued that he had enough room. As it turned out, he was right by a margin of three inches. We flew back to my command post.

Actually, our forces were all over Rome that day, but they had to engage in some sharp fighting at scattered points. Swift mobile units had thrust into the city against rear-guard opposition, and it was never exactly certain which of these flying columns was first in the city. They moved through scenes of great excitement and were often seriously delayed by cheering crowds as they crisscrossed the capital in an effort to seize as many as possible of the nineteen bridges across the Tiber—bridges we would need for pursuit of the enemy. By midnight most of them were securely in our hands, although some on both sides of Rome had been blown up by the German rearguard.

Meanwhile in the Alban Hills the last lines of German resistance were being mopped up, and our attention was turned to pursuit of the enemy past Rome. In the next twenty-four hours the whole battle moved on to the northwest. With the capture of the city, the Fifth Army had suffered 124,917 casualties in Italy, including 20,889 dead, 84,389 wounded in action, and 20,139 missing in action. Of the dead, 11,292 were American, 5,017 British, 3,904 French, and 176 Italian, with wounded in proportion to the dead. The men of the Fifth Army had paid a high price for liberating the Eternal City.

On June 5, with Gruenther and other officers, I drove along Route No. 6 into Rome. We didn't know our way around the city very well, but General Hume, who was with us, had suggested that the Town Hall on Capitoline Hill would be a good place for me to meet my four corps commanders for a conference on our immediate plans. We wanted to push on past Rome as rapidly as possible in pursuit of the retreating enemy and toward Civitavecchia, the port of Rome, which we direly needed for unloading supplies. There were gay crowds in the streets, many of them waving flags, as our infantry marched through the capital. Flowers were stuck in the muzzles of the soldiers' rifles and of guns on the tanks. Many Romans seemed to be on the verge of hysteria in their enthusiasm for the American troops. The Americans were enthusiastic, too, and kept looking for the ancient landmarks that they had read about in their history books. It was on that day that a doughboy made the classic remark of the Italian campaign when he took a long look at the ruins of the old Colosseum, whistled softly, and said, "Geez, I didn't know our bombers had done *that* much damage in Rome!"

Our little group of jeeps wandered around the streets while we craned our necks looking at the sights, but not finding our way to Capitoline Hill. In fact, we were lost, but we didn't like to admit it and we didn't care very much because we were interested in everything we saw. Eventually we found ourselves in St. Peter's Square, which delighted us all and which enabled Hume to get his bearings. As we stopped to look up at the great dome of St. Peter's, a priest walking along the street paused by my jeep and said in English, "Welcome to Rome. Is there any way in which I can help you?"

"Well," I replied, "we'd like to get to Capitoline Hill."

He gave us directions and added, "We are certainly proud of the American Fifth Army. May I introduce myself?" And he told me his name. He came from Detroit.

"My name's Clark," I replied.

We both expressed pleasure at the meeting and the priest started to move on. Then he stopped and took another look and said, "What did you say your name is?" A number of Italians had gathered around by this time and were listening to our conversation. When the priest told them I was the commander of the Fifth Army, a youth on a bicycle shouted that he would lead us to Capitoline Hill. He did, pedaling along in front of our jeep and shouting to everybody on the street to get out of the way because General Clark was trying to get to Capitoline Hill. This, of course, merely added to the excitement that we had felt everywhere we had gone in Rome, and by the time we reached a point opposite the balcony where Mussolini used to appear for his major speeches the road was blocked by curious and cheering people.

We finally broke a path through and twisted up the hill to the Town Hall. The door was locked and there didn't seem to be a soul around. Pounding on the big door, I reflected that it had been a curiously varied as well as a historic day. We had been lost in the ancient capital, which we entered as liberators after a long and unprecedented campaign. We had been welcomed and taken in tow by a priest and a boy on a bicycle. We had almost been mobbed by excited, cheering crowds; but now we couldn't even get in the Town Hall. I pounded on the door again, not feeling much like the conqueror of Rome. Anyway, I thought, we got to Rome before Ike got across the English Channel to Normandy. I was right about that, too, but by a narrow margin. I didn't know it, but even while I stood there Ike's army was embarking. We had won the race to Rome by only two days

16.

Pursuit to the Arno:

June 1944–October 1944

The meeting with my four corps commanders on Capitoline Hill in Rome that morning of June 5 will always stand out in my mind as a kind of turning point in the Allied attack on the soft underbelly of the Axis.

The meeting itself, of course, resulted in no momentous decisions. After a caretaker had appeared in response to our pounding on the door, General Roberto Bencivento, the Italian military commander in Rome and a splendid patriot, came to make us welcome. When General Truscott, General Keyes, General Crittenberger, and General Juin arrived, we quickly got down to the immediate problem of following up the badly battered Germans and giving them no chance for rest.

But to me the meeting was significant because of the men present and because of decisions, made in higher echelons, that were soon to affect all of us. On that morning I felt that the corps commanders of the Fifth Army made a great team; that we had finally developed a winning combination of leaders with the desire and the ability to conquer almost any circumstances. It was interesting that my three American corps commanders—Truscott, Keyes and Crittenberger—were originally all cavalrymen and that, in a time when the cavalry was disappearing, they had what it took to meet the stern tests of the war in the mountains of Italy. I already have told of my admiration for Juin—there never was a finer soldier.

There was no question in my mind that day that we could soon destroy the enemy in Italy and drive him beyond the Alps and go on to whatever objective was set for us. The Fifth Army, it seemed to me, had at last become a tremendous fighting machine and its horizons were unlimited.

That, however, was not the way it worked out. For various reasons, which will appear later, our team soon was broken up and the Fifth Army was sapped of a great part of its strength. A campaign that might have changed the whole history of relations between the Western world and Soviet Russia was permitted to fade away, not into nothing, but into much less than it could have been. These were decisions made at a high level and for reasons beyond my field and my knowledge; but I do not think that it is outside my bailiwick to discuss, from a military viewpoint, what might have been achieved had the Fifth Army been kept together and strengthened in the coming months instead of being torn apart.

Such speculation, I already have indicated, comes under the heading of Monday-morning quarterbacking. It's a lot easier to see mistakes when you look back at them; but in Italy there was plenty of opportunity to see what might be done, and the possibilities were exhaustively discussed before it was decided to ignore the opportunity they offered. Not alone in my opinion, but in the opinion of a number of experts who were close to the problem, the weakening of the campaign in Italy in order to invade southern France instead of pushing on into the Balkans was one of the outstanding political mistakes of the war.

I previously have pointed out that General Eisenhower naturally wanted to bring to bear against the Germans all the military pressure possible, and that from a purely military viewpoint the so-called ANVIL invasion of southern France was logical. Had I been in Ike's place, I would have insisted on it, too, for his job was to destroy as rapidly as possible the German forces opposing him; and he believed the attack into southern France would help him do just that; in thus shortening the war, he would in the end save Allied lives. Moreover, I know that at the time General Eisenhower suggested to the Prime Minister that an attack into the Balkans might be more productive in attaining British-American political objectives than would the attack through southern France. But he additionally pointed out that, if such political considerations were to affect this particular decision, the responsibility would necessarily be assumed, in democratic countries, by the highest political leaders. This attitude was undoubtedly correct, and there is, of course, the probability that General Eisenhower's opinion—which I know was shared by General Marshall—was sound as to the strictly military advantages.

I am firmly convinced that the French forces alone, with seven divisions available, could have captured Marseilles, protected General Eisenhower's southern flank, and advanced up the Rhone Valley to join hands with the main OVERLORD forces. The VI American corps, with its three divisions, could then have remained in Italy. The impetus of the Allied advance in Italy would thus not have been lost and we could have advanced into the Balkans.

In fact, I discussed this very subject with General Marshall when he came to visit us shortly after the capture of Rome. I then urged that the French alone do the southern France job, leaving the American element of the Fifth Army intact. He expressed his interest, but it was too late then, I suppose, to do anything about it. Our Government had committed itself to an attack, decided upon a year earlier at Teheran, without reevaluating the strategical situation in the light of new Allied successes in France and Italy.

As it worked out, the men, materiel, and air forces needed for ANVIL simply stripped the Fifth Army of its strength. I eventually lost the entire VI Corps, including the 3rd, the 36th, and the 45th Divisions, all of which I had picked for the job when I had been designated to go on ANVIL. In addition, the French Expeditionary Forces, naturally, wanted to take part in the return to their homeland; it was only through Juin's efforts that I did not lose immediately their great fighting strength. However, by the end of July they had all left.

Naturally, I am a prejudiced witness in this matter because it was my team that was being weakened; but I believe there is plenty of evidence from other sources to support my attitude. For instance, there was Marshal Kesselring, whose intelligence section was completely mystified in coming weeks when our great forward drive failed to take full advantage of its chance to destroy the beaten and disorganized German Army in Italy.

"It is incomprehensible why divisions were withdrawn from the front," according to one German general, whom we interviewed after the war. "Whatever were the reasons, it is sure they all accrued to the benefit of the German high command." It was some time before the Germans understood what had happened to the American troops in Italy; for weeks the Counter-intelligence Corps under the able direction of Lieutenant Colonel Stephen J. Spingarn were catching enemy agents who had orders to find out "where in hell" were various Allied divisions that were being sent to France.

The Russian viewpoint I also consider most interesting. Stalin, it was evident, throughout the Big Three meeting and negotiations at Teheran was one of the strongest boosters of the invasion of southern France. He knew exactly what he wanted in a political as well as a military way; and the thing that he wanted most was to keep us out of the Balkans, which he had staked out for the Red Army. If we switched our strength from Italy to France, it was obvious to Stalin, or to anyone else, that we would be turning away from central Europe. From France the only way we could get to the Balkans was through Switzerland. In other words, ANVIL led into a dead-end street. It was easy to see, therefore, why Stalin favored ANVIL at Teheran and why he kept right on pushing for it; but I never could understand why, as conditions changed and as the war situation changed, the United States and Britain failed to sit down and take another look at the overall picture with a view to eliminating or reducing the scope of ANVIL if something better was offered.

This wasn't done, although there was lots of talk about it, particularly by the British. I imagine Prime Minister Churchill was responsible for this talk and that it was not his fault it never developed into anything more than talk. After the fall of Rome, Kesselring's army could have been destroyed—if we had been able to shoot the works in a final offensive. And across the Adriatic was Yugoslavia, pretty much in the hands of Marshal Tito's forces, and beyond Yugoslavia were Vienna, Budapest, and Prague.

I am getting a little ahead of my story in order to explain the circumstances surrounding our failure to go into the Balkans, but it is necessary to an understanding, in particular of the attitude of the British. For on several occasions in the next few months, General Alexander came to me with the idea of planning to cross the Adriatic and move through Yugoslavia.

Marshal Tito had made a visit to Alexander's headquarters and had suggested that he could provide protected beachheads for a landing in Yugoslavia. Obviously, Tito's partisans would have been of great assistance in advancing through the mountain passes toward Vienna.

"Let's begin thinking about the possibility of making an amphibious landing in Yugoslavia," Alexander said on one occasion. "The landing could be made on protected beaches, and at the same time the Fifth Army could move up through northern Italy and along the coast through the Lubiana Gap."

General Wilson was strongly in favor of pushing some such operation in the Balkans and even King George, when he visited my headquarters, talked about the advantages of a thrust from Italy into Austria. There was no question that the Balkans were strongly in the British mind, but so far as I ever found out, the American top-level planners were not interested. It was generally understood that President Roosevelt toyed with the idea for a while, but was not encouraged by Harry Hopkins.

The circumstances and viewpoints outlined above developed rather slowly over a period of weeks or months, as far as I was concerned; but the net result was that after the fall of Rome we "ran for the wrong goal," both from a political and a strategical standpoint.

The political blunder involved has since been rather exhaustively discussed by several writers, including André Garteiser, who pointed out in an article in *Le Monde Français* that a military commander "must strive . . . above all to terminate the war in such a manner that the military situation at the end of the conflict should be the one which his country should desire to see realized for political reasons."

"The Russians," he added, "played their hand with a view to the future peace." But, he said, the failure in Italy to follow up the shattered German Army when victory was within our grasp was a great error.

"For the first time in history," Garteiser said, "the world was subjected to the spectacle of seeing an Army flying on the wings of victory and then suddenly giving the enemy, who was in headlong flight, a respite. . . . It is rare to find an instance where strategic incompetence is so openly admitted."

From a military standpoint I could only agree with Garteiser's well-stated conclusion, and from a political standpoint, I later came to understand, in Austria, the tremendous advantages that we had lost by our failure to press on into the Balkans. In view of Tito's attitude at the time, it seems to me that his break with Stalin might have come even sooner, and that our friendship with Yugoslavia could have been cemented by military cooperation then. As for the rest of the Balkan nations behind the Iron Curtain, the difference has since become only too obvious. Had we been there before the Red Army, not only would the collapse of Germany have come sooner, but the influence of Soviet Russia would have been drastically reduced.

As I have already said, the decision to steer clear of the Balkans was one that puzzled the German High Command for many weeks, because they could not easily understand why their Army was not being beaten to pieces against the high ridges of the Apennines in that summer and fall of 1944. It was a decision that is likely to puzzle historians for a much longer time.

These things, of course, were only a vague worry in my mind at my meeting with the commanders on Capitoline Hill. I knew that we were going to lose certain divisions, but at the time I am sure I did not realize how devastating the effect would be.

After the conference all of us went to the Excelsior Hotel. We had had enough experience with the Germans by this time to be a bit fearful that the hotel had been booby-trapped; but the proprietor assured us that Kesselring's military staff had moved out too quickly to permit anything of the sort, and I decided to spend the night there. Later we took the hotel over as a rest center for officers, while a rest center for enlisted men was set up in the Mussolini Sports Stadium, a huge affair that included a score of buildings, indoor and outdoor pools, gymnasiums, and living quarters. I directed that every man and woman of the Fifth Army who had participated in the long struggle to Rome should have a chance to enjoy its sights and opportunities for relaxation.

A luncheon had been prepared for us and rooms were set aside for our use at the Excelsior. There was a good deal of milling around, but I remember that finally I found myself alone in my bedroom. For the first time I stopped to think about all that had happened in the last week or ten days and how much it had meant in the long and bitter Italian campaign. I knelt down then to say a prayer of thanks, and I was just ready to rise when I felt a hand on my shoulder. I looked up and saw Juin standing beside me, smiling slightly and nodding his head.

"Good," he said. "I just did the same thing."

For the next two days we made every effort to capitalize on our success and on the disorganization of the enemy. The Air Force had played a tremendous role in the victories that led to the liberation of Rome, not only disrupting the enemy's reinforcements from the north, but, in the final phase, raining countless blows on his retreating columns. The loss in matériel, as well as men, was all but fatal to Kesselring and would have meant his complete defeat if a powerful force had been permitted to follow through in the attack.

The Vatican had been concerned lest a period of disorder take place in Rome after the departure of the German forces and before the arrival of the Americans. This did not occur, because the enemy had been pursued right through the city and across the Tiber bridges; but later the Vatican was interested in how long our headquarters would remain in Rome, fearing that our presence would inspire air attacks by the Germans.

The Right Reverend Monsignor Walter S. Carroll, of the Vatican Secretariat of State, had been the Pope's liaison with the Fifth Army during most of the Italian campaign, and on June 8 he arranged for me to have an audience with His Holiness. I took several of my staff along. We drove to the Vatican in jeeps, wearing our battle dress, and were escorted to the Pope's chambers by Swiss guards in their historic uniforms. The Pope invited me to talk with him alone before the regular audience; I found him greatly interested in as well as informed on military developments.

"I understand your headquarters are now in Rome," he said. "How long will you be here? I am fearful that your presence may bring retaliation from the Germans."

I said that I didn't believe the Germans were able to retaliate on anybody at the moment, but that in any event we would be in Rome no longer than necessary—at most a few days.

The Pope inquired whether I had had any contact with the Russians and expressed concern over the possible effects of Communism in central

Europe. Then he expressed the hope that American soldiers would be free to visit the Vatican and invited them to attend a special audience, which he was planning to hold each day. I thought that was an excellent idea and told him I would make arrangements for every soldier in the Fifth Army to be given a chance to come to the Vatican for these audiences. In the following months many thousands of them took advantage of this opportunity to see the Pope.

The Pontiff always seemed happy to talk about America and to discuss the trip that he had made as a cardinal to the United States. I discovered, however, that while his knowledge of America was extensive, he did not fully understand American attitudes. This came out some days later, when he asked me to call and brought up the subject of the audiences he was holding for large groups of our soldiers.

"You know," he said, with an expression of utmost seriousness, "I think your American soldiers do not like me."

Since soldiers of all faiths had been swarming to the audiences enthusiastically, I would have thought he was joking except for his serious expression. I could only stammer that I did not understand.

"Well," he continued, "I appear for these audiences after the soldiers have assembled in the courtyard. Now when Italians or other Europeans attend such audiences, I follow about the same procedure, and when I appear, they break into cheers and shouts of greeting and similar expressions of enthusiasm. But when I appear before your American soldiers, they do not utter a sound. They do not say one word."

I hastened to clear up his misunderstanding, although I am not sure I did a very good job of explaining the difference in religious attitude between Americans and the people in the Mediterranean countries. I assume, however, that I made it clear that the American soldiers were less demonstrative and that their background prompted them to maintain a reverent silence in the presence of the head of the Roman Catholic Church. At least he seemed to understand and to be pleased.

I saw the Pope on many occasions thereafter during my stay in Italy and developed a great admiration for his statesmanship, his wisdom, and his infinite humaneness.

Shortly after our capture of Rome, I moved my headquarters to the woods of the Villa Savoia, near the banks of the Tiber, and concentrated our immediate efforts on seizing and putting into working order the port of Civitavecchia. We badly needed this port to shorten our line of communications, which had become much too long in recent months, since Naples was still our main shipping base and practically all supplies had to be hauled by truck from there.

When the Germans were driven beyond Civitavecchia, I had Jack Walker pilot me there on June 9 in a new L-5, which was a little larger and a little faster than the type of Piper Cub we had been using. I wanted to survey the port from the air to determine how much it had been damaged by the Germans before their withdrawal. It looked pretty bad as we came over the port, so I told Jack to start circling and just keep on circling until I told him to stop.

As a result of this order, not only was I looking down at the water, but Jack was looking down too, and neither one of us saw an American barrage balloon that had just been run up as protection against a German air attack. There was a sudden grinding crash and the wing of our plane hit the barrage-balloon cable, which extended down to a truck at the edge of the harbor. The cable slid along the wing and caught on the air-speed indicator at its end. By the time I realized what had happened, gas was leaking from the wing tank and we were swinging wildly in a circle. My first thought was to bail out, but I remembered I had no parachute.

Jack pulled the throttle wide open as we swung in a kind of spiral, and we went around the cable in merry-go-round fashion several times, spinning toward the water. Then, happily, the cable broke while Jack could still straighten out the plane into a glide. Gas was all over the place by then, so he shut off the engine and drifted toward land. Neither of us ever figured out just how we escaped that time, and the men handling the balloon later said that it had seemed impossible that Jack ever could pull the plane out of it. In addition there was a bomb attached to the balloon that was supposed to slide down the cable and explode when anything struck the cable. The only reason we could imagine that it had not was because we were going at very slow speed in a light airplane.

Jack picked out a field not far from the water and set down the plane on it as tenderly as possible. When we crawled out, both of us were still shaking.

"Sir, you have just witnessed a miracle," Jack said, and it wasn't exactly a joke. "I really thought it was all over."

In the next phase of the Italian campaign, after Rome, Kesselring's purpose was to withdraw, behind such delaying action as he could provide, to a strong defensive belt, known as the Gothic Line, in the high Apennines some 25 miles north of the Arno River and about 175 miles north of Rome. Our hope was to keep on the enemy's heels and cut off as large a part of his forces as possible. For the first few weeks the pursuit was comparatively swift through the rolling country north of the Tiber, despite occasional bitter fighting by German rear-guard units. Later, enemy resistance stiffened in the hills.

In this period, and on to the Arno, the Fifth Army zone was along the Tyrrhenian Sea, with our front extending some forty-five or fifty miles inland, where it made contact with the wider Eighth Army front that ran on across Italy to the Adriatic. The Germans had lost some 1,500 vehicles, 110 pieces of field artillery, 125 self-propelled artillery and antitank guns, and 122 tanks since the middle of May. Much more equipment was abandoned in flight or destroyed by our Air Force, and we had taken some 15,000 prisoners. Only the Hermann Göring Panzer Parachute Division provided much resistance in the first weeks of pursuit. Our estimates of enemy battle casualties ran to 17,000 killed and 68,000 wounded.

One of our greatest difficulties was in keeping contact with our advance units, which were on the heels of the Germans. Sometimes they moved forward as much as ten or fifteen miles a day, and supply problems as well as communications became increasingly difficult. On one occasion in June, for instance, the 11th Evacuation Hospital was in its usual position about fifteen miles behind the front, but by the next night it was thirty miles behind. We resorted more and more to flying casualties from the front. During the advance to the Arno some 8,000 men were flown out.

Because opposition was by small units, our pursuit operated less on the Army level than on the level of divisions and regiments, which followed occasional Army directives but for the most part adjusted themselves to local conditions that were changing with great rapidity. The enemy methodically destroyed bridges and culverts, which averaged about one a mile along the coast, and our speed depended mainly on the ability of our engineers to make repairs. They worked miracles under the professional direction of Brigadier General Frank Bowman, my Fifth Army Engineer.

I have summed up this phase of the campaign briefly and in advance to make it clear that we had entered a very fluid period which did not present any definite pattern other than a pursuit to the Arno River—a pursuit that raised many problems and plenty of stiff fighting, but resulted in no large battles such as had been fought previously in the campaign. At this point our principal aim was to destroy the enemy divisions now opposing us and to draw more of them into the campaign in Italy.

My own problems and activities during the period extending into September reflected this condition on the front, and were concerned largely with the withdrawal of fighting strength from the Fifth Army for the invasion of France.

An excerpt from my diary in the middle of June illustrates what was happening:

I have known, of course, that the VI Corps would go [to ANVIL] as soon as we had captured Rome. I also knew that most of the French Expeditionary Corps would leave me. I assume that the Combined Chiefs of Staff making these decisions know what they are doing and that ANVIL will contribute more to the invasion and the second front than our continued effort in Italy. I am convinced, however, that their decision was made long ago and without realizing the great success the Fifth and Eighth Armies were to have in Italy. The morale of the Fifth is sky-high. The Boche is defeated, disorganized, and demoralized. Now is the time to exploit our success. Yet, in the middle of this success, I lose two corps headquarters and seven divisions. It just doesn't make sense.

The depressing part is the case of General Juin. He has performed magnificently. Yet he has heard nothing from his government [de Gaulle had come into power by this time] and he has received indications that leave him and his staff depressed.

At that time I felt that Juin was in disfavor with de Gaulle, and it was becoming obvious that he would not be given an opportunity to lead the French troops on their return to their homeland in connection with ANVIL. (This de Gaulle later confirmed when he paid a visit to my headquarters.) I asked Juin to come to see me. I told him that I understood his divisions were to be withdrawn for ANVIL, which meant that the rug was being pulled out from under him.

"I had been led to expect something of the sort," Juin replied. "I am strongly opposed to this idea."

"I am sorry about this," I said. "It is shameful that after this victory in Italy we will not be allowed to exploit it."

I told Juin that General Marshall would arrive in Italy within a few days and that I would bring him to visit Juin's headquarters.

"I will speak to General Marshall about the whole question," I said. "Until then, we should continue to push on. When your divisions are withdrawn, I will ask General Alexander to reduce our sector to conform."

"In my opinion," Juin said, "it is all a great pity. This will cause the loss of the battle of Italy because it is in the plains of the Po Valley that we must destroy the German reserves. History will judge this decision severely. . . . Well, events turn out as they do."

I urged him not to lose heart until there were more definite developments, although we both felt that the final decision had already been made.

On June 18, General Marshall arrived and was escorted to the new Fifth Army command post near Tuscania, where he was introduced to the corps commanders, including Juin. I had asked him to award personally some Distinguished Service Medals at this time, but knowing that he, as always, would be conservative about it, and wanting a number of the men who deserved such recognition to get it, I broached the subject to him privately. He said to give him the names. When I presented the names, he exclaimed, "You've got all your corps and division commanders on the list! It even includes Juin."

I said yes, but that they all deserved the medal.

"Oh, no," Marshall said. "We haven't got that many medals here."

"I'll get them. In fact, I've already got them."

"Well," he protested, "I can't give the D.S.M. to Juin. I can't give a decoration to a foreigner."

I said that if he couldn't give a D.S.M. to a foreigner, I couldn't think of anybody else who could. He weakened and finally gave in to my proposals. When the officers lined up for the ceremony I told Juin to get in line, and Marshall pinned on him the first D.S.M. to be awarded to a Frenchman in World War II.

Later I discussed with Marshall at some length the problems of the Italian campaign and the effect on us of ANVIL. He outlined to me the problems facing Eisenhower, whom he had just visited, emphasizing Ike's intense desire for ANVIL in order to open Marseilles as a port of supply. I said that if the decision was final and unalterable, I would do everything possible to speed the movement of necessary forces from Italy to France. I added, however, that I wanted him to understand that we were passing up an opportunity to strike hard at the enemy in Italy, because after our team here was broken up we could not be certain how far or how fast we could advance.

During July, I drove to Cecina for a conference with General Crittenberger, the IV Corps commander, and General Ryder, commanding the 34th Division, and from there went forward to within a couple of miles of the German rear guard. En route we encountered a number of Italian partisans, wearing red stars and other Communist insignia. They greeted us with clenched fists in the Communist salute. The leader of this group was a tiny, club-footed man. He said there were twenty-nine men in his outfit and about two hundred others in the Cecina-Livorno area. The commander of the area was a Captain Testa, whose headquarters were at Marina di Cecina. They told me that they had killed a number of Germans and otherwise harassed the retreating enemy, but they were unable to give any definite figures.

"Is there anything we can provide to help you?" I asked.

"There are many things we need," the leader replied. "We are trying to bury the dead and to police the area. We need medical supplies and food."

I told them I would see what we could do to help them. The partisans in this area were not so well organized as they were farther north in the Po Valley area, but they caused plenty of headaches for the Germans. As we moved north, we encountered them in increasing numbers; they proved a great help. Some of them were led by escaped Allied prisoners of war and others were rather informally attached to some of our units and fought alongside our soldiers. They were excellent at gathering information for us and often found German stragglers that our units had missed. On other occasions they exposed German soldiers who were trying to escape while disguised as Italians. The partisans also performed valuable policing work which enabled our units to concentrate on pursuit of the enemy without waiting for military-government officials to get organized. We maintained communications with these various groups by messenger and radio, and issued instructions to them that would coordinate their actions with ours.

After my command post had been moved several times as we progressed northward, Sergeant Chaney had a chance one day to look around the countryside. He came back with some fish for dinner.

"Where did these come from?" I asked him.

"I went fishing in a lake a few miles from here," he said.

Lieutenant Colonel Arthur Sutherland, my A.D.C. at the time, was with me, and we decided to take a couple hours off and go fishing later in the week. Art fixed it up with a local fisherman who said he had everything we needed and that we'd be sure to get some fish. The boat, as it turned out, was a leaky one, but it was a sunny afternoon and we set out happily on the lake with the fisherman as guide.

"Can we find any fish?" I asked him.

"*Si, si, signori.* Plenty of fish."

We rowed around for an hour or so, but had no luck. Every time I asked the fisherman, he would promise that we'd get some in just a minute. At the end of two hours I said I had to get back to work, fish or no fish. The Italian protested, but I said I could not spend any more time and told him to row us to shore.

"Just one minute," he shouted. Before anybody could stop him, he reached in a sack, pulled out a hand grenade, jerked the pin out, and threw it in the water. After it had exploded, four or five small fish floated to the surface.

"There," he exclaimed. "Fish!"

"Why, we ought to put you in jail," I told him angrily. "That's no way to get fish."

He merely pulled in the fish and shrugged. "I told you you'd get fish," he said. "Here they are. Anyway, that's the way the Germans fished all the time."

It was along about this time that Major General Fred Walker, who had been in command of the 36th Division, returned to the United States. There was some suggestion after the war, when controversy arose over the Battle of Rapido River, that I had been responsible for Walker's recall. This is not the case; in fact, what happened was that General Marshall sent a message to me saying that he needed a good man to put in charge of the Infantry School at Fort Benning and suggesting that Walker might be the man.

I took the message to Walker shortly after I received it and laid it on his desk.

"I just got this, Fred," I remarked. "It's up to you."

He said he would like to think it over for a few days. Later he sent me a message saying, "I'd like to do it." That, as far as I know, is why Walker went home.

We were, in the summer of 1944, getting many new faces in the Fifth Army, and losing some familiar ones. Lieutenant General Truscott and his VI Corps were relieved from the Fifth Army on June 11, and we arranged to move the 92nd Infantry Division, the first American Negro infantry outfit to go into action in the European war, up to our left flank in order to work it gradually into the line in the Leghorn sector. Later in the summer the French units previously earmarked were withdrawn for ANVIL; the remaining French forces shortly went on the defensive, and soon ended their part in the Italian campaign. They had been a tremendous factor in our advance and it was with great regret that I saw them drop out. In the period from November 16, 1943 to August 5, 1944, they suffered 5,246 killed in action, 20,852 wounded, and 1,943 missing.

Following the capture of Rome and during the flight of the Germans toward the Arno, I had received a great many personal messages in which my friends and various distinguished persons had said some pleasant things about the accomplishments of the Fifth Army. Naturally, I appreciated the messages, but I had kept looking for a letter from my son, Bill, who was a cadet at West Point. I had long since realized that he didn't write very often, but I had assumed that I would hear from him after he read about the fall of Rome. Sure enough, I got a letter after a certain length of time. I opened it with considerable pleasure. I suppose that, after all is said and done, a man is most interested in what his son thinks of his accomplishments. In that light, the letter was rather interesting. It said:

DEAR DAD:

It is June here and very pleasant. [That was enlightening, because it was June in Italy, too.] My studies are going along okay and I have very good marks this time. I have been made a cadet sergeant. We licked the Navy at baseball yesterday. I took a blonde from New York to a dance last night and we had a wonderful time. Sorry I can't write more, but I have to make a formation.

Love, BILL

P. S.—By the way, I see from the newspapers that you're doing all right, too.

The last phase of the drive to the Arno River began near the important port of Leghorn (Livorno), which was seized by the 34th Division on July 19 after severe fighting in the mountains below and around the city. The division now was under Major General Charles L. Bolte. Major General Ryder, its previous commander, had gone back to the United States as a result of my recommendation that he be promoted to a corps commander because of his great performance in Italy. I had asked for my old friend Charlie Bolte to take his place. He and his 34th Division likewise turned in a magnificent record of accomplishment during the remainder of the Italian campaign. The harbor was partly blocked by sunken ships, and the Germans had done a tremendous job of mining and booby-trapping the town. It later was discovered that three-fourths of Leghorn, comprising the area around the port and extending inland, had been cleared of civilians by the Germans almost a year before our arrival and had been designated as the Zona Nera, or Black Zone. This section had been blocked off by demolishing the houses around the line of demarcation in a way to make streets impassable. Barbed wire had been erected and signs posted in German and Italian warning civilians not to enter. Officials of the town said that no civilian had been in the Black Zone for almost a year and that they had no idea of conditions there, except that they believed it was the most heavily mined area in all Italy.

I entered Leghorn with the first patrols of the 34th Division and my impression was that the enemy was spending more and more time thinking up new booby traps. We had had a great deal of experience with all kinds of hidden and concealed explosives in the past, but Leghorn turned out to be filled with many new ones, all of them tricky. As soon as we mastered one trick, we immediately discovered that the Germans had another up their sleeve. Here they used articles such as chocolate bars, soap, a package of gauze, a wallet, or a pencil, which, when touched or molested, exploded and killed or injured anyone in the vicinity. Others were attached to windows, doors, toilets, articles of furniture, and even the bodies of dead German soldiers. We found over 25,000 of these hideous devices, and many of our lads were killed or injured as a result.

While we were cleaning up in Leghorn, the 34th Division continued on up the coast and four days later reached the famous city of Pisa, on the Arno. The Germans had destroyed all bridges across the river and prepared to make a stand on the north bank.

The other elements of IV Corps also reached the river. The 91st Division, commanded by Major General William G. Livesay, which had only recently arrived from the United States, had gone into the line earlier, and had advanced up the Era River valley to Pontedera. The 88th Division ran into some heavy clashes with the Germans, but reached the river line by the 23rd.

The French Expeditionary Corps had driven to within about ten miles of the Arno before being recalled to join the ANVIL invasion, turning their sector over to the British. By July 23, we stood on a thirty-five-mile front along the Arno, extending from the sea to the Elsa River, about twenty miles west of Florence. We had been rather thoroughly reorganized by this time and had the II and IV Corps with only two divisions each—the 34th, the 85th, the 88th, and the 91st. We had lost some of our most experienced American divisions and eleven of thirty-three corps artillery battalions. Kesselring had been able to restore some order to his battle lines, and the last miles of our 175-mile advance had shown that we could expect severe resistance on the Arno and in the mountainous bastions of the Gothic Line, which guarded the Po Valley. It was necessary that we pause for a rest and for regrouping along the Arno.

The shift of strength from Italy to France began seriously to affect operations of the Fifth Army. Our weakness in everything from men to ammunition became more and more apparent and we had to improvise constantly to continue the drive toward the Po.

> As you know [Alexander wrote me], my intention is to proceed with the destruction of the enemy's armed forces in Italy. . . . I intend to penetrate the Gothic Line roughly between Dicomano and Pistoia. It is essential to secure [these two towns] quickly, especially the very important road centre of Pistoia. . . I suggest that the best way of developing operations across the Arno would be to force a passage somewhere between Empoli and Pontedera and then to develop two thrusts, one on Pistoia and the other on Lucca. . . . It would suit me best if, as your next task, you could undertake the capture of Pistoia and Lucca.
>
> I fully realize how much your army has been reduced in strength and I have made a personal request to the Supreme Allied Commander verbally and in writing to supply the supporting and ancillary units you have asked for and to accelerate their arrival.
>
> I also realize and deeply appreciate the fact that three out of your four remaining infantry divisions have had a great deal of heavy fighting and that your armored division is in the process of reorganization. At the same time, I feel . . . that it will leave you sufficient troops to force the passage of the Arno east of Pontedera . . . [and] play a part in the attack on the Gothic Line in the area north of Pistoia in conjunction with the Eighth Army's attack further east.

When Alexander came to my headquarters a day or so later, I told him that three of my divisions were somewhat used up, but that I would take on the crossing of the Arno and seizure of Pistoia and Lucca after my troops had a couple of weeks' rest. I explained that we were using every device to make up for our deficiencies, including the use of Italian troops and the use of tanks, tank destroyers, and antiaircraft guns as supporting artillery, and antiaircraft artillerymen as "doughboys."

"It is going to be difficult," I said, "but I feel we should go on putting pressure on the enemy from all directions. He is fighting under severe handicaps. His morale is low. I think the war is nearing an end. We must take chances and pound him from all directions."

By the end of July, however, we were further handicapped by lack of supplies. Brigadier General Tate, my G-4, informed me that there were not sufficient service troops, particularly signal and engineer units, to support our proposed operation across the Arno.

"Also," he said, "the future supply of artillery ammunition makes it necessary that fires be concentrated on a narrow front. Strict allocation of ammunition is to be applied by the Service of Supply beginning August 1. We cannot expect an increase in monthly ammunition allocations in view of priorities established for other operations [Ike's in France] and the limited output in the United States. . . . Artillery ammunition supply in the future will not be sufficient to continue the heavy artillery concentrations employed in the past in support of advancing troops."

Late in July and during August, while we were preparing to cross the Arno, a number of distinguished visitors came to my command post in the Cecina sector. King George VI visited us to meet the commanders of the Fifth Army units and award a number of decorations, including the formal presentation to me of the medal of the Knight of the British Empire. At the same time, Archbishop Spellman of New York was spending some days with us during a tour of the Italian front. My command post was close to the beach and Sergeant Chaney served lunch for our distinguished guests in the open, which was pleasant except when a German mine exploded on the beach nearby, killing an enlisted man of my headquarters staff.

The King took a great fancy to Pal, the cocker spaniel I had brought with me when I returned from Washington prior to the capture of Rome. Pal became a fixture at my van and mingled carelessly with the famous people who came there, showing very little favoritism. On one occasion, when I was preparing to escort the King on an inspection trip in an open command car, Pal insisted that he wanted to go along.

"No," I said. "Go on back. Go back."

"Oh, let's take him with us," the King suggested. So Pal climbed over His Majesty's legs and sat sedately, but proudly, beside him on the seat throughout the trip.

Archbishop Spellman spent enough time with us to become thoroughly indoctrinated in the ways of the Fifth Army. We outfitted him in a GI uniform for his trips around the front, and every morning at breakfast he got a big laugh when we would make him stand inspection beside the table before he could eat. He always seemed to enjoy the time he spent with the Army, and his visits were of great interest and benefit to the men.

Other guests about this time were Lily Pons and her husband, Andre Kostelanetz, who were on a tour to entertain the troops. When they came to headquarters, there was an eager demand for her to sing, so we arranged an open-air performance in a wood not far away. The tiny singer seemed to fascinate the men and there was a big turnout—so big, in fact, that we finally had to get a box for Miss Pons to stand on so all could see her. I shall never forget that scene as she stood on the box in a wonderful pine forest, with the soldiers so quiet that for a moment all one could hear was the chirping of the crickets everywhere around us. When the famous coloratura soprano began to sing, it seemed to me that millions of crickets were singing with her in a fantastic but lovely duet under the pine trees.

Our entry into Pisa had been without much fighting, but the Germans held the part of the city that lies just across the Arno, and there was occasional artillery fire and some patrol action during the period of regrouping. Pisa, of course, was of great interest to the soldiers because of its famous leaning tower, which was on the German side of the river, and there were a lot of gags about how "our engineers will straighten that building up for them when we get across the Arno." We could see the tower plainly, and after a few days some question arose whether the Germans were using it for an observation post.

When we suffered casualties in the area, talk spread that it was being used by the enemy and there was considerable pressure on me to order the shelling of the famous tower. I ordered a most searching investigation to determine whether the Germans were in the tower. Later I got a report from Crittenberger, in which he referred to a feature story in the *Stars and Stripes,* which had quoted an officer as saying Germans had been seen there.

"The officer states that he was misquoted," Crittenberger's report said. "Observers with field glasses were seen in the tower on the morning of July 25. Although a close observation has been kept since then, no further observers have been seen in it and it is considered quite possible that the individuals originally sighted may have been in civilian clothes."

The report then quoted various officers as saying there would be no point in shelling the tower and that, anyway, there had been very little artillery fire in the area.

I might add here that later, after we had crossed the river, I went into the tower sector the same day. A large crowd had taken shelter in the nearby cathedral; from them I found out that the care of the tower was entrusted to an old man. He later appeared and unlocked it and escorted me to the top.

"The only German who ever came into the tower," he explained, "was Marshal Kesselring and he was a sightseer, just as you are."

When we got to the top I insisted that our party remain on our side of the tower so that there would not be any danger of the Germans seeing us there and using our presence as an excuse to shell the structure. Then, when we departed, I had the doors locked and ordered that no one be admitted.

By the end of the first week in August, the first elements of the 25,000-strong Brazilian Expeditionary Forces had arrived in Italy. We made plans to integrate them slowly into the Fifth Army. The performance of the Brazilians was, of course, important politically as well as militarily. Brazil was the only Latin American country to send an expeditionary force to take part in the European war, and, naturally, we were eager to give them every chance to make a good showing. At the same time, there was considerable difference in their training, and we felt that it was important to go slowly in bringing them into the line. It was always in our minds that a setback for these troops would have an unhappy political reaction in the Americas. The Germans had the same thought in their minds and, as will be shown later, made efforts to capitalize on the combat inexperience of the South Americans.

The two weeks' rest that had seemed necessary before crossing the Arno stretched out through most of August and involved changes in our planning. In the middle of the month Alexander called a meeting at the Eighth Army headquarters of General Leese and announced that the main attack was being shifted to the Adriatic coast, with the Eighth Army leading off.

"It is my idea," Alexander said, "that the Eighth Army attack first and be followed at the proper moment by the Fifth Army in a boxer's 'one-two' punch."

Both Leese and I agreed with the one-two idea, but we felt that it was essential that the Eighth and Fifth Armies attack as one combined effort instead of separate affairs. A point of disagreement arose, however, over whether the British XIII Corps, which was in the center of the front, should come under Fifth Army direction or be regarded as part of the Eighth Army. It was only natural that Leese, like any other commander, should dislike giving up a part of his command, but after some resistance he finally agreed that it should be under my command. Thus I received into the polyglot Fifth Army still another group of nationalities: the 6th South African Armored Division, the 6th British Armored Division, the 8th Indian Division, and the 1st British Infantry Division.

We indeed were becoming an international army. I had even borrowed some sixty miscellaneous pieces of British artillery and two battalions of Royal Engineers to make up for Fifth Army shortages. Just to make the picture complete, Prime Minister Churchill paid us a visit, on August 19, and took advantage of a chance to get in a personal blow in behalf of the Fifth Army. During his tour of the front I took him to a 240 mm. battery of the 697th Artillery Battalion near Nugola, where we were met by Brigadier General Paul W. Rutledge and the battalion commander, Lieutenant Colonel Christian. The battery was just preparing to open fire on a bridge target north of Pisa. When Christian explained the situation and had the gun sighted on the target, the Prime Minister stepped forward and pulled the lanyard to fire the first round. Six more rounds were fired, and an observation plane reported back that the target had been hit. The Prime Minister departed in high good humor.

Later he addressed units of the Fifth Army, including the Brazilian Expeditionary Force, the 92nd Division of Negro troops, and the Japanese-Americans.

"No operation could have been more fruitful in this theater than the work you have done by drawing away perhaps two dozen or more enemy divisions down into Italy, where they have been torn to pieces," he told them. "You have aided notably and most effectively the great battle now proceeding to its victorious climax on the fields of France."

By the end of the last week in August, we were set for the new offensive which, we hoped, would lead us into the Po Valley, where our armored divisions could chop up the remains of Kesselring's armies. General McCreery commanded elements of the Eighth Army, which stood on the Metauro River, from where they were to lead the first attack to the south bank of the Foglia River. This would bring them into position facing the Gothic Line. Their advance from then on would be into the main German defenses toward Rimini. Alexander hoped that this thrust would draw German strength from the Fifth Army front and permit us—if our advance were timed properly—to smash through from Florence and drive on a twenty-mile front in the direction of Bologna and Imola.

The Germans had been working for months on the Gothic Line defenses, using some 15,000 unwilling Italian laborers under direction of the Todt Organization. They had built antitank ditches, gun emplacements, machine-gun pits, and personnel shelters. The main defense line was laid out to take advantage of the rugged hills and the few roads that passed through the area. The line started in the vicinity of Massa, on the west coast, and extended southeastward through the mountains along the coast, thence eastward across the Serchio River and through the Lucca and Pistoia sector. This was the formidable half of the line that we had decided not to attack. The area of our attack was where the defenses swung in an arc around the headwaters of the Sieve River, crossed the highway below Futa Pass, and then extended along the main Apennine ridge in a southeasterly direction to the headwaters of the Foglia River. There it turned northeastward to Pesaro, on the Adriatic. Because of the rugged terrain and the elaborate defenses, some parts of this line were almost as strong as the German positions at Cassino. Along the most logical route of attack through Futa Pass, for instance, the enemy had built some of his most powerful defense works. Around the pass were concrete bunkers and pillboxes and, in addition to thousands of mines, there was one antitank ditch three miles long.

I visited the various units of the Fifth Army in the several days before the Eighth Army began its attack. I tried in particular to welcome the 92nd Division, which General Marshall was eager to give an opportunity to prove the ability of Negro troops in battle. I remember that when I was talking to one colonel of the 92nd, I asked whether he was having any major problems. He said that about the only thing they had to complain of was that promotions were slow for some of his officers.

"Give me an example," I said.

He turned and called a first lieutenant who was commanding one of the companies that we were inspecting. "Here's a good example," he said. "This man is far overdue for promotion."

I turned around to my aide and borrowed the captain's bars from his shoulders and pinned them on the lieutenant.

The next day I went to Vada to inspect a regimental combat team of the Brazilians, and was received by Major General Joao Batista Mascarenhas de Moraes (the Brazilian Expeditionary Force commander) and his staff. The combat team looked pretty good to me and the Brazilians generally were enthusiastic about getting into action. In fact, they were in such a hurry that they probably did not get the complete training that they needed after their arrival in Italy. But they were extremely cooperative and an atmosphere of strong friendship existed between our headquarters. The thing, I believe, that stands out most plainly in my mind about that day was when, after the ceremonies ended, the Brazilians suddenly burst into the strains of "God Bless America." Although most of the men spoke only Portuguese, they had memorized the words in English.

The British Eighth Army offensive began when the 1st Canadian Corps and the 5th Corps moved up beside the 2nd Polish Corps, which was on the Adriatic coast, and all three advanced on the night of August 25–26. Good progress was made until the Germans, aided by two days of heavy rain, slowed up the advance south of Rimini. The Eighth Army, however, had broken into the Gothic Line. After a few days of hard fighting, Kesselring shifted three of his best divisions to the British front and committed all his available reserves in the area. By September 6, the offensive thrust had progressed to a point where the Eighth Army was separated from the vital Rimini-Bologna road by only a single ridge. There the Germans made a powerful stand. The time had come for the Fifth Army to strike northward from Florence toward Bologna and thus crack the Gothic Line wide open.

Both IV and II Corps began the American advance, only to find that the enemy was falling back rapidly from the Arno River. There was little opposition to our crossing, and by September 3 we had reached the slopes of the hills that stood before the Sieve Valley. Again the Germans drew back and contact was difficult to maintain. It was not until September 10 that the Fifth Army was able to get into position to strike hard at the retreating enemy. By that time we were going up against the Gothic Line defenses, hidden high in the mountains beyond the Sieve Valley and almost twenty miles north of the Arno. It was decided to make our main effort to break through at Il Giogo Pass, which lies slightly to the east of the powerfully defended Futa Pass.

Il Giogo Pass is the area where Route No. 6524 passes through a break in the Apennine Mountains between the Arno and the Po valleys. The divide traverses the highest and most rugged area of the Apennine Mountains. It is divided up into many deep gullies and sharp peaks, covered with brush and pine forests, and there are few roads. The going would be extremely difficult, but by breaking through there we would be able to outflank the main German defenses at Futa Pass. From September 12 to 18, the 85th Division on the east side of the pass, and the 91st Division on the west, attacked stubbornly over the rocky mountain barrier, with powerful aerial support whenever the weather permitted. In the first two days they gained little ground and suffered rather severe losses, but they battered the defending German troops into a state of exhaustion. Mt. Altuzzo, one of the strong points defending the pass, fell on the 17th, and Mt. Monticelli, to the northwest, was taken a few hours later, giving us a seven-mile stretch of mountains on either side of Il Giogo. The enemy had no choice but to pull back from the pass. On September 21, the 85th Division drove northward to the town of Firenzuola and to the Santerno River on a front extending from

Firenzuola to San Pellegrino. Within approximately two weeks of hard fighting, the Gothic Line had been pierced and Futa Pass was in our hands.

This initial success had been the result of some excellent teamwork all along the front. The Fifth Army attack was timed just right to take advantage of the gains made by the British Eighth Army and to catch the Germans off balance while they were shifting their forces from one sector to another. Our thrust had been powerfully concentrated in a comparatively narrow sector, but it was so well concealed that the enemy could not prepare for it and had little idea where the main attack would come until it was well under way.

While the main attack was in progress, the other elements of the Fifth Army kept up the pressure on both flanks to harass the enemy and keep him occupied all along the front. The Brazilian 6th Combat Team, which hailed from São Paulo, under Brigadier General Euclideo Zenobio da Costa, went into action on a five-mile front, the first units from their country or from any South American country ever to fight on European soil. On September 15, their first day in action, they seized the village of Massarosa, north of Lake Massaciuccoli. Soon thereafter, General Eurico Gaspar Dutra, the Brazilian Minister of War (now President of Brazil), visited me. He expressed a desire to see action, so I set up what we called the "Dutra Task Force" and put the Brazilian Expeditionary Force, together with supporting American troops, temporarily under his command in a sector in the western part of Italy. I liked General Dutra. He cooperated in every way and backed me up to the limit in the tasks we assigned his countrymen.

As a result of the breakthrough in the Gothic Line, our next big objective became the city of Bologna, almost due north through the high Apennines and at the edge of the Po Valley. We therefore shifted the direction of our main attack from the Firenzuola-Imola road to Route No. 65 leading to Bologna and pressed slowly forward against stiff resistance. On October 3, I flew up to the 91st Division positions near San Pietro a Sieve and drove through Futa Pass up Route No. 65 to Monghidoro, which we had captured the previous day. The 91st, in its first real battle, had fought magnificently with Bill Livesay at its helm. From a vantage point in that town, I could see for the first time the Po Valley and the snow-covered Alps beyond. It seemed to me then that our goal was very close.

As a matter of fact, it was close, but that didn't mean it was easy to reach. Not only was winter coming on, but our strength was limited. On October 6, when we were only twenty miles across the mountains from Bologna, we were running so short of replacements that I sent a message to General Wilson's headquarters, as follows:

Infantry replacement situation is so critical that current operation may be endangered. Supply of infantry replacements and infantry overstrength in divisions only sufficient to maintain divisions at authorized strength through 9th or 10th of October. Losses in my four infantry divisions during past five days have averaged 550 per day per division over and above returns to units. Heavy fighting continues with enemy apparently rushing all available forces to halt our advance on Bologna. All divisions have been in heavy fighting twenty-three to twenty-six days under adverse weather conditions. Continuous supply of infantry replacements is imperative.

At this time we were also much concerned about the loss of manpower from psychiatric disorders; I sent a letter to General Marshall on the same day which summed up our experiences:

The incidence of manpower loss from psychiatric causes began to be felt in January when the combat forces available to the Fifth Army were so limited that it was necessary to keep infantry units in the line for very extended periods [in reference to the Battle of Cassino]. Our assaults against fortifications were made with divisions, which became materially understrength and could be given little respite as we pressed forward.

A similar situation confronts us today in the Apennines. My troops have been negotiating the most difficult mountain terrain we have had to face in Italy, involving the bitterest fighting since Salerno. Our only chance to rest the troops is within the divisions themselves. [We had inaugurated a system of having each division hold out one regiment and rotate the regiments in the line approximately every five days.] The decision that has faced me is one of halting our attack in order to rest or of pushing on in an all-out effort to gain our objectives before winter catches us in the Apennines. Fifth Army troops have made significant advances every day for more than two weeks.

I do not yet know the answer to the psychiatric problem. It appears clear from the report, based largely on Fifth Army experience, that susceptibility to psychiatric breakdown is directly related to the length of time in combat. I shall continue to take every practicable measure to give my troops the opportunity for rest.

This letter stated only part of my problem during the drive toward Bologna. More than ever I felt the adverse effects of losing men and equipment to the invasion of southern France. It seemed to me that our fighting strength was being sapped by our American representatives at AFHQ, who were supposed to be handling our supply and replacement problems, but instead were most interested in getting more and more of everything for ANVIL. Even the Japanese-American troops, which had performed so well in the mountain fighting in Italy, were shifted to the French invasion, as was much of my heavy artillery. My feeling was that I had been directed to cross the Apennines, but was not getting any backing from the Americans at AFHQ. In a somewhat desperate mood, I finally sent a message direct to General Eisenhower, who at that time, fighting in France, had no responsibility for our operation, but who I knew would be sympathetic, asking him to take over the ANVIL requirements so that some 5,000 infantry replacements in the Mediterranean Theater could be released to me instead of being diverted to southern France. I did not, at that time, feel that an appeal through ordinary channels would do much good.

"There seems to me to be no excuse for having so many large headquarters in Italy," I noted in my diary. "I would estimate that many thousands of military souls are tied up in these activities, contributing little to the battle. Again I say: never were so few commanded by so many."

Furthermore, there had been no significant progress on the Eighth Army front while we were driving toward Bologna. By the middle of October, with the Fifth Army advance elements fighting around Livergnano (which the doughboys called Liver 'n' Onions), exhaustion of our troops raised a serious question whether the Fifth Army could break through. We were so close to the Po Valley that every day we would tell ourselves, "Now if we can just push on a little farther today, then well make it. We are right at the edge of success."

It is difficult now to explain the agonizing hope we then felt that "just another mile" or "just a few miles" would do the job. By the time we had pushed on to within ten miles of Bologna in mid-October, the Germans had shifted their main strength again and had some seventy-two battalions opposing us. The Fifth Army had sustained 13,082 casualties and taken 7,087 prisoners. We had replacements available for only one more day. At a meeting that day with my corps commanders, I said, "The Germans have been sideslipping their divisions from other parts of the front to meet our main attack. . . . The four American divisions will continue their attack northward as long as they are able."

On October 16, the German 29th Division moved from the Eighth Army front to our front, and we were strongly counterattacked in the Belmonte area. General Howard, my G-2, informed me that the 90th Panzer Grenadier Division also was moving over to our front; this appeared to be more than we could handle easily.

"Of course," Alexander said, "if you think you should stop the attack, do so."

"I won't stop," I replied, "until we have to."

Under the most trying conditions, we did keep up the attack. I know that there were countless incidents of heroism and of unimaginably stubborn courage on the part of the men during those days. There was also the day that I visited Brigadier General Paul W. ("Bull") Kendall, who as a division commander,[*] should have had a promotion coming along. Kendall was commanding the 88th Division. I told him, "Bull, you see Mount Grande over there? Well, your second star is up on top of that peak. Go and get it."

The 88th got Mount Grande and Kendall got his second star.

On October 19, I received a message from Lieutenant General Jacob L. Devers,[†] who was the American deputy to General Wilson at AFHQ, in which he said,

> I have just seen your reported daily casualty list. Suggest you rest a division or regiments within a division, as your casualty rate will break down any replacement system. Your problem is one of using available troops to best advantage.

Since I felt that Devers had not been particularly energetic in pressing for fulfillment of our needs and since much of our strength had been shifted to southern France (where he commanded the 6th Army Group), I replied,

> Your radio indicates a lack of appreciation of our tactical situation, the terrain, enemy resistance, and my mission. Unfortunately, you have not been able to visit this front in approximately two months. I have been keenly aware of my casualty rate and have taken every possible opportunity to rest regiments within divisions consistent with the urgency of my mission. . . .
>
> Our success now hangs in the balance, and our growing infantry shortage may prove the decisive handicap. General Alexander took up directly with General Eisenhower a request for 3,000 replacements. General Eisenhower has notified us that they are available and arrangements are under way to fly all or part of them to this theater. I regret that you did not see fit to release to Fifth Army the ANVIL [Seventh Army] replacements in your depots as requested in my radio of October 9. Had you done so and arranged for the Seventh Army supply from SHAEF [General Eisenhower's headquarters] sources, it would have saved much time and obviated the necessity of shipping replacements from Italy to France and shipment back of an equivalent number to Italy.

In the latter half of October, the German build-up of opposition on the Fifth Army front progressed steadily and the exhaustion of our troops

---

[*] He had replaced Major General Sloan, who had returned to the U.S. because of illness.

[†] He was also commander of MTOUSA (Mediterranean Theater of Operations, U.S.A.), which was an administrative job with no tactical control of troops in battle. His primary mission was to relieve the Fifth Army of logistical burdens by keeping up the flow of replacements and supplies of all kinds to the front.

increased. Torrential rains that fell almost every day added to our difficulties as the 88th and 85th Divisions sought to expand a bulge they had made in the enemy lines northeast of Mount Grande. In that sector we were only five or six miles short of the last possible defensive line the Germans could hold in front of the Po Valley, and a final attempt was made to break through, starting on the night of October 22–23. Despite counterattacks, the 351st Infantry pushed forward a mile north of Mount Grande and, during the next night, Company G found a gap in the enemy lines and infiltrated into the village of Vedriano. The rest of the battalion was held back by the German defenses, however, and on the following day the enemy encircled Company G and wiped it out. When the attack was renewed the following night, it proved impossible to advance. Rain and mud completed the exhaustion of the infantrymen. Low clouds interfered with artillery and air support. A German counterattack in the Vedriano sector virtually destroyed two more companies, made up largely of fresh replacements. On the same day a flash flood knocked out the Sillaro River bridges and tied up all transportation there. Ammunition and rations were carried on mule back and by hand and with the aid of a breeches buoy across the swollen river to troops on the north bank. On the 28th, General Keyes ordered the 85th and 88th Divisions to pull back to defensible ground and dig in.

We didn't fully realize it then, but we had failed in our race to reach the Po Valley before winter set in. Our strength was not enough to get across the final barrier to which the enemy clung. In the period from September 10 to October 26, the 34th, 85th, 88th, and 91st Divisions had suffered 15,716 casualties, of which the spearhead 88th Division had sustained 5,026. It was understrength by 1,243 officers and men. Those who were left were completely exhausted and the 3,000 replacements that were flown from France to Italy were so delayed by storms that they arrived too late to take part in any but the final days of the battle.

The Fifth Army's offensive did not stop with any definite setback or on any specific date. It merely ground slowly to a halt because men could not fight any longer against the steadily increasing enemy reinforcements on our front. In other words, our drive died out, slowly and painfully, and only one long stride from success, like a runner who collapses reaching for but not quite touching the tape at the finish line. At the time, I felt that with a month of rest we might yet be able to break into the Po Valley before winter clamped down on the Apennines. After all the effort that had been expended, after all the casualties we had suffered, it seemed almost impossible to give up the idea of completing the breakthrough that fall. For the next few days we worked over many plans for renewing the attack as soon as feasible, but not later than

December 1. At the end of October, a tentative date of December 15 was set for renewal of both the Fifth and Eighth Army attacks toward Bologna, but we never kept the date.

The weather became steadily worse. Our troops on the mountainsides were able to maintain themselves only under severe hardships. Eventually, I had to face my most difficult decision of the war: we could not get into the Po Valley before winter.

I faced that prospect with bitterness and disappointment. We had failed, and of course, failure is a bitter tea for any commander, regardless of the circumstances that made it inevitable. But that was now a secondary consideration. We were stuck in the high Apennines for the winter. Looking out from an observation post near Futa Pass, I could see the snow sweeping across the dark crown of Mount Grande, and I knew that for the men of the Fifth Army it was going to be a hard winter, even if nobody fired a shot. It was the Germans who would spend the next few months in the protection of the Po Valley.

When I returned to my headquarters in Florence, the decision to dig in was made known. There wasn't anything else to do, but when someone—I don't even remember who it was—remarked that at least we at headquarters were lucky to be able to remain in Florence during the winter, I think I must have realized for the first time the real reason for my bitter reaction to our failure.

"The men of those divisions are going to spend the winter in the mountains," I said. "So is my headquarters."

The next day I had my van dug in for the winter at Traversa, near Futa Pass, one of the highest points in the Apennines.

17.

The Hard Winter in the Apennines:

November 1944–March 1945

The dawn of Thanksgiving Day on November 25, 1944, was dark and gloomy with the wind whipping a drizzling rain through Futa Pass. I was awakened in the semidarkness by an orderly who said that the British signal officer attached to my Fifth Army Headquarters wanted to see me. I got up in a hurry, forgetting the cold and dank morning. He didn't come to see me often at such an hour, but when he did it was important, usually a message from Prime Minister Churchill. In any event, it would be a highly secret message, and in those days it seemed to me that all important messages meant trouble.

I turned on the light in my little van, wondering what was wrong now, and got a pleasant surprise. The British officer's bright and shining face was in happy contrast to the weather. "This time," he said, "I've got good news for a change." He handed me a message from the Prime Minister. It said:

> It gives me the greatest pleasure to tell you that the President and his military advisors regard it as a compliment that His Majesty's Government should wish to have you command the 15th Group of Armies under General Alexander, who becomes supreme commander owing to the appointment of General Wilson to succeed Sir John Dill in Washington. [Sir John had recently died while on duty in our country.] I am sure we could not be placing our troops, who form the large majority of your command, in better hands, and that your friendship, of which you told me, with General Alexander will at once smooth and propel the course of operations.

When I saw General Eisenhower last week at his headquarters, I spoke to him about General Truscott succeeding you in command of the Fifth Army. He promised to release him [Truscott was then in France] if in due course he is approached by the United States authorities. I expect this will be agreeable to you and General Alexander specially desires it. Every good wish in your new command. We have the utmost confidence in you and in the goodwill which has always guided your conduct with your British comrades and Allies.

I must confess that the Prime's message made Thanksgiving morning in the high Apennines look immeasurably better. In reading over the message's reference to my friendship with Alexander and my attitude toward the British troops in Italy, it occurs to me that the reader might feel Churchill's statements were overdrawn in view of the events that I have related showing my disagreements at times with the British. If so, I would like to make it clear that our disagreements served to strengthen rather than lessen my friendship for General Alexander and most of his British colleagues. Our differences of opinion were very real and very important. Perhaps for that reason they tend in an account such as this to overshadow the routine of friendly collaboration which went on day after day in the Italian campaign, and which was such a paramount contribution to victory.

The change in commands was not to occur until the middle of December and was, therefore, Top Secret. When the workday began, however, I sent for General Gruenther and when he arrived, I confided: "Well, Al, I've been relieved."

The surprise and shock of this announcement showed so plainly on his face that I couldn't keep up the gag, and handed him the message. We tried to keep the change a secret, but, through some error, the British Broadcasting Company put the news on the air on November 27. By that time it had been decided that my new 15th Army Group Headquarters would be a tactical rather than an administrative setup, which would permit the largest part of the Eighth Army administration to deal directly with AFHQ rather than clearing through my headquarters. I also had decided that the 15th's headquarters would be moved forward from Siena to a wood near Florence.

We were, during November and December, planning to resume our drive toward the Po Valley; in fact, the Eighth Army did launch a limited offensive which advanced its lines on the Adriatic side of Italy to a position that was better related to the Fifth Army front, although it did not quite reach its goal, which was the Santerno River. The Fifth Army had been scheduled to attack a few days later, but the weather deteriorated so rapidly that traffic was almost impossible and the whole Italian front settled down into the mud. I do not want to give the impression that fighting ceased. There were strong patrol actions and occasional local attacks or counterattacks; but generally the front remained static except for one operation that will be related.

There were, however, a great many serious problems to keep us busy. The artillery-ammunition shortage, which had handicapped our drive toward Bologna, continued for weeks, and played a direct part in our failure to resume offensive action during the winter. I had been forced to reduce Fifth Army allotments of ammunition in mid-November to fifteen rounds a day per gun for 105 mm. howitzers, eighteen for 155 mm. howitzers, and eleven for 155 mm. guns. Neither was there much hope of soon building up reserves for offensive operations on a sufficient scale to reach Bologna.

"In view of information in messages from the War Department," I noted in my diary, "the ammunition situation in the United States is so critical that it has been necessary to resort to the scheduling of current shipments direct from loading and production lines to docksides. The War Department expresses grave doubt of its ability to meet the demands of Ike's command and mine, especially during the next three to six months. If our present rates of expenditure are continued, our reserve will be reduced to approximately 60,000 rounds at the end of the fifteen-day attack now planned for December. [This attack was later dropped.] This does not allow for ammunition expenditures to repel enemy counterattacks."

At the end of November, on an inspection trip to a battalion of Brazilians who were about to go into the line, I noticed that many of the men were wearing clothing that seemed too light. I commented on this to General Mascarenhas, and he explained that they had come from Brazil without the proper clothing for a winter in Italy. This gave us still another problem to solve and it turned up a surprising fact. The Brazilian soldiers had small feet in comparison to the Americans and we had great difficulty in getting enough small shoes to outfit them. We did, however, get combat jackets and winter underwear for them quickly, so that they were properly prepared to go into the line.

We arranged for men to be relieved from the front during the winter months as regularly as possible so that they could go to the various recreation centers we established in some of the larger Italian cities. One of these was Montecatini Terme, a famous Italian bathing resort with fine hotels. There were a number of noted theatrical personages in Italy that winter to entertain the men. These shows meant a great deal to our lads, and the entertainers usually seemed happy to put up with a certain amount of hardship and inconvenience in order to make their contribution to army morale.

I remember that the arrival of Katharine Cornell and her husband,

Guthrie McClintic, with the cast of *The Barretts of Wimpole Street,* resulted in a good deal of discussion about the type of entertainment that was most appreciated by the soldiers. I suppose that the answer was as varied as it is in civilian life, but I think it is important to emphasize that the serious shows were just as popular as the more frivolous ones, if not more so.

Miss Cornell was, I believe, a bit concerned when she first arrived at Montecatini about whether *The Barretts of Wimpole Street* would be popular with men who had been in battle for a long time and might be expected to look for rowdy entertainment when they got to a rest center. I attended the first performance and felt that it was greatly enjoyed by the GIs, and later I attempted to reassure Miss Cornell on that score. She didn't need my assurances.

"Oh, I know they liked it," she said. "I was a bit worried the first night, so I took advantage of a chance to listen to the remarks of some of the soldiers as they were leaving the theater. I heard one of them say to his companion, 'There now! Wasn't that better than going out with that dame?' After that I didn't worry."

Snow in the high mountains added to our problems in the early winter season and about all we could do was plan various operations, virtually none of which ever got to the active stage. In this planning, the eagerness of the British to go into Yugoslavia became more and more evident, and Alexander on several occasions outlined his idea of how it would be done. He wrote to me in connection with one plan:

> It is quite clear that no additional Allied formations will be available for operations in this theater now or in 1945. Nonetheless, it is the Allied intention to carry out a sustained offensive. . . . Plans which will now be taken in hand will be based on the assumption that during the next two or three months the advance of the Russian Armies in Hungary, combined with the operations of our light forces and the Partisans in Yugoslavia, will force the enemy not only to give up the ports on the Dalmatian coast at least as far north as Zara, but to withdraw from the mountains in the hinterland of those ports.
>
> It is the intention of the Supreme Allied Command in Italy to occupy the ports of Split, Sibenik, and Zara with commandos and other light forces as they are evacuated by the enemy and to develop operations in conjunction with the Partisans to gain control of the roads running inland over the mountains. As soon as these preparations are sufficiently advanced our main bodies will be brought in as quickly and secretly as possible for an advance on Ljubljana and Fiume. . . . This operation will be the task of the Eighth Army. . . . At the same time, these operations will have to be coordinated with those of Marshal Tito's forces, and possibly with those of the Russian southern army as well.

As a result of this planning, it seemed for a number of weeks that the Eighth Army would split off on an amphibious thrust into Yugoslavia, while the Fifth Army would follow an overland route designed to sweep across the Po Valley and curve northeastward toward Yugoslavia.

As it worked out, these plans went through a number of modifications. By the time I had taken over 15th Army Group Headquarters in the middle of December, we were reasonably certain that all our planning would be subject to thorough overhaul—at least by my Government—before the weather again permitted large-scale operations.

Before I left my Futa Pass command post to assume command of the 15th Army Group, Major General Souslaparov, the Russian representative in Italy, arrived for a visit at my headquarters, and presented me with the Russian Military Order of Suvarov, First Degree, which had been awarded me by Stalin as a result of our capture of Rome. The medal presented on this occasion was accompanied by two small books, which apparently were part of the paraphernalia of this Russian decoration. The pages of one of the books unfolded like an accordion and turned out to be a lifetime pass for travel on all Russian railroad trains. I am not sure how far it would get me on a Russian train today (probably a one-way ticket to Siberia) but I can report that on various occasions when I dealt with Russian guards at roadblocks or elsewhere in Austria after the war that little book came in mighty handy. When I was stopped by Russian sentries, as I was on several occasions, I usually whipped out my lifetime railroad pass and waved it under their noses as I walked confidently past the roadblock. I never did find out exactly what the Russian words on the book said, but they must have been impressive, because they never failed me in an emergency.

I have mentioned earlier that the Germans were particularly eager to take advantage of the inexperience of the Brazilian troops. The Nazi propaganda in Latin America obviously would try to make it appear that the United States was using the Brazilians as "cannon fodder" if General Mascarenhas' troops suffered heavy losses in a defeat. In the first part of December the Germans attempted to make capital along this line by swinging some hard blows at the Brazilians whenever they got a chance. As a result of this attitude on the part of the enemy, the rugged mountain terrain, and the inexperience of the Brazilians, there was a period of some weeks during which the BEF had a difficult time adjusting itself to the war in Italy. It was necessary, therefore, to regroup the Brazilian units and to give them an opportunity to build up slowly in order to meet both the climatic and military situation that confronted them. This was done just before I took over 15th Army Group Headquarters; later it was pleasing to observe the way in which the BEF progressed in the final stages of the campaign. They never complained and always were anxious to carry their share of our burdens.

On Christmas Day, Don Brann and I decided we would take a few hours off and go pheasant hunting. There had been virtually no activity along the front for some days and he had spotted an area near Siena where the hunting was supposed to be good. We were all ready to go when Gruenther came along.

"What makes you think you'll get any pheasants?" he asked. "I'll bet you ten dollars you don't come back with two."

"You're on," I said. "Two pheasants and you're out ten bucks."

Brann and I got started early in the afternoon. We hadn't been out long when two birds got up. Brann knocked down one of them; I missed. We were confident that we had Gruenther's money. But strangely enough, we didn't even see another pheasant. We kept on walking all afternoon and didn't turn back until it was almost dusk. No more pheasants. We were both pretty peeved about our lack of luck as we approached a farmyard at twilight. I saw a pigeon sitting on the top of the barn.

"Could that be a pheasant?" I asked Don. "The light is so poor, I can't tell positively."

Don was willing to agree that it might be a pheasant, so we knocked the bird off the rooftop.

When we picked up the poor pigeon, I said to Don, "I don't think Al will know the difference—and ten dollars is ten dollars."

We decided it was necessary to pluck both birds, but the result still was not entirely satisfactory, so we got a pair of scissors and trimmed the feathers still on the wings and on the heads so they looked pretty much alike. We took both birds back to headquarters and tossed them on the mess table in front of Gruenther.

"All right," I said. "Pay up."

Al examined the birds carefully and complained bitterly, but he finally gave in. Three days later, he came in with a smug look on his face. He sat around saying nothing much for a few minutes, but finally, with elaborate nonchalance, said: "I had a most interesting conversation today with Dick Moran [our signal officer]. Dick said that some unprincipled so-and-so had been shooting our homing pigeons. He thinks he'll have to take some official action to stop that kind of thing. Thinks probably some publicity in the *Stars and Stripes* might do the job." Gruenther paused and looked around at Brann and me. "You know," he went on, "it just happened that somebody shot our best pigeon—old Dickie—on the day you and Brann killed those two pheasants. Poor old Dickie."

We returned the ten dollars and paid the bet without a word and bought a round of drinks besides.

Meantime, we had some action along the front. I had been somewhat concerned about the strength of our positions on our extreme left flank, on the west coast of Italy. This sector, and particularly the Serchio River Valley, guarded the approach to Lucca and Leghorn, the latter our vital supply port. It didn't seem likely that the Germans could mount a large counterattack there, but there had been some heavy build-up in that area, so on December 23 I decided to play it safe and reinforce the 92nd Division with two brigades of the 8th Indian Division and two regimental combat teams of the 85th Division. I also sent two tank battalions and five artillery battalions from II Corps to the vicinity of Lucca.

On Christmas night a number of strong German patrols pushed into the Serchio Valley zone. On the following day the enemy made attacks along a six-mile mountain front astride the Serchio River, thrusting into the line held by the 92nd, which was our Negro division. German and Italian Fascist units probed along the west side of the river while stronger elements of the German 148th Grenadier Division moved forward east of the river against the towns of Sommocolonia and Tiglio. The forward elements of the 92nd gave ground and some units later broke, falling back in a state of disorganization. This left a gap adjacent to the river and made a more general withdrawal necessary.

The enemy attack was renewed on the 27th and again gained ground, forcing the 92nd from its second defensive line and extending the enemy advance to a total distance of around five miles. The German thrust, which began by feeling out our positions by reconnaissance elements, exploited quickly and effectively its initial success and might well have endangered Leghorn, but for the presence of the Indian forces near Lucca. The Indians moved forward, while elements of the 92nd Division passed back through during the night of the 27th. Before midnight the veteran Indian troops had made contact with the Germans and the enemy began to retire on the following day. By the end of the week, we had restored the original lines.

This performance by the 92nd—and it was a bad performance—has since been used on various occasions in an effort to argue that Negro troops cannot be depended upon to fight well in an emergency. Having commanded the only Negro infantry division in World War II, which was continuously in battle for over a period of six months, I feel I should report factually on its performance during that period. Of the ten American infantry divisions in action in the Fifth Army in Italy, the 92nd Division's accomplishments were less favorable than any of the white divisions.* On the other hand, there were many instances of individual heroism and successful action by smaller units, such as a company or battalion. Shortly after the war, when asked about the effectiveness of Negro infantry troops in battle, I replied that the 92nd Division performed a useful role and its presence on Italy's west coast assisted us materially in our final drive into the Po Valley.

At the same time, it would be dishonest and unfair to future Negro soldiers to overlook the serious handicaps that they had to overcome. Leadership was one of the biggest problems. There were many illiterates among the Negro troops; hence it took longer to train them, and there was, in general, a reluctance to accept responsibility for the hard, routine discipline that is essential in wartime. This failure I view not as a reflection on the Negro soldier or officer, but as a reflection on our handling of minority problems at home. The Negro had not had the opportunity to develop qualities of leadership. Most of all, perhaps, the Negro soldier needed greater incentive; a feeling that he was fighting for his home and country and that he was fighting as an equal. Only the proper environment in his own country can provide such an incentive.

It would be a grave error, however, to assume that no suitable officers can be found for Negro combat troops. In fact, they were found in Italy. When it became necessary to reorganize the 92nd in the following weeks, we were able to select certain battle-proven officers and men who responded to special training, and to build up battalion combat teams that participated much more effectively than before. I have decorated for bravery Negro officers and men of the 92nd Division and have known of others who were killed in extremely valorous actions on the field of battle.

Let me make it clear that I am opposed to discrimination. I believe there is a way to work toward a solution of the problems that handicap the Negro soldier, although I do not feel that at this stage of the game there should be an indiscriminate mixing of Negro and white soldiers in our Army. On the basis of performance in the last war, it would not produce the best fighting team and it would not be fair to anyone. I do believe, however, that there can be sound integration of Negro and white troops at the battalion and lower levels, that regiments could include one effective Negro battalion in any branch of the service, and that it could be provided with sound, responsible leadership. In fact, General Eisenhower told me after the war that he had occasion in France, at a critical time, to call for infantry volunteers from

---

* Colored service units (quartermaster, engineer, ordnance, etc.) and combat support units (tanks, field artillery, antiaircraft, etc.) in general demonstrated a high degree of efficiency.

among his hundreds of thousands of Negro troops. Large numbers offered their services and were organized into special combat platoons which were integrated into hard-fighting veteran infantry divisions and fought well.

I do not think that this system should be practiced in units larger than the battalion. Our experience in Italy did not indicate that a Negro division could perform as effectively as a smaller unit under the severe test of modern warfare. The 92nd Division was given the most complete preparation and training for action and provided with the finest equipment procurable. It gradually was brought into the line in a comparatively quiet sector and under the most competent leadership of Major General Ned Almond. In spite of all these advantages, it did not come up to the test when required to attack and when the Germans struck down the Serchio Valley. Regimental commanders were unable to exercise sufficient control over their troops in an emergency, largely because the rigid discipline required in battle was lacking and because junior officers often avoided routine responsibilities and lacked essential qualities of leadership. These are faults that can be corrected—and are being given full attention in our present training program—but time is required, and I must reiterate that it would be a grave error now for the Army to attempt the indiscriminate mixing of white and Negro soldiers.

On January 2, I moved from Siena, which had been Alexander's head-quarters, to a new command post near Florence, in the woods beside the Arno River. As commander of the 15th Army Group, I named General Gruenther as my chief of staff, and took several of my most able associates with me, men who had demonstrated their ability to operate well as a team.[*] Otherwise, the staff was a mixture of Britons and Americans. In the following weeks I spent a good deal of time getting acquainted with new units and with the Eighth Army, which now came under my command.

One of my visits was to the 6th South African Armored Division, under a most competent leader, Major General W. H. E. Poole. This outfit had pre-viously been shifted to the Fifth Army front and had performed splendidly under adverse conditions. It was a battle-wise outfit, bold and aggressive against the enemy, and willing to do whatever job was necessary. In fact, after a period of severe day-and-night fighting, the 6th had in an emergency gone into the line as infantrymen. When the snow stalled their armor, they dug in their tanks and used them as artillery to make up for our shortage in heavy guns. Whenever I saw them, I was impressed by the large number of decorations and honors they had earned the hard way. Their attacks against strongly

---

[*] Brigadier General Brann as G-3, Brigadier General William C. McMahon as G-1, Brigadier General Charles S. Saltzman as deputy chief of staff, and Brigadier General Richard B. Moran as signal officer.

organized German positions were made with great *élan* and without regard for casualties. Despite their comparatively small numbers, they never complained about losses. Neither did Prime Minister Smuts, who made it clear that the Union of South Africa intended to do its part in the war—and it most certainly did.

The South Africans were not the only armored unit to shift to the role of infantry during that winter in the Apennines. We had to undertake a large-scale job of retraining and reorganization, particularly in the Fifth Army, which meant that each major unit was out of the line for periods of a month or so. Thousands of American replacements were coming in at this time and many units had to be given an opportunity to integrate these newcomers into the team. In January, the Fifth Army activated the 473rd Infantry, made up largely of men from antiaircraft units, which were not now required since we had almost complete air superiority over the Germans. The 473rd was placed under command of Colonel William P. Yarborough, one of the finest combat soldiers produced in the war, and it later was moved over to the area north of Leghorn, where it became a prime factor in our breakthrough at the end of the war.

Meanwhile, the 10th Mountain Division began arriving in Italy and took up positions in the Pistoia area. This division, which included some of the world's famous skiers, had been trained at Camp Hale in Colorado and was equipped with weasels and other vehicles particularly adapted to use in snow and in the mountains.[*] It proved itself a great fighting unit in the final months of the war. It was commanded by Major General George P. Hays, a Medal of Honor winner in World War I. He was a great soldier, and under the spark of his leadership this division spearheaded our final drive to victory.

The story of how the 10th Mountain Division came to Italy was given to me later by General Marshall. He had offered it to other theaters, but because it had special equipment instead of the regular infantry equipment, other commanders had turned it down. Later, in a conversation with Marshall, one of the commanders indicated that there had been a mistake in regard to the message of refusal and that he would like to have the division.

"You're too late," Marshall told him. "I asked Clark if he wanted it, and almost before I could turn around I got a message back saying to start it moving."

I was happy to get any division at that time and, of course, the 10th Mountain was ideally suited for the high Apennines. We made several limited

---

[*] Minot Dole, president of the National Ski Patrol System, and Lowell Thomas had a lot to do with the organization of the 10th Mountain Division.

attacks to keep the enemy off balance during the winter and to clear several high ridges in preparation for our spring attack toward Bologna. In one of these the 10th Mountain Division and the Brazilian 1st Division punched some impressive holes in the German defenses in mid-February. The 10th moved toward high ground opposite Porretta on an eight-mile front near Vergato, miraculously scaling the 1,500-foot rocky cliff known as Serrasiccia-Campiano and seizing Mt. Belvedere and Mt. della Torraccia in a brilliant attack that caused the defense of the position by the 232nd Grenadier Division to collapse. The Brazilians took Mt. Castello and both outfits then pushed northeastward early in March in order to advance the right flank of IV Corps to a more favorable position in preparation for the spring offensive.

During the winter I also got back the 442nd Regimental Combat Team of Japanese-Americans. The 100th Battalion, as I have noted, had joined the Fifth Army at Naples. Just before we reached Leghorn, I received two other battalions of Japanese-Americans, which, with the 100th, made up the 442nd. They had been shifted to the invasion of southern France in September, but later, when I explained my needs to General Marshall, he asked Ike to release them. Ike generously agreed, and by the end of March they were back in Italy.

I remember particularly an able and hard-boiled captain of the 100th Battalion, who was among the first to arrive in Italy. He was Captain Young O. Kim, a Distinguished Service Cross winner, and he was always on the ball, very proud to be a veteran of the Fifth Army. Shortly after the other battalions of Japanese-Americans had arrived to form the 442nd Infantry Regiment and had gone into the line with the 100th, I visited the front and talked to Kim.

"How's the 442nd on your right flank getting along?" I asked him.

"I've been having a lot of trouble with those punks," he replied. "I'll have to check." He picked up the telephone, a dark scowl on his Oriental face, and rang up regimental headquarters.

"Where," he demanded when he got the connection, "are those goddam Japs that are supposed to be on our right flank?"

On another occasion I visited headquarters of the Cremona Gruppo, the first to be activated and committed of a new series of Italian formations trained by the Eighth Army. This organization held the extreme eastern sector of our line along the Adriatic coast, and was under the command of Brigadier General Clemente Primieri, an extremely able commander. The Italian regular units took some heavy losses and fought well in the last year of the war. And, as I have previously mentioned, the Italian Partisan groups also played an important role in attacking the rear areas of the German defenses in northern Italy. In fact, all through the war the Italian soldiers, Partisans, and civilian population fought bravely and made great contributions to our final victory. During the winter of 1945, I had approximately one hundred thousand Italian troops in the 15th Army Group

Crown Prince Umberto, as Lieutenant General of the Realm after his father's abdication, was Commander in Chief of the Italian Army, and was always highly cooperative. He spent much time forward with the troops and seemed eager to share in their hardships and to encourage their participation in the fighting.

About this time, the First Canadian Corps, under their fine leader Lieutenant General Foulkes, was taken away from us. It was going to join the First Canadian Army, which was fighting in Holland. These "Canucks," who talked our language, had built up quite a record of accomplishment during their eight months of fighting in Italy. We hated to lose them and sorely missed their fighting qualities during the spring offensive.

Our plans for renewal of the offensive were carefully developed as spring approached. Among other things, we worked out some elaborate cover schemes to keep the Germans confused about when and where the real attack would come. One of these, the cover experts decided, would be to let word leak out shortly before the offensive began that I was going to Rome for a short rest. To make it seem real, they planned to have me seen in Rome one evening so that enemy spies would be likely to send word to the Germans that I was away from the front and no offensive need be expected at that time.

In line with this scheme, they passed the word around that I would take a rest in Rome—and almost immediately got back word that there was a plot to assassinate me when I got there. I never was able to figure out whether the assassination plot and our cover scheme just happened to coincide or whether word that I was going to Rome stirred up the enemy agents. It was true, however, that there was a group of saboteurs who blew up an oil pipe line and caused other damage, and that word of the assassination plot came from one of our agents who had managed to work himself into the confidence of the gang. A number of arrests were made and my plans to be seen in Rome went out the window.

It was about this time that we suffered a painful calamity. I have frequently mentioned the exploits of my Cub pilot, Major John T. Walker. He had a fine combat record and had been decorated on more than one occasion for bravery. He was an able pilot, as has been demonstrated, had a pleasant personality, and always was willing and anxious to carry more than his share of the burden. He came from Springfield, Illinois, was married, and had a son born shortly after he came overseas.

I decided to send Jack home for a couple of weeks' rest, along with some other members of my staff who had seen long service in combat. He was to fly in a British plane to Caserta, where he would take an American plane for home. I had pinned the Legion of Merit on his coat and said goodbye before he went to the nearby airport. I never will know what happened, but a few minutes later a terrific crash indicated there had been an accident. I rushed to the airfield only to see his plane in flames. It had crashed shortly after the take-off. The heat was so intense that no one could get near it. Jack, as well as his companions and all the crew, had been killed instantly. We took him back to a cemetery near Florence and laid him to rest among so many of his comrades who were paying the great price for our victories.

In all our plans for the offensive, the Polish Corps figured prominently. I had high confidence in their fighting spirit, and they were moved into a vital spot along the north side of the road to Bologna when the advance started. Then early in February, we received word of the decision by the Big Three at the Yalta Conference that after the war Poland was to be divided along the Curzon Line.* The result was something akin to panic in the Polish Corps.

On March 2, General Anders came to my van to explain the attitude of his men, most of whom had lived east of the Curzon Line, had been prisoners of the Soviet Union, and had been able to reach the Near East and join the western Allies only after long delays and many hardships. The Allied decision to give the area east of the Curzon Line to Russia came as a terrible blow to all of them.

Anders' first reaction had been to send a letter to General McCreery, who was now commander of the Eighth Army as successor to Leese,† expressing his unalterable opposition to the decision and asking to be relieved from his front-line command of the Polish Corps. He even indicated that it would be desirable to accept the entire Polish Corps, which had fought so valiantly in Italy, as prisoners of war, because they could not accept the decision.

---

* The Curzon Line, named after Lord Curzon, British Foreign Minister, was established by the Allied Supreme Council of the Treaty Powers of the Treaty of Versailles on July 11, 1920, as the temporary eastern boundary within which Poland was entitled to establish a Polish administration, but subject to change by treaty negotiations. It was established in an effort to bring about some stability in the region in connection with the boundary dispute between Poland and Russia after World War I without prejudice, however, to the ultimate disposition of territory farther to the east. On March 15, 1923, the Supreme Council of the Treaty Powers accepted a boundary between Poland and Russia to the east of the Curzon Line.

† General Leese was transferred to command the 11th Army Group in the Southeast Asia Command under Lord Louis Mountbatten.

My sympathies were entirely with Anders, but I could see no advantage to impulsive action on his part and I certainly did not want to lose the Polish Corps on the eve of our spring offensive. He was very depressed and there were tears in his eyes when he discussed the decision with me.

"We are done for," he exclaimed, referring to the territory that was to remain in Russian hands. "My people come from there."

"What are you going to do about it?" I asked him.

He didn't feel that he could go on fighting under the circumstances.

"If you quit now," I said, "you will lose the respect of the Allied people, and they are your only friends. Your men will follow your lead. If you become a defeatist and indicate to them that all hope is lost, you will have failed in your duty as a commander."

Anders was pessimistic, but I insisted that the crisis had created an opportunity for him to show himself as a great patriot, to forget at least temporarily these new troubles, and to inspire his men to maintain their fighting standard. I expressed my own opinion that President Roosevelt—whose death was then only a few days away—would not take part in a deal that turned the Poles over lock, stock, and barrel to the Russians. If the Polish Corps would just stand firm, I added, I would be only too glad to do everything that I could to bring the situation to the attention of our President in an effort to achieve a remedy.

"You know," I went on, "when I was a cadet at West Point, I used to look out of my window at Kosciusko's statue. He was a great hero to us because of what he did for America. If you stay in this fight now, we will one day be putting up a monument to you."

Before leaving, Anders promised that the Polish Corps would maintain its defensive sector for the time being. A decision about the future would not be made, he said, until he had flown to England to consult with the Polish government-in-exile. That was the best I could do until he returned, and until then I worried about how I could replace the Polish Corps if it came to the worst. But when Anders came back, he was in better spirits. The Poles, he said, would fight on—and they did.

Later in March, after General Anders' return, I visited the Polish Corps for a special ceremony. Anders, who had been promoted to Commander in Chief of the Polish Army, was turning over command of the corps in a short time to Major General Zygmunt Bohusz-Szyszko, but he had arranged to present decorations to officers and men of the 2nd Polish Armored Brigade. During the ceremony, he promoted to the rank of lance corporal a young tank gunner whose service indicates something of the fighting ability of the whole corps.

The boy, whose name I do not know, had enlisted when he was sixteen, giving a false age in order to be eligible. He was the only surviving member of the crew of a tank that had been knocked out by a German gun, but he had killed an even dozen German infantrymen in action. It was not difficult to understand why I was eager to have the Poles take part in our final offensive into the Po Valley.

In the days leading up to the offensive, we were visited by a number of members of Congress, who were, I believe, surprised to discover how many different nationalities were represented in the Italian campaign. One of them was Representative Clare Boothe Luce, who took a special interest in our problems and stayed on to make a thorough tour of the front. When she returned to Washington, she made a speech in the House about the "forgotten front," telling what we were doing and how we were doing it. Her interest and efforts gave all of us a real lift and helped to clarify the Italian war in the minds of people back home.

I am not sure, however, that the picture ever could be made entirely clear, except by visiting the polyglot units that we had assembled in the high Apennines. I know that I devoted considerable time to trying to explain our problems to the War Department and that, finally, I took a calculated risk and deliberately disobeyed a direct order from General Marshall in an effort to get our story across.

Marshall had made a tour of the European Theater during the winter and had informed me of the date in February on which he would arrive in Italy. His message was brief, but specific, and it said, "Do not meet me at airport. I will come to your headquarters. No honors."

I replied that we would be happy to have him take a look at our front, that I would meet him at the Pisa airport, and that we would have a minimum of honors. I got back a quick reply, which left no room for doubt about Marshall's desires: "Don't meet me. No honors repeat no honors."

When the general arrived, accompanied by Lieutenant General Joseph T. McNarney, commanding general of MTOUSA,[*] I waited for him at my headquarters near Florence. He climbed out of the automobile that had driven him from Pisa and scowled when he saw not a small guard of honor, but a really big one. His lips pressed together in a thin line.

"Didn't you get my message?" he barked at me.

"Yes, sir."

"Didn't I say no honors?"

---

[*] McNarney had recently replaced Devers, who had gone to southern France. McNarney supported our operations with every resource available to him.

"Yes, sir."

"Well?"

"It will only take a few minutes and you'll not regret it," I said, suppressing a feeling that *I* might regret it in the end. There was nothing that the General of the Army could do about it except review the honor guard, and I led him over to the head of the line. There were men and women from a score of units standing stiffly at attention. Marshall paused and the frown vanished from his face. Nothing could have spoken more eloquently than this honor guard of the melding of units from all over the world into the 15th Army Group. In a single glance, he could see the problem of supply, the problem of different languages, the problem of different religions, the whole complex and tangled problem of making it possible for a dozen nationalities to live and fight as one team. I had lined up before him one squad (about ten men) from each nationality fighting in Italy.

"The 1st Battalion, 135th Infantry, 34th Division," I said as Marshall paused before one of the few squads that were familiar to him. I didn't need to explain anything to him about the 34th's grand performance; nor did I need to add anything when he stood before the next squad of rigidly erect Negro soldiers from the 92nd Infantry Division.

But from then on he was on comparatively unfamiliar ground:

"1st Division, Brazilian Expeditionary Force." (We had had to scramble to find Portuguese-speaking interpreters to man our tanks supporting Brazilian units in action.)

"1st Argyll and Sutherland Highlanders." (I sometimes felt, quite unjustly, that the British would stop in the middle of a battle for their after-noon tea. But at Anzio, when supplies were desperately short, we pulled the outstanding lend-lease deal of the war by trading American tea for British coffee. Everybody was happy.)

"3/8 Punjabs, 19th Infantry Brigade, 8th Indian Division." (The British Eighth Army had to maintain a herd of goats behind the lines to provide food for them. Their religion prohibited them from eating pork.)

"166th Newfoundland Field Regiment."

"Special Service Battalion, 6th South African Armored Division." (These were Field Marshal Smuts' "Springboks." They left their tanks and fought on foot.)

"24th Guards Brigade, Welsh Guards."

"2nd Battalion, Inniskillings, Irish." (Before one important battle on St. Patrick's Day, they insisted that a special plane bring shamrocks from Ireland for every man.)

"1st Armored Brigade, 1st Canadian Corps."

"Defense Company, Headquarters 2nd Polish Corps." (Most of them had relations in America.)

"26th Battalion, 2nd New Zealand Division."

"Italians—platoon of Partisans and 67th Regiment, Legnano Group." (It was a confusing war for them.)

"American nurses, 56th Evacuation Hospital." (They were shocked when the French Arabs refused to put on pajamas, and wore the pants as turbans.)

"Women's Army Corps, Fifth Army."

"American Red Cross women."

"Auxiliary Territorial women, 15th Army Group." (Referred to as ATs, these British girls carried with them into the field the proud tradition of the heroic contribution they had made as operators of antiaircraft guns in the great battle for England.)

"One Indian nurse, 18th Indian General Hospital."

"South African, British, and Canadian nurses from 107th South African General Hospital." (This hospital received the wounded of all nationalities. The task of the personnel was greatly complicated by the varying languages of their patients.)

General Marshall ended his inspection in a much better humor than he had started. He said he was glad I had ignored his instructions.

"All I regret," I told him, "is that it is impossible to have the French represented here. I am sorry; they have gone to France. I don't want you to think that we are intentionally holding anything out on you."

18.

The Surrender:

May 2, 1945

In the spring of 1945, the great battles of the European war moved swiftly to a climax. From the west, General Eisenhower's Allied armies were hammering at German defenses beyond the Rhine, and from the east the Red Army had rolled across Poland and through the Balkans to envelop Hitler's Reich in a giant nutcracker. It was then that we began to hear about the "Southern Redoubt."

The strength of the Nazi armed forces had crumbled, but Hitler still had a powerful fighting machine. In Northern Italy alone there were twenty-five German and five Italian Fascist divisions. If the Nazi forces in Germany withdrew southward to the Bavarian Alps and the thirty divisions in Italy joined them in that vast mountain stronghold, they might hold out indefinitely. By the beginning of April, information from prisoners made it clear that industrial machinery was being moved from Milan and Turin into the sheltered valleys of the Alps, apparently in preparation for manning the Southern Redoubt.

As a result, the task of the Allied armies in Italy was clear: destroy the enemy armies in the Po Valley before they could withdraw to the Alps and prolong the war by setting up a new defense line behind the almost impassable Adige River. This defensive position had been under construction since July 1944. At that time the Fifth Army had been pursuing the shattered German Army toward the Arno River after its defeat during the battle for Rome. The fact that he was starting a new defensive position behind the

Adige River, and so far from the scene of fighting, might well indicate how the enemy estimated our capabilities, lacking the knowledge, of course, that half our strength was being diverted to southern France. This new line ran between Lake Garda, where it linked onto the Apennine Mountains, through Verona to Vicenza on the Adriatic. It was a very strong position, made up of trenches, many dugouts, and machine-gun emplacements. The river was swift and swollen from thawing snow and was three hundred to five hundred feet wide.

As the weather improved, the Allied air force in Italy broke the grip of winter on the 15th Army Group front by striking almost daily at the German communication lines. The airmen did a great job. Bridges by the score crumbled under the attack. Rail lines were twisted and uprooted. Highways were smashed and pockmarked with craters. The Brenner Pass was battered by many tons of high explosives. The enemy was able to provide almost no opposition in the air.

In April, the effects of this aerial bombardment began to tell. The enemy could move troops only slowly, usually on foot and at night, whereas in the past he had been able to shift units with great rapidity. Although he was living off the rich granary of the Po Valley, his supply of many necessities began to dwindle. He resorted to countless tricks. Bridges were built under a few inches of water so that they could not be seen by our airmen. Others were concealed by day and swung out over the water at night. Radio-directed repair crews were organized to work on railroads and tunnels; again and again our bombers had to go back for a second or a third or a tenth time. But in the end, the weight of bombardment was strongly felt.

In the meantime, as the swollen streams went down and water drained from other areas that the Germans had flooded, the Fifth and Eighth Armies moved with extreme secrecy into the sectors from which they would strike the final, crushing blow. It had to be sudden and it had to be paralyzing in order to cut off the enemy from the Southern Redoubt behind the Adige River.

The Nazis' Army Group Southwest held a strong line defending the Po Valley. On the west they were entrenched near Massa, in the mountains north of Pisa, with the line extending eastward along formidable ridges to the vicinity of the wrecked town of Livergnano, south of Bologna, and thence northeastward behind the wide and steeply banked Idice, Sillaro, Santerno, and Senio rivers. A maze of dikes and flooded fields strengthened this eastern flank where it stretched across the Po Valley to the Adriatic at Lake Comacchio. Moving so secretly that often the men of one division did not know the identity of the divisions on their flanks, the 15th Army Group had taken up positions that would permit it to strike as soon as the ground would bear the weight of our armor. The Fifth Army front ran from Viareggio on the west coast to Monte Grande, ten miles southeast of Bologna, a distance of about ninety miles. On the left flank, touching the Ligurian Sea, was IV Corps, commanded by General Crittenberger. The IV Corps sector extended seventy miles inland through the mountains. The remaining twenty miles of the Fifth Army front was crammed with II Corps, under General Keyes. From Mt. Grande to the Adriatic was the British Eighth Army, with the 13th Corps under Lieutenant General Sir John Harding holding the mountainous left flank. The remainder of the line was held by the 10th Corps, under Lieutenant General J. L. I. Hawkesworth; the 2nd Polish Corps, under General Bohusz-Szyszko; and the 5th Corps, under Lieutenant General C. F. Keightley at the anchor spot on Lake Comacchio.

On April 5, General Truscott ordered the Fifth Army to begin execution of the plan of battle, a diversionary attack on the west coast where the Nisei 442nd Infantry and 473rd Infantry hit the Germans in their mountain fortifications and the 370th Regiment of the 92nd Division started up the coastal road. In the next six days, they captured Massa and, with the aid of Italian partisans, the town of Carrara. Meantime, on April 9, General McCreery's Eighth Army launched a powerful, stunning blow from the east coast to open the main attack.

Rested, revitalized and ready for the kill, the Eighth Army swarmed against the Senio River line in a drive toward Argenta and Bologna, with V Corps, the Polish Corps, the New Zealanders, and Indian divisions in the lead. At first the going was steady, but slow, because the vast network of rivers and canals aided the German defense. As the fighting progressed, however, the British 56th Division launched a daring and carefully planned amphibious attack across Lake Comacchio, using buffaloes (amphibious tanks) to sweep around a series of enemy lines and head for Bastia, which was a key to the whole defense area before Argenta and Bologna. Other units landed on the south shore of the lake at Menate and still others walked along a narrow bank between the lake and the land, which the Germans had flooded. By the 11th, the Senio and Santerno river lines had crumbled and Bastia was caught in a pincers from the east and south. In the next two days, heavy fighting and steady progress had broken a third river line—the Sillaro—and the flooded route to Bologna was almost opened.

While the drive was in progress, I broadcast a special message to the Partisan forces of northern Italy, telling them that the final battle for the liberation of Italy and destruction of the invader had started.

"You are prepared to fight," I said, "but the time for your concerted action has not yet come. Certain bands have been given special instructions. Other bands will concentrate on preserving their districts and towns from destruction when the enemy is forced to withdraw. . . . To those bands not given specific tasks for the immediate future: you are to nurse your strength and be ready for the call. Do not play into the hands of the enemy by acting before the time chosen for you. Do not squander your strength. Do not be tempted to premature action. When the time comes, one and all will be called upon to play his or her part in liberating Italy and in destroying the hated enemy." The services that the Partisans performed were many, varied, and important and included the capture of many towns and villages.

Another example of heroism by Italians that stands out in my mind followed a call for Italian soldiers to volunteer for a parachute jump behind the enemy lines in the Po Valley. We got about two hundred men to volunteer and told them that they were to be dropped at night along roads where they could strike at enemy transportation. They were then to lose themselves by daylight among the Italian population of the area. They did a fine job, killing a thousand Germans. One of them later told me that he had been dropped as his plane passed along a road that the Germans were known to be using heavily after dark. As he floated close to the ground, he heard trucks moving along the road, and before he knew it he had landed directly on a moving truck filled with German soldiers.

"The result," he said, "was unbelievable. I was one man descending from the darkness right into the hands of a score of heavily armed enemy soldiers. But when I hit them there was a great shout of surprise and consternation. They had no idea what was happening. The truck went out of control and ran off the road. All the German soldiers leaped wildly to the ground and disappeared into the darkness. I made off as discreetly as possible."

Early on April 14, General Truscott's Fifth Army front was blanketed in mist and fog from the Tower of Pisa to Mt. Grande. Anxiously, we waited for a break in the heavy clouds. At dawn it was hopeless. At seven o'clock there was little change. The tension increased all along the line from headquarters to the forward patrols. Everybody was waiting. We still were waiting at eight o'clock, but the clouds were breaking up. It was essential that we have close air support for our attacking infantry and tanks. Weeks of teamwork between my staff and that of Major General Benjamin W. Chidlaw, commander of the Mediterranean Allied Tactical Air Force, had produced a carefully coordinated plan for this all-out, air-ground attack. Through various intelligence means, including information from our agents, infantry patrols, and aerial reconnaissance, we knew what targets to hit. These were indicated to Ben Chidlaw, who assigned the necessary types and numbers of aircraft to do the job.

At eight-thirty, there came the welcome roar of fighter-bomber engines. Wave after wave came northward over the mountaintops and suddenly the front sprang into action. For almost an hour the Air Force hammered at the enemy positions and communication lines in the forward area. At ten minutes after nine, the artillery joined in, blasting selected targets in a nerve-shattering crescendo. At nine forty-five, the 10th Mountain Division moved forward from Castel D'Aiano across a valley and up a strongly defended and heavily mined enemy hillside while fighter-bombers guided by both ground and air-plane controllers flashed back and forth in front of the attackers, strafing the rocky slope until it seemed to rise slowly into the air in a swirling cloud of dust.

It wasn't easy going. The men of the 10th Mountain Division advanced by inches and feet; but by afternoon they had seized the high ground over-looking Route No. 64, and the veteran 1st Armored Division had captured the towns of Susano and Vergato. The Brazilians moved against Montese. All along the line the blows were beginning to fall. The Germans knew now that they were in for trouble in a big way.

It came the following night. The concentrated power of II Corps—rested, filled up to strength with replacements from the United States, and with its ammunition dumps filled to capacity as a result of conservation made possible by weeks of winter inactivity—jammed into a narrow corridor below Bologna, hit the enemy an hour and a half before midnight with a barrage that lit up the sky and obscured a pale crescent moon above Mt. Sole. Seventy-five thousand rounds were fired by artillery and tanks in thirty minutes; while the ground still shook, General Keyes sent the South Africans against Mt. Sole, and the 88th Division against a hail of machine-gun fire from nearby slopes. Mt. Sole was scaled and held against two heavy counter-attacks. Before daylight the 91st and 34th Divisions plunged northward through the hills on the right flank of the 88th. It was bitter fighting every step of the way, but these veteran troops performed miracles.

Throughout the next day, the intense fighting continued. The main effort was now obviously a pincers movement by Fifth and Eighth Armies, a broad encircling movement around and beyond Bologna. Throughout the mountains and down across the valley to the water barriers around Argenta, men and pack trains, armor and artillery, were edging forward. By the 18th, the Eighth Army closed in on Argenta, and the Poles, battering a path down Route No. 9, were firing heavy artillery into enemy positions at Bologna. Slowly, the enemy defenses began to crack.

Two days later the beginning of the end was in sight. Tired, dirty, but gaining momentum as they advanced from peak to peak, the 10th Mountain Division broke out of the Apennines on April 20, with the crack 85th Division, which had been held back in reserve initially, driving full-steam ahead on its right. And up from the east came the Eighth Army. By dawn of the 21st, troops of the Fifth and Eighth Armies were in Bologna, the 91st and 34th Divisions entering from the south at the same hour the Italian Legnano Gruppo and the Polish 3rd Carpathian Division entered from the southeast.

It was sweet revenge for the Poles, because the crack German 1st Parachute Division was at Bologna. It had been at Cassino, too, where it fought the Poles to a standstill time and again until repeated onslaughts by the Poles had made the town untenable. All the way up the coast, the Poles had been trying to get at the Germans again, but the Nazi veterans were tough and rough and not easy to take. They became a kind of taunting challenge to the Polish Corps—until Bologna. That was the end of the 1st Parachute Division. It simply fell apart. When the Poles captured the division's headquarters, they left almost nothing intact, and ended up by driving tanks over the wrecked tents and buildings. The few survivors of the division were taken prisoner. The only thing left when they got through was the divisional flag, which their great leader, General Anders, happily carried away as a prize.

After the capture of Bologna, I noted in my diary that we were just getting warmed up. "British, New Zealand, Indian, Polish, Brazilian, South African, Palestinian,* Italian and American troops will destroy the enemy," I added. "Bologna is a symbol [but] our most important objective remains the destruction of the enemy forces." We had, in fact, barely reached the point we had waited for so long: the point at which we could turn loose our armor and let it run across the plains of the Po Valley. On that same day, it began to run.

The 6th British Armored broke out of the Argenta area, after overcoming stubborn resistance, and smashed the German 1st Parachute Corps back into the arms of the Fifth Army. Prisoners were pouring into our cages or forming long, dejected lines on their march to the rear. On the 22nd, the Eighth Army had reached Ferrara, and by the next day Bondeno was in our hands. On the same day, the 10th Mountain Division raced far north past Bologna. It crossed the Po River near San Benedetto on the 23rd, completing an advance of seventy-five miles in eight days. The circle was drawn tightly around some seven thousand enemy troops in the Bologna area, and still the momentum of the attack increased.

---

* A brigade of infantry from Palestine had been added to the Eighth Army.

Paced by fighter-bombers that littered the roads with wrecked enemy equipment, our mobile, fast-moving spearheads thrust out in all directions to break up and cut off the enemy retreat toward the Alps. On the right flank, the 91st Division, the 2nd New Zealanders and the 6th Armored swung in a huge semicircle across the Po and the Adige rivers and on northward along the Adriatic coast toward Treviso and Trieste, with the South Africans sweeping farther northward toward Bolzano. From the Fifth Army front, the 85th and 88th Divisions drove straight north toward Verona and then on into the Alps, while the 10th Mountain Division dashed along Lake Garda to Trento, deep in the Alpine ridges. The 1st Armored slashed past Modena and carved a huge circle across the Po Valley in a magnificent final dash to Brescia and Milan, and the Brazilians skirted the southern edge of the Po Valley in a push of 130 miles to Alessandria.

During this climax to the Italian campaign General of the Army "Hap" Arnold came to pay me a visit. He brought with him from Washington Colonel Bill Darby of Ranger fame, who had been with us in Italy during the early days of our campaign. As usual, Darby was raring to see action. Knowing where he would find it, he asked to be attached to the 10th Mountain Division. Hap Arnold agreed and I sent him up to General Hays. As fortune would have it, the assistant division commander of the 10th, Brigadier General Robinson E. Duff, was wounded a day or two later, and Hays asked to have Darby permanently assigned to fill the vacancy created by Duff's absence. After radioing Washington for authority, and getting it, Darby fell heir to that important job. A couple of days later, while leading a task force along the east side of Lake Garda, he was killed instantly by a German shell. Word of his death shocked me greatly. I had sent him home originally because I felt he had had more than his share of combat and harrowing experiences, and I believed a demonstrated leader like Darby could do a lot on the home front in training new units for battle. He had written me often from the United States begging to come back to the Fifth Army, but Washington—quite correctly—would not turn him loose.

He died exactly the way he would have had it—out in front of his men in hot pursuit of the enemy. I asked General Marshall to promote him to a brigadier general posthumously, and he did—I believe the only such promotion made during the war.

In 1949, while commanding on our West Coast, I had the privilege, in the presence of his mother and father, Mr. and Mrs. Percy N. Darby of Fort Smith, Arkansas, of christening an army transport, the *General William O. Darby,* in honor of this great soldier.

Meanwhile, the Brazilian dash to Alessandria cut off the main avenue of retreat for the Germans on the Ligurian seacoast, who had been shattered by blows of the 442nd and 473rd Regiments from the Viareggio front. After making their original diversion, the 92nd Division had advanced against the German 148th Grenadier and Italia Bersaglieri Divisions, which also were squeezed from the northeast by the Brazilians and elements of the 34th Division. Then the Japanese-American 442nd Infantry and Colonel Yarborough's 473rd broke loose to spark a brilliant thrust up the Ligurian coastal road to Genoa, where the German garrison of 4,000 already had surrendered to Partisans, and on to Turin and the French border.

Everywhere the enemy was in disorder as the Allied armies, penned up for bitter months in the mountains, stretched their legs in magnificent strides across the plains. By the end of April, the prisoners were being counted by the tens of thousands. At Fornovo, the Brazilians caught up with the German 148th Division, which had handed them some stiff blows earlier, and captured its commanding general and 6,000 men. On the north, Fifth Army patrols were on the Swiss border, having failed by a few hours to catch up with Benito Mussolini, who was shot by Partisans at Lake Como. In the Ligurian zone, the 34th Division seized the 75th German Army Corps, adding some 40,000 prisoners to our bag. The Eighth Army, spearheaded by the New Zealanders and the British 6th Armored Division, on our Adriatic flank, was close to Venice; and the South African 6th Armored Division on the right flank of American II Corps was nearing Treviso, moving in the direction of the Yugoslav frontier. Even the Germans knew that it was all over, and Hitler's suicide in his underground bunker at Berlin merely made it official.

On May 1, my forty-ninth birthday, I issued a statement that I hoped would let the world know that the German military power in Italy was ended, not by any armistice, but by a decisive defeat on the field of battle. It said:

> Troops of the 15th Army Group have so smashed the German armies in Italy that they have been virtually eliminated as a military force. . . . Twenty-five German divisions, some of them the best in the German army, have been torn to pieces and can no longer effectively resist our armies. Thousands of vehicles, tremendous quantities of arms and equipment, and over 120,000 prisoners have been captured and many more are being corralled. The military power of Germany in Italy has practically ceased, even though scattered fighting may continue as remnants of the German armies are mopped up.

Negotiations for an armistice already had begun at Alexander's headquarters at Caserta with representatives of the German commander, Colonel General Heinrich von Vietinghoff, who succeeded Kesselring when the latter was shifted to the German western front before the final collapse. We later were informed that terms had been accepted for unconditional surrender, and on May 2 we intercepted the enemy's instructions to the German troops stating that they should lay down their arms at two o'clock that afternoon. It was the first time during the war that a German army group had surrendered unconditionally. I informed Truscott and McCreery of the developments and instructed them that "Allied forces of the 15th Army Group will cease firing forthwith except in event of an overt hostile act by the enemy."

It was the end of hostilities that cost America—as well as our Allies—a heavy price. A total of 189,000 Fifth Army casualties had been recorded since we landed at Salerno, and of these 31,886 were killed.*

There was, of course, some confusion in ending the fighting. Some elements declined to surrender because they had not received official orders, but these were only temporary delays. There was also considerable difficulty in keeping the Italian Partisans in line, because they had been nursing their hatred of the German invaders for many months and were inclined to take their revenge while they had a chance. This was particularly true around and in the big industrial centers, and the Germans, with good reason, felt they would be in considerable danger if they attempted to move about.

Von Vietinghoff, as commander in chief of the German forces in the southwest, had headquarters at Bolzano, high in the mountains near the Brenner Pass. The Partisans were so active in that area that he expressed belief they would wipe out his party if he attempted to come to my headquarters for the formal surrender of his troops. I therefore instructed him to remain with his staff at Bolzano and maintain order among his forces, sending his next senior as his representative to Florence to receive our instructions for the surrender of German land forces.

My office at Florence was a small, portable shack that had two rooms. I used the front room for working space and the back room for maps. On the morning of May 4, Generals Truscott, McCreery, and Chidlaw (commander of the air forces so ably supporting our final drive) arrived with their chiefs of staff. So did about twenty newspapermen, photographers, and movie cameramen who crowded into one corner of the little office.

We had been rather frantically looking up the rules for issuing surrender orders, but everybody was vague on the fine points of protocol. We did,

---

	Killed	*Total Casualties*
American	19,475	109,642
British	6,605	47,452
French	5,241	27,671
Brazilian	275	2,411
Italian	290	1,570
	31,886	188,746

however, decide that it was proper to remove our sidearms. We piled our belts and pistols in one corner of the office, which was getting pretty crowded by now.

At ten-thirty in the morning, General von Senger und Etterlin, commander of the XIV Panzer Corps, arrived, wearing a dark green uniform with an Iron Cross suspended by a ribbon around his neck. He was tall, thin, and obviously under great emotional stress. This strain may have been intensified by any one of several factors. He had, for instance, had some experience with armistice sessions early in the war when he was head of the triumphant German delegation to the French Armistice Commission. This morning, however, he was on the receiving end and finding out how it felt to be taking instead of giving the orders.

Another good reason for his emotional stress was the fact that his trip through Partisan territory from Bolzano was probably the most dangerous experience he had had during the war. Only two days earlier, Partisans had attacked von Vietinghoff's headquarters and killed forty Germans. On his trip down the Brenner Road, en route to Florence, von Senger's party had been harassed repeatedly and finally attacked by a band of Partisans who lay in ambush near a mountain pass. Von Senger's group would certainly have been killed but for the intervention of several American officers. As a final blow to his dignity, von Senger stepped on my cocker spaniel, Pal, as he entered the office, and Pal immediately retaliated by making a pass at his booted leg.

Standing very stiffly, the German emissary saluted and I returned the salute. I was laboring under considerable strain myself.

"General Clark," he said in perfect Oxford English, "as representative of the German commander in chief, southwest, I report to you as the commander of the 15th Army Group for your orders for the surrendered German land forces."

"I assume you come with complete authority to implement unconditional surrender terms," I replied.

"That is correct."

I handed him the instructions. "General Gruenther, my chief of staff, will now conduct a conference for members of my staff and yours to cover details of the plan," I told him. "If there are any subjects that cannot be settled, they will be brought to my attention."

Von Senger saluted again, about-faced, and started for the door. I suddenly realized there was something wrong with this picture. After a moment, I saw what it was. Von Senger was wearing side arms—a small pistol in a holster that snapped on to his belt at the back. I started to speak, but didn't. When he was out of the door, however, a reporter quickly said:

"General, you let that guy surrender while armed!"

"I didn't see it," I said; but I had to do something.

"Get him back here," I told a guard. Von Senger came back to stand in the doorway. He saluted again. "Get rid of that gun," I said.

Very stiffly, his face expressionless, von Senger took off the leather belt and let the gun holster swing downward. Very stiffly, he swung it toward the foot of a tree outside the shack and turned away as it thumped softly against the ground. Looking at his retreating back, I felt a kind of agonized relief. The tension was sliding away. This was the end. *Finito!* The war in Italy was over.

I turned to my aide. "Get me that gun under the tree," I said. "I can use that among my souvenirs."

Later I had a long talk alone with von Senger, who had been educated at Oxford and was married to an English-speaking woman. I asked him in great detail about various points of battle tactics during the Italian campaign: why didn't the Germans mass their entire force to overwhelm us at Salerno, rather than resort to the piecemeal attacks which Kesselring made; and had the Germans thought they could "drive us into the sea and drown us" at Anzio, as Hitler had instructed? Von Senger said that at Salerno Kesselring had been cautious because he feared that our landing might be a feint in preparation for a stronger attack farther up the coast. In regard to Anzio, he said the Germans had been supremely confident that they would wipe out our landing force because of their numerical superiority. But I was most interested in why the German armies in the Po Valley had permitted themselves to be destroyed when they might have fallen back to the Po River and then to the Adige, and fought on for a long time in the Southern Redoubt. They hadn't even made a serious effort to follow such a program until it was too late.

"Why did you stay south of the Po and be smashed?" I asked.

Von Senger shrugged his shoulders. "Hitler," he said, as if that told everything. "He ordered every man to die in his position, to hold the whole valley."

The surrender plans were soon completed, and we began collecting a large assortment of German generals, whose stories we wanted to hear. They, however, were not inclined to talk. Although we questioned them for several days, their answers were routine and we obviously were learning nothing. Finally, we fixed up a special villa for them, a pleasant, comfortable place. By the time they had moved into it, the house was wired for sound from top to bottom. There were microphones in every room, and in the basement we had a control board where stenographers and intelligence officers could hear everything that was said. After a couple of days, my G-2 came around with a disappointed look on his face.

"Nothing's happened," he said. "They don't say a word that amounts to anything."

"Well," I told him, "take a couple of cases of Scotch whisky over there. I think that may help them talk."

That afternoon the whisky was delivered to the German generals. About two hours later, the stenographers were working their heads off. The generals almost talked the microphones out of the walls. In disgusted and disgruntled tones, they complained of how Hitler had run the war in Italy by remote control, making unsound tactical decisions to hold to the last man when they should have withdrawn and lived to fight another day. They discussed the possibility of Hitler's committing suicide, and showed amazement at the offensive power in the mountains developed by the American divisions, particularly the 10th Mountain Division. The Scotch whisky certainly turned the trick.

General von Vietinghoff was cooperative in carrying out the surrender details, but there was a great wave of German desertions by men who decided to try to find their own way through the mountains and back home. Von Senger said that the German troops hated the Italians and didn't want to be brought back from the mountains into the Po Valley where they would be subjected to Italian insults. They also felt that the danger from Partisan groups was very great. I asked General Truscott to move his forces into the Brenner Pass area as rapidly as possible to round up the Germans, but it was impossible to prevent large numbers from deserting.

A detachment of the Fifth Army passing through Bolzano, von Vietinghoff's headquarters, found carefully stored away in a deep cavern thousands of cases of fine French champagnes and liqueurs. Each bottle was carefully stamped in German: "STOCKS RESERVED FOR GERMAN ARMED FORCES ONLY" You can imagine how much attention we paid to that. The wines were distributed to the men of the Fifth Army, and few needed any water for the next couple of weeks.

Meanwhile, our forces had fanned out to the French, Austrian, and Yugoslav frontiers, and we were beginning to run into trouble with our Allies. In order to assist our final drive into the Po Valley, we had asked the French forces on the Italian frontier to simulate an attack from that direction early in April. The French did more than simulate. They started active operations along the frontier where France and Italy had long disputed the ownership of a large strip of territory. On April 27, I told the French that they had achieved their purpose and should withdraw to their own frontier. The

French commander replied that he would halt his troops the next day—they had shoved forward in the Val d'Aosta region—but that he could not withdraw without the consent of his government. The area contained a large separationist party, and the presence of the French troops there aroused fear of conflict with the Italian Partisans, who were well armed.

The situation eventually developed into a sort of tug of war in which, as Truscott said, it seemed obvious that "political machinations are involved, looking toward the annexation of some of the communes or provinces adjacent to the Franco-Italian border." Truscott was as persuasive as possible, but unsuccessful in getting the French to withdraw. Of course, we had no intention of trying to force them out. About all we could do was stand firm and let the quarrel be settled at a high political level. The French finally withdrew without further difficulty.

A different situation existed, however, on the eastern coast, where my mission required me to secure the port of Trieste and to protect the lines of communications from Trieste into Austria through Gorizia and Tarvisio. Here we ran into Marshal Tito's Yugoslav forces, which were determined to seize as much Italian territory as possible.

In the final phase of fighting in Italy, Alexander had been in close touch with Tito and had sought to work out the way in which our forces would cooperate when they met on the Adriatic coast. These negotiations, however, were rather indefinite, and on May 1, I noted in my diary:

> The Province of Venezia Giulia is a hot spot between the Italians and the Yugoslavs. Alexander understood that Tito would not oppose the movement of my troops into this province, including the occupation of Trieste, Pola, and other naval facilities in the Istrian Peninsula. He assumed that Tito would place his troops there under my command.
>
> I have set up, under Eighth Army, a British corps commanded by General Harding, with Freyberg's New Zealand Division and the 91st Division under Major General Bill Livesay to occupy the port facilities of Venezia Giulia. I have directed that under no circumstances, if our troops are opposed by the Yugoslavs, should we come into armed conflict with them. I told our commanders that if Tito's forces are not willing that we advance into territory they hold, we will halt our advance and they are to report to my headquarters.

The next day Alexander received a message from Tito saying that Yugoslav forces had broken into the German defense line and were fighting in Trieste and the Fiume sector, having liberated almost all of the Istrian peninsula. He said that conditions had changed since he last talked with Alexander, but that "I am prepared for you to use the ports of Trieste and

Pola as well as the railway line from Trieste to Tarvisio for supplying your troops in Austria." He added, however, that his forces intended to establish their front along the Gorizia-Tarvisio line, which was the line I was supposed to occupy and protect.

In order to protect a line, in military operations, it is necessary to take a stand somewhere beyond the designated line, particularly if, as in this instance, you are instructed to protect a supply route. Thus I correctly foresaw that if the Yugoslavs intended to place themselves on the line we were protecting, there was going to be danger of trouble. In order to carry out our mission, we had to advance far enough to the east beyond the line to establish a defendable position.

Actually, we began to run into the Yugoslavs before we reached the designated line. At the same time General McCreery reported that confusion was growing over cooperation with the Yugoslavs in the Trieste area. The Yugoslavs seemed to be surprised to see our troops east of the Isonzo River. Simultaneously, Yugoslav soldiers were moving into Trieste and Gorizia in fairly large numbers. General Freyberg, in Trieste, was having trouble because he did not know exactly what port facilities were needed. McCreery finally decided to hold up our advance on Pola until the situation was clarified.

On May 5, I flew to Monfalcone and conferred with General Harding and General Freyberg, who later took me into Trieste. The city was quiet, but had an air of uncertainty and unrest. It seemed to me that the streets were full of every kind of uniform imaginable and some went beyond that limit. The New Zealand troops and Tito's forces had originally arrived in Trieste at almost the same time, and now there were many Partisans on the streets, plodding along on foot, riding bicycles and usually waving some kind of flag or carrying some kind of weapon.

There were occasional outbreaks of disorder in the town, and just before our arrival some of the city's 200,000 Italians had staged a demonstration against the city's 60,000 Yugoslavs, but the affair had been broken up by Yugoslav soldiers who fired into the air. The Allied and Yugoslav soldiers, each occupying part of the city and dock area, got along together well enough, but there was constant friction at higher levels where political problems made their influence obvious.

Tito obviously was moving as much armed strength into the area as possible in order to back up his claims to the territory. Companies and battalions were infiltrating across the Isonzo River to the west, where Italian property was being requisitioned and manpower conscripted. This action, designed to influence the elections that soon would be held in some towns, increased the danger of clashes with the Italian population. It seemed obvious to me that we would have great difficulty in trying to occupy all of Venezia Giulia without clashing with the Yugoslavs, something we were desperately trying to avoid. As a result, I decided to make a show of force by moving all of the American 91st Division into Trieste and Gorizia and shifting the British 56th Division eastward to the Isonzo.

Upon my return to my headquarters, I telephoned to Alexander,[*] telling him of the tense situation and expressing the belief that he and Tito would have to work out a solution. I suggested that he emphasize that we were going to protect the port of Trieste and our line of communication through Gorizia and Tarvisio into Austria, and that Yugoslav troops must not be permitted west of the Isonzo River. The only alternatives to this plan would be to act by force to establish our line or to get out of Venezia Giulia and supply our troops in Austria through Venice.

Alexander agreed generally and undertook further negotiations with Tito to establish our line of control, instructing me, meanwhile, that a strong attitude should be taken toward Yugoslav forces that infiltrated west of the Isonzo. After the German High Command surrendered all land, sea, and air forces in Europe on May 7, Lieutenant General Sir William D. Morgan, chief of staff to Alexander, met with Tito and discussed a solution. The Yugoslav marshal said, however, that he could not accept the proposed agreement, since he had conquered the territory and intended to claim this and other territory to the west under the peace treaty.

Tito added that he would give the Allies full and unrestricted use of the port of Trieste and roads and railways required for military needs. After some argument, he suggested that there should be a joint military command in the area. In his report Morgan said that he believed the political situation had put Tito in a position where he could not, even if he wished, accept our proposals without prejudicing his own position at home.

There was no inclination on Alexander's part to accept compromise with Tito, except in regard to a few details, and for several days the situation did not improve. I did, however, get word from Washington to occupy the Austrian towns of Villach and Klagenfurt, instructions that puzzled me at the time. McCreery's troops were moving in that direction and soon took over the towns. We then discovered that Tito had been seeking a zone of occupation in Austria and was trying to infiltrate his troops into Villach and

---

[*] This was about my last official contact with Alexander. Serving in close association with him through the entire war, I came to consider him an outstanding leader. He is also a man whose friendship I value. Alexander is now the Governor General of Canada. Of the other great battle leaders whom I knew in Italy, it is interesting to note that Bernard Freyberg is now Governor General of New Zealand and General Juin Governor General of French Morocco.

Klagenfurt in order to strengthen his claim. By this time the quarrel had almost ceased to be a military matter and was being threshed out at high government levels, while our troops held their positions somewhat short of the line that we needed to protect our communications route to Austria.

On May 16, receiving word that some action might be necessary to improve our position, I told Truscott to be prepared "in the immediate future to carry out operations to eject Marshal Tito's forces from southern Austria and all or portions of northeast Italy." The British Eighth Army was similarly alerted. On the 20th, with tension considerably increased, I decided it was essential, in order to protect our railroad line from Trieste to Tarvisio Pass, in Austria, that the Allied forces move forward several miles all along the front facing Yugoslavia. This meant, among other things, that we would have to take over the town of Gorizia, which was held by the Yugoslavs. Orders for this operation were issued by me. On May 22, I flew to Udine, where I met with General McCreery and General Keyes.

Our troops were out on the roads in our own zone by that time, ready to move forward along several roads that would take them to higher and defensible ground. We had brought up the 361st Infantry of the 91st Division besides other units, so that we would be able to make a strong show of Allied force, in the hope of avoiding any trouble. The order for the advance was given, and a short time later I drove in a jeep along the road followed by the main column in order to see how things were going. Approaching Gorizia, the road led under a railroad bridge, and there the Yugoslavs had set up a roadblock. Our column had halted short of the bridge, waiting for the time set for all the columns to make their advance simultaneously.

"When do you advance?" I asked the column commander as my jeep pulled up beside him.

"Right now, sir."

"All right, come along," I said, and motioned my driver to proceed under the bridge, where there was a gap in the road block wide enough to allow one vehicle to pass. We buzzed past the Yugoslav guards and the column followed us with no difficulty, although I must admit I held my breath for several minutes in fear that some reckless guard might fire a shot. Everyone else felt the same way; nobody wanted the distinction of being the *last* guy killed in World War II.

The columns on the other roads also advanced. I drove through Gorizia and inspected the high ground to the east where we were setting up our front line. In the afternoon, as we returned through Gorizia, I was stopped by a Yugoslav general.

"Why are your troops moving to the east?" he asked. "I don't understand what is happening."

"We're on maneuvers," I replied as carelessly as possible. "Just maneuvers." That didn't seem to satisfy him, but it stopped the conversation.

Later McCreery called me and said that the commander of the 13th Yugoslav Division had ordered our 361st Regiment to withdraw from Tarnova village. Colonel Rudolph W. Broedlow, commanding the regiment, replied that he had orders to remain there, whereupon the Yugoslav general said that if necessary he would force the 361st out. McCreery said that he could tell Broedlow to withdraw, but that reinforcements might be needed if we stayed put.

"Make no withdrawals," I instructed him. "Get General Keyes and go up there and explain to the Yugoslav general that we are going to remain in the town. Run some tanks up and down the road. Let them know that we mean business."

Needless to say, no attempt was made to force out the 361st. Several hours later McCreery telephoned me and said with a chuckle that everything was all right. When he and Keyes arrived at Tarnova, they quickly discovered that the main difficulty had been caused by the British Broadcasting Company, which had broadcast a news report that the Allied forces had advanced "without any opposition." The Yugoslav general regarded the broadcast as reflecting on his courage because he thought it meant that he had refused to fight. He then felt required to threaten to drive out the Allied troops in order to save face.

On that not-very-harmonious note, my military service in Italy came, more or less, to an end. For some time, I had been receiving indications that I would be the American commander of troops in Austria, and also the American high commissioner. However, there was a period of indecision about the Austrian appointment, and late in May I was ordered to return to the United States to take part in a victory celebration in Chicago.

I selected about ten officers and men of the Fifth Army to go back with me. Practically all hailed from the Chicago area. They had been decorated, and had fine combat records. Unbeknown to the enlisted men, I had arranged with Washington to have them discharged as soon as they hit Chicago. We had to come in over Michigan Boulevard at a specified time, where we were picked up by an Air Force escort. We landed at the Chicago Municipal Airport and were met by Mayor Edward J. Kelly. There followed a triumphant ride all through Chicago, down Michigan Avenue, along State Street, through the Loop District and eventually to the great Civic Stadium on the waterfront. The people of Chicago gave us a mighty fine welcome.

At the Stadium I had to make a speech. I had received word that Mrs. Clark was flying to Chicago to meet me, but as yet no one had produced her. I kept asking Mayor Kelly, "Where is Mrs. Clark?" He replied, "Just have patience, you will see her soon." When I arrived on the platform in front of the many microphones, still no Mrs. Clark. I was beginning to be a little peeved, so I turned to the mayor and said, "I don't understand. Where the hell is Mrs. Clark?" About that time someone had turned on the microphones, and the last part of my sentence roared out to the audience. They echoed my sentiments and started screaming, "Get Mrs. Clark"—that produced the results. We attended a big banquet that night, and next morning took off for Washington.

Luckily, I arrived in Washington in time to be present when my daughter, Ann, was graduated from college there; then I flew up to West Point for Bill's graduation, and I proudly handed him his diploma.

By that time it had become definite that I would go to Austria, but I had also received an invitation from the Brazilian Government to visit Brazil for official ceremonies in connection with the return of the Brazilian Expeditionary Force from Italy in July. It was decided, therefore, that I would return from the United States to Italy in the middle of June, remain there for about a month, and, after visiting Brazil, take up my duties in Austria. When I got back to Italy, there were a great many loose ends to be tied up during the remaining days of June and early July. My command post had been moved to Verona. We planned as far as possible the setup that we would have in Vienna, but otherwise things were comparatively routine, except for an interesting discovery by Major Joseph Kolisch, chief interrogator on my intelligence staff.

There had been a number of rumors that certain Nazis had concealed stolen treasure in Italy in the hope of one day coming back and getting it. We knew they had stolen plenty, but nobody knew just where it was hidden. Then one day a tip from a prisoner of war caused Kolisch to do some digging. A day or so later I was told that the treasure had arrived and had been placed under guard. I was asked to "Come and take a look."

I wasn't interested in whatever Kolisch had found and replied that I didn't have time. "Just be careful," I said, "that you don't stick your neck in a booby trap when you open it."

Several days later I was again asked to "take a look at the treasure." I went along and discovered that they had dug up five boxes, each measuring one foot by one foot by one and one-half feet. When the lid was lifted from the first box, it made me think of a trash basket—but a valuable one. It looked as though somebody had taken a shovel and dumped the box full of jewelry, gold coin, necklaces, bars of silver, watches, and I don't know what else. All five boxes were about the same, filled with jewelry and gold and silver coins and bars. Somewhere down in that mess of riches, they found several books of an old stamp collection, and in another box a large collection of old coins. I directed that the boxes be nailed up, kept guarded, and that the stuff be turned over to the Allied Military Government for return to the rightful owner.

"And," I said, "be sure you get a receipt!"

At midnight of July 5, the 15th Army Group was officially disbanded, and for five hours I was out of a job. At twenty-four minutes after five in the morning, I assumed command of the United States forces in Austria. I slept all through it.

Ten days later, with General Crittenberger, General Brann, other staff officers, and Sergeant Chaney, I flew to Brazil. From the time our plane touched ground briefly at Natal, where I reviewed an assembly of Army, Navy, and Air Force officers and men, our visit to Brazil was a constant round of excitement and official functions. From Rio de Janeiro, where Mrs. Clark joined me, to Bela Horizonte, to São Paulo, to Port Alegre, and back to Rio, we took part in a joyous welcome home to the first Brazilian soldiers ever to participate in a war in Europe.

Sometimes the crowds in the street were so thickly massed and so demonstrative that we were forced to move at a snail's pace from one official function to another, throwing the program far off schedule and keeping high officials waiting. Nobody seemed to mind. The returning soldiers could hardly push their way through the crowds when they attempted to parade through the capital, and it was late afternoon before the ceremonies were ended. At Bela Horizonte, after I had reviewed a parade, the crowd swarmed around so thickly that I literally was picked up off the street and carried back to my hotel. At São Paulo, which is supposed to be a less-emotional city than Rio, our automobile barely crawled through the crowds that rushed out from the curbs to block our path. Here I finally got the answer to a problem that had concerned me when the Brazilians first landed in Italy and we had turned over some of our fine 2½-ton trucks to their drivers. We had immediately been confronted with a traffic situation in regard to speeding. The men, part of the 6th Brazilian Combat Team, were from São Paulo. It was not until I had a chance to see that great and rapidly growing metropolis of South America that I realized the reason for their fast driving. Those Paulistos came from one of the fastest-moving cities in the world, and it is no wonder we had a problem trying to slow them down.

President Vargas, General Dutra, Foreign Minister Veloso, General

Mascarenhas, General Milton, and Roberto Marhieno, at whose home we stayed, joined with many other Brazilians to make our stay a memorable one. The people of Brazil had a right to be proud of the accomplishments and sacrifices of their fine Expeditionary Force under the able and understanding leadership of General Mascarenhas de Moraes.

By the last week in July we were almost exhausted and I was getting messages from General Gruenther that made me think it was about time I got back to Europe, for the Austrian situation was getting hot. Gruenther had been negotiating with the Soviets in an effort to arrange the first meeting of the Allied and Red Army commanders in Austria. The Soviets didn't seem to be coming to any definite decision about when we could get started, despite pressure by the Americans and the British. By the time we left Brazil, on July 27, it was apparent that all would not be peaches and cream in Vienna.

"Stalling continues," Gruenther radioed me just before we departed. "Had three-hour meeting this afternoon. Tough going in spots. Another meeting tonight. There are many headaches here."

I was soon to discover that Al was guilty of gross understatements.

19.

The Austrian Occupation and the Russians:

August 1945–November 1946

I knew that my new job as American high commissioner for Austria would involve many grave postwar problems requiring collaboration among the four Allied powers; but it was only after I had returned to Europe that I discovered our greatest immediate problem was persuading the Russians to let us get into Vienna and go to work. They were busy looting Austria at the time and didn't want to be bothered.

Marshal I. S. Konev, the Soviet High Commissioner, was known as an able battle commander, and I had looked forward to meeting him. As it turned out, I had to look forward for quite a while. Konev was ill, according to information that General Gruenther, who had gone to Vienna for preliminary talks, sent back to my Verona headquarters. All attempts to arrange a meeting of the British, French, Russian, and American high commissioners were useless until he recovered. The nature of Konev's illness remained forever a mystery, but at the same time it became obvious from Gruenther's conversations with other Soviet officials that they were awaiting instructions from Moscow on procedure—and Moscow apparently wasn't in any hurry to act as long as the looting of Austria was proceeding so successfully.

Early in August I sent a message to Major General John Russell Deane, head of the American military mission in Moscow, saying that we needed to get started in Austria and suggesting that he attempt to expedite our efforts to call a meeting of the Allied Council in Vienna. "During a staff conference late in July," I added, "some Russian staff officers stated that Konev was ill while others indicated his health was excellent."

I got my first taste of dealing with the Soviets in the reaction to this message. Konev's deputy in Vienna was a big, bull-necked man named Colonel General A. S. Zheltov, supposedly subordinate to Konev but actually a kind of Soviet political commissar for Austria, who, I believe, could over-rule Konev whenever he desired. Zheltov was high in the Russian NKVD, which was the People's Commissariat of Internal Affairs and the equivalent of the Nazi Gestapo or secret police. His power became evident later; on one occasion, when Konev agreed to a minor suggestion made at an Allied Council meeting, Zheltov snapped at him in Russian; "Why the hell did you do that?"

The contents of my message to Deane got back to the Russians in Vienna the following day. Zheltov went into a rage in talking to Gruenther, asserting that I had no business saying that the Russians were causing delay; that the only reason was Konev's illness. At that time I certainly was hopeful of working harmoniously with the Soviets in Austria, and I began to fear that my efforts to speed up action would create a suspicion in their minds that I was a ringleader of opposition to Konev. I therefore did my best to smooth over the affair, and I decided to get my headquarters moved from Italy to Austria without delay.

Austria, like Germany, was divided into American, Russian, French, and British zones. The Russians, who got there first, had the country's granary, known as Lower Austria, and Vienna.* The British were in the southeast and the French in the southwest. Our zone was the major portion of beautiful, but relatively nonproductive, Upper Austria, lying along the western boundary and including Salzburg. It is interesting to note that the American Zone of Upper Austria originally extended northward across the Danube River, giving us complete command of that vital transportation route from the vicinity of Linz to Passau. The Soviets, however, soon informed Washington that a serious error had been made and that they had intended to extend their zone all along the north bank of the river, which otherwise was entirely in their hands. Our Government immediately agreed, without reference to me, and a part of Upper Austria was cut off from our zone and turned over to the Russians, giving them the north bank of the Danube as far as the frontier of Germany.

---

* Lower Austria, Burgenland, and the part of Upper Austria lying north of the Danube, which comprised the Soviet zone, is about 96 percent arable land. It contains 43 percent of all Austrian plowland and normally produces more than one-third of all wheat, half of the rye and potatoes, and more than three-fourths of the sugar beets.

On August 12, I moved to Salzburg, in the American zone, on the theory that I could go to work in the territory allotted to us without waiting longer for the Russians to agree to begin operations in Vienna itself. My headquarters was at Schloss Klesheim, which once had been a residence for guests of Hitler when he was at his famous Eagle's Nest above nearby Berchtesgaden. Built by the Hapsburgs, the palace had been wonderfully modernized by the Germans and furnished with art treasures, mostly stolen from France. It was surrounded by fields and gardens and sparkling fountains; but I soon discovered that the beauty and the peaceful appearance of Salzburg was all on the surface. Underneath, the people of Austria were afraid, and mainly they were afraid of the Russians.

Our action of giving in to the Russians over the Danube boundary had created a wave of uncertainty. That change not only cut off from our zone a productive piece of Upper Austria, but it eliminated any connection between the American zone and Czechoslovakia. This severance from the Czechs was probably of greater immediate importance to the Soviet officials than any other question involved because they were preparing to take over that nation, but the speed with which we gave in to their demand was a jolt to the Austrians, too. They began to fear that we were not in earnest and that we would desert them at the slightest excuse. As a result I decided that it was important for us to act firmly and to demonstrate that we would do everything possible to carry out our mission, which included the drafting of a treaty that would assure the future of Austria as an independent nation.

Such a treaty, naturally, could not be written immediately. There were many urgent problems to be solved at once before we could consider peace terms and the withdrawal of the Allied armies of occupation. Foremost among these were the pressing tasks of caring for displaced persons, supplying food for a nation that was close to the edge of starvation, establishing a system of free elections under secret ballot, and disposing of former German assets in Austria.

The problem of food was the most urgent, and for weeks Gruenther had been taking part in talks at Vienna in an effort to establish a basis on which the Allied Council could agree.

A major stumbling block in the negotiations was the refusal of the Russians to move food to Vienna from Hungary and Rumania, as had been done in normal times. In other words, they sought to utilize for their own purposes most of the supplies that normally would feed the city. Thus the Americans and British had to import food from home to supply the population. Since at that time we had not been able to move into Vienna, it seemed to me that we could refuse to take up quarters in the capital until the Russians accepted a reasonable settlement on the food question. This course of action would force the Russians to accept full responsibility for the food shortage in the capital, and we knew that they were eager to avoid the adverse political repercussions that would be sure to follow. I suggested this course to Washington, but in reply I was told not to adopt such a rigid policy.

By this time the Russians were showing signs of being ready for the first meeting of the Allied Council; there were hints that Konev's illness was about over. Thinking it might be a good idea to get the four high commissioners together informally prior to the Council meeting, on August 19, I invited Konev, General McCreery, the British high commissioner, and Lieutenant General M. E. Béthouart, the French high commissioner, to be my guests at the Salzburg Music Festival. It turned out that Konev's recovery had not progressed that far, or perhaps there was another delay in the arrival of instructions from Moscow; in any case he sent his deputy, Zheltov, and the four of us were able to discuss the whole situation informally. There were some rough spots to get over, but Zheltov seemed cooperative and jovial. I had arranged to take the commissioners to Berchtesgaden on a sightseeing trip, and I made a point of riding there with Zheltov in one of the big bulletproof automobiles that had belonged to Hitler. En route I told him that I was eager to meet Konev, and that I sincerely regretted that illness had prevented the Soviet commander from attending our informal gathering. Zheltov seemed to appreciate my position and gave the impression that something might be done about it.

That night I entertained my guests at a dinner at American headquarters. I toasted the heads of our four governments and said that I anticipated a pleasant association with the high commissioners. I recalled my friendship and battle association with McCreery in Italy and remarked that I had known Béthouart during the exciting preinvasion days of North Africa. I added that although I had not had the pleasure of working with the Red Army, I was happy that in Austria I would have the opportunity of serving with the commander who had led an important part of that army so brilliantly to victory.

The others spoke briefly, but I noticed that Zheltov was stiff and formal. I didn't think much about it until some hours later when Gruenther came to my quarters and said he had been talking to Zheltov, who was much upset as a result of my remarks.

"He says that you emphasized your previous relations with McCreery and Béthouart," Gruenther told me. "He takes that as a sign that there is an Anglo-French-American bloc which is united against the Russians in dealing with Austria. He says he doesn't like it."

I told Gruenther to get Zheltov into my office the next morning as early as possible. When they arrived, I wasted no time in speaking my mind.

"Your attitude is completely unjustified," I said. "There is no bloc against Russia, and if there were the United States would not participate in it. The Americans here will side with the Russians whenever our policies coincide, and we intend to do our best to make our policies coincide."

Once Zheltov stood up abruptly while I was talking, and I thought for a moment he was going to decide that he was insulted. He made a move as if to walk out, but after a moment's hesitation decided to stay. By the time I was finished, he seemed to be satisfied, but it was only temporary. The pattern, I was soon to discover, was always the same. The Russians were always suspicious, always looking for an ulterior motive in our words and actions. It seemed to me that they were suffering from a combination of guilt and persecution complex.

Zheltov did not, however, change his mind about my desire to meet Konev. The next day I received word that Marshal Konev had extended an invitation to the other commanders to meet unofficially in Vienna on August 23; meantime, he asked me to visit him informally at his headquarters at Baden. I quickly accepted.

On August 22, I flew to Tulln Airport, near Vienna, where I was met by a delegation of Russians, with whom I drove to Baden. There, Zheltov took us to Konev's headquarters. The Russians had taken over most of Baden and their area was surrounded by barbed wire fences guarded by soldiers. For a considerable distance around Konev's headquarters, all Austrians had been made to leave their homes. Konev's office was on a city street, and he was waiting in front of the house, a stolid, bald man in a gray-green tunic, with the red star of a Hero of the Soviet Union on his chest. He smiled jovially and invited me to review a guard of honor. When we entered the headquarters, the vodka bottle immediately was produced, despite the fact that it was early afternoon.

I had hoped to talk to Konev about setting a date for a formal meeting of the Allied Council and about when we could take over our sector in Vienna. The Russians, however, obviously were prepared for an afternoon of drinking. My party was plied with vodka, and there was more liquor at the table when we went to Konev's residence for dinner about five o'clock. We managed to discuss some aspects of the food and fuel situation in Vienna, but it was obvious that the Russians firmly intended to get us "plastered." As soon as this became evident, I watched the servants pour the drinks and immediately observed that Konev was being served a white wine instead of the powerful vodka that was being served to the Americans.

My spirit of friendship goes only so far when it comes to drinking. I stopped the waiter the next time he started to pour me a drink. Turning to Konev, I said through my interpreter, "I'll go drink for drink with you, Marshal, but we'll have to drink from the same bottle. Just have him put the bottle on the table in front of us so we will be sure to get the same. You see, I've got but one stomach to give for my country."

This took some of the heat off me, because Konev obviously had no desire to put away a large quantity of vodka, but he was in a friendly mood and the dinner went on and on. At ten o'clock, it still was in progress and I wanted to go to bed. At that time Konev gave some signs of breaking up the dinner, and I permitted myself a sigh of relief, too soon. He immediately announced that he had ordered a group of Russian entertainers who were performing at the Baden Opera House to remain in costume and give a performance especially for us. I could not possibly refuse. We went to the Opera House and sat for an hour listening to Russian folk songs, watching Russian dances, and trying to keep awake.

Later I went backstage and talked to the entertainers. I urged them to come to the American zone for performances and suggested that American entertainers should go to the Russian zone. It was long past midnight by this time and I was aching to get to bed. Konev said good night—and added that he had arranged for us to see a motion picture, starting immediately, at the house where we were quartered. He left, but, possibly to make sure that we didn't go to bed instead of to the movie, Zheltov remained with us. We sat there for another hour or so, watching a Russian propaganda film; then Zheltov insisted that we have another meal before going to bed. It was between four and five o'clock in the morning when he finally indicated that we might retire, but in the same breath he said he would call at eight o'clock in the morning to keep a date for a swim.

"All right," I said. "We've had a wonderful evening. See you at eight o'clock."

I decided that the Russians were trying to wear us out before the commanders' meeting that evening, but I felt that I could take it. When Sergeant Chaney woke me up at seven-thirty the next morning, however, I was not so sure. I pulled myself painfully out of bed and looked at Chaney, who seemed a little shaky too.

"What time you get in last night, boss?" he asked.

"Pretty late," I said. "When did you get to bed?"

"Oh, I don't have any idea," he said weakly. "They sure showed me a great time." He paused and shook his head as if wondering whether it was still fastened to his shoulders. "Boss, did you drink some of that kerosene, too?"

I had to admit that I had had my share, but I had no intention of being worn down by old Russian customs. I went out with Zheltov and took a swim; then I drove to Vienna to look over the situation and be prepared for the commanders' meeting at eight o'clock that night. I felt that it was worth going through a Konev party in order to get our work started, although for technical reasons the session was not officially regarded as a meeting of the Allied Council.

The entire setup in Austria was as awkward and, I suppose, as unwise from our point of view as the occupation setup in Germany. Vienna, like Berlin, supposedly was ruled by all four occupation powers, and we did establish a joint police force and otherwise conduct a four-power government; but the city actually was surrounded by Russian-occupied territory and subject to Russian pressure. It seemed to me that when the division of territory was originally agreed on at the British-Russian-American commission meetings in London prior to the end of the war, our representatives either were ignorant of the Austrian situation or were motivated by a desire to reduce our commitments and get our troops home as rapidly as possible. In other words, we hadn't known precisely what we wanted to do.

On the other hand, the Russians knew exactly what they wanted. Mainly, they wanted control of the Danube, of the big Zistersdorf oil fields and of the areas—Lower Austria and Burgenland—which produce most of Austria's food. They got what they wanted; and even after we were established in Vienna, the Russians had control of everything—railroads, roads, airfields, and even the telephone system. Thus they could cut in on all of our communications except radio, and they could make it as difficult as possible for us to use the airfield allotted to us at Tulln, some seventeen miles outside Vienna. From time to time, as will be seen, the Russians sought to take advantage of this situation, and it was not long before we learned that our basic uncertainty about what we wanted to do in Austria had let us in for many grave difficulties.

I say it was not long before we learned, because in the beginning we got along fairly well. Konev was jovial and often cooperative in the first weeks after we got the Allied Council into operation in Vienna. He also was subject to considerable political pressure. On the problem of food, for instance, the Russians were reluctant to raise the content of the daily ration from 800 to 1,550 calories, which our experts regarded as a mere subsistence level.* I made it clear, however, that we were going to achieve that level in the

---

* The average American's diet is over 3,000 calories per day.

American zone. The Russians had to come along because they hoped at that time to win the friendship of the Austrian people. Actually, they usually stole the food from the Austrians originally, and what the Red Army did not consume was then turned into the four-power pool as the Russian share. That was at least better than removing most of it from Austria.

By firm action we also were able to keep in line the amount of money that the Russians levied against Austria for support of the Red army of occupation. When the subject of occupation costs first came up, Konev announced that the Russians were "going to charge Austria a certain amount each month."

"This is a matter of common concern," I said, "and all four powers should agree on the costs that will be charged to the Austrian Government."

"No," Konev replied, "it is only our affair what we charge them. If we made the cost of occupation a public matter, we would be revealing military information because the amount would indicate the number of Soviet troops in Austria."

My arguments got nowhere, but later I advised the Austrian Provisional Government, which was headed by Dr. Karl Renner, not to honor drafts to the Russians for occupation costs until the Allied Council agreed on the question. Before long the question of the Austrian budget came before the Council, and it was agreed by all four powers that the budget should be subject to approval by the high commissioners. When the Russians agreed to this proposal, the problem of making known their occupation costs became simple. Such costs had to be included in the budget in order to be paid, and Konev thus had to disclose the sum that the Red Army had demanded. It was far greater than the costs of other Allied occupation armies, and we declined to approve the budget until it was brought into line.

There were other occasions that provided an interesting contrast between the action of the Russians and the other Allied powers, a contrast not lost on the Austrians, I am sure. For instance, during the war Hitler had seized the Austrian crown jewels, the coronation paraphernalia, and various national art treasures. The Russians had been looking for these riches, but fortunately they finally were found in a salt mine near Salzburg in the American Zone. I arranged to have them returned to the Austrian Government at a public ceremony. The Franz Josef Palace, from which most of the treasures originally had been stolen, was occupied by the Russians, so I had them taken to the National Bank Building where we had our headquarters. Renner and other officials came down to the bank vaults and I officially restored the treasure to them. The Austrian Government expressed to me the nation's gratification, but Renner also asked me to put the priceless articles back in the bank vaults at once and lock them up under American protection. The Austrians had no intention of risking them in the Franz Josef Palace during the occupation.

Late in August, before I had moved into Vienna, I had made arrangements to use a lodge at Hinterstoder, where I could do some hunting and fishing whenever I could afford a day off. The lodge was in a valley surrounded by high mountains and laced with good fishing streams. I decided it would make a good rest camp and made a trip there to complete arrangements. There was at Hinterstoder a big aggressive German who was working as an interpreter for the American officers in the area. He did a good job and I used him occasionally, although I noticed that he did an unusual amount of talking and asked a great many questions.

On this occasion he inquired several times about where I would live in Vienna, and finally said that he had an apartment there that he would be glad to have me use until I completed my own arrangements.

"I haven't seen it recently," he added. "I was a leader against the Nazis and spent most of the war in a concentration camp. I thought you might be able to make some use of my services in Vienna."

He seemed a likable man, and I told him to give me a memorandum about his qualifications as well as his record of service with the American Army, which he did. On one or two occasions he rode with me in my jeep around Hinterstoder. I noticed occasionally that residents of the town gave me a peculiar look when they saw him in my company, but nothing was said. The interpreter, however, talked so much that I had just about decided I didn't want him in Vienna when the Counter-intelligence Corps came around and arrested him. The man had been a big shot in the Nazi party throughout the war and was on our list of wanted characters. We quickly put him in detention, but it was some time before the residents of the town were completely sure that we weren't going to put the Nazis back in power.

In the fall of 1945, I suffered a serious setback when General Marshall decided that it would be a good idea to make Gruenther the assistant commandant at the National War College. I had to agree that it was a good idea as far as the College was concerned, but I was extremely reluctant to lose Gruenther at a time when we were facing such major difficulties. Throughout the war in Italy and during the negotiations in Vienna he had done a tremendous job, and I had depended heavily on him. I urged Marshall to delay the transfer, but he felt that it was necessary. I had no choice but to accept his decision. I did, however, manage to get it delayed until I had returned from a trip to the United States in October.

One thing of interest occurred during that trip. Soon after our arrival in Austria, the Russians had halted all shipping on the Danube River. At that time I discovered that the Germans had moved all Austrian, Yugoslav-Hungarian, and other river barges up to Linz in the closing days of the war; they were therefore in the American Zone. When, as previously related, the Russians persuaded Washington to extend their boundary to the Danube in that area, I moved the barges up the river to Passau, in the American zone of Germany, thus keeping them under American control. It seemed to me that they would be a kind of ace up our sleeve in bargaining with the Russians, since the barges would be essential when river traffic was resumed.

There was almost immediate pressure brought for the return of these "captured" barges; the Yugoslavs in particular soon were demanding their return. When I was in Washington, I discussed the subject of the barges and gained the impression that everyone concerned agreed about holding on to them.

After I returned to Vienna, however, one of the first messages I received was from the Department of State, instructing me to return the Yugoslav barges. I replied that I didn't understand, because I was under the distinct impression that my move had been approved and that I was to hold the barges as a bargaining point. A couple of days later, I got another message. The Secretary of State said to turn these barges over to the Yugoslavs or else. I turned them over.

One day about this time, I returned to my office from a short trip and was told that General Patton had tried to reach me on the telephone from Heidelberg, Germany, where he was in command. I had my aide call him back, and when I was told Patton was on the telephone, I picked up the receiver and yelled, "Hello, Georgie!"

A deep voice said, "Georgie who?"

"I am trying to get through to General Patton in Germany," I said.

The voice replied, "Get off the line—it's busy."

"Wait a minute," I snapped. "This is a priority call which must be put through to General Patton."

"Get the hell off the line!" The voice was louder this time.

"Who are you?" I demanded. There was a moment's pause. Then the voice asked, "Who are you?"

"This is General Mark Clark—and who are you?"

There was a longer pause this time, and then—mockingly—the voice asked, "Wouldn't *you* like to know"—and bang! went the receiver.

I often wondered who the culprit was, and still do. I never did complete the call to Patton, and the next day he was in a fatal automobile accident. I found out later that he was calling me to request my support in recommending certain officers for promotion. Georgie always was thinking of those who had served him well in combat.

Gruenther departed after my return to Vienna, and I selected Major General Don Brann to succeed him as my deputy. Don was my close friend, and his assistance during the war in Italy had been highly important in our victory. We had been hunting and hiking companions for years and frequently were competitors on the shooting range. In Austria I had done a little hunting in the American Zone, but Don had been so busy he had had little opportunity to do much shooting. When I told him about the chamois I shot in the mountains, he assured me that he could do better. Soon after he became my deputy, I arranged at Christmastime for him to go to a lodge where I had hunted to see whether he could get a chamois. With a guide he climbed through snow patches up the mountainsides around the beautiful valley that had been Franz Josef's hunting preserve in the Tyrol. They had bad luck for some hours, failing to find any game. Don finally had stopped at the top of a cliff to rest when several chamois were sighted. He stood up quickly, in some excitement, and fired. Then, as he stepped forward, he lost his footing and plunged over the side of the cliff, suffering fatal injuries.[*]

His death was a heavy blow to me. On many, many occasions during the Italian war I had depended on his steadiness, his common sense, and his sound tactical knowledge when the going was at its worst; but as I look back, I can see that there was something even more important. There were more than a few times in the midst of our rigorous endeavors, in the midst of tens of thousands of soldiers engaged in a tumultuous war, when I was strangely, almost desperately lonesome. By some trick of intuition Don Brann usually seemed to know how I felt, and in the evening I would see him coming toward my van, a big, peaceful man with a startling shock of white hair. He would drape himself over a chair, perhaps we'd have a drink and talk for an hour or so about almost anything except the war, and then he'd go about his business. Things usually seemed better after that.

Our major difficulties with the Russians had begun to appear on the horizon before Brann's death, and even before Gruenther's departure. Although relations at the top level, particularly between Konev and myself, continued friendly on the surface, it was becoming obvious that there would be trouble over the disposition of former German assets in Austria. At the time of the *Anschluss*, Hitler had decreed that all Austrian Government property was German property. The Nazi seizure of Jewish property also applied to Austria, as did the later seizures of the property of foreign nationals,

---

[*] Brigadier General Ralph Tate, who had been my able Fifth Army G-4 in Italy, succeeded Brann as deputy.

including some large American companies. In other words, the Nazis stole a great deal of property in Austria.

The three-power conference in London in 1943 agreed that the Allies would cooperate to return such stolen property to its rightful owners. Later, at Potsdam, it was agreed that the Russians should be given, as reparations, all actual German property in their zone of Austria. This, however, did not include property that the Germans had stolen.

The Russians never lived up to the London or Potsdam agreements. They attempted to declare that almost everything the Germans had stolen in Austria was legitimate German property and, therefore, should be turned over to the Soviets as reparations. These properties included many thousands of acres that the Germans had confiscated to use as military training grounds, all mineral rights, property of foreign nationals, and property seized from Jews. Most important of these properties was the Zistersdorf oil fields, in which Americans and Britons held about 50 percent of the investment.[*]

The Soviet approach to this problem was to claim everything and then challenge the Austrians and the other Allied powers to prove that it had not been legal German property. When we did submit the proof, they vetoed it in the Allied Council. In this way they removed vast amounts of coal, oil, and machinery from Austria immediately after the war in a period of looting that all but wrecked the national economy beyond hope of reconstruction; and they used their rights as an occupational power to seize 120 factories in their zone—factories which still are producing for the Russians five years after the end of the war, although most of them are considered to have been wholly or partly Austrian before the *Anschluss*.

This question of German assets in Austria became—and still is—the paramount issue in our long-term objective of writing a peace treaty. The Russians knew that we, as well as the British and French, were eager to formulate a treaty as soon as possible and they sought to blackmail us into agreeing to their looting of Austria as a condition of the treaty. Or, more accurately, they refused to agree on a treaty unless it included a clause that

[*] Statistics regarding the Russian looting of Austria are indefinite. The Russians usually asserted that they had removed no more than 10 percent of the country's assets as reparations; other estimates ran up to 40 percent. Actually, these figures were not as important as was the fact that the Russians looted the key industries on which the rest of the Austrian economy depended. Figures at the end of 1946 showed that 120 industrial enterprises had been, seized, of which only 47 had been regarded as wholly or partly German-owned. These seizures were greatest in textiles, machinery, electrochemicals, nonferrous metal milling, hard-coal mining, rubber, rayon, petroleum and river shipping. A total of 76 agricultural properties were seized, of which 75 were regarded as non-German. As a result of Russian seizure of the Zistersdorf fields, they controlled 72 percent of Austrian oil production and virtually all desirable oil exploration lands as well as half of the oil-refinery capacity.

legalized their rape of the Austrian economy.

This situation began to emerge in September of 1945 when my staff discovered that the Soviets were exerting pressure on the Renner government to agree to an Austro-Soviet Oil Corporation to exploit the Zistersdorf oil fields. At that time there was in Vienna a special Soviet delegation headed by Deputy Minister for Foreign Trade Kunikin. He ordered the Austrians to sign the agreement by September 10—the day before the first meeting of the Allied Council. The Austrians were also told to keep the negotiations secret.

We, of course, learned of this and advised the Renner government to stall off the negotiations, if possible, until I had an opportunity to bring up the matter at the Allied Council meeting on the 11th. But on the 10th, Renner was called from a Cabinet meeting to Soviet headquarters, where he was presented with a contract for his signature. He gallantly refused to sign it, saying that his Provisional Government could not speak for all of Austria and that it was essential to consult other members of the Allied Council. The Russians threatened that they would "report him to Marshal Konev," that his attitude would make impossible any future trade agreements, and that the Russians might, therefore, feel that they no longer could support the Renner government. They told him to return in the evening and sign up, but he declined.

This halted formation of the projected Austro-Russian company; but since the oil fields were in their zone, the Soviets merely seized them under their own unilateral misinterpretation of the Potsdam reparations agreement, and even claimed exploration rights to petroleum still in the ground. They argued that this property had been a German external asset and that it, therefore, became available as reparations to Russia. Such an interpretation of the Potsdam agreement made it impossible for the Allies to carry out their promise to create a firm economic foundation for an independent Austria, because it robbed the country of a key industry. This was a policy that the Russians followed consistently despite the repeated, strong protests of other members of the Allied Council.

It was not often that we were able to frustrate such seizures, although I discovered before long that Konev and his staff were wary of publicity that might reveal what Russia actually was doing in central Europe. On one occasion I was tipped off by my alert public relations officer, Colonel Stanley J. Grogan, that the Soviets were going to seize the building of the Austrian Ministry of Interior for their own use. This seemed a senseless act of intimidation to me, so I had Grogan give the American and British newspaper correspondents the exact details of the Soviet plan, warning them not to reveal the source of their information.

When the Russians arrived at the Ministry building at the scheduled hour to take over, they found themselves surrounded by our correspondents and photographers. Pictures were taken and the correspondents jotted down details of every move, particularly of the Soviet general who was supervising the seizure. This publicity embarrassed not only the general in charge, but the whole Soviet staff in Vienna; about an hour later, they moved out of the Ministry and returned it to the Austrians.

Another example of Soviet tactics stemmed from the fact that the Red Army, when it entered Austria, seized all German reichsmarks in Austrian banks as war booty. Not long afterward, the Russians "loaned" 400,000,000 of the stolen reichsmarks to the Austrian Government, which was planning to convert this German currency into specially overprinted reichsmarks for use as official Austrian currency. After the loan was made, however, the plan was dropped because the establishment of four-power control in Vienna led to an agreement to use Allied military schillings until a new Austrian national currency was issued.

The Austrians then attempted to return to the Russians the reichsmarks that they had "borrowed." The Russians made no response to this offer. Some time later, in December of 1945, the Austrians established a new Austrian national currency. The following month, the Russians demanded the repayment of the 400,000,000 reichsmarks "loan," and demanded that it be paid in the new Austrian schillings. By that time, of course, the old reichsmarks were worthless as a result of conversion to the new Allied-controlled currency, and the Russians merely sought to profit by that change. The 400,000,000 reichsmarks which they had "loaned" had cost them nothing in the first place.

When I heard of this attempt to undermine the Austrian finances, I wrote to the Renner government stating that if the Russian demand was met, I would demand payment in the new currency of almost two billion Allied military schillings which the United States had advanced for the conversion of the currency. Like the reichsmarks, these military schillings had been legal tender at the time the advance was made, but they had no value after the conversion. I knew that the Austrians could not repay both loans and that they would be unable to repay the Russians without also repaying us, so that they could only decline both demands.

The real end of anything other than pretended collaboration by the Russians dated from November 25, 1945, when the Austrians held a free and democratic election for a national parliament and provincial legislatures. About 93 percent of the registered vote was cast, and the People's party (formerly the Christian Social party) won a majority of the seats everywhere except in Vienna and Carinthia, which went Socialist. The Communist party was third, but it was a very poor third, receiving only about 5 percent of the total vote cast. Dr. Renner became President and Dr. Leopold Figl, of the People's party, a courageous and competent little fellow, became Chancellor.

The Soviets were both surprised and angered by the failure of the Communist party to show any strength. They obviously had been supporting the Austrian Government in the belief that it would lead to the establishment of a pro-Communist state; when they found that the opposite was true, they began to change their attitude toward the Austrian people. Within a short time they had begun to restrict the freedom of Austrian authorities in the Soviet zone, and eventually political meetings were permitted only when the Soviet officials approved and had an observer present. Administrative offices were rejuggled to give Communist officials greater authority, many former Nazis who switched to Communism were permitted to hold important jobs, and Communists generally were accorded special favors and privileges. It might be added, however, that these measures had very little effect on the Austrian people, who had seen Communism as practiced by its originators and who still, five years later, show their desire to have none of it.

There also was a steady deterioration in Soviet relations with the Americans, British, and French following the establishment, at the end of 1945, of the new Austrian regime. Russians who had shown themselves friendly toward the Americans seemed to disappear from Vienna, presumably transferred back to the Soviet Union. Those who replaced them were stiff and formal in their contacts with Westerners and resisted all efforts to establish anything other than an official relationship.

I mentioned earlier that the Russians were able to cause us a great deal of trouble in regard to communications. We controlled the Tulln Airfield, but it was of little use to us if we could not get over the road from Tulln to Vienna. For long periods of time, the Russians blocked the direct road on one excuse or another. As a result we usually were forced to use a much longer and circuitous route to and from the airport. Eventually, I established what we called "The Mozart Express"—a train that ran between Vienna, Tulln, and the American zone, making a trip each way once a day to carry American personnel.

The train was marked with American flags and carried signs in Russian and German saying it was for the exclusive use of American personnel. Despite this, Russian soldiers often insisted on interfering with the operation of the train when it passed through the Soviet Zone, and there was considerable trouble and stealing from time to time. I didn't like it, and I advised Konev in writing that the Russians had no business interrupting this train service. Furthermore, I said, I had issued instructions to our military police to keep them off after a specified date.

One day, later in the winter of 1946, several Russian officers and enlisted men forced their way on to the train while it was in the Soviet Zone. One of them was Captain Klementiev and another was Senior Lieutenant of the Red Army Salnikov. They encountered Technical Sergeant Shirley B. Dixon of the U.S. military police, who in line with my orders told them to get off the train. There was an argument, but after a few minutes the Russians left the train. As it started up, however, they got on the next car and came back through the vestibule to the car where Dixon was stationed.

As Dixon stepped toward them, Klementiev drew his pistol, put it against Dixon's mouth, and threatened to kill him. Dixon persuaded him to put away the gun. A few seconds later, however, the Russian captain made a move toward his gun and Dixon shot him fatally. Lieutenant Salnikov moved to draw his pistol and Dixon shot again, wounding him. The other Russians jumped off the train.

Konev immediately demanded that Dixon be punished, charging that he had shot the two men in cold blood. He said that the case should be tried in a civil court or in a joint Russian-American military court. I had no intention of doing either and told him that the sergeant would be tried, without prejudice, in our American military court. I appointed the best counsel and the best prosecutor available and put my most competent officers on the court. They acquitted Dixon.

I then received a letter from Konev in which he demanded a retrial and said that "the acquittal of the murderer, whose guilt was proved beyond a reason of a doubt, cannot be construed in any way other than as an un-friendly act toward the Red Army." I declined to consider a retrial and moved Dixon out of Austria as soon as possible, but for the next six weeks Konev kept on writing me long and vindictive letters. I answered every one of them, and sometimes I wrote even more words than Konev. The net result of this, of course, was nil, except that we engaged in a long and heated discussion of jurisprudence, which served only to demonstrate how far apart are the American and Russian ideas of justice.

Later, even more serious incidents arose in connection with flights of American planes to Tulln. The Russians had stipulated that our planes must follow a narrow corridor while flying over Soviet-occupied territory. This, of course, was inconvenient, but we observed the rule. As relations deteriorated, however, our craft began having trouble with Soviet planes that suddenly would appear along the route, flying close to ours as if intending to crash them and, eventually, firing their guns in the direction of our planes.

On several occasions I officially informed Konev of these incidents and asked him to put an end to them. In each case he replied that he had investigated and found that there were no Russian planes anywhere near the scene of the alleged incident, and that, since no Russians were there, they could not possibly have fired on or otherwise harassed our craft. No matter what was said, he always came back to that point—no Russians were there. At one time, when a number of witnesses were available to show that Soviet antiaircraft had fired on American planes, Konev blandly replied that there was no Soviet antiaircraft in that area. After a number of such incidents, I decided that only force would do any good. There was no question in my mind that the Russians were making the attacks, because my own plane had been fired on. So I ordered the American planes armed and I formally advised Konev that from that day on any Russian plane that made a threatening gesture at an American plane would do so at its own risk. I added that my instructions to the American gunners were to shoot first if they felt they were in danger. We didn't have a single aerial incident after that.

The meetings of the Allied Council, even after relations became strained, usually were conducted with an outward show of friendliness—at least when the session started. It was customary for the top commanders and their deputies to gather a few minutes before the meeting and greet each other informally. However, I noticed that at one meeting Zheltov gave all of us Americans a distinctly cold shoulder. He glared at me and didn't even nod. I had no idea what was bothering him, but during a lull in the meeting I sent an aide around to make some inquiries. The question of what was troubling him was broached as tactfully as possible.

"Have you," Zheltov snapped at my aide, "seen the last issue of *Time* magazine?"

As a matter of fact, I had seen a copy of *Time*, because it had my picture on the cover, but I had not had a chance to read it carefully, and I still was mystified until I got a copy and checked up. In a story about the Austrian occupation, the magazine said:

> To Vienna the chief villain is General Alexei Zheltov, Konev's second in command, who is believed by most observers to be more powerful than Konev. Zheltov . . . was once a wrestler and is usually described by U.S. correspondents as bullnecked. Recently, he insisted on finding out what the word meant, was furious when he did.

The word "bullnecked" was the only adjective I ever knew to get under Zheltov's thick skin. He couldn't stand it and he showed his attitude all through the meeting. I felt I had stood about enough, and at the end of the session I said, "The attitude that has been taken by General Zheltov at this meeting is insulting." I then suggested that we go into his office and see what was what. When we had closed the door, I turned to Zheltov and asked:

"Are you insulting me or are you insulting the United States?"

He again referred to the article in *Time,* which he insisted should not be permitted to make insulting remarks about Soviet officials. This was the usual Russian tactic; about all I could do was deliver a short lecture on freedom of the press and depart, which I did.

The feeding of Austria continued for months on a kind of day-to-day basis. The Red Army had illegally confiscated food supplies, livestock, and farm equipment and was, of course, virtually living off the land, refusing to carry out promises to give the Austrians control over indigenous food supplies in the Russian Zone and refusing to permit exports from there to other parts of Austria. The Soviet Zone normally produced 65 percent of all the country's agricultural products and was the "breadbasket" for Vienna, in particular. Livestock was about all that was produced in the American Zone, and I had authorized shipment of stock to the Soviet Zone. It was only after months of argument that the Russians finally agreed during an Allied Council meeting to recognize the right of the Austrian Government to control all indigenous resources of the country and to utilize them fully in the Austrian economy.

When I made it clear that I intended to provide 1,550 calories per person per day in the American zone, I not only put the Russians on the spot, but I caused difficulties for the British, who were short of food everywhere. (The French share was being supplied by the United States.) As a result both the Russians and the British were eager to have UNRRA move into Austria to help feed the population. Seventy-three percent of the cost would thereby fall upon the United States, for we were by far the greatest contributor to UNRRA. I was not too happy to have UNRRA take over the responsibility of feeding the Austrians, for I felt that more effective controls than it could offer should be maintained to see that the food and supplies of all kinds reached the Austrian people and were not siphoned off by the Soviets.

The UNRRA policy was that no account should be taken of the zones of Austria, but that the supplies should be distributed generally, with UNRRA agents checking on their delivery. This method was put into practice in theory, but checking was impossible in the Soviet Zone. It merely permitted the Russians to start stealing again. Within a short time my intelligence agents had proof, including specific railroad car numbers, that food and tractors and other supplies were being sent out of the Russian Zone and into Rumania, Hungary, and Czechoslovakia. I protested to UNRRA, but got nowhere.

Learning that Fiorello La Guardia, then head of UNRRA, was going to be in Switzerland, I persuaded him to come to Austria and supplied him with complete data on what was happening. I urged him to apply sanctions against the Russians to prevent these thefts, but again nothing happened.

One other major problem in Austria should be mentioned—the displaced persons. As the Red Army moved westward in the final stages of the war, it was preceded by millions of persons who for one reason or another did not want to fall into Russian hands. These included White Russians, Balts, Poles, Yugoslavs, Jews, Ukrainians, and many other nationalities. In all, there were an estimated 750,000 of them in the American Zone of Austria immediately after the war. Their presence posed a tremendous problem. Merely sheltering and feeding them was a severe strain on a country that had suffered as much as Austria; the job, therefore, fell mainly to the occupying forces. We had to use any buildings available, which included some that had been German concentration camps, and conditions certainly were not good in the beginning.

The number of refugees decreased in the following months. We managed to repatriate many thousands voluntarily. Others moved on to Palestine or other countries and many moved into the American Zone in Germany in the hope of reaching the United States or some other haven. This movement to Germany, in fact, became so large that General Lucius Clay, then high commissioner in Germany, became alarmed and finally threatened to post guards along the frontier unless we stopped the migration, which was greater than could be absorbed there. When I left Austria, there were still some 400,000 displaced persons in the country, about 30,000 of them Jews. None of them wanted to return to their homes, which had fallen under Soviet domination.

We adopted the policy that none of the refugees would be forced to return to areas under Soviet control, where many feared they would be severely punished or killed. The Russians insisted that many of them should be forcibly returned, on the grounds that they were war criminals or deserters from the Red Army, and it finally was agreed that we would send them back if the Russians could prove to our satisfaction that they were in either of those categories.

As a result of this agreement, I was instructed by Washington to permit a Russian Repatriation Mission to enter the American Zone to attempt to persuade refugees to return home or to assist in identifying war criminals or deserters. I had nothing but trouble with this mission. Instead of attending to its business, it caused unrest among the refugees, tried to force the return of persons who did not want to return, and spent a great deal of time engaging in espionage. I informed Konev of these facts on several occasions and finally wrote him that the mission would have to leave the American Zone. He agreed, but asked permission to send in a new mission, suggesting that we try it for a thirty-day period to see whether things went better. I said that we would try it.

Shortly before the old mission departed, however, our counter-intelligence received a tip that an attempt would be made to kidnap one of our key counterespionage agents, an Austrian citizen. Our counterintelligence had had plenty of trouble with the Russian mission and was only too happy to see in this plot a chance to strike back.

On the night of January 23, 1946, several automobiles without lights crept close to the house where the U.S. counterespionage agent was living. Several men got out of the cars, entered the house, and threatened our agent with a pistol. At that moment our military police appeared. Lights that had been carefully hidden around the house were switched on, making it impossible for any one to escape the guards stationed there. Our trap was remarkably successful. Several members of the Soviet Repatriation Mission were in the raiding group. One officer wore the complete uniform of the U.S. military police, and the lining in his helmet was marked to show that it had been stolen from the 250th U.S. Military Police Battalion in Salzburg. Another officer wore a civilian overcoat over his Red Army uniform and a civilian hat. A third wore a civilian overcoat over his uniform, but still had on his Red Army cap, although the insignia had been removed. An enlisted man driving one automobile wore the Red Army uniform. All of them were armed, and one of the officers had his pistol drawn when he was seized.

I notified Konev the next day that we had his men in custody and that they would be shoved over the line into the Russian Zone at Linz at two o'clock the next afternoon. I explained the circumstances and said that we did not want any more repatriation missions in the American zone.

Our difficulties with the Russians increased, but I never really blamed Konev. He obviously was merely carrying out instructions. He even had a sense of humor about it occasionally. Once when we were discussing Austrian politics, the name of the Communist party leader, Ernst Fischer, was mentioned. Jokingly, I said: "Well, I don't like him because he is a Communist."

Konev grunted. "That's fine," he said. "I don't like him either because he's an Austrian Communist."

On another occasion, I decided to give Konev, who liked to hunt, a custom-built rifle, with a silver plate on the stock inscribed "To Marshal Konev, from his friend, General Clark." I wasn't sure he would get it if I simply delivered it to his headquarters, so I had an officer take it to him. I didn't even get an acknowledgement from Konev, although I saw him on various official occasions. Finally, about three weeks after I had sent the gun, I walked to lunch with him after the commissioners' meeting. Speaking through an interpreter, I asked if he had received the gun.

"Yes."

"Ask the marshal whether he liked it."

"Yes."

"I just wondered," I said. "I hadn't received any acknowledgement."

"Well, you didn't send any ammunition."

Quickly I said, "Special ammunition is being made. You'll get it soon."

"Fine," Konev replied.

A few days later I sent the ammunition by special messenger, but I never heard a word from Konev about it.

In the summer of 1946, Marshal Konev was withdrawn from Austria and succeeded by Colonel General V. V. Kourasov. I was sorry to see Konev leave. Some months later I met him at a reception in Moscow and we talked for a while in friendly fashion, but not about Vienna. He then was described to me as holding a job equivalent to the commander of Ground Forces in the United States—a job I was to take over eventually in America.

Some months after I had given the rifle to Konev, I had another interesting experience involving a gift, though this time I was on the receiving end. I already have spoken of how Crown Prince Umberto of Italy had insisted upon sharing the front-line experiences of Italian troops who fought with us. Actually, it sometimes seemed to me that Umberto was constantly laboring under what he felt was the necessity for repairing the damage done to Italy's national honor by the Mussolini-Hitler partnership. It crossed my mind more than once that, as the representative of the House of Savoy, not only was he prepared to die in battle against the Nazis, but on many occasions almost deliberately invited death.

During the summer of 1948, a national election was held to determine whether the monarchy would be retained. While the election campaign was in progress, Umberto invited me to Rome for a ceremony, which, it seemed to me, might have improperly influenced the voters in his behalf, and I was forced to decline. I did, however, go to Rome on other business at the time of the election and saw him privately. The next day, the election resulted in the end of the monarchy, and shortly thereafter Umberto went into exile in Portugal. On the day of his departure a messenger brought to my hotel a flat leather box that he said was from the exiled prince. When I opened it, I found a small automatic pistol which Umberto had worn throughout the war.

An engraved plaque on the box had this inscription: "To the son of General Mark Wayne Clark, from a friend of his father."

I think it might be well to include here an excerpt from my diary, which concerns a report I made late in the winter of 1946 on our efforts to pave the way for a sound and independent Austrian Government and to create conditions favorable to a peace treaty. It fairly well sums up the progress—or perhaps the lack of progress—made during my service as high commissioner, although I remained in that post for more than a year longer.

It is clearly evident to me that the Soviet policy is to prevent establishment of Austria as an economic entity without strong ties to Soviet territory or Soviet-controlled areas. While the governments of the three Western powers are attempting to reach agreement on the vital question of German assets, the Soviets are removing many important plants, resources and other economic assets from their zone. In other cases, such as the Zistersdorf oil fields and the Danube Shipping Company, they are taking over control in such a way that Austria must remain dependent upon Soviet influence for years to come.

Whole plants essential to the existence of Austria have been stripped of machinery. Others have been put to work solely on production of items most needed by the Red Army. The Soviets have acquired control of the Danube in Hungary and Rumania by their recent agreements with these countries to establish joint shipping interests. Their intention is to extend this control of the Danube to include Austria.

The Red Army has placed a demand upon the Austrian government for approximately 60,000 acres of farmland in Lower Austria for use by the Red Army to raise vegetables and other garden produce to feed their troops. Our experts estimate that this acreage is sufficient to feed 60,000 to 100,000 persons for a year at 1,550 calories. Withdrawal of this land from the Austrian economy will indirectly mean that UNRRA [i.e., the U.S.A., as its largest contributor] will be feeding the Red Army, because greater food imports will be needed to meet the deficiency in Austrian diet caused by loss of this land.

Because of the strength of the Soviet position, it is becoming more evident that the Austrian Government recognizes the inability of the Western Allies to cope effectively with this position. Prominent Austrians in Vienna realize they are surrounded by Soviet-held territory and there is little hope of economic liberation.

While I recognize the responsibility of the United States toward Austria, I am of the opinion that little can be accomplished toward the discharge of that responsibility until the governments of the four powers adopt a uniform policy to carry out their avowed intentions. The Western Allies are blocked by the Soviet veto power in the Allied Council and can give only lip service to the Austrian Government on any policy the Soviets choose to adopt which is contrary to our policy. The economic gains being made by the Soviets can result only in eventual political strangulation if Soviet policy is allowed to continue.

I made another trip to Washington in September of 1946 and had a chance to talk with Eisenhower, who was then Chief of Staff.

"Want to come home?" Ike asked at one point.

"I certainly do," I answered. "I've been away almost four and a half years."

"I think you should," he went on. "We can probably fix it a little later. Where do you want to go?"

"I understand Joe Stilwell is going to retire," I said. "That will leave the Sixth Army job open and I'd like to spend some time at the Presidio."

"Sounds reasonable," Ike said. "I'll try."

Before I left the United States, I had one interesting experience. John Steelman called me from the White House and said that he hoped I could talk before a group at the White House on the following day.

"I'm sorry," I replied, "but I have to leave town."

There was a brief silence and then Steelman hung up.

About three minutes later, my telephone rang. It was Secretary of War Patterson.

"Is this you, Clark?" he asked. "Do you feel all right? Anything wrong with you?"

I assured him I felt fine.

"Well, I wasn't sure," he went on. "I was given to understand that the White House called you to make a speech and you refused."

I started to agree that I had, and then it struck me—a little belatedly—that I hadn't really been *asked* to make the talk. I had been *told*.

"I didn't know," I told Patterson, "that it was a command performance."

"Well, it is. Will you call Steelman back?"

"Yes, sir."

I called, and I made the speech. I also decided that perhaps I had been away from Washington so long I had forgotten the rules. Maybe I ought to get back to Austria before I really put my foot in it. I left the next morning.

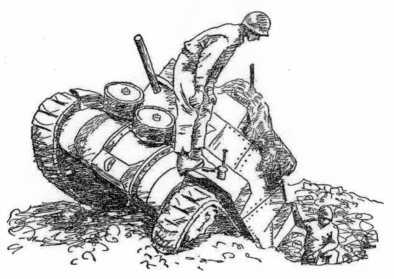

20.

The Moscow Conference:

March 1947

I got back to Vienna on November 4, already counting the days until we
would be transferred to the Presidio. So was Mrs. Clark And as usual it
didn't work out that way. I went to Moscow instead.

Shortly before Christmas, Secretary Patterson radioed that Secretary of
State Byrnes wanted me to act as his deputy during the London negotiations
of the Council of Foreign Ministers to draw up the basis for an Austrian
peace treaty, which would be concluded later at Moscow. General Stilwell had
died at that time, and arrangements, even to the formal announcement, for
my transfer to the Sixth Army had been completed, with General Keyes
scheduled to succeed me in Austria. When I received the formal request from
Byrnes, however, I could only accept. I had a strong desire to see that the
Austrians got a fair break.

I immediately cabled Byrnes that I would go to London with my staff of
experts in the fields of Austrian economics and political affairs. Much to my
surprise, I received a quick reply saying that my staff in London would be
furnished by the State Department from Washington and that I didn't need
anyone except a secretary. As far as I was concerned, that message arrived
too late. I already had arranged for my staff to fly to London, and I told them
to go ahead, informing the State Department that I could not then change my
plans. Besides, I felt it was essential to have with me in London men who, I
knew, were familiar with the situation in Austria; I did not want to have to
rely upon men from Washington who probably had only a theoretical

knowledge of our problems. As a result, when I arrived in London, I had two staffs.

My Austrian staff included Colonels Frank Oxx and Ed Howard;* Lieutenant Colonel James Rundell, economics adviser; Arthur Marget, financial adviser; and James Garrison, adviser on reparations. My Washington staff included Frances Williamson, political adviser; Charles Rogers, economics adviser; and Leonard Meeker, legal adviser. Ware Adams, a member of my political section in Austria, also joined me in London.

As we got down to business, it seemed to me that the attitude of some of the State Department representatives put Austria in about the same position as the satellite countries.† There was an inclination to make the same kind of treaty and, in many instances, to use the same clauses; in other words, we must get a treaty at almost any cost. One of the main difficulties in framing the treaty, as I pointed out earlier, was the Russian demand that we accept their definition of German assets in order to legalize their looting of Austria. At that time it was already apparent that in making treaties with the Russian satellite countries we had agreed to too much that the Russians wanted. Furthermore, we more or less had sold those countries "down the Danube." We had not fully understood at the time what the Russians were trying to do or the manner in which they were seeking to gain complete domination over central Europe. In Austria, however, the picture had become only too clear. Austria was an entirely different matter, and I was determined to do all that I could to guarantee its independence, based on a sound national economic setup rather than on one controlled by Soviet interests.

The London conference lasted for almost two months and didn't make any substantial progress, largely because the most controversial issues depended upon first reaching agreement on the definition of German assets in Austria.

Both the Austrians and the Yugoslavs, who were claiming territory and reparations from Austria, were permitted to send delegations to the conference, and one of our early problems was to decide the procedure for hearing them. The Russians felt there was no point in hearing the Austrians, whereas I insisted that they be heard. I felt that it would bolster Dr. Renner's prestige at home if his regime made a presentation of his country's case. Since the Russians wanted the Yugoslavs to be heard, we managed to reach a compromise by agreeing to hear both delegations. The Yugoslavs were heard first, on a day when the Russian deputy foreign minister, Feodor T. Gusev, was

---

* Both had been "busted" from brigadier generals in accordance with our demobilization plans. They had been with me all through the war and served me exceptionally well.
† Hungary, Rumania, and Bulgaria.

presiding over the conference table.

The Yugoslav case clarified an incident that had occurred at the end of the war when the State Department, for reasons then unknown to me, told me to get troops into the Austrian towns of Villach and Klagenfurt as soon as possible. I did get them there just before a Yugoslav force tried to infiltrate into Lower Carinthia, the province in which these towns were located. At the London conference, the Yugoslavs claimed that Lower Carinthia should be turned over to them; the Russians supported their claim, presumably because it would strengthen the Communist approaches to Italy. If the Yugoslav troops had occupied the two towns, it might have been hard to oust them peacefully. Since they had failed, however, it was easier for the Western powers to defend their opposition to Yugoslav claims when they were presented at the peace conferences.

The next day the Austrian delegation was heard. Dr. Karl Gruber, the Austrian foreign minister, ably presented his government's case. On that day I was presiding over the conference, the arrangement being for the chairmanship to rotate daily among the four deputy foreign ministers. As soon as Gruber had concluded, he was closely questioned by Gusev and other Russians, who were obviously hostile.

During this questioning a secretary brought me a letter from the Yugoslav Embassy but, I imagine, written by Gusev. The reason I imagine it was written by Gusev is that when I finished reading it, I looked up and found that he was watching me closely as if he expected me to do something. The letter said that the Yugoslavs strongly protested the appearance of the governor of Carinthia as a witness with the Austrian delegation on the grounds that he was a Nazi. It obviously was intended to create a political bombshell at the session, interrupt the Austrian delegation's testimony, and generally cause confusion and embarrassment. Since I had had considerable experience with such tactics in Austria, I merely laid the letter aside and permitted the Austrians to proceed.

When we had heard the Austrians, I asked the other deputy foreign ministers to remain and, when the Austrians and Yugoslavs had left the room, I told them of the protest.

"I decided that the right thing to do was to show you this protest and ask what the conference desires to do about it," I added. "When the Yugoslavs were here yesterday, nobody brought up any question about whether they were Nazis or anything else. They were permitted to tell their story. The Austrians are supposed to continue their testimony tomorrow. I suggest that we do nothing and permit them to continue."

Gusev insisted that the governor of Carinthia should be barred, and he added: "I move that we vote on whether to seat him."

This motion was also familiar tactics to me because the Soviets had used it frequently in Vienna, taking advantage of the "veto" arrangement that requires unanimous consent of the four powers. The motion was so worded that Gusev's vote alone could bar the man.

"Just a moment," I said. "I am chairman of the meeting today. I will put the motion. It seems to me that the man already has been seated. Therefore, it is more proper to vote on whether to throw him out, and I so move."

By putting the motion in that form, the veto advantage was on our side instead of the Russian, and the governor of Carinthia retained his seat.

As I have stated above, the London sessions didn't accomplish much other than to make it clear that our main problem at Moscow would be to agree on a definition of German assets in Austria. The foreign ministers of the four powers were to conduct the Moscow sessions, but while we were still in London, Byrnes resigned and was succeeded by General Marshall. I immediately received a cable from Marshall saying that he wanted me to continue to act as deputy and accompany him to Moscow. The question arose again whether I could take some of my own staff. After several exchanges of cables, I was told in a message signed by Marshall that I could take only a couple of men. Later the general told me that he had never seen the messages, which were handled by his subordinates in the State Department. I managed to take along John G. Erhardt, my political adviser in Austria; Colonel Frank Oxx; Arthur Marget; and my secretary and interpreter.

I had a few days in Austria before the Moscow meeting and on March 8 flew to Berlin to join Marshall's party, which included John Foster Dulles, Benjamin Cohen, Robert Murphy, and General Lucius Clay. I felt that it must have taken a great deal of courage for Marshall to step into the job of Secretary of State and then leave almost immediately for Moscow to deal with many intricate problems before he had had time to familiarize himself with the essential details. I was amazed, however, when we met in Berlin, to discover that we didn't have a definite program of action. On the eve of the most important conference since Potsdam, everybody still was discussing what we should do in Moscow.

We flew to Moscow the next day, picking up a Russian Air Force officer at Berlin in order to conform with the Soviet regulations that no planes could fly to the capital unless a Russian navigator was aboard. Actually, our own navigator did the work of getting us there, while the Russian sat at the window and occasionally pointed out some town or farmhouse that he recognized.

I can't say that I enjoyed my visit to Moscow, although I was tremendously interested in seeing the city and its people when I had an opportunity. Most of the time, however, we were busy and usually we were frustrated; and we were, of course, more or less surrounded by the apparatus of the Soviet system throughout our stay.

The telephone in my room at the Moscow Hotel, for instance, seemed to ring incessantly during the night. Usually when I answered it, a feminine voice would inquire about my health and general disposition and wonder if there was anything that I needed or whether I would like to go out and see the sights. Such incidents occurred time after time until finally I wrapped the telephone in a bath towel and put it in a desk drawer, where it would not be heard.

Most of our rooms were wired for sound, with microphones of the secret police concealed at various strategic spots. Sometimes we carried on long and ridiculous conversations purely for the benefit of the microphone listeners, and occasionally we made remarks hinting that some good, faithful Communist official in Austria had been working for us as a spy or a saboteur. Whenever we really wanted to talk about anything important, we went to the American Embassy or strolled up and down the streets. I eventually developed a regular routine for conferences—a stroll around the Kremlin walls.

The foreign ministers had a long agenda, of which the Austrian treaty was only a part. Until that subject came up, the deputy foreign ministers in charge of the Austrian treaty renewed their efforts to reach an agreement, without any greater success than at London.

In the first place, the Russians objected to going on record with the other three occupying powers that none of the four would violate the independence or territorial integrity of Austria. The Russians previously had subscribed to the establishment of a free and independent Austria, but at Moscow they contended vaguely that the proposed guarantee of independence was a function of the United Nations rather than of the occupying powers.

Second, the Soviets finally agreed that Austria should be permitted to raise an army of 53,000 men to maintain internal security and protect her frontiers after the Allied occupation terminated; but in the same breath, they added that the formation of an army could not be started until the occupying powers withdrew their troops and that Austria must then equip this force "with weapons of national manufacture only." That, of course, was virtually impossible. I pointed out that it would be foolish to wait until the nation had no protection by occupation troops before starting the difficult process of raising and training an army. Furthermore, all war factories in Austria had been destroyed by the Allies, so there was no immediate way in which the country could produce its own armaments.

At this point I ran into white-haired, vitriolic Andrei Vishinsky. When I argued that the Austrians should be permitted to purchase arms wherever they pleased, Vishinsky made a long speech in reply. The gist of his argument was that no self-respecting sovereign nation would think of stooping to the purchase of arms from some other country.

"I can think of one that did," I replied, recalling the vast amounts of armaments which the United States had sent to Russia under Lend-Lease during the war. I also knew the Russians had never admitted to their soldiers that these arms and equipment were of foreign manufacture, and that the Red Army soldiers in Austria thought every jeep they saw was the handwork of the Russians. This belief was so strongly imbedded that it may, or may not, have accounted for the fact that they stole countless American jeeps until we put armed guards around our parking lots.

The foreign ministers' sessions dragged on for weeks. I took advantage of one lull in the negotiations to make a hurried trip back to Vienna, where I cleared up my desk and even got in one day of hunting at Hinterstoder. Our wire-haired terrier, Snooty, was an expectant mother and not very happy about it. The veterinarian who was taking care of her was worried and said that a Caesarean delivery might be necessary. He knew we were very fond of Snooty, and he had consulted with other veterinarians and finally with one of the leading surgeons of Vienna. By the time I had heard all the details, you would have thought our dog was in danger of becoming an international incident. She was still looking unhappy about it when I flew to Berlin, en route back to Moscow.

I had delayed my return until the last hour, but all arrangements were confirmed and I didn't expect any delays. When we reached Berlin, however, the American officer who met me at Tempelhof Airdrome said that the Russian navigator we were supposed to pick up there had vanished.

"He was here a half hour ago," he added. "Now I can't find him."

We made telephone calls in an attempt to find him, but without any success. It was getting late and we had to get started if we were going to get to Moscow before dark.

"Can you fly to Moscow without a Russian navigator?" I asked Colonel Howard Moore, my pilot.

"Why not? Anyway, my copilot can speak Russian."

We departed at once, ignoring the Soviet regulation that we must be accompanied by a Russian navigator. Our arrival in Moscow at dusk caused quite a commotion. A large group of officers and soldiers surrounded our plane and began shouting at us. When the sergeant opened the door, they refused to let him get out.

"Nobody can get off this plane!" an officer in the group shouted at the sergeant.

I walked back to the door and put my hand on the sergeant's shoulder. "Get out of the way—just in case," I told him. Then I jumped squarely into the middle of the crowd. I explained that our Russian navigator had vanished and that I had to be present at the Foreign Ministers' Conference the next morning. Then I got the crew off the plane and took them to town. The Russians made quite a fuss about it, and a few days later I got a request through the State Department to explain the "incident." It was quite a while before we got everything smoothed out, but at least I was back in Moscow on time.

General Marshall had had so little opportunity to study up on various issues coming before the Conference of Foreign Ministers that he usually held a briefing session at the Embassy each morning at ten o'clock. He would go over the subject of the day with various experts and then drive to the conference with someone, who would continue giving him details.

Ben Cohen was supposed to be the man who had the broadest background in problems relating to the proposed treaties. He had played a large part in the satellite-treaties conferences. Actually, during the German treaty negotiations, Murphy and Clay devoted many hours each day to making sure that Cohen, who acted as a kind of funnel for information to the Secretary, knew the right answers so he could properly brief Marshall on the details.

It seemed to me that this procedure was a bit cumbersome, so when the Austrian treaty came before the foreign ministers I tried a new one. I prepared a small booklet for General Marshall, with a section devoted to each clause of the proposed treaty. On the first page of each section appeared our version of the clause. On the next page I stated the positions of the British, French, and Russians, making it as brief as possible. Then I set down how far I thought we could go in compromising on that clause without endangering the fundamental principles on the treatment of Austria to which we were committed.

Furthermore, I had one advantage. I knew Marshall well enough to go to his room each morning before he was dressed. While he was getting his clothes on and having breakfast, I would go over the particular points that were scheduled for discussion that day, explaining to him what I believed the British or the Russians or the French were likely to say and also giving him the answers to the anticipated arguments where conflict existed. As a result, when the usual morning briefing was held at the Embassy at ten o'clock, Marshall was fairly well warmed up to the subject and the discussion moved along with greater speed.

The crux of the whole treaty discussion still was the definition of German assets in Austria. On the morning that we were to discuss that question, it had become apparent that any hope of success depended on finding ground for a compromise that would avoid the surrender of the Austrian economy to the Soviets.

"General Marshall," I said at the briefing session, "this is the principal issue in the treaty; if we can agree on it, all the other questions will fall into place and can be solved. I have typed out here what I think should be our minimum position in order to avoid legalizing the Russian seizure of and control over the backbone of Austria's economy. I don't think we can go an inch farther."

I handed copies of my memorandum to Murphy, Cohen, and Dulles.

"What do you think, Mr. Cohen?" Marshall asked after a few minutes.

"The Russians won't accept it," he replied.

"Mr. Dulles?"

"They won't accept it."

"Well," Marshall asked, "what do we do?"

"I recommend," Cohen said, "that we adopt the language used in the satellite treaties."

I had been afraid that this was coming. The language he favored was vague and subject to misinterpretation, and, of course, the Russians already had misinterpreted it in order to take over assets and assume extraterritorial rights in the satellite countries that it had never been intended to give them. One look at the situation in those countries today is sufficient confirmation of this.

"I'd like to say a final word," I interrupted. "I have worked hard to try to make Austria independent. I'm going to say what I believe. If you accept Mr. Cohen's proposal, you will be selling the Austrians down the river. They will become nothing more than a Russian puppet state. The assets clause in the satellite treaties is one that the United States never should have accepted in any treaty. Furthermore, the situation in Austria is different. I can never agree to acceptance of that language, and I don't believe the British or French will accept it either."

Marshall looked at his watch and said, "It's time to go."

"General," I said, "we must be prepared to decide this question at the afternoon session."

"Well, you dictate a statement incorporating your viewpoint," Marshall said. I already had one prepared.

That afternoon I gave Marshall the statement and we went over to the conference room, where the foreign ministers and their aides sat around a huge oval table. Marshall was presiding; Cohen and I sat on either side of him. Bevin, Bidault, and Molotov were there with their advisers. Everybody had given up hope of reaching an agreement, and we were just waiting for the signal to break up the negotiations. Marshall gave it.

He began by noting that the British, French, and American delegations had put forward many proposals, because they were sincerely striving to find a common ground for solution of the problem of German assets in Austria. He expressed regret, however, that the Russians had not offered to make any compromise or even to submit any proposal other than the one they had made at the London conference. There was no hope, he added, that an agreement could be reached if the Soviet delegation would make no greater effort. As a result, he felt that further progress was impossible, unless the Russians had some concrete suggestion that would make it clear that German assets do not include assets which in justice and equity should be restored to their rightful non-German owners. The United States, he concluded, did not believe that the Soviet attitude was consistent with the pledge made by Russia at Potsdam that war reparations would not be taken from Austria; nor was it consistent with the pledge Russia had made to reestablish Austria as a sovereign, independent, and democratic state.

On that note the efforts to write a peace treaty for Austria ended. Four-power negotiations on a lower level have continued for the past three years, but the Russians have never suggested any real basis for an agreement. Consequently, no progress has been made. Our country will not be a party to a treaty that makes Austria a satellite of the Soviet Union.

On that note, too, my European service ended. There were a few formalities remaining, but the work was over as far as I was concerned. That night we went to the Kremlin and walked up a long flight of stairs to a landing where Generalissimo Stalin greeted us and led us to a banquet table. I sat next to Konev, and when the vodka was produced I made them put the bottle on the table and pour our drinks from the same bottle. We joked about Konev's old habit of substituting white wine for vodka, but after two drinks we called it a draw and didn't pour any more, even when we went through the motions of drinking the many toasts that were proposed. It didn't really matter, because the toasts to our various governments and our future friendship were just as empty as Konev's glass or mine.

Feeling very discouraged, I went back to my hotel to pack. I was going to Vienna, but it would be only a stop on the way home. Ike had kept the Sixth Army job open for me and I was thinking about the Presidio and the Golden Gate with its good fishing and the way the cable cars crawl up the hills of San

Francisco. America seemed a long way away and, in my mind, it had never looked better.

At the hotel I was told that a message had arrived during my absence. I hurried up to my room and found a radiogram carefully pinned to my pillow. It was from Vienna and I hurriedly ripped it open.

"Snooty birthed five pups," it said. "Mother and offspring doing fine."

I read it over again. Well, I thought, that's great. We'll take them all home with us. At least Snooty had five pups. That's more than we got out of our sojourn in Moscow. The next morning, with Mrs. Clark and our daughter Ann, who had flown in several days previously, we took off for our return trip to Vienna, with a stopover for lunch in Warsaw.

World War II was an era in which America came of age as a world power. We had and we still have many lessons to learn. It was not surprising, perhaps, that we celebrated a victory when in reality we had not won the war. We had stopped too soon. We had been too eager to go home. We welcomed the peace, but after more years of effort and expenditure we found that we had won no peace.

In the Italian campaign we had demonstrated as never before how a polyglot army could be welded into a team of allies with the strength and unity and determination to prevail over formidable odds. But in Austria and elsewhere in postwar Europe, we had learned another lesson about allies. The Russians were not interested in teamwork. They wanted to keep things boiling. They were ready to resort to lying, to betrayal, to the repudiation of solemn pledges. They were accustomed to the use of force. They were skilled in exploiting any sign of weakness or uncertainty or appeasement. This was their national policy.

Once I said to Konev, "You've made ten demands at this Council meeting that we can't meet. But suppose I should say, 'All right. We agree to all ten demands.' Then what would you do?"

"Tomorrow," he said, "I'd have ten new ones."

Having seen the Red Army and Russian diplomacy in action, my own belief is that there is nothing the Soviets would not do to achieve world domination. But I am convinced also that they respect force; perhaps they respect nothing in the world except force. And when confronted with strength and determination, they stop, look, and listen.

The unbelievably difficult task of making policy to guide the destiny of our country is not and never has been mine; nor do I desire to hear the rattling of any sabers in Washington. But, on the basis of such experiences as I have had, I feel that it would be folly to ignore the threatening facts that confront us. We can survive only if our own team pulls together; only if our

Army, Navy, and Air Force collaborate and are given the means to make and keep us strong. As chief of the Army Field Forces, with the responsibility of training our Army for any emergency, I know that this is not a simple or easy task. It requires the assistance and support of all the people of America—but we must build a national military team that will make it unavoidably clear that anybody who endangers our way of life will risk destroying himself. We must give notice to the world, and to anyone in our own country who would change our form of government, that we intend to be strong; that we intend to preserve the blessings of freedom for which the men and women of the Fifth Army, and millions of other Americans, fought and died.

Index